SOCIOLOGY FOR HEALTH PROFESSIONALS
IN IRELAND

Sociology for Health Professionals in Ireland

ABBEY HYDE, MARIA LOHAN AND ORLA McDONNELL

INSTITUTE OF PUBLIC
ADMINISTRATION

First published 2004
by the
Institute of Public Administration
57–61 Lansdowne Road
Dublin 4

British Library Cataloguing in Publication Data

ISBN 1 904541 14 3

Cover design by M & J Graphics
Typeset by Computertype Limited, Dublin
Printed in Ireland by ColourBooks

Table of Contents

Preface

The objective of this book is to be a comprehensive sociological text for health professionals[1], health researchers, and those undertaking sociology at undergraduate and post-graduate levels in the health and social science disciplines in Ireland. In particular, we hope that this book will be of interest to lecturers and students in the areas of nursing, midwifery, occupational therapy, physiotherapy, radiography, and medicine. In order to be comprehensive, we sought to produce a book that would outline the fundamentals of sociology as a discipline and to show how sociology has been developed to inform understandings of health and healthcare. We cover four main themes: health professions and sociology; sociological understandings of health and illness; experiences of healthcare; and the social context of healthcare. In our quest to make this book relevant to health professionals in Ireland,[2] we have sought, where possible, to incorporate Irish research on health and illness and a detailed analysis of the social and policy context of health and healthcare in Ireland. The social and policy context of health and healthcare in Ireland is situated in European and global contexts. We hope that the novice reader will find it accessible and that the *glossary of key terms* may act as an accompanying resource. We also hope that the more experienced reader of sociology of health and illness may find this textbook a refreshing analysis of this exciting area of sociology.

Structure of the book
In Part 1, *health professions and sociology*, the links between health work and sociology as a discipline are explored, and the theories and methodologies that underpin sociological knowledge are examined. In Chapter 1 of the book we begin by defining the discipline of sociology and presenting a case as to why sociology might be of interest to health

---

1 We use the term 'health professionals' broadly, to include those working in a range of occupations in the health and voluntary services. The notion of what constitutes a profession has been the subject of sociological analysis, and will be explored in depth in Chapter 12.
2 Unless otherwise indicated, references to Ireland refer to the Republic of Ireland.

professionals. Here, the origins and purpose of sociology are explored, and the specific contribution of sociology over and above other scientific disciplines allied to healthcare is considered. In making connections between the world of the health professional and the discipline of sociology, we describe how the sociology of health and illness contributes to an understanding of the nature of health and illness, the experiences of health and illness and the social context of health and illness services. We argue that sociology is a subject that is worth pursuing for those in health-related disciplines. In Chapter 2, we introduce the reader to some of the primary theories in sociology. We discuss the explanation of social processes that these social theories offer the understanding of health and illness that they reflect, and the role of the health services that they propose. In this way, the connections between social theory and patterns of health and healthcare are made explicit. In Chapter 3, we move on to look at what research methodologies – data gathering tools and the philosophical principles that mediate them – are used to create sociological knowledge. Again, we draw on examples from health and illness research to explore how sociological knowledge about health and illness is produced and defended.

Part 2 (Chapters 4-6) of the book is about *sociological understandings of health and illness*. In Chapter 4, we consider how patterns of health and illness may be understood through a sociological analysis of health inequalities, particularly in relation to social class, gender, and ethnicity. Here, the manner in which these social divides account for diverse patterns of health status is discussed. In addition, the main explanations for the link between social inequality and health and illness are presented and evaluated. In Chapter 5, we expand the focus to the wider global context, and consider what the main determinants of health and illness are on a world-wide scale. In addition, drawing on the notion of globalisation, we explore the linkages between local contexts and global trends in health status. The influence of the spread of neoliberal individualism as a political doctrine across the globe is also discussed. Tensions that have arisen between prominent global organisations that are central players in regulating health are explored. In Chapter 6, we consider how, with the benefit of a sociological analysis over and above common sense perspectives, biomedicine may be understood in a rather different way. Drawing on the work of social theorists, we consider the extent to which biomedicine has been effective in bringing about improvements in the health status enjoyed by those in industrially-developed countries over the past century. Furthermore, we explore biomedicine's role in creating and maintaining collective norms in society. The challenge to biomedicine posed by complementary and alternative medicines is also discussed.

Part 3 (Chapters 7-11) focuses on people's *experiences of healthcare*. In Chapter 7, a number of significant developments in theoretical thinking about the body in sociology and their application to the area of health and illness are presented. The current interest in the body within sociology is explored, and various sociological perspectives on the body are considered. Specifically, we explore how the body is perceived in relation to the experiences of chronic illness, body impairment and experiences of disability. In addition the various ways in which medical discourses construct womanhood in terms of fertility and bodily processes are examined. A central insight emerging from the areas explored in this chapter is that the body can be analysed as a social construct and that wider social and cultural relations permeate and shape our experiences of the body. In Chapter 8, the nature of relations between lay people and health professionals is discussed, and the extent to which such relations are 'objective' and impartial is considered. In particular, we review the manner in which the social divides of gender, socio-economic status, ethnicity and age mediate professional-patient interactions. In Chapter 9, various phases of the lifecycle from childhood to death are considered, particularly in relation to how they have been affected by the processes bound up with modernity. The chapter begins with an account of childhood socialisation, and is followed by an analysis of discourses on the family, ageing, and dying and death. In Chapter 10, the issue of mental illness is explored, beginning with a review of the range of competing models and perspectives that prevail in healthcare contexts. This is followed by an outline of the main sociological approaches to the study of mental illness, and in particular, how the relationship between mental illness, social class, and gender is interpreted within these approaches. The shift in emphasis from institutional to community care for the management of mental illness is then explored. The chapter closes with an account of the ethics and politics of mental healthcare from the perspective of mental health users, and the dominance of the psychiatric profession and the pharmacological model in dealing with mental illness. Chapter 11 is about the way in which the extension of science and technology in healthcare threatens to overtake our moral perspective of the body and raises issues about eugenic thinking. Within the sociology of science and technology, questions are raised about how and why particular technologies develop in a particular manner. The way in which economic and cultural power mediate developments in science and technology in healthcare is also examined. Case studies on technologies of childbirth and New Reproductive Technologies (NRT) provide a social context to explore the theoretical issues.

In Part 3 (Chapters 12-14) the *social context of healthcare* is examined. Chapter 12 focuses on the healthcare division of labour, with particular emphasis on relations between nursing and medicine. The issues of gender and professional power that cross-cut relations between nursing and medicine are explored. The extent to which the professional power of the medical profession in Ireland is under threat is then considered, as is the extent to which nursing in Ireland has made gains in terms of professionalising. A review of empirical studies in clinical settings follows in which the power of nurses relative to doctors is examined. Chapter 13 focusing on health policy, opens with an overview of the central transformations that have occurred in understanding the provision of health and healthcare. The development of the Irish healthcare system and current health policy reform are explored. The current system of Irish healthcare, characterised by a mix of public and private provision, is then outlined. Finally, the reorientation of health policy since the mid-1980s is reviewed, and three important elements in terms of the future of health policy and healthcare – equity, the structural reform of primary care and health consumerism – are addressed. The final chapter, Chapter 14 focuses on the increasing dominance of health promotion as a strategy of contemporary health policy. The chapter demonstrates how the current preoccupation with health echoes wider socio-economic and cultural changes. The New Public Health movement is explored, and the themes within the sociology of health promotion such as the body and consumer culture, risk society, surveillance and the self-care ethic are examined. The main sociological critiques of health promotion as a public health strategy are presented. The chapter closes by considering existing dilemmas and tensions within health promotion.

Collectively, in these chapters, we attempt to take on board the rapidly shifting theoretical debates within sociology and integrate them with empirical examples from sociological scholarship and policy in Ireland.

Acknowledgments
The authors would like to thank the following people who have contributed to this book by commenting on various chapters: Phil Barker, Damien Brennan, Claire Coleman, John Garry, Agnes Higgens, Anne Marie McGauran, Tony McNamara, Kathleen Murphy, Joe Sloan and the anonymous referees.

Glossary of Key Terms

Absolute poverty: Circumstances in which people do not receive enough resources to support a minimum of physical health and efficiency. Absolute poverty is often contrasted with *relative poverty*, which refers to living standards *relative to* others in the same society.

Agency: The capacity of a social actor (human) to act upon and create the world independently of *social structures* (see below).

Behavioural disorders: These include eating disorders, alcoholism and substance abuse and are a more ambiguous category of mental disorder since they have no proven biological cause, but are nonetheless medicalised as pathological conditions.

Biological determinism: The view that the human self and human societies are an outcome of the characteristics of our biology.

Biomedicine: A shift in thinking in the seventeenth century, suggesting that there was no essential relationship between the mind and the body, prompted a new way of perceiving the human body. The body began to be seen as a collection of parts, each of which could be 'fixed', independently of the workings of the mind, if it failed to function.

Bureaucratisation: The move towards the creation of bureaucracy. A bureaucracy is a type of administration run by officials and characterised by clearly identified rules. A hierarchical structure is in place and relations in the hierarchy are impersonal, with an emphasis on pursuing organisation goals.

Community rating: This refers to standardised health insurance premium rates across age, sex and health status and eliminates the distinction between high and low risk groups for insurance purposes.

Division of labour: Work divided into diverse occupations, in which people specialise.

Dramaturgical techniques: Associated with the work of Erving Goffman, this refers to the manner in which people 'act' or stage manage the impressions they give off when they interact with one another, depending on the social context.

Embodied self: The notion of embodiment is derived from the phenomenology of Merleau-Ponty who argued that the manner in which humans experience external reality involves their bodily experiences of the world. In addition, this school of thought suggests that how individuals relate to their own bodies is not an external, objective and neutral relationship.

Empirical study or research: A study that draws on data or evidence in making inferences or conclusions (Harvey et al, 2000: 11).

Enlightenment: This is a broad philosophical movement across the arts, sciences and humanities which challenged modes of living based on tradition, modes of reason based on religion and modes of governance based on monarchical rule which originated in eighteenth century Europe. Enlightenment thinking advocates individual and societal progress through rational reasoning.

Epidemiology: A branch of medical science research which investigates the social distribution of health and illness (*who gets what illnesses where*) and the identification and quantification of the individual 'risk factors' leading to ill-health.

Epistemology: The study of the underlying principles of how knowledge can be produced.

Essentialist notion: A notion that assumes that particular phenomena have common traits and behaviour arising from biological structures or nature.

Ethnicity: Ethnicity is a form of cultural identification with specific groups in society, usually with reference to culture, language, ancestory or nationality.

Ethnomethodology: 'The study (*ology*) of people's (*ethno*) methods of creating social order' (Craib, 1992:103), or the methods used by people to give meaning to the world around them.

Feminist theory: A set of theories concerned with understanding and explaining the manner in which women are systematically disadvantaged in modern societies through gender differences and *patriarchy* (see below).

Gender: Gender is usually distinguished from sex. Sex refers to the biological differences between men and women. Gender is the cultural construction of types of masculinities and types of feminities.

Gene therapy: The insertion of genes or genetic material into cells in order to genetically modify the function of a cell. The treatment, cure, or prevention of disease is based on the idea of altering the expression of genes.

Genome: The entire genetic material of an organism found in the chromosomes; humans have twenty-three pairs of chromosomes.

Germ cells: Cells that develop into the reproductive cells of sperm and eggs.

Gross Domestic Product (GDP): Refers to the total goods and services produced domestically by a nation during a year.

Human Genome Project: An Anglo-American research programme the objective of which is to identify all of the possible 30,000 genes in human DNA (deoxyribonucleic acid), the agent which transmits human genetic traits.

Ideological effect: Refers to the effect of ideology, a contested concept that usually refers to a set beliefs, attitudes and opinions, which may be 'true' or 'false' and which are presented by the most powerful groups in a society.

Individualism: An outlook on the world which promotes individual choice, freedom and responsibility.

Ideology: A term much debated within sociology that refers to a cluster of beliefs, attitudes and opinions related to one another to a greater or lesser extent.

Individualist theories: A set of theories which views the individual psychological and personality traits as the explanatory system of human behaviour (Jones, 2002: 200).

Internal market: An arrangement whereby, within a structured system, the free market with principles of competition and efficiency is mimicked.

Labour power: A concept from Marx' works to refer to a labourer's *capacity* to work. Marx noted that under capitalism, the employer buys the worker's labour power, rather than the value of his or her labour.

Late or high modernity: (see *modernisation* and *modernity* below) Theorists such as Anthony Giddens consider that contemporary societies are influenced by the same forces that constructed the 'modern age', and, therefore, they challenge the view that society has entered a phase of *post*modernity. Theorists that take this position tend to see the current phase as one of late or high modernity rather than *post*modernity.

Labelling theory: The idea that 'deviance' is produced in social interaction through the successful identification of certain behaviours as deviant.

Life expectancy: The average number of years, statistically, a person is likely to live in a given society at a particular time.

Macro level: Macro level in sociology refers to the analysis of large collectivities (for example, government, or the medical profession as a whole) in addition to more abstract social systems or structures.

Means of production: The means of producing material goods of a society. The means of production include the *forces of production*, or technology, factories, machinery buildings etc, to manufacture goods, and *relations of production*, that is how people relate to one another at work.

Medicalisation: The manner in which medicine increasingly claims expertise over everyday aspects of life such as death, birth, eating, drinking, and sleeping.

Mental handicap: Refers to people suffering from an impaired bodily function, such as Down's Syndrome, senile dementia and other learning disabilities. These conditions have a known biological origin, although paradoxically they are the 'least responsive to medical treatment' (Taylor and Field, 1993: 136).

Mental illness: Psychotic and affective disorders such as schizophrenia and depression.

Micro level: Micro level in sociology refers to the analysis of interactions and social processes in small groups and in face-to-face encounters.

Modernisation: The processes and patterns of social change in societies initiated with industrialisation.

Modernity: The term used to distinguish particular attributes of modern societies (see *modernisation*, above). These attributes relate to the economic, political, social and cultural systems, and are often contrasted with these realms in pre-modern societies.

Monogenic disorder: A single gene disorder, for example, Huntington's Disease or Cystic Fibrosis.

Morbidity: A measure of the death rate of a population.

Mortality: A measure of the illness rate of a population.

Multifactorial disorder: A disorder that is understood to arise from the effects of several genes as well as environmental factors.

Negotiated order: A term first introduced by Strauss et al (1963, 1964) to capture the process of social order they found in research into two North American psychiatric hospitals. They noted that while negotiation (bargaining, compromising, or colluding) contributed to social order, social order facilitated interaction processes such as negotiation. The concept of negotiated order challenged an established view of organisations as rule-driven stable structures, instead conceptualising social order as more fluid and continually being re-constituted.

Neoliberal individualism: This political doctrine is characterised by a commitment to individualism and a capitalist-orientated enterprise culture. Its political agenda is to claw back on welfare benefits and reduce the influence of trade unions over work practices. The word 'liberal' here refers to freedom of the market to function without regulations which critics of the doctrine argue are necessary to protect those most vulnerable.

Normalisation: The philosophy of normalisation has been developed in the context of people with learning or intellectual impairments. The concept of normalisation has undergone different modifications since it was first introduced in Denmark in 1959 and it generally refers to making social roles, behaviours and living conditions that are culturally normative (or valued) available to people who are learning impaired.

Norms: Expectations about how people ought to act or behave. They refer to the most acceptable patterns of behaviour in a society that may or may not be the most frequently occuring.

Partriarchy: The dominance of men over women, whereby men gain and maintain their dominance and power over women.

Perinatal mortality rate: Number of still births (post twenty-four weeks) plus number of babies who die before seven days.

Phenomenology: A branch of philosophy concerned with how individuals actively attribute meanings to aspects of everyday life. In sociology, it lies within the social action school of social theory.

Political economy: A branch of social theory associated with focussing on how capitalist economies create socio-economic inequalities in society.

Polygenic disorder: A disorder that is understood to arise from more than one gene.

Positivism: 'Positivism is one way of knowing the social world. Positivism attempts to apply a natural scientific approach to the study of the social world. The approach seeks to identify cause and effect relationships. It is assumed that for each social phenomenon there is a social cause' Positivism also assumes that we can rid ourselves of any preconceptions that we might have in order to produce 'factual information' (Lee et al, 2000: 30).

Postmodernism: A branch of social theory which rejects the values of modernism, namely the ability to establish truths about the world, the logic of progress of society and meta-theories which claim to know what unites people in societies.

Post-structuralism: A branch of social theory which views discourses (languages of knowledge) as being embedded in social and political contexts. In order to understand society, we need to understand how particular forms of knowledge become prevalent.

Private realm: Generally used to refer to the family, domestic and household sphere.

Public realm: Generally used to refer to the world of work, politics and areas beyond the household.

Qualitative research methods: Methods which can inquire into people's interpretations of aspects of society. Qualitative methods try to tap the quality of experiences of aspects of society.

Quantitative research methods: Methods which can produce numbers to measure (quantify) social phenomena in society.

Risk equalisation: The claim costs of less healthy members are shared by all insurers operating in the market according to the market share of the companies and the amount of claims that they pay. As a regulatory principle this is intended to act as a disincentive against insurers targeting younger and healthier members.

Sex-mortality ratio: The ratio of male to female deaths in a given age group.

Social action theory: The belief that society is composed through the interaction of individual meanings and actions.

Social Class: A means of classifying the power over resources (especially income and prestige) people hold in a society.

Social constructionism: It proposes that 'realities' are created or constructed by human cognitive activity rather than being derived from an objective status or nature.

Socially constructed: Practices derived from socio-cultural processes rather than nature.

Social structure: This concept has not been clearly defined within sociology, but generally refers to enduring, orderly and patterned relationships between the dimensions of a society.

Social theory: At its simplest, statements about how or why something is the way it is (Lee et al, 2000: 7). Social theories are used to explain patterns or changes in patterns in society.

Sociological imagination: This term was coined by C.W. Mills (1970) to describe the sociological model of thinking through issues which occur in society. We think sociologically when we draw linkages between personal issues and events we encounter in everyday life and broader issues and occurrences in society at large.

Somatic cells: All body cells except reproductive cells.

Special needs: The philosophy of special needs is based on the idea that people may have special educational or social support needs depending on the nature and severity of their impairment.

Standardised mortality ratio (SMR): This is the measurement used to compare death rates in different populations. The mortality ratio is the ratio between the normal expected deaths for a population and that which is observed. It sets normal mortality at 100, such that a figure below that is less than what is expected, and above that is more than expected. 'Standardised' means that the mortality ratio has been adjusted to take account of factors such as age and sex which could distort the statistics.

Stem cells: Undifferentiated cells that develop into specialised tissue cells, for example, muscle, liver, heart, kidney etc. A distinction is drawn between **embryonic stem cells** derived from five to seven-day-old embryos known as blastocysts, and **adult stem cells** derived from adult tissue.

Stigma: The identification of a negative difference in someone.

Structural functionalism: A branch of social theory which views society as a system of inter-connecting and inter-dependent parts which create a structure for society in order for it to function well.

Symbolic interactionism: A branch of social action theory which views society as being socially (re)constructed in the interactions of everyday life.

Total institutionalisation: This concept is used by Goffman (1961) to describe how asylums and mental hospitals were designed from the perspective of institutions rather than from the perspective of individual care. Within such institutions patients' lives are tightly structured by institutional rules and routine, and therapeutic interventions create docile patients who comply with the institutional regime.

Triangulation: A process of using multiple research techniques in order to tap the one research question.

Worldview: A set of beliefs collectively comprising a perspective on the world that is held by a particular social group, for example, those in the pro-choice or alternatively pro-life movements who share a common outlook on the world.

Section 1
Health professions and sociology

ONE

What is sociology and why might health professionals be interested?

The purpose of this chapter is to define the discipline of sociology and to argue the case as to why sociology might be of interest to health professionals. In the first part of the chapter, the origins and purpose of sociology are explained, and we identify the uniqueness of sociology compared to other scientific disciplines allied to healthcare – notably the biological sciences and psychology. In the second part of the chapter, the discipline of sociology is linked to the world of the health professional. We argue that knowledge of human societies should be a central part of the theory and practice of healthcare professionals. Specifically, in this chapter, we describe how the sociology of health and illness contributes to an understanding of:

- the nature of health and illness
- experiences of health and illness
- the social context of health and illness services.

Overall, the meaning of sociology is introduced in this chapter and it is argued that healthcare professionals have much to gain from studying the sociology of health and illness.

What is sociology?

Sociology is the social scientific discipline that studies society. It is the study of how people and the society they live in are moulded through the interface of people acting on society and society acting on individuals.

Sociology emerged as an academic discipline over 200 years ago. The inspiration behind the discipline was the social and political upheaval occurring in European societies which accompanied the socio-political revolutions and industrialisation or **modernisation**[1] of eighteenth century Europe. The changes occurring in society at this time provoked questions

---

1 The meaning of words appearing in bold font (other than headings) is explained in the Glossary of Key Terms.

about how societies could or should be organised and how emerging forms of society affected relations between groups of individuals in society. Before the modern period (pre-industrialisation), people typically lived in small groups and produced their own food. In the 1700s and 1800s, countries such as Britain, Germany and France experienced an 'industrial revolution', which had far-reaching effects on family and working life. The move from most people working on the land to most working in industry altered the most basic aspects of daily life, including the basis for marriage, which prior to industrialisation was related to economic concerns, while after industrialisation changed to romantic love (Giddens, 2001a). Medical advice was also not routinely sought in pre-industrialised societies because the medical profession was thought to be poorly equipped to deal with the perceived causes of disease, namely acts of God or acts of witchcraft. Instead, according to Porter, people medicated themselves or changed their lifestyle (Porter, 1992 cited in Lupton, 2003: 89). Karl Marx (1818-1883), one of the most influential theorists in sociology, believed that in order to understand society, one had to understand the development of capitalist economies based on industrialisation. He emphasised the inevitable conflict which was emerging in capitalist societies between those who owned the economic resources (the bourgeoisie) and those who did not (the proletariat).

The French Revolution also inspired an awareness of society as an organised entity that had changed over time and could be constructed by human actors in different forms. Society was no longer understood as having a natural order but was rather subject to change by human agents, for better or worse. Auguste Comte (1798-1857) is credited with having coined the discipline of sociology as 'the science of society'. Comte developed the discipline in order to understand how society operates – how society is held together (which he referred to as *social statics)* and how society changes (which he refers to as *social dynamics*, Comte, 1974 [1830-1842]). The pioneering French sociologists (notably Auguste Comte and Emile Durkheim 1858-1917, the first Professor of Sociology, appointed to the Sorbonne in 1915) were influenced by **Enlightenment** thinking as a new way of understanding the natural and social worlds. The new intelligentsia of the Enlightenment sought explanations for patterns in the natural and social worlds by rejecting religious (or supernatural) and metaphysical (or natural) explanations in favour of the development of scientific and rational explanations. Enlightenment thinking was proving very successful in the development of scientific and technological innovations. The pioneering French sociologists sought to develop a science of society in which data about the social world would be collected and analysed akin to the manner the natural scientists were pursuing in the natural world. Comte, in particular, thought sociologists would strive to identify social patterns in the world and prescribe ways of improving the social world through the application of this knowledge.

Contemporary sociology has much in common with its early antecedents. The core concern of sociology remains rooted in understanding how patterns in society are created and how they change over time. In addition, a central concern remains the dialectical or reciprocal relationship between the impact individuals can have on the society in which they live and the impact society can have on individuals. There are, however, some notable differences between sociology's early and contemporary concerns. Contemporary sociology is less interested in offering solutions to social problems, or social engineering, as was proposed in the original writings of Auguste Comte. Instead, sociology is more concerned with increasing understanding about how particular social patterns and social problems have emerged, are sustained and challenged, so that a number of alternative scenarios may be imagined. Sociology asks questions about who holds power to interpret society and define society and how this power is challenged by other groups. In so doing, sociology gives us a better understanding of how society operates and the role of individuals and groups in social processes. Contemporary sociology has also broadened the early methodologies of sociology that effectively mimicked the methodologies of the natural sciences. Max Weber (1864-1920) was a German sociologist whose work has influenced sociology and the social sciences more broadly. Weber argued that social scientists need to understand the motivations and interpretations of individuals' actions in society. His writings have given rise to the development of a range of 'interpretative' social scientific methods, most usually developed in qualitative research. Contemporary sociology uses both positivist research methodology, adapted from the original natural sciences, and interpretative research methodology which has been developed within the social sciences. (See Chapter 3 for a discussion on research methodology in sociology).

What is unique about sociology?

Sociology raises questions and issues which are overlooked by other scientific disciplines allied to healthcare, such as the biological sciences and psychology.

The biological sciences offer an understanding of the individual and the individual's health by reference to biology (anatomical and physiological components). The mind is theorised as being separate from the body (for a further exploration of this issue, see Chapter 6). In psychology, the mind takes precedence over the body. A common debate in psychology is the 'nature versus nurture' debate which may be seen as two opposite ends of a continuum. At the nature end of the continuum is neuropsychology, which offers an understanding of the individual and individuals' health status as a product of organic biochemical processes. At the nurture end of the continuum is social psychology which is closer to sociology. At this end of the spectrum of psychology, the individual's mind is understood as being developed in interaction with the social world he/she lives in. Nonetheless, psychology as a discipline is primarily interested in understanding the individual and individual's health through an understanding of the person's mind. Sociology is different, in that it seeks an understanding of individuals and their health by reference to the society in which they live. Consider, for example, the image of the health status of privileged people living in the developed world compared to that of people living in deprived areas of the developing world in order to understand the effect society can have on our health. Sociology joins up the mind and body and sees both as a product of the relationship between individuals and the society in which they live. It is an analysis of the relationship between the individual (for example, experiences of one's body, motivations, ambitions, understandings) and structures which may exist in society (for example, types of economy, healthcare system, religious and education systems).

Sociology is thus not just about human societies, it is also a *way of thinking* about human societies. A famous sociologist, C. Wright Mills, wrote a book called *The Sociological Imagination* in which he described what it is to *think sociologically*. Essentially, Mills describes sociology as the study of the links between 'the personal troubles of milieu [or personal circumstances] and the public issues of social structure' (Mills, 1978: 21). Let us consider the example of the practices of childbirth. At one level this may seem like a very 'natural' event guided by our bodies or an individual event guided by our wishes. However, society can create structures and expectations for individuals. For example, in contemporary Ireland most women attend pre-natal screening and give birth in hospitals. At the same time, it is possible to consider how much the practices of childbirth have changed over time in Ireland. The practices surrounding childbirth also currently differ across different parts of the world. This historical and cross-cultural variation suggests that individuals/groups of individuals can effect change in society and alter the structures and kinds of expectations around giving birth. Thinking sociologically further implies considering whether there are particular groups in society (for example, midwives, obstetricians, women of different social class backgrounds) who have more power to effect change than others. (See Chapter 11 for a further discussion of changing norms around childbirth.)

Above, we have distinguished the uniqueness of sociology compared to other academic disciplines. However, since sociology focuses on issues we encounter in everyday life, it might also be fruitful to identify how sociology is distinct from common sense theories of everyday life. Sociology moves into the realm of an intellectual discipline because conventional wisdom is scrutinised though rigorous research. The scientific basis of sociology is developed through methodical examinations of the social world we live in. There are two essential resources that sociologists draw on to conduct methodical studies of the social world: *social theory* and *research methods*. As noted above, sociology has contributed to, and shares with, other social sciences (such as political science, economics and psychology) methods of research that are used to acquire knowledge about the social world. The function of social theory in sociology is precisely to better explain issues in individuals' lives, or general patterns in society. (The scientific resources of sociology will be further elaborated in Chapters 2 and 3.)

The *reason* why sociologists draw on research methods and social theory has much to do with wanting to know why aspects of society are the way they are and to model alternatives. Sociological studies seek to move beyond individual subjective understandings in order to ask how others might understand the same processes differently. Sociologists have 'a sceptical attitude' and generally seek to challenge common sense understandings. In particular, sociology as a discipline is sceptical of explanations of the world that rely on the sentiment 'that's just the way things are' or 'that's human nature' (Marsh et al, 2000). For example, it was once thought that women's 'natural place' was in the home until sociologists and feminist movements more broadly began to challenge women's 'natural' affinity to housekeeping and lack of suitability to the workplace, particularly once married. However, sociologists also point out that it is often not easy to disrupt common sense, particularly because it usually means shifting balances of power and resources in society. For example, Germov has pointed out that in Australia, as in other places, health inequality between different social groups is *common place*, but it is not *common knowledge* (Germov, 1999a: 4, emphasis in original). There are generally interests at stake in seeing the world only through particular perspectives, or in maintaining the status quo.

Why might health professionals be interested in sociology?
In this section, we are moving away from describing sociology in general towards the application of sociology specifically to the field of health. The sub-discipline of sociology that deals with health is known as 'the sociology of health and illness'. The sociology of health and illness is the largest sub-discipline of sociology in Great Britain and the US. This is not surprising given that health commands large resources and is one of the biggest economic sectors in most Western societies. The constant imperative to improve the health of populations raises the social profile of health issues. In this section, we will elaborate the relevance of sociology and particularly the sociology of health and illness to the concerns of health professionals. We argue that sociology can increase health professionals' understanding of:

- the nature of health and illness (the social causes and social distribution of **mortality** and **morbidity**)
- experiences of health and illness
- the social context of healthcare.

ders will note that these issues are reflected in the remaining sections
book, where each of the themes is explored in greater detail. Running
ıgh all three themes is a critique of **biomedicine**. The biomedical model
of healthcare is a sociological definition of the type of medicine which has
grown in dominance in Western societies over the past two hundred years.
The biomedical approach conceptualises illness as being due to a specific
pathology or malfunction in the body. It relies upon medical specialists
largely within a hospital setting to treat illness with drugs and mechanical
procedures. Sociological critiques have contributed, in particular, to the
development of more holistic approaches to health by relating health and
illness to the society we live in.

*1. The nature of health and illness (the social causes and social
distribution of mortality and morbidity)*
Studying the sociology of health and illness can enable health professionals
to appreciate how the social realm of life cross-cuts physical health. The
core argument here is that what happens in our bodies is very much a
product of the kind of society we live in. Social divisions present in
society create divisions in the distribution of mortality and morbidity or
inequalities in health. Take for example, the following health findings for
Ireland:

- Based on statistics collected for 1989 and 1998, those in the lowest
  occupational groups (such as the long-term unemployed, unskilled
  labourers and cleaning staff) were up to twice as likely to die prematurely
  than those in the higher occupational groups (such as doctors, the higher
  legal profession and university lecturers) (Balanda and Wilde, 2001).

- There was a steep gradient from the poorest to the richest for all major
  causes of death – circulatory diseases, cancers, respiratory diseases, and
  injuries and poisonings (Balanda and Wilde, 2001).

Ireland is not unique in relation to such inequalities in health and
mortality trends (statistics on causes of death). Similar patterns have been
identified in other industrialised nations. For example, Giddens (2001a)
summarises two recent nation-wide health reports conducted in the UK as
follows:

Individuals from higher socio-economic positions are on average
healthier, taller, and stronger and live longer than those lower down the
scale. Differences are greatest in respect to infant mortality (children
dying in the first year of life) and child death, but poorer people are at
greater risk of dying at all ages than more affluent people (Giddens,
2001a: 145).

Sociologists believe that some of the reasons behind the above he findings cannot be regarded as biological reasons. Rather, some groups in society get sicker and die younger because of the social conditions (socio-economic, cultural and political factors) of their everyday lives and social values. Some groups of people adopt health behaviours (for example, smoke or eat an unhealthy diet) because the social conditions to which they are exposed lend themselves to behaviours that undermine health. (The issue of inequalities in health will be explored more fully in Chapter 4.) Sociology elaborates this relationship at the level of the physical society (for example damp housing) influencing physical bodies, or at the level of meaning – showing how social factors impact on how we understand health and illness and everyday behaviours that influence our health (Lupton, 1998). The sociology of health and illness helps us take on board, and yet go beyond, individual explanations – biological or psychological causes – in order to explain individual symptoms by having recourse to sociological explanations. We argue, in short, that sociology should be of interest to health professionals because it elaborates the impact of society on our bodies (health and illness) and the way we think about our health and illness.

The implication of understanding health as an outcome of the social fabric of society is that health problems need also to be addressed at the level of society and not just at the level of the individual body, as in contemporary biomedicine. In support of this argument of the importance of social factors in 'treating' illness, sociology can draw on an established body of interdisciplinary scholarship which has concluded that increased life expectancy and improvements in health in the Western world owe less to advances in science and medicine than to improvements in wider society, such as in nutrition, public hygiene and the decline in birth rates. (See Chapter 6 for a discussion of the seminal work of McKeown (1976), Szreter (1995) and Illich (1976) on this point.) Sociology has thus been concerned to point out that the biomedical framework of understanding health and the treatment of health is too narrow in its focus. Biomedicine treats symptoms as they emerge in individuals within healthcare systems. Sociologists point out that the reduction of ill-health should start at the level of the reduction of poverty and inequality in society, and by improving the quality of life in our communities and towns, particularly in deprived areas. Health professionals need to be aware not only of the relationship between poverty and poor health but also the political dimensions of poverty so that health professionals can be advocates of better health for those most in need.

2. Understanding experiences of health, illness and healthcare
The importance of patients' perspectives on health and illness have become increasingly important in the light of the changing healthcare context. As a result of the social changes in the Western world, a concern for infectious diseases that have threatened humanity over time has been superseded by a

concern for chronic and degenerative diseases. Consequently, with the changing nature of health and illness in the Western world, the concept of cure has been superseded by care, monitoring, rehabilitation and prevention.

Nettleton (1995) summarises this transformation in health and medicine as one from disease to health, from hospital to community, from acute to chronic, from cure to prevention, from intervention to monitoring, from treatment to care and from patient to person. A second feature of the social and health policy context that has prompted an interest in the experiences and perspectives of patients is the rise of consumerism in healthcare. Klein (1989) describes a shift in health policy from paternalism to consumerism, whereby patients are increasingly viewed as consumers who have health demands which the health services should strive to meet (see Chapers 8 and 13).

Sociology can contribute to an understanding of patients' experiences of health and illness within the changing context of health and healthcare. Because sociology is concerned with studying the workings of the wider world around us, it offers health professionals the opportunity of stepping outside the immediate health professional-patient situation to a fuller understanding of the patient's social and cultural context. For example, Porter (1998a: 2-3) says of nurses in particular:

> Instead of confining our interest in sick people to their inner pathologies, nurses now accept that persons' health status is determined by many factors, including their physical, cutural and social environment.

Whilst sociology acknowledges that all humans experience birth, death, pain and illness, sociology also acknowledges that some people's understandings of these experiences vary, and sometimes to a considerable extent (Lupton, 1998). 'Sociologists argue that, in many cases, the reasons for these differences are not simply anatomical, but are also social and cultural' (Lupton, 1998: 122). Being ill is intimately related to one's sense of self (Lupton, 2003). Patient perspectives on the ill or healthy self are influenced by social factors such as the development of gendered identity, social class identity and the ethnic identity of the patient. The term 'biographical disruption' (Bury, 1982) is often used by sociologists to chart how patients make sense of a broad range of issues, like what it means to be 'a man', a 'good mother', a 'productive worker' or a 'sexual being' during the onset of an episode of acute or chronic ill-health. Such issues of how the **embodied self** links to perceptions of the self may need to be re-constituted by the patient and, as such, the renewal of self may be a central part of the renewal of wellness.

Sociology has become particularly central in the education of nurses and
ıpts to develop an autonomous body of knowledge known as 'new
, theory' (Salvage, 1990). 'New nursing theory' refers to a more

holistic system of caring for patients. Within this model, health status is not simply defined by the pathophysiological factors of disease, but also by the psycho-social dimensions of health problems. In addition to informing the holistic care of patients, sociological studies have been central to understanding communication between health professionals and patients. In particular, sociological studies have critiqued the relative power imbalance which health professionals have traditionally held in interactions with patients. This theme of understanding patients' experiences of healthcare and communication between health professionals and patients is taken up in Chapter 8 of this book.

3. Context of health and illness services

Looking at the context of health service provision, sociology has addressed two main questions. The first relates to how the health services can be organised and the second is the study of health professionals themselves and how changes in inter-professional relations (for example between physicians and nurses and midwives, nurses and care-workers, radiographers and physicians) can affect how healthcare is practised in a society. These two questions will be addressed separately below.

(i) The organisation of healthcare

The core argument of this section is that sociology illustrates how the organisation of healthcare services is interwoven by social factors and social priorities. Sociology asks questions about the ways in which medical knowledge is produced and organised; how medical knowledge is linked to the spaces in which it is carried out[2] and the professions involved. Sociology can help health professionals and health policy workers analyse organisational models of health services and, in each case, ask questions, such as, who is included and who is excluded? In particular, sociology has concerned itself with the dominance of biomedicine in the organisation of healthcare in Western societies, and with contemporary key changes in the context of health and illness services, which we will consider briefly further on.

Sociological studies have challenged conventional understandings that suggest that biomedicine is the rational approach to health problems. Sociology has instead illustrated how biomedicine is a system that has succeeded because of its organisational dominance in healthcare. In effect, as Illich (1976; 1995) has pointed out, illness as we know it is a biomedical construction, that is, it is *created* by biomedicine, that *then* dictates a biomedical solution. The writings of the Michel Foucault (1926-1984), especially in *The Birth of the Clinic* (1973), have been particularly important to understanding the historical development of biomedicine as

---

2 For example, the body of medical knowledge about ageing has given rise to a specialism called gerontology, and hospitals are physically organised so that all gerontology patients are housed in the same place (the geriatric ward).

the dominant system of interpreting and treating illness in contemporary Western societies. Foucault describes the origins of modern medicine as an outgrowth of the modernisation of society, in which the profession of medicine along with other new professions of criminology, penology (the study of punishment), psychology and sociology developed in response to the need for a new type of administrative power in society. As part of the modernisation of societies, referred to earlier, administrative power replaced violence as a means of controlling populations who were concentrating in large numbers in urban spaces. Foucault's argument in *The Birth of the Clinic* is that the development and institutionalisation of modern biomedicine (as the focus on inner pathologies) which replaced earlier models of disease (such as the Galenic humoral model – disease as a disturbance of the body's balance, and the theory of miasma – disease as a result of polluted air and water) was not because of the rational progress implied in the development of biomedicine. Rather, Foucault (1973) argues that it was the result of modern medicine's development of the 'clinical gaze' which produced a new way of seeing the body – the so called new 'anatomical atlas' of the body. In late eighteenth century Europe, the medical profession introduced the concept of the medical examination of the live body (the physical examination) using the stethescope, and the dead body (the post-mortem) using the microscope, and the hospital was invented to make these processes efficient for the new biomedical professions of anatomy, psychiatry, radiology and surgery (Lupton, 2003: 23). The development of this new view of the body using the new technologies of biomedicine allowed biomedicine to define and treat medicine in its own terms. In Chapter 6, the role of biomedicine in contemporary understandings of health and illness is re-evaluated and contemporary challenges to biomedicine are examined.

In further exploring how sociology contributes to an understanding of the organisation of health services, we have chosen for the purposes of this introduction to also mention, briefly, contemporary key changes in the context of health and illness services, namely health promotion, community care and the rise of consumerism in healthcare delivery. In relation to health promotion, Thorogood (1992) has distinguished between a sociology *as applied* to health promotion and a sociology *of* health promotion. This means that sociology can help to extend health promotion and/or critique it respectively (Nettleton, 1995: 234). The main body of sociological studies applied to health promotion are sociological studies of lay health beliefs. Such studies investigate what the body of beliefs are, how they are related to the people's social and cultural milieu, for example, family circumstances, community or race, gender, generation, sexuality and so forth, and/or investigate how people perceive and respond to health messages (Frankel et al, 1991; Task Force on the Travelling Community, 1995; McKinlay, 1993; Collins and Shelley, 1997). In the more critical vein of sociology of health promotion, sociologists and social psychologists have pointed to the core idea of **individualism,** rather than social conditions, which is implicit in health promotion (for example, McQueen, 1989; Thorogood, 1992; MacLachlan, 1998). Essentially, this means that individuals are asked to take responsibility for changing particular behaviours or lifestyles. Yet, often these particular behaviours are part of the wider web of people's lives, their culture, their families, their communities and the infrastructures available to them. Ultimately, although health promotion looks beyond the biological as the factor determining an individual's health, it still tends to treat health problems as individual rather than social problems (Graham, 1984; MacLachlan, 1998). (A fuller discussion of this tension in health promotion is discussed in Chapter 14).

The development of community care as a policy trend is a feature of health policy in Western industrialised countries, particularly in the post-war period, and most especially in Ireland in the last two decades. This shift has been especially evident in psychiatric care. Sociologists have studied the origins, development and impact of this policy for mental health (for example, Busfield, 1986; Prior, 1991 and Chapter 10 of this text). Sociologists have also examined the experience of community care from care-givers' and care-receivers' perspectives (Ungerson, 1987; Thomas, 1993; O'Donovan, 1997; Fox, 2000). Sociology has shown how the development of community care is, in particular, interlinked with change (and stability) in family structures in society (O'Donovan, 1997; Edmondson, 1997; Saris, 1997; Finucane et al, 1994; Lundström and McKeown, 1994).

In relation to the development of consumerism in healthcare services, sociology has made a particular contribution to examining the trade-offs for groups in society (for example Hadley and Clough, 1991; Jones, 1998; McAuliffe, 1998; Gabe and Calnan, 2000). In particular, these sociological studies have shed light on the tension between a universal health system, based on the principle of equity, and a health system based on what people want and what they can pay for (a free-market). In addition, sociology has examined the exchange of power amongst different groups – between different groups of health professionals and between health service providers and health service users – in consumer-oriented health policies. These organisational dimensions of health services are taken up in greater detail in the later chapters of this book.

(ii) The changing role of health professions

The organisation of health professionals as groups of individuals within the health service is also crucial to understanding the social context of the health services in any given society. Sociology is at the heart of making sense of the changing role in health professionals, both in terms of what the new roles mean to professionals themselves and the implications for the recipients of healthcare. It is possible to identify a number of trends in the health and social policy context which are provoking changes in the role of health professionals and to which sociological knowledge has been applied.

One is the professionalisation of nursing. Sociological analyses of the professionalisation of nursing provide a critical appraisal of the transition from the vocational ideal of service, stereotyped by images of ministering angels and handmaidens of the doctor, to the ideals of nursing as a profession. Some commentators (for example, Witz, 1994, and Walby and Greenwell, 1994) have questioned whether the new professionalism (based on a distinct body of knowledge and research competence) and the values it inspires – autonomy and self-development, along with the weakening of traditional authority structures – can sustain the care ethic and the skills needed for the practical tasks of nursing. As nursing gains professional status and is developed in terms of new specialisms, the basic practical tasks of nursing are increasingly being taken up by healthcare assistants.

A second trend is the increase in managerial professions in healthcare, or managerial-led healthcare. Sociologists have identified the potential for this trend to lead to the 'de-professionalisation' of physicians (Freidson, 1970a; 1994; Haug, 1973), whereby the clinical leadership role of physicians is weakened. This is because health managers are increasingly in a position to make decisions about how healthcare institutions are run and to direct healthcare provision more broadly. A third trend is the rising costs of healthcare and the concerns of centre-right governments to gain value-for-money in healthcare. This trend raises questions over the correct 'professional-mix' required on the ground. In particular, which groups of healthcare workers, such as physiotherapists, radiographers, midwives and nurses can, or could in the future, replace their more expensive physician colleagues? This feature of the health policy context has also emerged because of the enforced reduction in junior doctor working hours. Sociologists have studied the development of new professional roles, such as in the nurse's role, and the emergence and limitations of new inter-professional relations on the ground in healthcare settings. The 'doctor-nurse game' is a seminal sociological study of the characterisation of nurse-physician relations (Stein et al, 1998 [1967]). The study described the essentially hierarchical relationship between physicians and nurses in healthcare settings. More recent studies (for example, Stein et al, 1990; Porter, 1999; Manias and Street, 2001; Hartley, 2002) have re-assessed this profile of nurse and/or midwife-physician relations and provide an excellent opportunity for health professions to reflexively understand the socio-structural conditions of their everyday work. (The changing role of health professionals is discussed in greater length in Chapter 12.)

Summary

What is sociology?
• Sociology is the social scientific study of society.
• Sociology is the study of the mutual shaping processes of how society influences individuals/groups of individuals and how individuals/groups of individuals influence society.

- The discipline of sociology was initiated in nineteenth century Europe to understand the transitions occurring in society during industrialisation.
- *Thinking sociologically* involves drawing linkages between personal issues and wider patterns and structures at large in society.
- Thinking sociologically also generates a sense of curiosity about why aspects of society are the way they are and challenges taken-for-granted understandings of society and everyday life continuously.
- *Doing sociology* or sociological studies involves systematic studies of the social world using research methods to collect information and social theories to explain patterns in society.

Why should health professions be interested in sociology?
We have presented key areas of health and healthcare to which we think sociology makes a significant contribution:

- *The nature of health and illness.* Sociology enables people to understand the social causes and social distribution of mortality and morbidity. The core argument presented in this section was that what happens in our bodies is very much a product of the kind of society we live in. The social conditions of our everyday lives are an important determinant of health and consequently improvements in our social environment, such as a reduction of poverty, improved housing, sanitation and nutrition have been more influential than improvements brought about by biomedicine in reducing levels of mortality in the past century.
- *Understanding experiences of health and illness.* The core argument of this section was that sociology is central to understanding how health and illness are defined and experienced differently by different individuals and groups in society. Sociology points to social and cultural reasons to explain variations in experiences of well-being and illness. The importance of understanding the social context of patients in order to deliver quality care is accentuated by the shift in health services to prevention, care and rehabilitation.
- *The social context of healthcare.* The core argument of this section was that sociology helps health professionals understand the manner in which healthcare services are interwoven with social factors and social priorities. This can help health professionals understand inclusion and exclusion in health services.
- It is to sociology that we turn to question dominant definitions of health and illness; to understand changing social trends and their impact on health; to broaden assessments of the appropriateness of healthcare systems for individuals and population groups; and to explore and evaluate alternative options for achieving health. In addition, sociological studies of the organisation of health professionals themselves can increase awareness of the factors inhibiting and/or enhancing inter-disciplinary healthcare delivery on the ground.

Topics for discussion and reflection
1. Read through the definition of sociology as presented in the first part of this chapter. Does it capture the meaning of sociology, as you understand it?
2. In this chapter, reasons were presented as to why sociology might interest health professionals. Are you convinced?

TWO

The sociologist's tool-kit, part 1: social theory

The objective of this chapter is to provide a route map to the primary social theories with the health professional reader in mind. Each social theory will be explained briefly in terms of the *model of social processes*, the *understanding of health and illness* and the understanding of the *role of health services* it presents. The strands of social theory outlined are: *structural functionalism, political economy theory, social action theory, post-structuralism* and *post-modernism*. These theoretical positions however are not exhaustive of all of the major schools of thought available through which to understand health and illness in social context. The reader will be introduced to *critical theory* in relation to research methodology in Chapter 3, and again in exploring lay and professional interactions in Chapter 8. *Feminist theory* will be introduced briefly in the present chapter in the context of social theory more generally, and will be revisited throughout the book as it relates to the substantive issues of various subsequent chapters.

In the previous chapter, sociology was defined as the study of the mutual shaping processes between individuals acting on society and society acting on individuals. Social theory is the body of knowledge used to explain how this mutual shaping occurs. Social theory and research methods form the back-bone of sociology. Together they create the scientific basis of sociology. The scientific strength of social theories is that they offer the social scientist a number of systematically worked-through perspectives on how the social world is organised – models of societal and individual interaction. Such models of how society operates can then be used to help understand a wide range of issues in contemporary life including patterns of health and ill-health, the way we organise our health system and our subjective understandings of health and ill-health. The interplay between social theory and research will be the subject of the next chapter. In later chapters we expand on how social theory is interwoven into understandings of health and illness under key themes.

What is social theory?
Social theory is about understanding the organising principles, or underlying mechanisms, of the societies we live in. The objective of social

theory is to draw out understandings about the societies we create and how the societies we live in influence our lives.

Another way of understanding social theory is to show what it is not. Social theory may be contrasted to naturalistic and individualistic theories of human understandings and human behaviours (Jones, 2003). Naturalistic theories seek to understand the organising principles of our biological make-up. Such theories purport that the way we understand ourselves and our human behaviour is a product of our innate animal or biological constitution. Naturalistic theories are also referred to as **biological determinism,** meaning that human life is *biologically* driven. Social theories dispute the idea of pre-determined human behaviour and feelings because of the on-going and active interpretive processes engaged in by individuals and groups in society, which is evident in the variation in human cultures across the world. Biological determinism has gained renewed interest, especially since 2001 when scientists achieved a total draft of the human genetic map in the **Human Genome Project.** However, this new knowledge of genetics can also inspire new knowledge of society and culture (Shostak, 2003). For example, a leading geneticist, Professor Steve Jones of University College London, recently remarked that considering we share almost 50 per cent of our genetic make-up with bananas and 98.8 percent with chimpanzees, there has to be something more than genetic constitution which can account for the vast differences between humans, bananas and chimpanzees (BBC Newsnight 26 March 2003). Furthermore, although genetics has become useful in tracing different states of genotype in humans across generations and cultures, this too makes the social and cultural influences all the more apparent. The values and beliefs we hold and the lifestyles we lead can be very different across generations and between different cultures. Human cultures could not change in diverse ways were human cultures pre-determined through our biological make-up.

The example of perceived differences between men and women is an illustrative case. Gender differences between men and women are frequently attributed to a biological basis of sex differences. Yet, as proponents of **feminist theory** have highlighted, the changing relations between men and women, and the changing spaces in human culture which men and women are allowed to occupy, points to the way in which biological differences are interpreted through social lenses. The twentieth century has seen remarkable changes for men and women in Western societies. In particular, early feminist movements had to overcome the exclusion of women from educational institutes, a practice that was justified on the basis that educating women would physically alter their ability to bear children. The status of women was not just perceived as biologically determined but determined, in particular, by their reproductive organs. 'Too much development of a woman's brain was said to atrophy the uterus, hindering the very function for which women were designed by nature' (Lupton, 2003:

134). Nonetheless, this biological determinism was challenged in Irish society, as elsewhere. Women were admitted to Trinity College Dublin for the first time in 1904 and in 2003 represented 60 per cent of the student body. Female students were permitted to live in the same university halls of residence as male students in 1972 and only by the early 1970s were female students in University College Dublin permitted to wear trousers. What this example points to is that social, cultural and political frameworks have reconfigured what male and female biology means.

Individualist theories are similar to naturalist theories in that they too look to aspects of the individual to explain human behaviour and human culture. **Individualist theories** purport that human understandings and behaviour are the products of our individual psychological constitution that creates innate natural drives. For example, warfare is a human behaviour that individualist theories invoke as evidence of our innate aggression. However, if people can also be peaceable, it is necessary to have a broader – or social – explanation that can explain the social circumstances in which aggression is likely to lead to warfare (Pilnick, 2002: 33). Pilnick suggests that, at best, we can only talk about a potential for aggression under particular environmental conditions (Pilnick, 2002: 33). In this sense, both naturalist and individualist theories lack a means of theorising socio-environmental conditions. They depend upon attributes of the self to produce the self *and* human culture. Social theory by contrast looks at the *interaction* between the social world and the individual in order to understand both. Social theory is about exploring the nature of who we are, what we believe in, and how we behave through understanding the nature of the social world and how it impacts upon our lives.

There is more than one social theory of how the social is constituted and interacts with individuals. In this chapter, we will elaborate five main strands of social theory that have become established in sociology and in the social sciences more broadly. What is common to all social theory is this concern with how the social world is ordered and how it influences patterns of individual understanding and behaviours. What differentiates the main strands of social theory is *what* are identified as the primary organising principles of society and the *manner* and *extent* to which the social influences patterns of individual behaviour.

The splits and divisions within sociology and social theory have led some to the view that sociology is worthless for practical healthcare (Sharp, 1994). Others (Porter, 1998a) have argued against this standpoint and instead assert that nurses (and other healthcare workers) assess social theories as other social scientists do and can discern which social theories best explain individual health and illness issues. Indeed, health professionals are not unaccustomed to discerning between competing theories of disease, competing theories of organisational management or competing theories of care, as in nursing theory (Porter, 1998a).

Main strands of contemporary social theory

Structural functionalism: how does society cohere?
Structural functionalism offers the following model of how society operates:

- Function and structure: different aspects of society function to maintain a basic structure (a structural consensus) for society.
- Society influences the way that we think (our beliefs) and the way that we behave (norms).

Structural functionalism is so called because within this perspective is an interest in how aspects of society *function* to maintain the overall *structure* of society. Society is theorised as a system of inter-dependent parts, analogous to the structure of the human body (Durkheim, 1964a [1895]). The emphasis within structural functionalism on how stability and consensus of meaning are established in society is most clearly inherited from Emile Durkheim (1858-1917). Durkheim was interested in how order and function in society could be maintained in the period of rapid changes which accompanied the rise of capitalism and industrialisation in European societies (see Chapter 1). It became very popular in the United States in the post-war period when sociologists embarked on programmes of research to explain the factors that bind individuals and groups together leading to social integration in society. This period of structural functionalism is notably associated with Talcott Parsons (1902-1979).

The essence of structural functionalism is that society is a system into which people are socialised (Harvey et al, 2000). The emphasis on social structures influencing people is referred to as a structuralist approach in sociology. Durkheim argued that our personalities, our likes and dislikes, thinking and emotions are shaped by the societies we grow up in. He believed that individuals come together in a society and create a collective consciousness which in turn becomes a structure which guides the way people think about the world (Durkheim 1964b [1893]). Thus collective consciousness and social institutions, such as the family system, educational system, and economic structures, are created in a society to uphold collective values and become a social reality that in turn acts to structure our society and constrain us. In twentieth century structural functionalism, Parsons refers to the norms of society as 'the socially accepted rules which people employ in deciding on their actions' and to values as 'beliefs about how the world should be' (Craib, 1992: 38).

Structural functionalism: understanding of health and illness
Structural functionalist social theory contributes to an understanding of health and illness by focussing on how a sense of wellness is an outcome of levels of belonging in a society (social cohesiveness). This social theory was developed through one of the most important health studies in sociology to

date – Durkheim's study of suicide (1952 [1897]). Durkheim concluded that the phenomenon of suicide – usually thought to be a highly individual act – has social causes. Suicide could be explained by individuals' degree of social cohesion in societies and levels of regulation in society. As we will show, he argued that over-integration and regulation can be as damaging to one's health as under-integration and regulation.

Durkheim's study draws on suicide data from eleven different countries and was one of the first studies in the social sciences to be based on the organised use of statistical methods (Simpson, 1952; see also Chapter 3 on research methodology). He identified that rates of suicide within particular societies were relatively unchanging over time, and that the rates varied between societies and between groups in society. Thus, the question became, 'Why does suicide vary by social context?' For example, Durkheim observed that Catholic countries (and Catholic areas within countries) had lower suicide rates than Protestant countries and also that Jews had lower suicide rates than Protestants. He also observed that married people and those with children had lower rates of suicide than those unmarried and men had higher rates of suicide than women. He noted that suicide rates were higher in societies in economic transition (in times of economic boom as well as slump) and political upheaval where the political climate was less established. Drawing on these patterns, Durkheim theorised that suicide was related to levels of social integration and levels of social regulation in society. As religions, Catholicism and Judaism act to cohere people into a collective consciousness whilst Protestantism is an individualist-oriented value system. Suicide rates were higher amongst those divorced, and especially among male divorcees since, according to Durkheim, men benefit more from the regulative effects of marriage than do women. And finally, the rise of suicide rates identifiable in times of economic and political upheaval is related to the transition from more integrated traditional societies to modern industrial societies.

From this theory of the relationship between social cohesion and rates of suicide, Durkheim identified two types of suicide which were characteristic of modern industrialising societies:

- *Egoistic suicide*: Resulting from insufficient integration into social groups/society (such as the case for certain religious groups and unmarried people).
- *Anomic suicide*: Resulting from insufficient regulation of individuals in society (such as in times of major political and economic change).

In addition, he identified two types of suicide characteristic of pre-industrial or traditional societies:

- *Altruistic suicide:* Resulting from excessive integration of individuals into a society.
- *Fatalistic suicide:* Resulting from over-regulation of individuals into society.

Altruistic suicide was identified by Durkheim in societies and among those with religious beliefs where sacrifice of life was regarded as a noble act. The so-called 'suicide bomber' made infamous by the 2001 September 11 attacks on the US and the suicide bombings which have become a characteristic part of the Israeli-Palestinian conflict are arguably modern-day versions of this type of suicide. Fatalistic suicide is a result of a society being experienced as an intolerably restrictive force. Durkheim imagined this type of suicide to be more of historical interest, for example it has been related to the time of widespread slavery.

Durkheim's study of suicide has of course been criticised. In particular Douglas (1967) criticises Durkheim for assuming that the available data on suicide are accurate, despite the cultural taboos around suicide that may have led to numerous omissions or mis-recordings. Nonetheless, Durkheim's ideas on suicide and the impact of social integration on health and well-being remain current. In particular, Durkheim's work has been rejuvenated in the concept of *social capital*, made popular by the contemporary book *Bowling Alone* by Robert Putnam (1995). The idea of social capital is that participation by individuals in local organisations creates social cohesion at a local level, which is good for your health. Healthy communities are those which develop physical and social amenities to facilitate such social interaction (Lomas, 1998; Putnam, 1995; 2000). (See also an account of David Coburn's argument about the impact of the loss of a sense of community on health in Chapter 5)

Structural functionalism: understanding of the health services
In this school of social theory, the health service is theorised in terms of the role it plays, along with the health professions it comprises, in the overall functioning of society. In structural functionalist theory, the role of the health professions, especially physicians, is to impartially regulate ill-health. Why did Parsons believe that sickness was something that needed to be regulated? Concurring with the principle concerns of structural functionalism, Parsons thought about sickness in terms of its effect on social integration amongst people. He was of the view that the state of sickness could interfere with the normal everyday carrying out of tasks and responsibilities. Thus, sickness could be dysfunctional not only for the individual but also for society, as people could opt out of their usual obligations. In order to prevent the dysfunctional aspects of sickness, Parsons observed that societies have created a *social process* surrounding sickness, namely customs and rules that have become routinised and that involve duties and obligations, which he labelled 'the sick role'. As Parsons noted, '[I]llness is not merely a 'condition' but also a social role' (Parsons, 1951a: 452). The sick role attempts to explain how individuals and societies cope with illness and is elaborated further in Chapter 8. Parsons' work was influential because he was writing at the time when there was an increased interest in psycho-somatic illnesses and in the role of motivation

in presenting or coping with illnesses (Annandale, 1998; White, 2000).

The role of the medical profession was also directly addressed by Parsons (1951b). He believed that it was the legitimate role of the medical profession to impartially regulate sickness and to identify those deemed to be in need of respite from work, and legitimately in need of the health services. The professions, he believed, were a group in society whose work was not predominantly defined by the value of capitalism, namely profit-seeking and utilitarian self-interest, but rather by the values of service and altruism (White, 2000; Annandale, 1998). His view of the medical profession as a service-oriented and altruistic institution came from the characteristics that distinguish professions from other groups in society, such as their lengthy education, professional culture and ethic of service to the community. Parsons' benign view of the health professions as altruistic and impartial service-providers has of course been contested. (See Chapters 8 and 12.)

Political economy: how in rich societies can so many people be so poor? (Macionis and Plummer, 1997: 76).

The political economy perspective offers the following model of how society operates:

- Based on Marxist theory, the political economy perspective purports that the economy is the defining structure of society.
- The perspective focuses on inequalities, especially class-based inequalities, in society as the basis of injustice and inevitable conflict in society.

The political economy approach became particularly popular during the time of the social movements of the 1960s and 1970s in Western societies, as well as in the academic social sciences where it challenged structural functionalist theory for ignoring inequalities in society. The ideas of a political economy approach are based on the thinking of Karl Marx (1818-1883) whose work has informed not only sociology but also economics, philosophy, political science and indeed political movements. Marx advanced a theory of society that held that whilst individuals have choices, these choices are limited by the society in which they live – or, more correctly, by the *economy* in which they live. According to Marx, humans[3] make society but not solely in the order of their choosing.

Men make their own history, but they do not make it just as they please; they do not make it under circumstances chosen by themselves, but under

---

3 Marx, in keeping with practices of the historical period in which he was writing, used the term 'men' to denote the human population. In current sociological scholarship, this would be considered unacceptable because it reinforces the marginal status of women.

circumstances directly found, given and transmitted from the past (Marx, 1954 [1852]: 10).

Marx was writing during the time of the development of capitalist society, an economic system he strenuously opposed. Marx believed that the way in which the production of goods and services is organised is fundamental to understanding the broader structure of society and the relations that individuals have to one another. He argued the economy created an *infrastructure* around people's lives and formed the basis for other institutions, such as religion, the family, systems of education or health, which he referred to as a *superstructure*. By this he meant that in capitalist societies wider social structures reflect and reinforce the ideals and values of the capitalist classes. Marx' emphasis on the power of structures in society to shape people's lives was, in part, a response to the common belief at the time (and now) that being poor is one's own fault. Marx believed this to be a form of 'false consciousness' whereby individuals were blamed for social problems that were created by the economic system in which they lived.

How, in a society so rich, could so many people be poor, was a central question for Marx (Macionis and Plummer, 1997: 76). The conflict was essentially a class conflict between a small group of people who owned the resources for production – the factories and other enterprises (the capitalist class or bourgeoise) – and the majority of the population who, in order to survive, had to sell their labour to earn a living (the proletariat). Marx believed that this conflict would eventually lead to a proletariat revolution and an end to the capitalist system. Thus, for Marx, the huge schism between the rich and poor is not inevitable, but rather would be changed by re-organising the system of production in a society. As Marx noted, 'The philosophers have only *interpreted* the world in different ways, the point is to change it' (Marx, 1963 [1845]: 83). Although many contemporary social theorists (for example, Holton and Turner, 1989; Lash and Urry, 1994; Beck, 1992) argue that the model of class divisions as advanced in Marxism has become weakened and paradoxically more complex, such that we should not speak of the traditional class system as the defining structural feature of society, the concept of class-based inequality remains a central concern within the social sciences. Moreover, Marxist analysis of class-based inequalities has been elaborated to understand other axes of the structural relations of inequalities such as gender and ethnicity. This issue will be explored in Chapter 4.

Political economy: understanding of health and illness
The central argument of the political economy approach to health is that capitalist economies based on profit-making create ill-health in society. The argument implies that the nature of our socio-economic environment is a primary determinant of our health. Political economists argue that capitalist

economies create ill-health because, in such economies, the *individual* is forced to deal with the social costs – now often referred to as the risks – of capitalist economies (Beck, 1992). Examples of the social costs of capitalist or market-driven economies are unemployment, raising families and facing retirement with limited support, lack of public transport, the high costs of housing and education, pollution through lax environmental controls on industry, chemical-rich and contaminated foods, and even the effects of wars, which are frequently economically-motivated. Critics of the political economy approach state that the argument of the political economists is illogical because it is in the *interests* of capitalism to promote a rise in the standards of living and environment in order to secure a healthy labour force and market place for capitalism to prosper (Hart, 1982). The question remains, nonetheless, as to why capitalist societies tolerate such inequalities in the levels of morbidity and mortality between the wealthiest and poorest members *within* countries. Furthermore, why are these differentiations of health status strongest within capitalist-dominated societies? (See Chapters 4 and 5 for a discussion on health inequalities.) Within contemporary Western democracies, there is a tacit recognition of the social costs or health risks of Western capitalist-based economies but there is variation in the ways in which governments 'shield' their citizens. For example, Europe is regarded as having a more socially democratic state system with stronger state welfare measures to protect at-risk or economically marginalised groups than the United States. In Ireland, the question is frequently asked if we should follow a Berlin or Boston style of socio-economic governance.

Political economy: understanding of the health services
The central argument of the political economy approach regarding health services is that capitalist-based medical services (or biomedical practices in capitalist-based economies) are damaging your health. This argument can be broken down into two main components: first, capitalist-based medicine is pursued for profit and is inequitable in terms of access; second, capitalist-based medicine detracts attention from the socio-economic bases of ill-health and creates an ideological dependence on biomedicine. These two points are elaborated below.

Political economists, notably Navarro (1980), argue that medicine under capitalist systems is pursued for profit and is inequitable in terms of access. This is because medicine in capitalist economies becomes a form of corporate investment such that new medical technologies and treatments are themselves only pursued to make a profit. For example, private biotechnology companies have been criticised for availing themselves of the publicly funded research under the human genome project, whilst retaining the results of their own research for profit-making (Pilnick, 2002: 101). This is the case in relation to new genetic testing for a pre-disposition to breast and ovarian cancer. A US biopharmaceutical company (Myriad Genetics)

, the patent on the method of diagnosis, putting it out of the reach of .ie healthcare providers, notably the UK National Health Service (NHS) ılnick, 2002: 105). From a global perspective, it is estimated that only 10 per cent of the global health research budget goes to tackle diseases such as malaria, tuberculosis (TB) and HIV/AIDS that constitute 90 per cent of the world's health problems (Editorial, *Guardian* newspaper, November, 2002). (A debate on global health inequalities is taken up in Chapter 5.) Similarly, many Western countries include privatised systems of healthcare whereby access to wealth enables one to have greater access to health services (see Chapter 13 on this issue in relation to Ireland). Political economy theorists point to the fact that cures are only developed for those who are able to pay for them. As such, Tucker has described the health industry as a 'self-perpetuating sickness industry rather than a service designed to ensure maximum health for all' (Tucker, 1997: 38). According to the political economy approach, however, there is an alternative: 'a socialized system of healthcare in which the state provides care for all free of charge (Lupton, 2003: 10), and where medical cures are not pursued for profit.

The second part of the argument is that capitalist-based medical services divert attention from the socio-economic causes *and* cures of ill-health. The work of McKeown (1984, 1995) and Szreter (1995) has shown that the reduction of morbidity and mortality over time has mostly been effected by improvements in nutrition and social conditions and public health interventions. Further, it has been established that the major causes of contemporary Western mortality and morbidity such as heart and lung diseases, various cancers and diseases of the central nervous system, are related more to socio-environmental conditions than biological agents and that such diseases are not curable via the application of intensive care or use of drugs (Tucker, 1997; White, 2000). Not only have researchers in this tradition shown that biomedicine – because of its failure to address socio-economic conditions in an integrated fashion – has been less than successful in the reduction of mortality and morbidity, they have also highlighted the immediate damage done by the healthcare industry. It is argued that medical treatments and drugs have created more ills than cures (Illich, 1976). Examples include drug related injuries from trial drugs, medication errors, misused drugs, contaminated drugs and so forth. According to Morrall (2001), up to 20 per cent of all hospital admissions in the UK are due to adverse drug reactions and, according to D'Arcy and Griffin (1986), half the amount of money spent on prescription drugs is spent on drugs to correct adverse reactions.

The inattention to social and economic issues and the focus on the individual as the source of the problem is an example of Marx' notion of *false consciousness* as outlined above. Political economy researchers argue that capitalist medicine has an **ideological effect** on the way we understand our bodies, namely that capitalist medicine focuses on *the individual* and the *biomedical solution* – and diverts public attention from the social and economic climate that underpins a vast range of sicknesses and which, if addressed, would be a powerful route to preventative health medicine. Recent and contemporary writers within this tradition, especially Ivan Illich (1976), Kenneth Zola (1972, 1984) and Vicente Navarro (1980) formulated a sociological challenge to the power and indeed the worth of biomedicine in society, which will be explored more fully in Chapter 6.

Social action theory: how do individuals' thoughts and actions create society?
Social action theory offers the following model of how society operates:

- Society is made up of people's understandings of the world and their behaviours based on these meanings (what people think and what they do).
- Societies have the potential to change because people's understandings of the world and their actions are open to re-construction in the interactions of everyday life.

The *social action* or *interpretive* school of social theory is fundamentally different to the schools of social theory discussed so far, principally in the way it views the structure-action relationship, or the power individuals have in shaping the society they live in. Social action theory is concerned *less* with how structures – such as capitalism, in the case of the political economy perspective or the intricate web of inter-related institutions in the case of functionalism – shape people's lives and *more* with how individual actions and beliefs shape societies. Social action theory has also a different concept of social change to the more structuralist theories of structural functionalism and political economy. Since action theory does not view society as being *shaped* by large-scale systems in society, large-scale systems in society are not held responsible for *change* in society. The 'action' in social action theory implies that societies have the potential to change because societies are the result of on-going meaningful actions by the members involved (Jones, 2002: 21).

This school of thought is linked to classical social theory through the work of Max Weber (1864-1920). Both Marx and Durkheim looked to the structures and social institutions in society in order to understand the actions and the social conditions of individuals. Weber argued instead that in order to understand society, we must inquire into how individuals give meaning to their actions. Although Weber did not deny that social structures existed, he believed that social structures, such as organisations and religion, were created and recreated through individuals' social actions (Weber, 1978 [1929]).

This theoretical approach launched a research agenda of exploring subjective understandings and the situated interactions between individuals in the context of everyday-life (what is called the *micro* level) rather than the study of large-scale social systems (the *macro* level*)*. Thus, once again, adjusting the social theory lens can imply an adjustment of what is considered important in social research. However, more than the other theoretical approaches discussed so far, social action theory is a broad church encompassing the sub-divisions of *symbolic interactionism, labelling theory* and *ethnomethodology*. Below, we will introduce symbolic interactionism and labelling theory under *social action theory: understandings of health and illness* and ethnomethodology under *social action theory: understandings of the health services*.

Social action theory: understanding of health and illness
The social action theory approach makes a key contribution to an understanding of health and illness by opening up a body of research into the subjective meanings and experiences of health and illness. Research in this area has focussed less on health or wellness *per se* but has covered diverse groups of people and groups of illness (Lawton, 2003). Examples of such studies include research on chronic illness (Anderson and Bury, 1998; Williams, 2000), those with critical illness (Rier, 2000), pain (Bendelow, 1993; Bendelow and Williams, 1995), autism (Gray, 1994) and AIDS/HIV (Ciambrone, 2001). Research on the subjective experience of health and illness will be elaborated on in Chapter 8.

As well as exploring the subjective understandings of illness, the social action theory approach opens up an exploration of *inter-subjective* understandings of illness. The social action approach is concerned with the way in which categories of health and illness are not pre-given objective or concrete realities, but rather social constructs which are negotiated in interactions between people (or in inter-subjective relations). This principal of 'meaning created in interaction' is grounded in the work of the founding father of **symbolic interactionism,** George Herbert Mead (1863-1931). Mead was interested in how a view of the 'self' or identity is co-constructed in interaction with others. Erving Goffman was also a pioneering figure of symbolic interactionism. His work broadly explored the **dramaturgical techniques** of 'impression management' in which people engage in order to present aspects of themselves to others in everyday life. This is the work we do to create a meaning of ourselves in correspondence with others. Goffman was particularly interested in the management of stigmatised or spoiled identities, that is, where there is an identification of 'undesired diferentness' (Goffman, 1968). His work explored the differences in identity management strategies of those who have a visible stigmatising condition (such as blindness) and mostly invisible stigmatising conditions, such as diabetes (Goffman, 1968). Goffman's concept of **stigma** (Goffman, 1968) has been developed in an array of health studies to explore the social production of 'healthy' and 'ill' or 'spoilt' identities in the interaction techniques of people with physical and mental illnesses in their daily intercourse with others. Such studies have included those with epilepsy (Scambler, 1989), AIDS,

(Alonzo and Reynolds, 1995; Surlis and Hyde, 2001), sexually transmitted diseases (O'Farrell, 2002; Taylor, 2001; Green, 1995; Lee and Craft, 2002), diabetes (Hopper, 1981), visual impairments (Davis, 1975), deafness (Higgins, 1981), disability (Susman, 1994) mental illness (Hall et al, 1993; Herman, 1993) and pregnancy among single women (Hyde, 1998; 2000a; 2000b).

Becker (1966) developed this broad theoretical position of symbolic interactionism into a well-known specific theory of how *deviant* identities are produced in social interaction, called **labelling theory.** Becker's work contends that deviance (or deviant identities) may be socially *produced* by others through the application of labels. Symbolic interactionism stresses identity creation as a two-way interpretative process. Labelling theory, by contrast, emphasises less the creative role of managing one's identity that is apparent in Goffman's work and in symbolic interactionism as a whole, and more the ability to have a meaning imposed on certain groups of people (Jones, 2003: 105). In fact, labelling theory is more interested in how sometimes people become *victims,* because of the power of others (usually powerful groups in society) to define the normal from the deviant (Jones, 2003: 105). Whilst Becker's (1966) work was developed in relation to crime, Thomas Scheff (1966) developed labelling theory in relation to mental illness. Here too the emphasis was on the label of mental illness being an outcome of the power of some members of society (for example, psychiatrists) to *define* the behaviours of others as deviant or pathological. An example of the power of labelling was shown in a famous experimental study involving eight researchers presenting themselves for treatment to 12 different psychiatric hospitals in the US (Rosenhan, 1973 reported in Grbich, 1999: 42). All of the researchers reported (faked) symptoms of hearing voices and particular words; all were hospitalised for up to fifty-two days, with an average of nineteen days, and seven of the eight researchers were diagnosed with schizophrenia and put on large amounts of medication (over 2,000 tablets between eight persons). All of the researchers pursued writing during their hospitalisation which, in some sites, appeared in the clinical notes as pathological behaviour. Labelling theory is thus critical of conventional psychiatric care for underestimating the potential for misdiagnoses and the negative domino effect labels of mental illness can have on individuals' identities. An evaluation of this theory is discussed at greater length in Chapter 10 on mental illness.

Social action theory: understanding of the health services
The social action theory approach contributes to an understanding of the health services by focussing on the micro-context, or the everyday social interactions within the health services. In particular, the social action perspective in health studies has most commonly been advanced in research inquiring into lay rather than health-professional perspectives. This research agenda is also often used as a political agenda for democratising the

healthcare system, promoting greater patient voices and elucidating imbalances of power within healthcare systems.

Ethnomethodological studies are particularly significant in social action led research on the health services. '**Ethnomethodology** is the study (*ology*) of people's (*ethno*) methods of creating social order' (Craib, 1992: 103). Thus, ethnomethodological studies differ somewhat from the broader social action approach in that they are much less interested in *what* the social world means to individuals and more *how* it is constructed in everyday settings. Ethnomethodological studies have been developed to explore how individuals *accomplish* social order in everyday settings, focussing on the habits, rules and rituals that structure everyday life. Harold Garfinkel, who was significant in the development of empirical studies in this field, described ethnomethodology as an interest in the 'organized artful practices of everyday life' (1967: 11). In his classes in 1960s USA, he encouraged his students to carry out experimental games, such as attempts to bargain with cashiers for goods in a department store and going home in the evening to their parents and pretending to be a lodger in their own homes (Craib, 1992: 104). In this way, he purported to show the fragility of the social accomplishment of everyday life and how, as individuals, we have choices about actively sustaining social order or disrupting it.

A body of work has developed in the ethnomethodological tradition which examines interactions between patients and healthcare systems. Accordingly, the concern is much less with addressing the patients' or doctors' perspectives, but specifically in uncovering the rules of method which individuals use to socially produce the 'successful' medical encounter. Emerson's (1970) study of the female gynaecological examination by male doctors is a well-known example of an ethnomethodological study. Her analysis exposes the use of conventions, rules and rituals to create a medical context for the gynaecological examination and thus the avoidance of the 'heterosexual context' of a male touching female genitals. The study reveals how the medical context, although anticipated by client and doctor, is not automatically given but is re-constructed in each professional-patient encounter through the organisation of the physical space, the presence of a female nurse, the demeanour and clothing of the staff, the use of language and body language which are worked upon to prevent the potential for misinterpretation. Further studies, such as those by Mishler (1984), Atkinson and Heath (1981), Heath (1981; 1984) and Atkinson (1995) have addressed the perceived power imbalance within encounters between health professionals and patients. These studies have explored how encounters between patients and doctors can follow a routinised sequential ordering to facilitate the health pofessional rather than the patient. Research in this area will be further elaborated in Chapter 8 which deals with lay-patient interactions.

The main criticism of social action theory arises from its variance from the structuralist approaches heretofore reviewed. The social action perspective focuses on agency rather than social structure – that is how individuals interpret events and create social order and power relations – on the spot rather than the historical and wider social context of those events. The emphasis on flexibility and uniqueness may be said to obscure stability and consistency in individuals' actions and social settings, failing to explain the background to people's motives and goals or why people continue to act the way they do. For example, the social action perspective strips sociology bare of many of its analytical concepts such as structural relations of gender, class, age or race, institutional socialisation through religion, education, family values and so forth. Interactionists, therefore, are accused of looking at interaction 'in a vacuum' (Haralambos and Holborn, 1991: 805) or indeed as being potentially 'blind and stupid' (Craib, 1992: 90). However, the criticism of this approach must be balanced with its achievements. First, as will be discussed in the next chapter, it gave impetus to a whole new system of qualitative research methods within the social sciences that emphasise the detail of people's lives. Second, social action theory presents a challenge to the theoretical frameworks of the political economy approach and structural functionalism in terms of how social structures are believed to impose meanings on individuals' lives. Social action theory suggests that we need to be sensitive to individuals' own meanings.

Post-structuralism and Michel Foucault: how does language influence the way we see and judge the world?
Post-structuralism (also called *discourse theory*) offers the following model of how society operates:

- Language or discourses are deemed to be the source of people's mindsets, influencing how they view the world at a particular time in history and place in the world (Jones, 2003: 125).
- Social change may be understood by comprehending the origins of particular discourses (for example medical discourses) and how they come to dominate ways of thinking about the world. In thus revealing how discourses are **socially constructed**, oppositional discourses (or knowledge systems) can emerge.

Michel Foucault (1926-1984) was a French social philosopher and social critic and was the most famous post-structuralist theorist. As will become apparent, his many books included significant works on the body, health and society: *Madness and Civilization* (1967), *The Birth of the Clinic* (1973) and *The History of Sexuality* (1990 [1978-86] [3 volumes]). As a post-structuralist, Foucault theorised language as the defining structuring force in society, in the same way that Durkheim referred to social institutions in society, and Marx referred to the economy as predominantly influencing social life. Post-structuralists do not understand language in the linguistic sense – as the languages we speak – but rather as representing bodies of knowledge, or discourses, which can become a language for interpreting and defining the world around us (Jones, 2003: 145). Foucault regarded the way our beliefs and ways of life are influenced through knowledge systems as 'a *knowledge based way of thinking*' (Jones, 2003: 25) and as the defining aspect of modern society. As knowledge is seen as the defining structuring influence in modern societies, knowledge is inextricably linked with power for the poststructuralists. However, unlike Marx and Weber, Foucault did not believe that power necessarily resides with, or is wielded by, any one group (for example, the bourgeoise) or institution (for example, the state) in society. Rather, power exists within *all* social relations.

How is social change to be understood in post-structuralist theory? The view that our beliefs and behaviours originate in and are shaped by knowledge systems seems very remote from the subjective consciousness as the locus of interpretation in social action theory. In post-structuralist theory, individual thought is considered to be constituted through discourses more than through the act of individual consciousness. Indeed post-structuralist theory is frequently referred to as representing the 'death' or, at the very least, 'de-centreing' of the 'actor' or 'subject' (Jones, 2003: 140-141). Nonetheless, poststructuralist power is not absolute and Foucault theorises spaces of human agency in the mobilisation of social change. He does this in three ways in different periods of his work. The first is analogous to Newton's *Third Law in Physics – for every action there is an equal and opposite reaction*. Foucault (1990) [1978-86 [3 volumes]) argued that groups that are targeted by professional knowledge such as mentally ill people, prisoners, and homosexuals, have the resources to resist, precisely *because* they are targeted. In this sense, Foucault believed that power is a productive (or creative) force in society. To be targeted by a professional discourse can, and is, according to Foucault, a necessary condition to generate resistance – a strike in the opposite direction. This is interesting in light of the more passive account of labelling theory purported by Becker (1966) and Scheff (1966) (as discussed under symbolic interactionism above) and the counter emergence of patient self-advocacy groups, especially in the field of mental health, which will be discussed in Chapter 10.

The second source of agency – or resistance to structural power – in Foucault's work derives from his notion of the relativity of knowledge. Foucault elaborated a lineage within philosophy (Nietzsche, 1967 [1901]; Fleck, 1935 [1979]; Kuhn, (1970 [1962]) that alleges that knowledge is not inherently correct or true. Rather, knowledge is conditional on a constellation (system) of social relations at a particular point in time. Foucault carried out real-world research into this theory of knowledge (see below). Foucault's work was about rendering visible that which we take for granted by showing how it used to be different in the past (Giddens, 2001a) and excavating the bases of contemporary knowledge. Foucault's scholarship was based on what he referred to as the 'genealogical method' (2001 [1970]), or the 'archaeology of knowledge' (1972), a methodology which investigated how systems of knowledge came to be established at particular times and places. By revealing the conditional bases of knowledge, the knowledge/power complex becomes less absolute and more open to intervention and change (Delanty, 1999). According to Foucault, the necessary conclusion is that if the basis of power (knowledge) is relative, so too is power itself.

The third source of agency or source of resistance to societal power arises in his later work (later volumes of the *History of Sexuality*) under the concept of the creation of subjectivity. In this Foucault describes how, as individuals, we can interact with dominant discourses (such as the imperative in modern medicine to exercise, eat certain foods, sleep at certain times) in a reflexive manner. We can thus engage with our own sets of priorities and in doing so create new identities. This reflexive engagement and active construction of identities is achieved through what Foucault refers to as 'techniques of the self' or ways of constituting our own identity. This idea is more fully developed in postmodern theory (see the next section below).

Post-structuralism: understanding of health and illness
Foucault's work has made an important contribution to understandings of health and illness, primarily because he provided social scientists with a provocative way of thinking about the body. We are accustomed in sociology (through the work of other social theorists discussed heretofore) to thinking about how social factors, such as inequalities in the case of political economy approaches, or social systems in the case of functionalist approaches, affect health (or the natural body). Both these approaches acknowledge that social factors and the natural body are *interrelated* but generally theorise the body and the social as *separate* entities. Foucault's work goes further. He maintains that the body (the natural) is a *social* construction. What is deemed to be 'natural' is interpreted differently in different historical and cultural settings and is therefore a product of our social worlds (as opposed to the something *onto* which the social world acts). Looking at our bodies, health and illness from this perspective imply that we can only know what our body means, and what it means to be healthy or unhealthy, through the meanings we ascribe to aspects and symptoms as derived from our culture and contemporaneous knowledge systems. Some commentators have argued that reducing the biological to the social is as wholly an inadequate theory as reducing the social world to the biological (see Cheek and Porter (1997) for a debate on this issue). In other words, in challenging the popular naturalistic idea that we are biologically determined, Foucault's theory ends up being socially deterministic by not giving due recognition to the physical aspects of our bodies. However, in the brief outline of Foucault's work that follows,

we also get a strong argument on how we (from lay and scientific perspectives alike) create an understanding of the physical through the social.

In *The Birth of the Clinic*, Foucault (1973) argues that disease does not have an existential (or real) existence other than how we know diseases through the discourses available to us. Foucault analyses the history of ideas in the medical understandings of the body which, he argues, do not show a linear model of knowledge progression, such that we may speak of 'advances in medical science'. Rather, he argues, they are products of socio-cultural values of their time and a presentation of different discourses or knowledge systems of the body structure or 'anatomical atlases'. For Foucault, definitions of the body and the reality of disease are *creations* of the medico-scientific gaze. Similarly, in *The History of Sexuality*, (1990 [1978-86 [3 volumes]), Foucault challenges the commonly accepted idea that the modern period has released us from the sexual repression of the Victorian era. In fact, he argues the reverse – that sexuality is much more controlled in the contemporary era, precisely because of the surveillance made possible by our obsession with talking about our sexuality, the developing of classifications (such as homosexual and paedophile) and treatments for sexuality. (An evaluation of Foucault's work on the body, health and illness is presented in Chapter 7.

Post-structuralism: understanding of the health services
Foucault views the health professions as being among the new regulators of social life, 'a disciplinary power' superseding the role of religion and morality in traditional societies. For Foucault, the development of modern sciences, such as the new biomedical sciences and psychiatry, as well as the social sciences of criminology, penology, psychology and sociology, has created a modern regulatory system over the body. As described above, poststructuralist theory is an investigation in to *why* and *how* particular knowledge systems emerge. Foucault regards the new sciences as being effectively recruited by the modern state to help it confront two major challenges of the modern world: urbanisation and the needs of industrial capitalism (Jones, 2003: 124-125).

In terms of how these knowledge systems become powerful, Foucault points to two key ways. One is the regulation of bodies *en masse* which he refers to as 'bio-politics'. This is achieved through the collection and organisation of data about individuals directly by the state (such as the national census), through a wider network of private organisations (for example, from places of employment and health insurance companies) and through public organisations (such as hospitals, universities and health and safety authorities). The second is the regulation of the individual body, which he refers to as 'anatomo-politics'. This is achieved through the internalisation of rules and ideas of the modern sciences (for example, the rules of healthy eating, or a healthy sex-life) and through supervision within institutions of the state such as hospitals, factories and prisons.

Particularly disturbing for Foucault was the expansion of medical practice (or the 'clinical gaze') into the socio-emotional realm, especially in the field of psychiatry and the ways in which modern medicine requires the patient to be passive, yet confessional. Foucault's studies of medical history laid much of the bases for the sociology of health and illness and, in particular, the sociological critique of the biomedical model. The anti-psychiatric movement in many countries also took up Foucault's ideas on the **medicalisation** of madness. However, Foucault did not always agree with this (O'Farrell, 1989). His work is political in the sense that it shows how powerful discourses come to define notions of the self and the body but the 'resistant' expert account (for example a sociological critique of biomedicine or the anti-psychiatric movement) is, for Foucault, merely another competing expert discourse. There are no heroes in Foucauldian sociology, just an examination of the pedestals on which they stand. (The medicalisation of the body is taken up as a theme in several chapters later in this book; see, for example, Chapter 6 on challenges to biomedicine, Chapter 9 on the sociology of the lifecycle, and Chapter 11 on science and technology in medicine.)

Postmodern social theory: how does society continuously emerge in surface productions?

Postmodern social theory offers the following model of how society operates:

- Postmodernist social theory challenges 'modernist social theories' which emphasise how social ordering in society is established through enduring structures (such as the economy or inter-connecting social institutions) by instead emphasising the transient and surface-level nature of society. Metaphorically speaking, there are no roots to society in postmodernist social theory.
- Postmodernist theory draws attention to the fragmentation of social life (the fact that we do not all experience social life in the same way), instability in who we are and the multiple nature of our identities.

Postmodernist theory is associated with social theorists such as Jean-François Lyotard (1924-1998) and Jean Baudrillard (1929-present). Postmodern theory is about being able to understand aspects of our lives (such as notions of the body) in advanced Western societies in which change is constant, and stable notions of what society is like or should be like are undermined. Therefore, it tells us more about how, as individuals, we negotiate our lifestyles and life chances from a plurality of modes of living in a globalised world. The central tenets of postmodernist theory can be made more explicit by comparing it to modernist theories. Further below, we highlight how postmordernist theories have elements in common with post-structuralist theory and action theory.

Modernist thinking is a product of the Enlightenment (see Chapter 1 for an introduction to the notion of modernity). This was a broad philosophical movement across the arts, sciences and humanities that emerged approximately 200 years ago. Enlightenment thought advanced the merits of liberalism and the need to move away from restrictive practices. It promoted scientific inquiry and the scientific mission of uncovering the logic of how the social and natural world works. It promoted the development of democracy and the nation state. Most fundamentally, the spirit of the Enlightenment was the advancement of a belief in individual and societal progress through rational thinking rather than tradition. Enlightenment thought is very apparent in the foundations of sociology. The theories of Marx, Comte and Durkheim and the ensuing political economy and structural-functionalist approaches are modernist social theories. They are characteristic of modernist social theory in three main respects: (i) society is viewed as having a historical trajectory (a specific origin and future) and is based on a logic of progress resulting in the betterment of society (the reader may recall Marx' alternative economic system and the development of new forms of social cohesion for Durkheim); (ii) they are based on what is known as 'meta-narratives' or grand social theories; modernist social theories lay claim to being able to talk about how societies work as a whole as though society has an identifiable overarching logic; (iii) Comte's and Durkheim's sociology and the structural functionalism of the twentieth century was based on creating certainty about society through the application of scientific principles (see Chapter 3 for a further discussion on this issue). Postmodernist theory challenges all three of these principles.

The problem as far as postmodernists are concerned is that modernity's idea of paths to progress simply did not materialise – a new moral order as Durkheim had predicted did not emerge and neither did Marx' revolution (Porter, 1998a: 206-207). Postmodern theory vehemently rejects the notion of the grand theory *of* society or *for* society. Instead of a grand theory *of* society, postmodern theory focuses on the transient and superficial nature of contemporary life, such as fashions, trends and media images. Instead of a theory *for* society the whole idea of freedom in postmodern theory is bound up with the idea of freedom from prescriptions. As Jones puts it: 'For modernist thinkers, we can only become free if we live as they tell us we should, whereas for postmodernists we will only be free when nobody feels able to tell us how to live' (2003: 162).

A key contribution of postmodernist theory, then, has been to challenge the way we theorise society. Instead of looking for stability in enduring relationships or structures in society, such as those of class, gender and age, postmodern theory encourages researchers to look for change and contingency. Postmodernist thinking defies reductionism of the social identities of individuals and social groups. Instead of using the accepted categories of modernist social thinking such as black/white, homosexuality/heterosexuality, disabled/able-bodied, post-modern theorists try to show difference and diversity within these categories. In the writings of Lyotard (1984) in particular, the rejection of the meta-narrative is a politics of rejection of dogmatism, or the reduction of the heterogeneity of humanity into homogenous ideas about the world. 'Trying to squeeze humanity, in all its diversity, into the confines of an overarching model, or meta-narrative' as Jean Francois Lyotard (1984) terms it, inevitably leads to the subjugation of those who do not fit in with our ideas of the way forward' (Porter, 1998a: 207).

This abandonment of meta-theories of and for society is based upon postmodernist ideas about truth and knowledge. As mentioned, modernist theory was based on the use of reason and science to discover the reality of the world, which is termed a *realist* position. Postmodernist theory (in common with post-structuralist theory) is instead deliberately *relativist*, meaning that different ways of knowing the world are just that – different (Porter, 1998a: 208). Postmodernism and post-structuralism share a common interest in deconstructing how ideas about the social (and natural world, as we will see below in relation to the body) are merely accepted (but transient) versions of social reality. Drawing from Friedrich Nietzsche (1844-1900), a philosopher whose writings are most influential on contemporary postmodernism, there are multiple ways of viewing truths about the world and there is no privileged position from which we can judge which way of knowing is more truthful or real than others. The 'will to truth' is described as the 'will to power' (Nietzsche, 1967 [1901]). Having one's position persuaded to be a truth is based on the power of promotion. Postmodernism is thus only concerned with interpreting representations and images of reality in contemporary life.

Postmodern social theory: understanding of health and illness

In the above discussion, postmodernist theory has been described as a rejection of looking for underlying structures and realities in society in favour of a sociology of constantly-emerging surface productions. The core contribution of postmodernist theory to understandings of health and illness then is to conceptualise the body as a social artefact or creation. Similar to Foucault's theorising of the body[4], the body, in postmodernist theory, is no longer regarded as having a true essence but rather is capable of being produced and re-produced in different ways. In effect, the body becomes an instrument of make believe. The body as make believe in postmodernist theory is derived in particular from the writings of Baudrillard (1981) whose

---

4   In the latter works of Foucault (latter volumes of the *History of Sexuality* (1990 [1978-86] [3 volumes]), there is some discussion of the refashioning of the body as a form of agency by 'techniques of the self' or individual power.

work has been described as 'a sociology of appearances' (Jones, 2002: 235). For Baudrillard, 'life is made up of images and signs – the hyper-real – that has no reality other than its own' (Jones, 2002: 235). This opens up for sociological analysis the contemporary preoccupation with bodily appearance where bodies can become an image of how we want them to be. According to Annandale:

> Under conditions in which it is no longer possible to distinguish 'the real' and 'the image', the body becomes ripe for reconstruction. Kroker and Kroker (1988) assert that in the postmodern condition the natural body becomes obsolete, no longer needed in the technologically advanced capitalist age (Annandale, 1998: 51).

The attainment of an image of the *appearance* of health (toned and fat-free body) can become more important than the attainment of health *per se* (Monaghan, 2001 cited in Lawton, 2003: 33). Postmodernist theorists point to the emergence of technologies for slimming, as well as technologies of body building, technologies of gender alteration, cosmetic enhancements and even genetic design as evidence of ways in which the body and ideas of health have become an important commodity and system of signs in contemporary society.

Postmodernist theories of health do not of course go un-criticised. Criticisms of postmodernist theorising of the body arise from precisely its self-professed aim of focussing on appearances to the neglect of how the *self* experiences the body and health and illness (social action approach). Furthermore, some feminist approaches criticise postmodernist theory for ignoring the patriarchal dimensions of the pressure on women, in particular, to appear beautiful. As Naomi Wolf, a popular contemporary feminist writer, has pointed out: 'During the past decade, women breached the power structure; meanwhile eating disorders rose exponentially and cosmetic surgery became the fastest growing medical speciality' (1991: 10). This suggests that some of the categories of modernist thinking such as gendered relations between men and women remain relevant to understanding how bodies and health are re-fashioned in contemporary societies.

Postmodern social theory: understanding of health services
Postmodernist theory takes the view that forms of medical knowledge and the health services based on these knowledges are forms of commodity products. The central idea of the relativism of medical knowledge, as discussed earlier in relation to Foucault's poststructuralist ideas, also continues to be a major theme in post-modernist theorising. There is perhaps a subtle difference between the poststructuralist and postmodernist approach, however. For Foucault, biomedicine has developed as a particular discourse and we can make sense of how this discourse or knowledge system emerged by reference to a wider socio-historical context (urbanisation and

Table 2.1. *Overview of social theory: models of social processes and of health*

Theory Strand	Model of Social Processes	Understanding of health and illness	Understanding of health services
Structural Functionalism	Society is a system of interconnecting functions (roles) bound by a social consciousness.	Sickness/disease is determined by levels of social coherence in society.	Health professionals as legitimate regulators of health and illness.
Political Economy	Social structures are bound up with economic structures. Capitalist economies cause class-based conflict in society.	Capitalist economies cause ill-health	Capitalist-based medicine is damaging to health.
Social Action Theory	Society is made up of human actions and human meanings.	Health and illness are subjectively and inter-subjectively attributed concepts.	Health services depend on the social acceptance of 'medical knowledge' and 'health professions'.
Foucault/ Post-structuralism	Knowledge is a form of power. Different forms of knowledge (discourses) create different ways of social life.	Knowledge of health and illness is not progressive but merely a product of different discourses.	The discipline of medicine and health professions act as a disciplinary power on the body (anatomo-politics) and public health (bio-politics).
Postmodernism	Society, in so far as it exists at all, is made up of transient and superficial representations of life which can appear 'real' through the power of promotion.	As it is no longer possible to identify 'the real', notions of the body, health and illness are simply ideas available for consumption.	Orthodox medical knowledge and medical services are commodities we choose/choose not to consume.

the development of industrial capitalism). By contrast, postmodernist theorising does not look for the underlying structures of *why* a particular knowledge system emerges (a logic of progression) rather it concentrates on *how* it is sustained through promotion and image.

Postmodernist theory views health systems as being promoted like any other commodity such as financial institutions, universities and so forth. The argument in relation to health is that there is increased individualisation in society in terms of how we choose to live (ranges of healthy and unhealthy lifestyles) which question the idea of a universal health system. In many contemporary Western societies, it is possible to buy healthcare today as one might buy a holiday or any other consumer good. Healthcare is delivered with consumers (individuals with needs) rather than citizens (pre-defined universal needs) in mind. Not surprisingly then, postmodernist theorising may be set in opposition to the political economy approach. The latter, as described earlier, criticises the individualising of health problems to the neglect of their social causes. In addition, postmodernist theories of health services may be contrasted to the political economy approach for neglecting the issue of unequal access to healthcare, including the resources of body enhancement technologies it highlights and, finally, for its preoccupation with cosmetic issues to the neglect of diseases of poverty. Approaches to healthcare provision are further discussed in Chapter 13.

Summary

- A number of key sociological theories provide various explanations as to how societies are organised and how they operate. (See Table 2.1)
- Since each of the theories presents a different view of how the social world is organised, each consequently brings out different under-standings of health and the treatment of health in society. This capacity to offer differing interpretations of the social world is, in fact, the contribution of social theory to the social sciences.
- The role of social theory in the social sciences is to provide us with a range of 'camera angles' on the relationships of self and society, with each camera angle bringing certain aspects of society into focus. For example, the political economy approach emphasised economic relations in society and in particular how capitalist economies could create inequalities, including health inequalities in society. The social action theory approach emphasised the role of subjective consciousness in creating society and thus emphasised that concepts of health and illness are not simply objective pre-defined categories but are interpreted within biographical and social contexts.
- Social theory does not just present social scientists with one account of how the social world operates, but several. In so doing, it offers the social scientist a number of different and competing approaches to interpreting society, health and illness.

- Social theories make a contribution to understanding society, health and illness precisely because they are not held as truths about society relevant for all times and in all places. Rather, they provide social scientists with theoretical propositions which can be validity-tested in the experiences of healthcare in everyday life as well as in social research.

Topics for discussion and reflection

1. Do you think we need social theory to explain how human culture is created or can we rely on biological and individualistic theories instead?

2. What new ways of thinking about contemporary local health issues (such as the decline in the uptake of the MMR vaccine or the shortage of hospital beds), or global health issues (such as differences in the way AIDS may be treated) might the different theoretical perspectives present? Are some of the theories more useful than others?

THREE

The sociologist's tool-kit, part 2: research methodology

This chapter is about research methodology. Questions of methodology are questions about how a researcher chooses research methods for a particular research project. These methodological questions relate to, on the one hand, pragmatic decisions about issues such as access, resources, type of information required and the sorts of techniques that are practicable and, on the other hand, with philosophical ideas on the nature of social reality and how it ought to be researched. The objective of the chapter is to further facilitate the reader in making sense of how sociological knowledge about health and illness, such as that presented in the rest of this book, is produced and justified. This chapter is structured as follows. We begin with an introduction to some of the primary research methods and briefly identify their strengths and limitations. We continue with an outline of the three main philosophical traditions that underlie research methods, namely positivism, interpretivism and critical theory. The implications of these philosophical traditions for research design will in turn be outlined. We conclude the chapter with a discussion of both the philosophical and practical reasons that influence choices of research method in social research.

The chapter also has a broader application to the social sciences. Although much of the popularly used research methods were developed originally within sociology, for example Emile Durkheim was the first to apply natural science research methods to the study of society, sociologists share the development and use of the research methods outlined in this chapter with the social sciences in general, including diverse subjects such as economics and nursing studies. Therefore, in this chapter we will speak of methods of *social* research rather than simply sociological research.

Outline of commonly-used research methods
This section introduces some of the popularly-used research methods (methods of data collection) in the social sciences. We adopt Sandra Harding's (1987) useful manner of summarising social research methods into three main types (see Treacy and Hyde 1999: 7):

- listening (or interrogating) subjects: for example, using interviews and surveys

- observing: for example by participant observation.
- documentary research: for example, official historical records or Internet sites.

However, we will also note that there are leaky boundaries between research methods. For example, participant observation may also involve asking questions, or informal interviewing may occur *whilst* observing, and focus groups are opportunities to observe as well as listen. The research methods we explore below may also be used in a variety of ways and in a variety of combinations, depending on whether one is using a quantitative research design, a qualitative research design or a combined approach. Quantitative and qualitative research designs are distinguished as follows:

- *Quantitative research* designs use methods that produce numbers to measure (quantify) social phenomena in society.

- *Qualitative research* designs use methods that inquire into people's interpretations of aspects of society. Qualitative methods try to tap the quality of people's experiences of aspects of society.

Table 3.1 presents the research methods that will be covered in this section of the chapter and outlines how they may be used in either qualitative or quantitative research approaches. The discussion below outlines the key strengths and limitations of each of the research methods.

Listening (or interrogating) methods

The survey questionnaire
There are few of us who have not been asked to fill out a questionnaire, whether it occurred as we walked down the street, by a postal invitation to complete one, or indeed via a telephone call. It involves answering a set number of questions, often with a range of pre-selected responses (closed-ended questions) and sometimes includes a limited number of questions where we are asked to give our opinion unprompted by responses (open-ended questions). As well as facilitating information gathering from a large number of people, researchers using surveys usually endeavour to generalise or scale up findings to an even larger population, for example, to a national population. The extent to which the findings of a survey are generalisable to a larger population depends on the number of people included (size of sample), the range of people covered in the sample (distributions in the sample) and the way in which people are selected to be included (sampling strategy). The results are computed with the assistance of statistical software packages.

The questionnaire survey is perhaps the king of quantitative methods because, relative to other methods, it facilitates the inclusion of a large

Table 3.1 *Common types of research methods and their application to quantitative or qualitative research*

Quantitative Research	Qualitative Research
Survey research using questionnaires (series of questions: face-to-face, postal or telephone)	**Interviews** (open-ended/in-depth or semi-structured)
Survey interviews (structured, face-to face)	
	Focus groups (group interview)
Content analysis of text (measuring the incidence of particular words/topics)	**Conversation analysis** (analysing structures in language) and **discourse analysis** (analysing the social construction of meaning in texts)
Observation (numerical records of occurrences)	**Participant observation** (participating in an environment in order to observe – overtly/covertly)
Diaries (numerical record of events or thoughts)	**Diaries** (detailed record of thoughts and reflections)

amount of people in a short space of time. Other key strengths are consistency (everyone is systematically asked the same questions under the same conditions), and the numerical measurability of the results. It also has the ability to make statements, such as how many people and what types of people behave in a particular way, or hold a certain attitude. However, the survey questionnaire also has limitations, most notably arising from the relative rigidity of the instrument. Once the questionnaire is drawn up, a set number of questions and usually only a set number of responses are possible. This implies also that it is a researcher-controlled data-gathering instrument. In addition, surveys cannot imput information in terms of the context of the respondent and how the respondent chose his/her responses (for example, respondent X may feel rotten on the day she filled out the questionnaire, and report herself as chronically depressed!) The risk of non-returns and non-responses is also high in survey questionnaires, generating a whole literature on how to improve response rates (see Edwards et al, 2003 for review).

Interviews
There are many types of research interview that researchers can conduct, ranging from quantitative-oriented structured interviews (all set questions asked) to qualitative-oriented open-ended in-depth interviews where only the broad theme might be set in advance of the interview. In *in-depth*

interviewing, the types of questions asked and time involved are usually negotiated within the interview itself. Such interviews are usually recorded and transcribed. The contents of in-depth interviews are analysed according to a range of techniques of analysis in qualitative research, such as thematic coding or the constant comparative technique as used in *grounded theory* research design (see interpretative research designs below). Coding of interview data can also be assisted by computer software.

The strength of in-depth interviewing lies in the scope or depth it potentially allows in exploring aspects of everyday life, the potential to probe and clarify meanings, the integration of the social context of the meanings and the social context of the interview itself (for example, level of rapport established with the interviewee and the conditions of the interview). The key limitation of conducting in-depth interviews is that, because of their labour intensity in terms of research resources (conducting interviews, analysing data and so forth), the number of interviews that can be conducted for a study is reduced, limiting the empirical scope in terms of breadth. This makes it difficult to scale up from a small amount of interviews to make generalised statements about a larger population over and above the number of respondents under study. However, as the definition of qualitative research offered above implies, measuring extent and generalisability are not key aims in qualitative research. Rather, the focus is on developing an understanding of how meanings are constructed. Furthermore, as in other types of qualitative research, a broader application of the results may be achieved through the use of theoretical explanations (known as theoretical generalisation). This implies linking findings in research to explanations of wider phenomena, as available in social theory. In comparison to other qualitative methods, such as participant observation, a limitation of in-depth interviewing is that it is usually not possible in interviews to verify behaviours – what people say they do is not always what they do. However, researchers might find out about the manner in which individuals present themselves and report behaviours.

Focus groups

Focus groups have become a mainstay in market research and are also increasingly used in social science research. They are effectively group interviews which are also usually audio-taped and sometimes video-recorded. Video-recording aids the capturing of the important body language interaction of individuals during group discussions, as well as highlighting who chose to speak when. Thus, the distinction between listening and observing can be very blurred in focus groups. Focus groups often involve an interviewer and a moderator, a researcher to ask the questions and a researcher to observe. The key strength of focus groups is the generation of ideas about a research topic that can occur in a group situation and the capturing of the group dynamic itself. Also, the researchers may be able to gauge the extent to which there is agreement or disagreement with particular viewpoints within and between focus groups, although caution must be exercised, as silence may not mean agreement. The key limitations are that not all topics are suitable for group discussions, due to privacy or ethical considerations, and that there is not always enough scope to explore individual understandings and rationale within the group. In addition, as in any group, some people may feel more confident speaking out than others.

Methods of observation

Observational techniques are more usually associated with qualitative research designs but this technique can also be used to do straight forward headcounts, such as how many people entered an accident and emergency department on a particular night and what their main characteristics were. In order to make statements about the representativeness of one night's observation, one would have to get an idea of how typical that night was by comparing it to other nights.

Participant observation

Participant observation is a key research technique in the social sciences and may be conducted overtly (where the observed are in full knowledge that they are being observed) or covertly (where the observed are not informed). The researcher usually spends a sustained period (often up to a year) 'in the field' or research environment, and usually covers periods when the environment might change, such as during different staff shifts or summertime/ wintertime. The researcher usually keeps a detailed daily diary and may take photographs. The researcher may also conduct formal or informal interviews so as to probe meanings behind observed actions/interactions in the research context.

The key strength of participant observation is the sustained immersion into the context of the research environment that it allows and the potential for the researcher to grasp a holistic view of the research environment. The key limitation lies in its characteristics of 'entering' the research site. This limitation pertains, first, to the difficulty of getting access to specialised spaces such as hospital wards or factory floors for the purposes of research. Second, relative to other methods, there is the potential of contamination of the research site or the 'observer effect' of the researcher being present and the effect this might have on those being observed, especially in overt participant observation. Third, the case of covert participation usually raises ethical concerns over the observed's right to know.

Diaries

Diaries are a means of self-observation which can then be shared with the researcher. When used in quantitative research, the respondent is usually asked to self-record frequencies, such as the amount of times a research subject took medication, or to record feelings and motivations that later become subjected to numerical analysis. When used in qualitative research, diaries are often used to provide a detailed record of thoughts and reflections. The primary strength of this research approach is that it can allow a picture to develop over time, as opposed to a single snapshot, as in a survey or a single interview. (*Panel* surveys, or interviews where the same respondent is interviewed at separate time points are also sometimes used to add a time dimension to research). The primary limitation is in terms of compliance. It is not unusual for a researcher to suspect that a respondent's diary, if filled out at all, was filled out altogether at the end rather than at individual time points. Finally, diaries can be saved over time and can effectively become a resource for documentary research.

Documentary research methods

Some research can, of course, be done without ever asking anyone any questions. Documents, such as web pages, telephone recordings, patient records, hospital mission statements and historical archives are all sources of information. Content analysis, conversation analysis, and discourse analysis are the most common strategies used to analyse documents and texts.

Content analysis

Content analysis is a technique sometimes associated with qualitative approaches, such as in exploring meaning and content of a text (see conversational and discourse analysis below for examples of this type of content analysis). However, content analysis can also be simply a method of counting regularities within texts, such as the number of times hospital mission statements mention 'equality of treatment' or 'efficiency' or 'individuality' or even words such as 'care' over 'treatment' (See Laver and Garry (2000) for an example of computer-assisted measurement techniques of large texts). The strength of this approach is that it allows an objective measurement within and between texts of the types of language and topics included. The limitations are similar to other quantitative methods, in terms of the absence of context of why and how certain words and subjects come to be included or omitted.

Conversation analysis

Conversation analysis is a research technique that developed from **ethnomethodology,** a branch of sociology that we introduced in Chapter 2. As indicated in Chapter 2, ethnomethodology is concerned with understanding how the rules and routines of everyday life are constructed and maintained in interactions between people. Conversation analysis involves the analysis of transcripts of conversations (recorded telephone conversations such as sales talk, helplines or recorded naturally-occurring conversations, for example the conversations between patients and health professionals). The analysis may focus on *how* conversations begin and end, the turn-taking of speakers, and on how agreement/disagreement was reached or avoided within the conversation. The analysis rigidly stays at the level of micro-analysis (the details of the conversation only), rather than encompassing the wider social context of the conversation. The strength of this approach is the way that it opens up for analysis that which we normally do not think about – the taken-for-granted ways we produce and re-produce the rules of everyday life in daily interactions. The limitation of conversational analysis is the fact that it also closes off for analysis the way in which language in everyday interactions is linked to broader power structures in society.

Discourse analysis
Discourse analysis, by contrast to conversational analysis, analyses the way we use language in relation to the wider social context. Discourse analysis involves an analysis of what is said or written (oral or written text) and a further level of analysis of the cultural ideologies (such as medical knowledge, scientific expertise, youth subcultures) in society which influence the languages available to us. Discourse analysis tries to uncover the 'interpretive repertoires' (Potter and Wetherell, 1987; Potter 1996) or related sets of ideas which influence how we use language. Foucault's work (1973), presented in Chapter 2, is an example of exploring beneath surface appearances in language to show how they are linked (and give credence) to wider cultural structures, such as the institutional power of medicine. The strength of this approach is also in disrupting the taken-for-granted use of language. Language is usually regarded as neutral and value-free but discourse analysis points to the way that languages are drawn from particular **worldviews**. In addition, discourse analysis, particularly when linked to postmodernism as will be described below, shows how different interpretations of a single text are possible and that the act of defining the text in a particular way is an act of power. The main limitation of this approach is, as in other forms of documentary research, that it does not seek out individuals' interpretations of what language means to them and what worldviews individuals think influence their use of language. Rather, it is a system of reading meanings from texts.

Philosophical foundations of research methods
Research methods, as outlined above, can be distinguished by their characteristics and use value but research methods are not value-free tools. Instead, they have developed from different philosophies of how we can research and know the social world. The philosophical foundations will make much clearer the strengths and limitations of the research methods and the process through which research methods are chosen for research.

Firstly, we offer an explanation of the terms readers will encounter in discussions of methodology. A term which is often used in this context is **epistemology**. The term epistemology is derived from the Greek word for 'knowledge', *episteme*, and the word for 'the study of', *logos*. Epistemology, therefore, is the study of the logical process of how knowledge may be produced, or how we can know what we know. Epistemological questions are crucial to any scientific endeavour such as sociology, mathematics, nursing or biological sciences that make ontological statements (statements about the nature of reality). Scientists make claims about aspects of the world in statements, for example that there is a relationship between genetic structure and forms of cancer, or that 2 and 2 equals 4, or that that inequality is linked to ill-health. Epistemological questions ask: What is the basis to such 'truth' claims and what are the broad resources scientists use to legitimate their claims about reality? In short, why should we believe them?

There are three *methodological paradigms* across the social sciences. Methodological paradigms are research approaches that are made up of philosophical traditions and the research methods or techniques that have developed to practice the philosophical ideas in doing research. The three dominant research approaches in social science are *positivism*, *interpretivism* and *critical theory*. The relationships between these perspectives are mapped out in Box 3.1. The defining characteristics of the methodological paradigms are summarised in Table 3.2 and will be elaborated in the discussion below.

Box 3.1 *Key terms in understanding methodology*

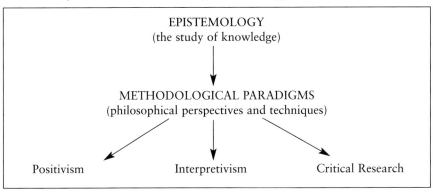

Positivism
1. Epistemological foundations. Positivism originated in the natural sciences. The positivist process in the natural sciences sets out to uncover the facts or *laws of nature* through the identification of stable relations of cause-and-effect between aspects of nature. The application of positivism to the

Table 3.2 *Summary of characteristics of methodological paradigms*

	Positivism	*Interpretivism*	*Critical Research*
Epistemological foundations	Basis lies within natural science	Rejection of natural science methods	Knowledge through critical consciousness
Technique	The observation and measurement of social phenomena and the identification of patterns of cause-and-effect in social behaviour	The identification and understanding of the ways in which individuals construct and interpret the world around them	A holistic understanding by researching structural accounts (measurement of phenomena) and interpretative accounts
Objectivity	Assumes objectivity	Rejects objectivity in research either as being possible or desirable	Values partiality and objectivity

social world (the pursuit of the identification of laws of society) in nineteenth century France by Auguste Comte (1798-1857) gave birth to the original sociology (1974 [1830-1842]). Comte's vision for sociology was 'that society could be understood through the methods of science, that is, observation, experiment and calculation, and, by these means, the universal laws which govern society and its workings could be uncovered' (Hughes et al, 1995: 10).

2. *Techniques.* The techniques of the positivist methodological paradigm are observation, measurement and the identification of cause-and-effect relationships between social phenomena. Contemporary positivist explanations of cause-and-effect relationships in social phenomena are primarily based on a deductive model of reasoning known as the *hypothetico-deductive method* or hypothesis testing. Hypothesis testing is a process of testing the relative strength of plausible explanations (theories) for a particular social pattern. (See Box 3.2.)

The deductivist hypothesis testing model of positivist science is attributed to the philosopher of science, Karl Popper (Popper, 1980 [1959]), and was developed as a research design by the Columbia School of Sociology (Lazarsfeld and Rosenberg, 1955; Lazarsfeld, Pasnella and Rosenberg, 1972). The hypothesis testing model is also known as the *falsification* model after Popper's argument that science should not base itself on the production of universal laws (as was made popular by inductive reasoning of the seventeenth century philosopher Francis Bacon) but rather on scientific statements that have not yet been falsified (Harvey et al, 2000). Popper

Box 3.2 *Hypothesis testing of cause-and-effect in positivist research*

> To illustrate hypothesis testing of cause-and-effect in positivist research, imagine the example of a known health phenomenon such as sex differences in the occurrence of heart disease. Scientists must choose firstly what theories might explain the greater incidence of heart disease in men over women and then go out and collect evidence (empirical data which represents these theories in the real world). Current theories on the causes of heart disease are drawn from both biological and social sciences, for example: genetic predisposition, attitudes of patients to healthcare, smoking patterns, diet and exercise and weekly hours of paid employment. Positivist research, then, uses statistical techniques to test the relative explanatory power of the competing theories. *Multivariate* statistical techniques facilitate a measurement of the relative strength of the theories – such that we may answer which theory best explains sex differences in chronic heart disease, the general order of strength of the theories and, indeed, if any of the theories is redundant.

(1980[1959]) argued that this model was a way of building a greater level of critique into the scientific process because plausible theories can always be proven wrong in the process. He (1980 [1959]) offered the simple and effective example of the colour of swans to illustrate the limitations of science in identifying universal laws. Swans were frequently and extensively observed as being white, such that it became a truism that swans were white until a black swan was observed in Australia.

3. *Objectivity.* Positivism asserts that it is possible to produce objective ontological truths about the world, albeit, as described above, truth statements that are constantly refutable. Positivism purports that objectivity can be gained through the scientific research process (Macionis and Plummer, 1997). Positivist research assumes that the techniques of scientific research are capable of controlling and standardising (making even by eliminating biases) the subjective aspects of research. These subjective aspects include the socio-demographic characteristics of the researcher, interactions within scientific teams, or the wider framework of the research, for example, the purposes of the research, who is funding it and who might benefit or lose from research.

Implications of positivist epistemological theory for research design

- There is a desire to *produce facts* about social phenomena by identifying patterns and structure in social behaviour.
- There is a desire to *explain* these patterns by measuring relationships between different phenomena.
- There is a desire to do large-scale research which can be used to draw conclusions about a large number of people or to be *generalisable* to a larger population.
- Usually *quantitative* research methods are utilised.

Interpretivism

1. *Epistemological foundations.* Interpretivism is principally about understanding the ways in which individuals interpret the world around them. Interpretivism rejects the epistemological foundations of positivism for the production of knowledge or truths about society, because it asserts that the social world is entirely different to the natural world. In the social world, scientists are studying, acting, thinking individuals. Therefore, human actions or responses cannot be read off (observed) as a reaction to external stimuli. Interpretivism asserts that human attitudes and behaviour need to be understood as a conscious and ongoing interpretation process of social context. The aim of interpretive social science, then, is to elaborate and understand interpretations of reality, rather than the measurement of cause-and-effect relationships. Social reality is complex (varies considerably) and multiple social realities (valid perspectives) are possible at any given time.

2. *Techniques.* Interpretivism is a broad church leading to variations in research approaches within it. In order to explain the primary techniques of interpretivism it is necessary to consider specific approaches separately within the broad banner of interpretivism. Each approach within interpretivism has a particular lineage in terms of philosophical roots (see Box 3.3) which we will now explore further.

Box 3.3 *The early philosophical development of the interpretive approach*

INTERPRETATIVE APPROACH			
Interpretative	*Phenomenology*	*Interactionism*	*Postmodernism*
M.Weber	E.Husserl	G.Simmel / G.H.Mead	J.F Lyotard/ J. Baudrillard
Verstehen model	Transcendental phenomenology	Symbolic Interactionism	Anti-realism

Max Weber (1864-1920) was a founding father of the interpretive tradition through what became known as the *Verstehen* model of sociology (derived from the German term 'to understand'). Weber's key contribution to the interpretive tradition was his emphasis on the need to understand values and meanings – the acting, thinking actor that positivist science neglected. Among the range of interpretative approaches, Weber's model of social research is closest to the positivist paradigm in that he too emphasised the importance of the social scientist identifying cause-and-effect relationships in society. However, unlike positivist science, Weber emphasised the role of values and meanings in giving rise to (cause) our actions. Weber (1978) argued that the fundamental objective of the social sciences was to understand motives (cultural values and ideas) behind actions or *erklarendes verstehen*.

Phenomenology is a school of philosophy that has also made key contributions to the interpretative tradition of social research. Indeed, the whole interpretive tradition is sometimes called the *phenomenological tradition* or *phenomenology*. Phenomenology owes its origin to the philosopher and mathematician, Edmund Husserl (1859-1938), who coined the word 'phenomenology' from the Greek word for 'appearance' (Husserl, 1960[1929]). For Husserl, 'knowledge was created in the way the world first *appears* to the human consciousness' (Porter, 1998a: 106). At its most fundamental level, the key contribution of phenomonological philosophy to the interpretive tradition is that people are conscious beings and, through this consciousness, engage in interpretation of their social world.[5]

Phenomenology was developed further in the research of Alfred Schutz (1899-1959). Schutz (1962) combined Weber's interest in values and Husserl's phenomenological ideas of individual conscience and 'appearance' of the world. He developed the phenomenological research approach which pays particular attention to understanding how individuals make choices on the basis of their unique biographies, the specific features of the situations in which they do so *and* in relation to individuals' interactions with others (Harvey et al, 2000: 62). He set forth a project for the social sciences on how understandings of social reality are actively and routinely constructed in everyday life. Phenomenology plays a significant role in health research. The core emphases of individual consciousness and interpretation of experiences has informed holistic ideas of caring in nursing research in particular (see, for example, Beck, 1994; Crotty, 1996; Giorgi, 2000; McNamara, 2000; Caelli, 2001).

The third philosophical underpinning of the interpretative tradition comes from interactionism and the work of Georg Simmel (1964 [1950]) and G.H. Mead. Mead was a social psychologist who further developed Simmel's ideas in an influential book entitled *Mind, Self and Society* (1934). Mead, as a psychologist, focussed less on society and more on how individual identities are a product of our interactions with others. His ideas were developed into the sociological approach known as *symbolic interactionism* by his student Herbert Blumer. This methodological approach launched a programme of micro-level studies of interaction between individuals and groups in society. Erving Goffman's work on stigma (1976[1963]) and constructs of mental illness (1961) are examples of symbolic interactionist work, which will be discussed in Chapter 10 on mental health.

---

5   For a more detailed understanding of phenomenonology, the reader should note that there are three distinct schools of thought in phenomenological philosophy: Husserl's *transcendental phenomenology*, Heidegger's *hermeneutic philosophy*, and the *existentialism* of Merleau-Ponty and Jean-Paul Sartre. These are sometimes reduced to two categories: *the German phase* and *the French phase* (see Holloway and Wheeler, 2002). For a more detailed discussion see, for example, McNamara (2000) and Caelli (2001).

As charted in Box 3.4, interactionism was later developed further in ethnomethodology (which was introduced in Chapter 2) as pioneered by Harold Garfinkel (1967). It is similar to the aforementioned approaches in that society is viewed as being constructed through everyday life interactions. However, in ethnomethodology the subjective understandings (interpretation) are not as important as in Schutz's phenomenology of everyday life programme or in the symbolic interactionist perspective. Rather, it is the rules and routines of everyday life which occupy the central focus. For example, in an ethnomethodological study of healthcare decision making, the researcher would focus on the *processes* of making decisions about the care and treatment of a patient, rather than on what the content of those decisions might *mean* to the health professionals or patients.

Box 3.4 *Detailed map of interpretative approach*

INTERPRETATIVE APPROACH			
Interpretative/ Verstehen model	*Phenomenology*	*Interactionism*	*Postmodernism*
M.Weber (1864-1920) Verstehen model	**E.Husserl** (1859-1938) Transcedental phenonmenology	**G.Simmel** (1858-1918) **G.H.Mead** (1863-1931)	
		H. Blumer (1900-1986) Symbolic Interactionism	
	A. Schutz (1899-1959) Phenomonology of everyday life		
		H. Garfinkel (1917-present) Ethnomethodology	**J. Baudrillard** (1929 -present) **J.F. Lyotard** (1924-1998)

Postmodernism has significant implications for doing (interpretative) research. Although postmodernism could be separated out as a methodological paradigm itself, it is also closely linked to the interpretative paradigm in the way that it challenges positivist constructions of knowledge about the world. The following points summarise the methodological issues implicit in postmodernism. (For an introduction to the theoretical basis of postmodernism, see Chapter 2.)

Firstly, postmodernism has an anti-realist epistemology, that is to say, the postmodernist perspective rejects the idea that positivist or any other type of science can produce the truth about reality or an aspect of the natural or social world. What then, one might ask, is the point of doing research, if we cannot draw conclusions about reality? The point, from the postmodernist perspective, is that research can map out how reality is constructed, yet abandon making statements about reality. In so doing, the postmodernist perspective can develop insights into how interconnections between different actors and values work to produce a way of knowing the world.

Secondly, the postmodernist perspective focuses on the social construction of reality through *language* (or discourse) and ideology. This is because 'language is considered to be an active medium for shaping our interpretation of the world, rather than a neutral process of representing the world' (Harvey et al, 2000: 70). What we say is a way of creating meaning about the world and, in turn, the languages available to us are based on particular ideologies or knowledge systems of the world. The objective, then, of postmodernist research is to *deconstruct,* or analytically take texts apart (including language, writing, audiovisual material and symbols) in order to show *how* the texts represent reality.

Thirdly, postmodernism is characterised as having an apolitical epistemology. Although, as described above, postmodernists are interested in showing how reality is produced, the postmodernist perspective does not make assertions on which version of reality is preferable. The argument is that if the researcher were to stake a claim as to what was right, wrong, good or bad, it would contravene the central idea of the uncertainty and relativity of knowledge and lead to the privileging of the researcher's perspective. At this point, we can return to dealing with all the different schools of interpretivism together.

3. *Objectivity.* Interpretivism rejects the positivist notion of objectivity in the production of (scientific) knowledge. The separation of knowledge of reality from our perception of reality is known as the *subject-object dualism* and is a principle of positivism. Based on the phenomenological philosophy of Husserl, interpretivism asserts that our knowledge of the world cannot be separated from our consciousness of it. Interpretative research does not assume objectivity and so an analysis of the position of the researcher and the relationship between researcher and researched is often included as part of the research project. This usually involves a form of reflexive thinking on the researcher's values, the values within the research programme, and the process of the interaction between researcher and researched. Arguably, by building reflexivity into the research process, interpretative research can produce a form of 'strong objectivity' (Harding, 1991) in that forms of subjectivities are worked through and made explicit, rather than assumed to be implicit in the research process, as occurs in positivism (Lohan, 2000).

Implications of interpretative epistemological theory for research design

- There is desire to capture *perceptions* of reality – or how individuals view reality rather than objective measurements of reality.
- There is a desire to analyse data *thematically* rather than numerically and usually inductively – using theory development rather than theory testing approaches. One such research design was developed initially through a study of death and dying and is known as *Grounded Theory* (Glaser and Strauss, 1965, 1967; Strauss, 1987; Strauss and Corbin, 1998; Glaser 1992). In brief, this involves developing an explanatory theory, grounded in the data from the field (research site). This occurs by coding, comparing, and grouping items of data, and analysing these data to produce theoretical insights.
- The objective is not to generalise to a broader population but to gain more *in-depth knowledge,* 'rich data' of a specific group of people.
- Usually *qualitative* research methods are utilised.

Critical research

1. *Epistemological foundations*. So far, we have indicated that positivism and interpretivism can be recognised in an oppositional relationship. Positivism, on the one hand, is informed by a theory of knowledge that states that we can know the social world, just like the natural world, by identifying regularities and patterns of cause-and-effect. Interpretivism, on the other hand, rejects positivism and develops a theory of knowledge that states that we can only understand the social world by understanding people's interpretations of realities. Critical research stands outside of this oppositional relationship and says something quite different. Critical research is informed by a theory of knowledge that states that we can only know social reality through a 'critical consciousness' of the social world. A critical consciousness, after the philosopher Immanuel Kant (1724-1804) and Theodor Adorno (1903-1969), means not accepting reason or knowledge uncritically but rather looking for the conditions that make knowledge and reason possible (Porter, 1998a). Critical research is an attempt to cross-examine interpretations of social phenomena (events, actions and meanings) with reference to the wider socio-historical context of those interpretations, to understand links between structure and agency, and to generate change. Readers may note that the objective of deconstruction in critical theory shares similarities with postmodern interpretivism as outlined above. However, there are also fundamental points of difference between interpretative postmodernism and critical theory. The first is that critical theory is originally derived from the work of social theorists whose perspective is overtly political and who sought change in the world, most notably Marx and Hegel. This politically-motivated scholarship is further developed in the current period by a

prominent group of theorists, including Jürgen Habermas (1929-present), at the Frankfurt school.

2. *Techniques.*Critical research involves a process of unravelling or deconstruction to reveal the inter-relatedness of interpretations of social life and socio-historical influences. Harvey and MacDonald refer to this as '*going beneath the surface* of what appears to be going on' (2000: 105, emphasis in original). It involves looking at an array of evidence to find out how things are put together in the social world, so as to provide alternative routes for re-building (Harvey et al, 2000). As such, critical theory can be distinguished from positivism and interpretivism in two key ways: (i) it seeks a more holistic account of social phenomena, an account that can combine interpretations of social reality (the micro) *and* one that can account for macro socio-historical influences on interpretations (the macro); (ii) it is a more pragmatic and inclusivist approach to using positivist or interpretative research methods.

Take, for example, a study seeking to explore patients' understandings of recovery from cancer and mastectomy. A critical social research approach would endeavour to research individual/group interpretations of recovering from cancer and mastectomy and go beneath the surface of those meanings to explore the socio-historical influences on such interpretations. The socio-historical influences on recovery from cancer and mastectomy might plausibly include cultural constructions of sexuality in our society, cultural constructions of femininity, the status of cancer research, ideology in medical training, and the socio-economic ordering of the local and national healthcare context. This contrasts with interpretative and positivist research design approaches. In an interpretative design, the researcher is generally focusing only on how individuals or groups themselves interpret the experience of cancer recovery and mastectomy. In a positivist design, the means through which to explore patients' understandings of cancer recovery and mastectomy are through a quantitative analysis. Positivism, however, is limited because it is dependent on obtaining measurable data and it is difficult to create measurable data for issues such as the cultural constructions of femininity or ideology in medical training. Therefore, there are limitations in the range of factors that positivism can use in its explanations.

3. *Objectivity*. Critical research is overtly political. It usually seeks to change consciousness and practical aspects of the social world. In order to do so, it needs to hold on to the concept of objective truths about the nature of the social world, for example realities such as inequality or patriarchy (gendered oppression by men over women) that require change. However, in the research process, the researcher him or herself is far from an objective or impartial bystander. In Porter's words, the researcher is much less a disengaged commentator and much more an intellectual activist (Porter, 1998a: 152). In this sense, the researcher is engaged in practical reflective action or *praxis* as Marx (1977 [1887]) coined it.

Implications of critical epistemological theory for research design
- There is a desire to seek beneath-surface meanings in order to engage critically with how meanings are constructed, usually through both macro-analyses (examining socio-historical structures in society) as well as micro-analyses (looking at how individuals and groups re-constitute relations and the social world in everyday life).
- Critical social research is also linked to what is termed *action research* designs through its emphasis on conscious change. The objective of action research is, as the name implies, one of research *and* action (or social change) and usually involves the researcher working in partnership with the researched on an agreed aim.
- Critical social research can involve a variety of methods, such as discourse analysis, interviews, focus groups, documentary analyses, reading of histories, and often employs a combination of methods that will allow an understanding of interpretation and context.

Choice of research methods: mixing philosophy and pragmatism
The differences in the positivist and interpretative approaches to research are often described as amounting to a 'methodological brawl' in social science research (Haralambos and Holborn, 1990: 718). Yet, many social scientists can see the epistemologies being complementary in accessing different forms of knowledge. Already within critical research, one can see bridges being built, especially in terms of a pragmatic approach to using both quantitative and qualitative research methods. This final section of this chapter explores how some further bridges can be created between positivist quantitative research designs and interpretative qualitative research designs and some of the further practical considerations that influence how research designs are put together.

The first consideration influencing research design is: *What is the research question?* Is it, for example: How do medical students support themselves financially in college? Or: How do recently immigrant women experience maternity care services in Ireland? Both of these questions could be answered either through a positivist or interpretative framework. Thus, the important question becomes: *What sort of information do I need?* Do I want to be able to measure numerically the extent of patterns and make generalised statements? In relation to the first question this would require a tool to determine how many doctors finance themselves in certain ways, or in relation to the second question, how many immigrant women feel a certain way? Or, do I want depth of experience and to allow research respondents to speak for themselves rather than presenting them with categories of answers? The choice of research design also relates back to the philosophical underpinnings of research paradigms and whether or not the researcher is a *paradigm purist* or *paradigm pluralist*. Paradigm purists may be defined as those who believe there is only *one* way to research the world. Paradigm purists usually raise research questions or seek out research which is compatible with their paradigm preference.

It is, of course, possible to *mix and match* research tools, and there are generally two methods of doing this. One is called **triangulation** and the other is called method mixing. Triangulation is a process of using multiple research techniques in order to tap a single research question. Triangulation can occur by mixing researchers, methods (or data collection techniques) and theories (explanatory systems). Triangulation is, of course, a wonderfully pragmatic way of going about research and, as indicated in relation to critical theory, can give a much more holistic account of a social phenomenon. However, it can also lead to one central problem, namely, when key differences arise from the different methods/researchers (especially when mixing paradigms), which account should take precedence? The reason this problem can occur in the first place is that triangulation tends to be rooted in the positivist paradigm and in the belief that there is an objective knowable reality that can be better uncovered using multiple research techniques, creating stronger validity for the results. However, within the interpretivist paradigm, and especially through the influence of postmodernism as discussed above, there is a belief that there is no single reality and that the role of researchers is to show how realities come to be defined.

Mixing methods is different to triangulation in that it involves using different methods to look at different aspects (or sub-research questions) of the research question (Holloway and Wheeler, 2002). DePoy and Gitlin (1993, cited in Holloway and Wheeler, 2002: 19) identify three main ways of doing this, namely (i) by *a nested strategy*, that is, the use of a particular methodology to pick up on a sub-question within the overall research project; (ii) by using a *sequential strategy*, that is, the use of a method such as focus groups to explore the topic initially in order to construct a questionnaire, and then go on to use an exclusively quantitative approach; and (iii) by the *parallel strategy*, that is, where both quantitative and qualitative methods are used. However, unlike triangulation of methods as described above, parallel methods are used to illuminate different perspectives rather than validating the findings arising from one method by use of another.

A further consideration is the question of appreciation of research findings in terms of being *scientific* or *non-scientific*. The positivist approach is often conflated with being the 'scientific' approach to the study of the social world because, as discussed above, positivism emerged from the application of natural scientific methods, which were established as 'science', to the social world. The implication is that interpertative research methods are non-scientific and, for some interpretative researchers, happily so. However, according to Bowling (2002: 125):

> It is increasingly accepted that social science becomes scientific not by using the basic experimental [positivist] model, but by adopting research methods that are appropriate to the topic of study, that are rigorous, critical and objective and that ensure the systematic collection, analysis and presentation of the data (Silverman, 1993).

According to Robson (2002: 18), what defines whether or not research is scientific is less the adoption of positivist or non-positivist research designs, and more the adoption of a 'scientific attitude'. A scientific attitude is similar to Bowling's criteria above and implies that research should be carried out systematically, sceptically and ethically. Systematic research implies a thorough thinking through of the logic of the selected approach and research process. Sceptical research implies scrutinising and critiquing observations and conclusions and ethical research implies adherence to a code of research conduct that protects the rights of those taking part (Robson, 2002: 18).

The practical aspects of research must also be considered. These include time and resources, know how, dealing with the politics of research funding and ethical considerations. Every project must take into account available time and resources. For example, negotiating access to a protected space such as a hospital ward can be time-consuming. So too can doing an in-depth interview project as the main researcher is usually required to undertake (at least some of) the interviews. By contrast, in survey research, the researcher can often contract out the data-gathering and data input stages. The point is that every research strategy implies use of time and money and most researchers have to create a research strategy with limitations on each in mind. Know-how is also a consideration. Perhaps because there is a paradigm split between positivist and interpretative approaches, researchers are often more highly competent in either quantitative or qualitative research. Another consideration is that of research funding. This can bring the researcher into a whole new set of negotiations over the validity of certain research methods, what can be achieved through the analysis of the results and issues such as intellectual property rights over the results. Last, and by no means least, every research project will involve considerations of what constitutes ethical research practice. In researching real lives there can be real repercussions for those being researched. (See Hyde and Treacy (1999) and Corrigon (2003) for a discussion on the ethics of doing research). In every research project, the rights of those who are researched (such as confidentiality and informed consent) must also be balanced with the interests of the research to a wider society (Harvey et al, 2000: 120). In practice, guidelines are usually available to help steer researchers, such as the ethical guidelines of social science professions, and ethical research committees to adjudicate on ethical considerations of proposed research projects.

Summary

- Research methods are conventionally divided into quantitative and qualitative methods, depending on whether their main focus is to quantify the extent of a social phenomenon or whether they are trying to focus on social context and the interpretation of reality.
- The distinctions between quantitative and qualitative methods are not accidental, rather, they arise because they are embedded in two different epistemologies or understandings of how we know the social world.
- The philosophy of positivism, with its emphasis on quantifying social phenomena and theory testing of cause-and-effect relationships of different social phenomena, is united with quantitative methods into a single methodological paradigm.
- The philosophy of interpretivism with its focus on interpretation of social reality is bound with qualitative methods in a very different methodological paradigm.
- Critical theory uses a variety of quantitative and qualitative methods but is underpinned by a belief that knowledge can only be achieved through critical consciousness. Critical consciousness involves examining how meanings and structures are constructed in everyday life and reveal the socio-historical influences on social life.
- In real-world research, it is possible to be a methodological 'paradigm purist' or 'paradigm pluralist'. Paradigm pluralists start with a variety of research questions, and may triangulate or mix methods. They may adopt a scientific attitude, as opposed to holding an oppositional stance between so-called scientific and non-scientific research but, like paradigm purists, their choice of research methods will be also be influenced by the practicalities of doing research on time and within budget.

Topics for discussion and reflection

1. Are research methods value-free tools for investigating the social world?

2. What might a researcher consider when making a decision about which methodological approach to use for a research study?

Section 2
Sociological understandings of health and illness

FOUR

The social determinants of health and illness: class, gender and ethnicity

In chapter one, we noted how some people suffer more from ill-health and die younger than others. In this chapter, we explore in greater depth this phenomenon of inequality in health and illness. We show how patterns of health and illness need to be accounted for not just in biological terms, but also in social terms, by taking into consideration the socio-economic and cultural context of our lives. This chapter focuses on three key social divides, namely, **social class, gender** and **ethnicity** that research has shown significantly influence patterns of health and illness in society. We consider why social factors are so clearly related to health outcomes. We present four main explanations for the link between social inequality and health and illness: a social selection/biological explanation, an artefactual explanation, a materialist explanation and a cultural explanation, and review the evidence to support these different causal explanations of the social patterns of health and illness. Finally, we close this chapter by looking at linkages between class, gender and ethnic-based differences in health and discuss the implications for health professionals of this knowledge base on inequalities.

Social class and health

What do we mean by social class? There are differences among people in the amount of access they have to the resources of wealth and prestige in most societies. Such differences among people in terms of income and status are usually referred to as social class differences. In contemporary social science, social class is most commonly measured by occupation. Box 4.1 shows the current Irish social class classification system based on an individual's occupation. The classification of occupations into rankings is similar to the UK national statistics socio-economic classification (see the UK Office for National Statistics at www.statistics.gov.uk), in so far as they are both derived from the Goldthorpe scheme (Goldthorpe and Hope, 1974; Goldthorpe, 1980), which ranks occupations in terms of levels of responsibility and autonomy as well as type of work. Notably, however, the Irish based social class scheme also differentiates between types of farmers.

The upper groups of professional, executive and administrative workers form what is known as the middle classes (higher and lower), also referred to as white-collar, and the lower groups on the scale are known as working class, or blue-collar.

Box 4.1 *Social class scale in Ireland*

Middle class
(higher middle and lower middle-class)

1. Higher professional and higher managerial (e.g. doctor, accountant, company director, senior government officer) and farmers owning 200 or more acres.

2. Lower professional and lower managerial (e.g. school teacher, nurse, sales manager) and farmers owning 100-199 acres.

3. Other non-manual (e.g. clerk, secretary, dental nurses) and farmers owning 50-99 acres.

Working class
4. Skilled manual (e.g. building site foreman, supervisor of cleaning workers) and farmers owning 30-49 acres.
5. Semi-skilled manual (e.g. plumber, electrician, fitter, driver, cook, hairdresser) and farmers owning less then 30 acres.

6. Unskilled manual (e.g. machine operator, assembler, waitress, cleaner, labourer, driver, bar-worker, call-centre worker).

Source: O'Hare et al, 1991

The categories that people have been assigned to by virtue of their occupations have been compared with patterns of illness in society, and the two are found to be closely associated. The lower your place in the social class scale, the worse is likely to be your health status and visa-versa. There is an abundance of literature demonstrating a link between inequalities in health and socio-economic status internationally (see the account explaining class-based inequalities below). Box 4.2 presents some key findings from a recent Irish report (Barry, J. et al, 2001) on inequalities and health which demonstrate a link between social class and health in Ireland.

Explaining social class patterns in health
Four key explanations have been advanced to account for social class patterns in health. These are: the artefact explanation; the social selection/biological explanation; cultural/behavioural explanations; and materialist/structuralist explanations.

Box 4.2 *Socio-economic grouping and health status in Ireland*

- Unskilled manual men were twice as likely to die prematurely as higher professional men.

- Unskilled manual men were eight times more likely to die from an accidental cause than higher professional men.

- Persons in the unskilled manual category were almost four times as likely to be admitted to hospital for the first time for schizophrenia than those in the higher professional category.

- In the early 1990s, women who were unemployed (and in the lowest socio-economic group) were over twice as likely to give birth to low birth-weight babies as women in the higher professional group.

- Persons within the socio-economic group 'unskilled manual' have worse health than professional groups in all years and for all the conditions which are analysed in this report.

Source: Barry, J. et al, 2001: 7

The artefact explanation

The artefact explanation suggests that the strategies that social scientists use to measure social class and **morbidity** and **mortality** may be flawed, artificially skewing the figures or statistics. Proponents of this position suggest that the statistics on the relationship between social class and health status are inaccurate and artificially inflate or exaggerate class-based health inequalities (Moore and Porter, 1998: 103). They argue that the alleged gap in health status between rich and poor people is founded on false premises, or is an artefact (something created by people) of weakness in the way in which statistics are gathered and presented. The primary perceived problem here is that the methods of measuring occupational class artificially inflate the size and importance of health differences. For example, one problem identified in UK statistics is that occupational classification schemes and the nature of occupations have witnessed transformations in recent decades such that comparisons with earlier decades this century could be rendered meaningless (Whitehead, 1988). For example, in the UK in the 2001 Standard Occupational Classification (SOC), nursing as an occupation was moved upwards into the category 'associate professionals' because of the expectation that most nurses will have university degrees; this alters the status of their occupation. A similar occupation classification shift occurred in 1961 when, in the former socio-economic group (SEG) classification scale, postmen were re-classified from class III to class IV (Miers, 2003: 35-36). In other words, in long-term comparisons, you are not comparing like with like in terms of the nature of occupations. However, researchers in the

UK have also demonstrated that social class differentials in mortality remain unchanged whether earlier SEG classification (the 1971 model) or later (the 1985 model) classification systems are used (Davey Smith, 1994: 32). In addition, when various other classification systems are used, such as educational level or household surveys of material goods and material conditions, a similar relationship between social inequality and health emerges. This strongly suggests that the relationship between health and inequality is unlikely to be an artefact of changing occupational classification systems (Davey Smith, 1994: 132).

A more substantive problem is that of who is included and excluded in social classification systems. As reported above, social class schemes are derived from classifications of occupations, but this can be problematic. In the recent Irish study of social inequalities and health described above (Barry, J. et al, 2001), the researchers found a large category of 'unknowns' – people who could not classify themselves as part of the formal labour market, and for whom little additional information was available. The authors concluded that it was likely to signify an underclass of people, a group of people alienated from the labour market and who are likely to have a significantly lower standard of living compared to the general population. In addition women have often (especially in the past) been classified in relation to the 'head of household', or primary earner, which was usually a spouse where present, regardless of their own occupation.[6] Dissatisfaction with conventional social class classifications has provoked sociologists to develop alternative modes of analyses of the relationships between class, gender and the conditions of both domestic and formal labour, under changing historical circumstances (see Williams, 2003 for a review). Such research has upheld social class-based patterns of inequalities in health but it gives a more 'fine grain analysis' (Macintyre, 1997; Popay et al, 2003) of social class differences in health between people in similar types of occupational groupings. The term 'fine grain' refers to the fine levels of social differentiation in terms of access to resources between people of similar occupations or social class groups. For example, it may seek to measure differences in financial resources, such as levels of inherited wealth, financial commitments, the number of young or elderly dependents, as well as lifestyle pursuits, such as membership of sports or social clubs. Fine grain analysis may also incorporate the history of how people came to occupy certain occupational categories (Popay et al, 2003). Thus, a key way of addressing some of the crudeness of occupationally-based socio-economic groupings, as highlighted in the artefact explanation, is to combine different measures of resources to

6. In the current UK social class scheme (NS-SEC), a household reference person has been defined as the person owning or responsible for accommodation and in the case of joint ownership, it is the person with the most income and in the case of equal incomes, it is the older person who is used as reference (Miers, 2003:37).

give a more fine grain analysis within quantitative measures of inequalities and health.

In spite of problems with using various strategies to measure social class, the artefact explanation is generally considered by sociologists to be a very weak explanation in accounting for reported inequalities in health. It has been used by right-wing politicians in the past to avoid dealing with structural inequalities, such as those relating to poor income and inadequate housing (this issue will be expanded on below).

Social selection/biological explanations

This explanation is basically proposing that good health is likely to enhance your socio-economic status, while poor health is likely to pull you down the socio-economic ladder (Moore and Porter, 1998: 103). According to advocates of social selection or biological theories, it is ill-health that causes poverty, and not the other way around. Extensive research has not produced a great deal of evidence to support the notion of social selection as a major explanatory factor of health inequalities (Whitehead, 1988; Davey Smith, 1994). For example, a study which simultaneously estimated the relative effect of health on changes in social position (social class) and of social position on changes in health, reported that the effect of health on social position was minor by comparison with the effect of social position on health (Chandola et al, 2003). The research was based on a large-scale longitudinal study, known as 'the Whitehall study', conducted on over 10,000 civil servants in the UK.

The inadequacy of the social selection explanation according to Bartley et al (1998) is because early life experiences do not have the same effect on the later health of all people, since those with greater social advantage may be better able to shrug off early health problems, by comparison to those with a combination of health and social disadvantage. To counter the more simplistic assertion of the social selection explanation, that health at one point in time can affect social status at multiple points in the future, a life course approach has been advocated in recent research (Acheson et al, 1998; Graham, 2002; Blane, 2003). A life course approach is one which concentrates on 'the process by which health and material advantages and disadvantages accumulate across the life course' (Blane, 2003: 123). This will be further explained under materialist/structuralist explanations below.

Cultural/behavioural explanations

Studies demonstrate that there are lifestyle differences (patterns of social behaviour closely associated with culture) among various socio-economic groups (SEGs). Those in lower SEGs are more likely to smoke, drink alcohol heavily, and have less healthy diets than those in higher SEGs (see Marmot et al, 1991; Davey Smith et al, 1996; O'Shea and Kelleher, 2001). Cultural/behavioural explanations have largely emerged from the discipline of **epidemiology** since the middle of the twentieth century. Epidemiology is the branch of medicine concerned with the identification of risk factors associated with particular diseases. The cultural/behavioural explanations that have emerged from this discipline, however, have tended to fuel a 'culture of poverty' thesis (Lewis 1961; Murray, 1989), which proposes a self-destructive culture among poorer people, which in turn is associated with specific attitudes and values, and ultimately behaviour that undermines their health (Moore and Porter, 1998: 104).

Differences in lifestyle among groups do account for some of the social class gradient in health. However, the 'risks of death from many causes of death which have not been related to "lifestyle" are higher in less privileged groups, which suggests that a wider range of explanatory factors should be explored' (Davey Smith, 1994: 138). The best known study that demonstrated that factors over and above lifestyle have an impact on health status is one of the early phases of the Whitehall Study described above (Marmot et al, 1984). It investigated coronary health disease (CHD) risk factors among various grades of over 17,000 civil servants in the UK. While 29 per cent of those at the top grade smoked compared with 61 per cent of the lowest grade, there were large mortality differentials noted for causes not considered to be smoking related. In considering non-smokers alone, CHD was still strongly linked to grade. Also, differences in smoking, blood pressure, cholesterol, glucose intolerance, height and prevalent disease could not account for the considerable differences in cardio-vascular and (all-cause) mortality according to employment grade and car ownership. This suggests that other factors also play a part. Similar results have been reported in US studies (Berkman and Breslow, 1983; Kaplan, 1985 as cited in Whitehead, 1988). In particular, the link between socio-cultural and material circumstances needs to be explored, that is, how people's behaviour is strongly associated with the context of their lives.

Materialist/structuralist explanations
As noted above under the cultural/behavioural explanation, post-war epidemiology has identified a number of behavioural risk factors such as diet, smoking and exercise. The materialist/structuralist argument points out that risk factor epidemiology is based on the assumption that individuals, once knowledgeable of these risks, have the freedom to make healthy choices. However, the assumption of freedom to choose may not correspond to people's experiences (Bartley et al, 1998; Williams, 2003). Materialist/structuralist explanations instead point to a wider set of material and environmental factors that shape people's lives and choices.

Low income is perceived to be a critical structural barrier to good health in a range of different countries (Kosteniuk and Dickinson, 2003; Lynch et al, 2001; Lobmayer and Wilkinson, 2000; Shaw et al, 1999; Ecob and

Davey Smith, 1999; Kawachi, Kennedy and Wilkinson, 1999; Krieger and Fee, 1994; Dahl, 1994; Davey Smith et al, 1996; DHSS, 1980). A recent national study of health in Ireland also showed income (measured in terms of eligibility for free general medical service (GMS), 'the medical card', to be the most significant predictor of self-reported state of health. Self-reported state of health was worse amongst those who were eligible for free medical service. The authors contend that since access to the GMS scheme is strictly means-tested, it acts as the best available proxy marker of disadvantage (Kelleher et al, 2003: 484).

Despite a relative consensus on the importance of income there is some difference of opinion as to *why* it is so important. Some have argued that it is not just low income per se which causes health inequalities in a society but rather *unequal* incomes or inequality in a given society. This is known as the relative income theory (Hoskins, 2003). Authors such as Wilkinson (1996) and Kawachi et al (1999) argue that socio-economic differences can create psychosocial reactions which change people's vision of self-esteem and forms of social cohesion or trust (social networks/social involvement) in society. They propose that this in turn leads to unhealthy coping behaviours, such as excessive drinking and smoking, and poorer health status. Others (notably Shaw et al, 1999 and Lynch et al, 2001) refute this mainly psychological argument, instead asserting that health differences are primarily related to the lifetime material well-being of social groups, including factors such as access to good quality accommodation, diet, and leisure pursuits, and not to the psychological effects of positions within hierarchies. This argument is also know as 'absolute income theory' and suggests that increasing individuals' low incomes is the primary means of combating inequalities in health (Hoskins, 2003). It is likely that both explanations, income inequality in the relative income theory and low income in the absolute income theory, are important to understanding the link between income and health in individuals' experiences. However, the absolute income theory has received further momentum in a third explanation, known as the neo-materialist argument (Hoskins, 2003) or lifecourse approach (see above). This explanation suggests that it is the cumulative effect over time of low income in combination with other indicators of poverty such as low birth weight, poor educational attainment and poor employment conditions that accounts for inequalities in health (see Shaw et al, 1999 and Lynch et al, 2001). Reducing inequalities in health from this perspective requires a multi-faceted approach to reducing poverty in order to moderate health inequalities, which also includes addressing occupational and spatial aspects of poverty.

Exposure to hazards in some occupations: people in manual occupations are at greater risk of work-based hazards such as those associated with machinery, chemicals and industrial waste (Jewson, 1997). Jewson notes that occupational diseases associated with manual work include various cancers linked to exposure to certain chemicals, respiratory diseases associated with dust inhalation, skin diseases, infectious diseases and poisoning. Furthermore, other family members may be indirectly exposed from products being carried in work clothes and so forth. In addition, recent research has shown that exposure to an adverse psychosocial work environment, in terms of job tasks, defined by high demands and low control and/or by effort-reward imbalance, elicits sustained stress reactions with negative long-term consequences for health. This is more likely to occur and to have more adverse effects in the occupations of the lower SEGs (Siegrist and Marmot, 2004: 1463). Unemployment has also been found to have a detrimental effect on physical as well as mental health, not merely because unemployment leads to poverty, but also because of the way in which unemployment removes the person from a web of social relations (Bartley et al, 1998; Nolan and Whelan, 1997; Blane, 2003).

Poor quality housing and areas of deprivation affect physical and mental health. Whitehead (1988: 298-299) cites several studies demonstrating a link between poor housing and poor health (more chronic illnesses, more recent illness and more depressive illness), even where lifestyle factors are controlled. In addition, more affluent areas tend to be better resourced in terms of quality foodstuffs, recreational facilities and public services (Macintyre, 1993; Cohen et al, 2003). Shaw et al (2001) using premature mortality rates (deaths under sixty-five), identified the fifteen worst and thirteen best health areas of Britain. These areas closely corresponded with the material wealth of the areas. Those in the worst areas of Britain were over two and a half times more likely to die prematurely than those in the better areas.

Gender and health

What is gender?
It is common within sociological scholarship to distinguish between what is meant by the sex of an individual and gender. Sex refers to the biological differences between men and women, whereas gender refers to the socially constructed differences of what it means to be a man or masculine, and what it means to be a woman, or feminine, in given societies at particular times. Gender also sheds light on differences between women and between men. (See Chapter 2 for an introduction to the notion of biological determinism.)

Explaining gendered patterns in health.
As we did for social class, we will now examine evidence for the explanations as to why there are inequalities in **life expectancy** and in rates of illness for men and women (see Boxes 4.3 and 4.4 respectively). In particular, we will pay attention to the emerging closing of the gap in health

Box 4.3 *Gender and mortality*

- In developed countries women presently live longer than men. For example, in Ireland, the **average life expectancy** for women born between 1995 and 1997 is 6.5 years longer than that of men (79.5 years and 73 years respectively) (CSO, 2003a), with the corresponding figure in the UK being 5 years (80 years for females and 75 years for males) (ONS, 2002). In the US, men die nearly 7 years younger than women and have higher death rates for all 15 leading causes of death (DHSS, 1996, cited in Courtenay, 2000: 1385).

- There is, however, a closing of the gap in the life-expectancy of men and women. For older adults in northern and western Europe and northern America and Canada, the gap was decreasing over the 1980s (Lahelma et al, 1999).

- In contemporary Ireland (based on statistics collected between 1989 and 1999) men are more likely to die prematurely than women for most major causes of death. Men were especially more likely to die of homicide/assault (over twice as likely) and were over three times as likely to die as a result of transport accidents (Balanda and Wilde, 2001: 12).

- The highest causes of death for young men from lower occupational classes are homicide/assault and transport accidents (Balanda and Wilde, 2001: 12).

Box 4.4 *Gender and morbidity*

- It had become a truism in research on gender and inequality in the latter part of the twentieth century that women had higher levels of morbidity, giving rise to the popular assessment that women are sicker but men die younger (Verbrugge and Wingard, 1987; Lorber, 1997)

- In recent times, research on physical well-being is showing a marked decline or a lack of evidence of gender inequality in morbidity. Women are at least as likely to report good health as men, as evidenced in Ireland and the UK (see for example, Kelleher et al, 2003; ONS, 2002; Arber and Cooper, 1999; Emslie et al, 1999; Macintyre et al, 1999; Mathews et al, 1999).

- Women in Western countries, however, are still more likely to have poor psychosocial/mental health (Lahelma et al, 1999). Women are especially more likely to report and seek help for depression and anxiety, but men are more likely to suffer behaviour disorders such as violence, drug or alcohol abuse and are more likely to commit suicide (Doyal, 1995; Macintyre et al, 1996; Emslie et al, 1999; Shilton, 1999; Busfield, 2002).

inequalities between men and women. We explore artefactual explanations (the way statistics are collected and interpreted); biological explanations (anatomical differences between men and women); cultural/ behavioural explanations (lifestyle differences); and materialist explanations (the conditions of people's lives).

Artefactual explanations
The artefactual explanation for gender differences in health status has focussed on the claim of women's propensity to suffer more illness (especially milder forms of illness), a claim which dominated research on gender and health in the 1990s. The artefact explanation suggests that this finding of excess female morbidity may not reflect actual differences in health status but rather is a product, or artefact, of how data on morbidity are collected. In particular, research has suggested that gender processes operate at the level of data collection, with women more likely to report illness to research interviewers, whilst male stoicism may prevent men from doing likewise. (Self-reported health is a global health status indicator.) In addition, it has been suggested that doctors are more likely to observe and diagnose symptoms in women and that women attend medical surgeries more frequently because of our culture of predominantly female responsibility for childcare and for family planning (Graham, 1984; Verbrugge, 1985; Radley, 1994).

However, research has also contested the argument of over-reporting of women's illnesses relative to men's (Macintyre, 1993; Popay et al, 1993; Macintyre et al, 1999). Macintyre (1993) studied men's and women's reporting of symptoms of the common cold. She found that contrary to over-reporting symptoms, the data supported more the phenomenon of 'the whingeing male'. At a given level of symptoms, men were more likely to complain. The research nonetheless confirmed that investigators expect to find more illness among women. In addition, Macintyre et al's research demonstrated that the lack of over-reporting by women is consistent with studies of other more serious conditions in men and women. She notes that:

> Female excess is only consistently found across the lifespan for more psychological manifestations of distress and is far less apparent, or reversed, for a number of physical symptoms per conditions (Macintyre et al, 1996: 621).

Biological explanations
Biological explanations for the differences in health status of men and women point to the following identifiable biological patterns:

• women's greater immuno-responsiveness to ward off viral and bacterial agents that cause death;

- women's greater susceptibility to auto-immune diseases such as rheumatoid arthritis and lupus (Nathanson, 1994; Ramey, 1997) (cited in Murphy-Lawless, 2003: 16).

Female reproductive health does account for some of the differences in reported morbidity levels between men and women but even when this is separated out, women still report higher levels of morbidity.

The known variations in biological predispositions of men and women towards certain conditions do not fully explain women's greater levels of morbidity. Social scientists do not find this surprising as they challenge the idea that sexual anatomy equates with gender inequalities in health. If inequalities in health were due to biology alone, the same inequalities between men and women should appear globally and historically. The interesting question in relation to biology becomes: how does our biology interact with the society and physical environment in which we live? Just taking life expectancy alone, we know that at the start of the twentieth century in Ireland, men had an equal life expectancy to women, but at the start of the twenty-first century this has changed (CSO, 2004a). It is notable that the shift in women's disadvantaged mortality ratio at the start of the twentieth century to a mortality advantage today emerged alongside a remarkable improvement in their social status and economic circumstances (Annandale, 1998: 128). These changes and differences in men's and women's health over time and space suggest that environmental and cultural factors influence men's and women's health and that environment and culture may place different strains on men's and women's bodies. In the following two explanations of gendered health patterns, the ways in which our Western society is gendered – split into tasks and spaces appropriate for men and women that in turn genders our health and life-expectancy – is considered.

Behavioural/cultural explanations

Behavioural and cultural explanations suggest that aspects of our behaviour influence our risk of disease. Within this explanatory framework, the conventional wisdom within sociological scholarship has been that women are more likely to adopt health-promoting behaviours and men are more likely to adopt health-damaging behaviours. However, recent research has begun to challenge this conventional wisdom, with a decline in health differences between men and women beginning to be reported. This may be accounted for by an evening up of health-related behaviours between men and women in recent years. Let us first consider some findings from the wider body of research on gender and health before exploring some recently-emerging trends.

That men are more likely to adopt health damaging behaviours including the 'holy four' of smoking, drinking, poor diet and lack of physical exercise (McQueen 1987, cited in Lahelma et al, 1999) and avoid seeking help through primary health services has become a relatively robust finding in this field of research (Blaxter, 1990; Prättälä et al, 1994; Doyal, 1995; Waldron, 1995; Shilton, 1999; Courtenay, 2000; McEvoy and Richardson, 2004). Gender has also been shown to be relevant to levels of sexual health knowledge, and to availing of the sexual health services for sexually transmitted diseases (Banks, 2001; Green and Pope, 1999). Men have been shown to be particularly reluctant in the uptake of clinical and support services for sexual health problems such as testicular cancer (Moynihan, 1998), prostate cancer (Cameron and Bernardes, 1998) and infertility (Meerabeau, 1991; Throsby and Gill, 2004). Similar to research on women, however, it is important to acknowledge that 'men' are not a homogeneous group, but rather, male health behaviour is cross-cut by factors such as class, ethnicity and marital status. For example, men in middle-age and men in lower SEGs are more likely to engage in negative health behaviour compared to men as whole category (Wilson, 1998; Roos et al, 2001; Prättälä et al, 1994.). A study of the 'well person checks' in the UK revealed that male attendees were more highly educated, less likely to smoke or drink to excess, and more likely to have positive views about their ability to influence their own health. Marital status has also been found to make a difference in some but not all studies (Waller et al, 1990 cited in Wilson, 1998: 263). These findings on differences in health behaviours among men as a broad category suggest that materialist explanations are important to understanding which men adopt which type of behaviours (see further below).

Research has also challenged the stereotype (and, as stated above, relatively robust research finding) that women are more likely to engage in health promoting and health preventing behaviour. Kane's (1994) prediction that that the effects of changes in women's behaviour in the last thirty years, notably increased consumption of alcohol and cigarettes, along with the materialist explanation of the dual burdens of paid and domestic work (that we will discuss below), may now be emerging as an explanation of the closing gap of morbidity and mortality patterns amongst men and women. In addition, certain health risk behaviours of women need more critical attention. An example of a relatively hidden health risk behaviour has been a pre-occupation with ideals of thinness, which can manifest in constant and excessive dieting, including eating disorders and cigarette smoking as a means of weight reduction (see Inhorn and Whittle, 2001 for a review of studies). European Union statistics indicate that conditions of underweight to severe underweight affect 15 per cent of women compared to 5 per cent of men. Furthermore, the age group most likely to feel the compunction to diet is the age group of 13-15 years. Thirty-seven per cent of girls of this age group in Ireland report they they feel the need to diet (Eurostat, 2000 cited in Murphy-Lawless, 2003).

As noted in relation to the artefact explanation, recent research has also questioned the idea that women are more likely to seek medical consultations in responding to symptoms and chronic conditions (Hunt et al, 1999; Wyke, Hunt and Ford, 1998; Adamson et al, 2003). There is a particular concern that chronic heart disease (CHD) has been constructed as a male disease in the eyes of health professionals and lay persons, causing an inequality in the early detection and treatment of heart disease amongst women in both the US and the UK (Dong et al, 1996; Mark, 2000; Pollard and Hyatt, 1999; Lockyer and Bury, 2002; Emslie, Hunt and Watt, 2001). CHD is a major cause of premature death in the Western world, with Ireland having twice the EU average death rate from CHD (Kelleher et al, 2003). The research suggests that there are poorer levels of detection, referral and treatment for women with cardiac disturbances compared with those of men, and that there is a greater need for research and health programmes which are woman centred. A woman centred approach would take into account prevention strategies for cardiac problems occurring in women, investigate what diagnostic testing is appropriate to detect cardiac disturbances amongst women[7] and engage greater research into women's responses to treatment (Woods and Jacobson cited in Murphy-Lawless, 2003: 24).

Materialist/structuralist explanations

The materialist position acknowledges that men and women have different behavioural patterns in relation to health promotion and treatment but materialist explanations suggest that it is aspects of society primarily beyond the control of individuals that may structure – or cause – different health behaviours and health outcomes. The materialist/structuralist position is premised on the idea that the structural reality of men's and women's lives, and especially the unequal position of women in society, creates additional strains on women's health. Therefore, greater equality for women (in the paid labour market and in the home in terms of distribution of domestic and care labour) could alleviate some of the materialist burdens on women's health.

> From the structuralist position it is plausible that the extent that men's and women's social positions, such as their employment status, family roles and social relation, do approach each other in the future, convergent trends of gender differences in illhealth can be expected (Lahelma et al, 1999: 10).

Indeed studies that have specifically explored men and women with similar working, social and material circumstances show a reduction or absence of gender-based morbidity (Emslie et al, 1999; Umberson et al, 1996; Hraba et al, 1996; Mathews et al, 1999; Arber and Cooper, 1999). Recent trends in the gender division of labour in the the home will be explored in Chapter 9.

---

7. Women tend to present with cardiac problems at an older age and frequently in co-existence with other conditions (Wenger et al, 1993 cited in Murphy-Lawless, 2003:23).

An important debate relating to materialist/structuralist explanations of gender inequalities in health has been the effect of employment status on women's health. Some research has shown that women who are full-time housewives have poorer health, especially poorer psychological health than those who are employed outside of the home (Kane, 1994; Nathanson, 1980; Sacker et al, 2000; Kelleher et al, 2003). Feminist materialist research has explained this in terms of the health effects of material deprivation, the lack of economic independence and the social status and social networks that accompany employment (see for example, the seminal work of Oakley, 1974). However, feminist research has also shown that employment outside the home does not automatically reduce strains on health and may, instead, compound strains (see for example, Arber, 1991, 1997; Bartley et al, 1992; Hall, 1992; Macran et al, 1996; Sacker et al, 2001). This research suggests that it is important not only to look at differences among women in terms of their employment status but also how that is combined in their lives with their life-stage and responsibility for children. Moreover, in understanding differentials between men's and women's health in materialist terms it is also important to look at materialist differences among women themselves. For example, feminist research suggests that women in higher occupations are likely to have more financial resources and benefits to manage the different responsibilities in their lives. In other words, the gender role strain that women may experience, and which is said to affect health outcomes, varies by social class.

This sociological focus on how gender relations affect health has, until recently, primarily explored the ways in which women's lives and health status are shaped by gender relations. Gender issues were regarded as women's issues. As a result, the health risks associated with the gendering of men in society or masculinity have remained largely unproblematised and taken for granted as part of the way men are. The study of masculinities and health has begun to explore the way gender is implicated in men's health behaviours, attitudes and health status (see for example, Sabo and Gordon, 1995; Cameron and Bernardes, 1998; Stakelum and Boland 2001; Saltonstall, 1993; Watson, 2000; Courtenay, 2000; Doyal, 2001; Riska, 2002; McEvoy and Richardson, 2004). As noted earlier, men (especially working-class men) have traditionally manifested themselves as more likely to adopt health-damaging behaviours and are less likely to attend health prevention services. It was also noted that this trend is showing signs of change. The materialist explanation would suggest that the reality of men's lives, such as the structure of paid employment, their greater involvement in high risk manufacturing and construction industries, creates a system which encourages negative health behaviours and prevents men attending health services. In addition, a cultural/behavioural explanation points to how cultural ideas of what it means to be a man or ideals of masculinity are interwoven in health behaviours. Cultural ideals of gendered behaviour are also influenced by other structural aspects of our lives such as ethnic and class identities producing differences, for example, between masculinities in different ethnic communities as occurs between men of working-class or middle-class backgrounds. According to Courtenay (2000), men often use the resources of assuming their physical and mental health to be strong and invulnerable and, crucially, more powerful than women's, to construct masculine identities. Adopting high-risk behaviours and a lack of fear in relation to one's health is a key means of demonstrating manliness in contemporary society.

> Men are demonstrating dominant norms of masculinity when they refuse to take sick leave from work, when they insist that they need little sleep, and when they boast that drinking does not impair their driving (Courtenay, 2000: 1389).

As individuals, we are self-aware of enduring gendered practices and gender ideologies in the expected behaviour of men and women which can act as a guiding frame – or structure – in everyday interactions. Changing health behaviours may thus involve questioning gender ideologies which are perpetuated in institutions in society and in daily living.

Ethnicity and health

What are race and ethnicity?
The concept of 'race' is a relatively recent innovation in European thought (Smaje, 2000). According to Annandale (1998) it first entered the English language at the start of the seventeenth century, but it was not until the late eighteenth century in Europe and North America that it began to refer to phenotypical (observable) differences between people. These differences include skin colour, hair texture and head shape, characteristics which have been used to legitimate discrimination and inferior treatment of certain groups. Race has historically been associated with hatred and has been used to justify inequalities. The notion that there were a number of distinct races whose members had a particular biological make-up that influenced their capabilities and behaviour was well-established by the mid-nineteenth century (Annandale, 1998). This view that different biological races exist has since been strongly contested. Although we still talk of different races of people, it is no longer considered valid to suggest that any group exists that is so biologically distinct from another to be called a race (Culley and Dyson, 2001). This is because it is now acknowledged that a great deal of variation exists within so-called races, and considerable overlap across races (Culley and Dyson, 2001: 4). The term race has been largely superseded by the term 'ethnic group' and 'ethnicity' in the health and social sciences (Aspinall, 2001: 830). Ethnicity, according to Culley and Dyson, means the '*socially constructed* differences, grounded in culture, ancestry and language

rather than in supposed physical or biological differences' (2001: 4, emphasis in original). Definitions of ethnicity emphasise the ongoing dynamic construction of an ethnic identity reflecting self-identification with cultural traditions that provide personal meanings and define boundaries between groups of people in a society (Karlson and Nazroo, 2002). The word race continues to be used in sociological literature,[8] but is usually placed in inverted commas to indicate that it is being used to denote social rather than biological dimensions (Culley and Dyson, 2001), and racism continues to concern sociologists. Since the seventies and eighties, the term 'black' has been widely used to refer to all people who are not white. However, there are problems with this blanket use of the term. People from the Indian subcontinent, for example, do not define themselves as black (Culley and Dyson, 2001: 4). Furthermore, the black-white dichotomy assumes that a neat divide between an oppressed black minority and a dominant white majority can be made. This simplistic divide ignores differences in identities across the black population as well as differences across the white minority group, for example, the Irish in Britain.

Ethnic diversity in Ireland
Travellers are an ethnic minority group of Irish people. There are estimates of around 30,000 Travellers living in the Republic of Ireland, with about 1,500 more living in Northern Ireland (Pavee Point, 2003). They are widely acknowledged as being one of the most marginalised and disadvantaged groups in Irish society and, as we will examine further in the next section, have generally poorer health than the settled Irish population (see Box 4.5).

Box 4.5 *Irish Traveller health*

- The life-expectancy rate for Traveller women is 65 years and for men 62 years (much lower than the national average).
- The infant mortality rate for Traveller children is 3 times the national average.
- Sudden Infant Death Syndrome among Traveller families in 1999 was 12 times the national average (DoHC, 2002).

Prior to the 1990s, migration into Ireland was very low and confined mainly to Irish people returning from abroad (Mac Éinri, 2001). Since the mid-1990s, Ireland has experienced an unprecedented increase in migration, predominantly returning Irish migrants, and EU and US citizens (Mac Éinri, 2001). There was also a large increase in the number of immigrants from

---

8. See Smaje (2000) for an argument as to why we should continue to use 'race', as in 'racialised identity'.

the rest of the world, excluding the US and UK, rising from 11 per cent of total immigration in 1996 to 35 per cent of total immigration in 2002 (NCCRI, 2002). However, the figures are still comparatively small. In 2003, 5.8 per cent of the population of Ireland was composed of non-Irish nationals but fewer than 2 per cent of this was composed of immigrants from non-EU states (Africa, Asia and USA) (CSO, 2003a). This rise of inward migration in Ireland follows closely the experience of other nations in that it can be seen in the light of a government policy of active recruitment of workers in the EU, the US and the rest of the world (Immigrant Council of Ireland, 2003).

The number of people seeking asylum in Ireland has also increased dramatically in recent years, although these represent just a small proportion of the overall number of migrants. For the year 2003, the top six countries from which asylum seekers migrated were Nigeria (39.4 per cent), Romania (9.8 per cent), Democratic Republic of the Congo (3.7 per cent), Moldova (3.1 per cent), Czech Republic (2.4 per cent) and Somalia (2.3 per cent) (Department of Justice, Equality and Law Reform, 2004). The National Consultative Committee on Racism and Interculturalism (NCCRI) (2001a) refutes the assertion that the increase in those seeking refugee status is because Ireland's 'Celtic Tiger' economy (at the time of writing in decline) was attracting economic migrants posing as political asylum seekers. Instead, they point to the growth in restrictive practices across European countries that have made it increasingly difficult for migrants to seek asylum in such states. To support their argument, they note that the countries from which most asylum seekers originate are countries that have experienced a great deal of political upheaval in recent years (NCCRI, 2001a).

Even before the increase in migration, racism in Ireland and emanating from Irish people was noted (MacGreil, 1996). The NCCRI has described recent acts of racism in Ireland as follows:

> The type of racism most often commented upon are incidents of harassment, racially motivated attacks or the expression of racist hatred on the street, through graffiti or in late night radio phone-in programmes. Labelling and scapegoating of groups are also common expressions of racism. In relation to refugees and asylum seekers the most recurring labelling includes the exaggeration of the overall numbers ('floods', 'tides' etc); the stereotyping of refugees as 'scroungers' who are unwilling to work or labelling of refugees as people likely to be involved in criminal activity and the linked assertion that most are 'bogus' and are in reality economic migrants (2001a: 6).

Racism among Irish people has also been noted in a number of other writings (Fanning, 2002; Lentin and McVeigh, 2002; Lentin, 2001; Boucher, 1998; McVeigh and Binchy, 1999; Begley et al, 1999). In addition, press reporting in the Irish media has been identified as representing refugees and asylum seekers in a negative light (Collins, 1997; Watt, 1997; Pollack, 1999). However, measures have been taken in Ireland that attempt to counteract racism. A National Consultative Committee on Racism and Interculturalism (NCCRI), referred to above, was set up in 1998 by the Department of Justice, Equality and Law Reform, with the aim of developing programmes and taking actions to develop an integrated approach against racism and to advise the Irish government on race-related policies (NCCRI, 2001b). The Immigrant Council of Ireland is an independent organisation set up in 2001 working with and for immigrants in promoting their rights through information, advocacy, and awareness. Other non-governmental local anti-racist groups have also developed throughout Ireland, such as the *Anti-Racist Campaign* (ARC) in Dublin, *Immigrant Solidarity* in Cork, and *Mid-West Against Racism* in Limerick.

Box 4.6 *Migrant communities and health*

- There is little research available on the health status of immigrants in Ireland. However, studies from Britain suggest that minority ethnic groups have a poorer health status compared with the white British population (Nazroo 1997; Karlson and Nazroo, 2002; Dyson and Smaje, 2001).

- The poorer health status of ethnic minorities in Britain includes people born in Ireland and living in the UK (Greenslade, 1997; Wild and McKeigue, 1997; Abbotts et al, 1997; 2001). There is also evidence to suggest that second and third generation Irish are also affected by poorer health status relative to the majority population (Williams and Ecob, 1999; Harding and Balarajan, 1996; 2001).

- There are differences not just between the health status of white indigenous British people and those from ethnic minority groups in general, but also among people from different minority groups. For example, compared to people residing in Britain (irrespective of the country in which they were born), death rates for suicide are higher for Irish migrants, and lower for Caribbean migrants, and significantly lower for migrants from the Indian subcontinent (Dyson and Smaje, 2001: 39). Mortality from all causes was low in Caribbean immigrants, largely due to low mortality from coronary heart disease (CHD)(Wild and McKeigue, 1997). Analysis of the Fourth National Survey of Ethnic Minorities in the UK showed that, while a South Asian group had a greater risk of indicators of CHD, once the group was broken down into constituent parts, this only applied to Pakistanis and Bangladeshis – Indians had the same rates as whites (Nazroo, 1998: 156).

- The mortality rates of ethnic minority groups are cross-cut by gender and SEG, giving rise to differences in mortality rates within specific ethnic groups.

Explaining ethnic patterns in health

The artefact explanation

The artefactual explanation is of little explanatory value in relation to ethnic patterns of health. As indicated in relation to other types of inequality, this explanation would suggest that reported ethnic inequalities in health are due to the way in which statistics are collected. However, it is widely acknowledged that the main problem in relation to statistics on ethnic communities has been the lack of available data (thus leading to a probable under-measurement rather than an over-measurement, as the artefact explanation implies). The relative absence of data on ethnic minorities has been compounded by the crudeness of measures of ethnic identity which have been characteristic of many of the large data bases available (Aspinall, 2001). Such problems include:

- the non-inclusion of dwellings such as hotels and hostels, spaces where many migrants and especially asylum seekers live, in the large household panel studies;
- inappropriately defined ethnic categories such as 'immigrants' 'black', 'south Asian', or 'country of origin' (as used in death certificates) rather than ethnic identity. Such categories do not allow adequate identification and comparison across ethnic groups (Nazroo, 1988; Fenton and Karlson, 2002)

Researchers have suggested that there is a need for less crude and more sensitive strategies in the research design of large surveys, such as allowing individuals to define their ethnic group in their own terms, which avoids the construction of ethnic boundaries on the basis of the ethnocentric assumptions of researchers (Nazroo, 1998: 153).

The biological explanation

While genetic factors may explain to some extent the health variations between ethnic groups, they should not be over-emphasised. As indicated earlier, it is now accepted that no identifiable racial group exists where there are consistent gene frequencies across a group. Only a small proportion of genetic characteristics such as skin colour and hair texture are observable. As Dyson and Smaje (2001: 51) suggest, there is of course geographical variation within the human species in genetic constitution. However, there is a highly imperfect association between social groups who have given racial labels and some genetic traits.

Behavioural/cultural explanations

There is an acknowledgement in social science literature that ethnic identities/cultures are likely to be implicated in ideas about health and the ways in which we respond to illness (see for example, Smaje, 2000; Culley,

2001; Karlson and Nazroo, 2002). However, as we will briefly elaborate below, it is widely believed within social science scholarship that this explanation for inequalities in health has been over emphasised and over-simplified in medical science and especially in health promotion.

This over-emphasis on cultural explanations as a primary explanatory factor in ethnic inequalities in health has occurred even though there has been little evidence to support this theory (Karlson and Nazroo, 2002). In a recent study in the UK it was the socio-economic context and experiences of racism which proved to be the most powerful predictors of the health of ethnic minorities, as opposed to cultural identification with a group (Karlson and Nazroo, 2002). Writers such as W. Ahmad (1996) argue that professional ideologies in health and social care focus too heavily on cultural differences as an explanation for ethnic inequalities in health. The resolution of health problems and inequalities is then seen to lie in re-socialising ethnic minorities into the norms of white society. Victim-blaming by health professionals may occur, whereby cultural attributes may seem pathological in the face of mainstream values (Pearson, 1986b). The problem with using cultural values as the primary explanation for health outcomes is that, as previously discussed under class and gender, the context of people's lives which shapes cultural values can be ignored.

Cultural explanations can be over simplified when claims about the values and practices of ethnic groups become stereotypes that simplistically assign particular cultural characteristics to specific ethnic groups and which are regarded as unchanging. The formation of ethnic identity through generations is likely to change in relation to the social, economic and political environments of the host community, but the consequences of these changes on health behaviours are poorly understood (Harding and Balarajan, 2001). The challenge for the health professional and health scientist is that ethnicity should not be equated with a specific set of behaviours. As Culley (2001: 110) notes: it is 'not that cultural differences in health beliefs and behaviours do not exist, but that they cannot be assumed'. Instead of a static set of characteristics, ethnicity should be regarded as being a fluid social construct which for individuals may be modified depending on the context a person is in and those whom he or she encounters (Wallman, 1986). In addition, Ahmed (1996) highlights that the differences between people in relation to health behaviours within the same cultural group are mediated by other factors such as socio-economic class position, gender and age. Below we examine how cultural values can be related to one's material circumstances.

The materialist/structuralist explanation
People from ethnic minorities frequently live in circumstances of material deprivation. The discussion below will highlight how relative material deprivation can account for a large part of the inequalities in health between ethnic minorities and the majority population, as well as among different

ethnic minorities. However, it will be argued that ethnic patterning of health cannot be reduced to socio-economic factors alone and that the experience of migration and racism adds explanatory value to an understanding of ethnically-based health inequalities.

Material deprivation: Nazroo's (1997, 1998) studies of the health status of ethnic minority groups in the UK demonstrated that material deprivation contributed to their poorer health status compared to the white population. She found that when standard of living was controlled, a large improvement in the health status of ethnic minority groups was noted. Dyson and Smaje (2001: 58) drew on a number of studies on the effects of socio-economic status among ethnic minorities, and similarly concluded that direct measures of material deprivation accounted for a good deal of variation in the health status of ethnic minorities. Standard of living indices that took into consideration the nature of accommodation, access to amenities and consumer durables were strongly associated with health status (Dyson and Smaje, 2001: 58). Ethnic minorities are not, however, a homogenous SEG. Considerable variation in material circumstances of ethnic groups living in Britain is also apparent (Nazroo, 1997; 1998; Karlson and Nazroo, 2002).

It is frequently assumed that immigrants, especially asylum seekers, may expect a better standard of living in their host country. However, many asylum seekers and refugees experience a fall in living standards following migration. Many migrate to Ireland and other countries to avail themselves of poorly paid work, and adverse and sometimes unregulated working conditions. A study of Vietnamese and Bosnian refugees in Ireland showed that only 17 per cent of Bosnian respondents reported an improvement in living standards since arriving in Ireland, while 40 per cent reported a noticeable fall (Refugee Resettlement Project, 1998). A study by the Holy Ghost Congregation (cited in National Consultative Committee on Racism and Interculturalism, 1999) on asylum seekers in Ennis, County Clare, showed that while asylum seekers were generally healthy, their long term health status was of concern in light of the low incomes they were forced to survive on. Kennedy and Murphy-Lawless (2003) researched the needs of refugees and asylum seekers in relation to the maternity services in Ireland. Their findings suggest that some respondents did not have basic toiletries like sanitary towels, in spite of the fact that women bleed for weeks after the birth of a baby. Many study participants did not have cots for their babies, nor access to a bath. Following the baby's birth, these mothers often shared single beds with their other children in hostels. British evidence suggests that rather than 'carrying over' poor health from the time spent in the mother country, ethnic migrants to the UK actually experience a decline in health after they re-locate (Nazroo, 1997; Williams, 1993; Dyson and Smaje, 2001: 53). This suggests that the material disadvantages migrants experience after re-location are an important factor in their health status. We have little evidence from Ireland as to how migrants fare over time once they arrive in Ireland (however, see below in relation to Irish migrants in Britain).

Migration: Research has shown that additional contextual or structural features in the lives of ethnic minorities, especially the experience of migration itself and racism encountered in the host society, also explains the poorer health of ethnic minorities. Dyson and Smaje (2001: 52) suggest that the experience of migration, experienced by many of those in ethnic minority groups, may adversely affect a person's health. First, the effects of a person's social conditions in the previous culture or country may continue to affect a person's health in the country of re-location. Second, the actual process of migration may undermine health, for example through the loss of support networks, increased stress, experience of racism, financial difficulties, and lack of local knowledge to access services. Begley et al's (1999) study of the experiences of those seeking asylum in Ireland found that asylum seekers feel isolated, vulnerable and powerless. The authors also noted that anxiety, depression and sadness were predominant aspects of asylum seekers' lives. Boyle et al (1998) trace the typical refugee experience from the initial threat in the home country, to the fleeing process and arrival at the country of destination. They note that a feeling of initial euphoria after a safe arrival quickly gives way to a profound depression associated with separation from their families and loss of identity and their homeland. Even years after their flight from threat, refugees may experience post-traumatic stress disorder (Boyle et al, 1998).

The negative effect of migration on health has also been experienced by Irish people migrating abroad. Williams and Ecob's (1999) research over time on Irish migrants living in England and Wales concluded that the raised mortality rates of the Irish living in those areas (and not found amongst the Irish at home) could not be explained wholly by the socio-economic conditions of the area but rather was associated with their status as migrants. Harding and Balarajan's (2001) research has traced the health of first, second and third generation migrants in Britain. They concluded that although socio-economic disadvantage lessened between generations of Irish people living in England and Wales, mortality of third generation Irish people remained high relative to the white English and Welsh population, and that the negative perceptions of Irishness with consequent unfulfilled expectations and lack of control in these people's environments and lifestyles are likely to be important contributors (Harding and Balarajan, 2001: 467) (see also Raftery et al, 1990 and Harding and Balarjan, 1996 for similar earlier findings on first and second generation Irish people in Britain). The experience of being a migrant group was also found to be significant in relation to alcohol misuse by the Irish in Britain (Foster, 2003).

Racism: How might the experience of racism be detrimental to health? In Chapter 8, the question of whether and how racism permeates the delivery of healthcare is addressed. In this section, we concentrate on how the experience of racism may affect health status. Although research linking

racism to health is not yet well-established (LaVeist, 2000; Karl
Nazroo, 2002) studies have shown a relationship between experie
racism and poorer mental and physical health (Krieger and Sidney
Benzeval et al, 1992). In particular, a number of studies have found stress-
related symptoms among those encountering racist attitudes. Armstead et
al, (1989) noted that experience of direct racism was associated with an
increase in blood pressure, and racial harassment at work has been linked
to both acute and chronic illness (Benzeval et al, 1992). Krieger and Sidney
(1996) reported that black women who remained silent about perceived
unfair treatment were more likely to suffer from hypertension (high blood
pressure). Indeed, exposure to racism is now being considered as a possible
primary etiological factor in race differences in mortality and morbidity, and
more thorough research on this topic has been recommended (LaVeist,
2000; Karlson and Nazroo, 2002).

Inequalities in health: the status of research and implications for health professionals
It is possible to draw some links across issues raised in the chapter at this
point. It is clear that the social hierarchies in society based on gender, class
and ethnicity are clearly manifested in people's health in Ireland as
elsewhere. The empirical data presented in the chapter has identified that all
three major social factors are independently related to health outcomes. The
data has also shown that in everyday life, social class, gender and ethnicity
are interwoven in a complex web that is bound up with our social identities,
creating a complex nexus of social inequalities in health. The over-riding
message of the chapter has been that the influence of social divides on health
is neither unchanging nor inevitable. Rather, there is the possibility of
addressing the social bases of poor health and tackling health inequalities.
     The explanations as to why social factors are so clearly related to health,
elaborated in this chapter, have been drawn from an influential report *(The
Black Report)* on class inequalities in health in the UK, published almost
twenty-five years ago (DHSS, 1980). Although these explanations
originated in class-based inequalities in health, the chapter has
demonstrated that these explanations also have relevance to explaining
gender and ethnic inequalities in health. The weight of the explanatory
evidence for social inequalities in health lies in the nexus between
cultural/behavioural explanations and materialist/structuralist explanations.
However, there is a greater need for research and research collaboration
which can explore how these explanations interact to produce inequalities
in health. Research to date on explanations of inequalities in health can be
crudely summarised by a schism between epidemiological research which
has identified risk factors in individual behaviour which are associated with
ill-health (cultural/ behavioural explanations) and sociological/social policy
research which focuses on how society shapes the context of our lives

(materialist/ structuralist explanations) or, as Graham has put, it 'how people got where they are' (Graham, 2002: 210).

One explanation for the schism in research between these two explanatory frameworks is the different disciplinary backgrounds from which they emerge. Epidemiological research, as indicated earlier, is a branch of medicine concerned with the distribution of disease and the identification of risk factors. Post-war epidemiological research is influenced by what Inhorn and Whittle refer to as biomedicine's myopic focus on the micro-level causes of diseases in individuals, that is, pathological agents that translate into a 'single-disease-single-risk factor' model of understanding health (2001: 554). As such, epidemiology frames the social distribution of disease in terms of individual risk factors, such as level of exercise and diet and as attributes of isolated individuals' lifestyles for which individuals must take account. Sociological research, by contrast, has been more concerned with showing how the social context of people's lives such as the experience of migration, poverty, gender norms and hierarchies, as highlighted in this chapter, are central to understanding the social shaping of lifestyles and the choices people make about their health.

There is a renewed interest in the research community which focuses on inequalities in health to move to more inter-disciplinary or collaborative research (for example, between disciplines such as social geography, social history, epidemiology and sociology) so that the interconnections between behavioural and materialist models of understanding health inequalities can be addressed (see, for example, Macintyre, 1997; Bartley et al, 1998; Frohlich et al, 2001, Graham, 2002; Williams, 2003). There is a need for much more on-the-ground type of research that explores how people in different types of communities make choices about their lifestyle and health over time and how forms of social inclusion and exclusion are built up in social groupings (such as in social class, ethnic or gender groupings) or in spatially-based communities and especially in deprived areas (Blaxter, 1990; Popay et al, 2003; Bolam et al, 2003). Indeed, the issue of health inequalities needs to be considered in the context of the age-old sociological problem of structure and agency (see Chapter 2 for an explanation of structure and agency). In this sense, the question needs to be framed as follows: *Why is it that people located within the social structures where we find them behave in the way that they do* (Bartley et al, 1998: 6, citing Wilkinson et al, 1998)?

What are the implications of a sociological understanding of health inequalities for health professionals? First, there is a need for health professionals to be knowledgeable of the primary determinants of health and illness. Social factors are incontrovertibly a powerful determinant of our health and chances of reaching the average life expectancy for our society. Second, sociology suggests that a broader approach is required to tackle inequalities in health. Contemporary health promotion and health preventative strategies are overwhelmingly targeted at raising awareness at individual-level behaviours, such as smoking cessation programmes or healthy exercise programmes. A sociological understanding of health problems suggests that there is a need to go beyond health promotion and raising health awareness in individuals and instead to involve health professionals in raising awareness and developing interventions that address societal level factors (the social and physical environments) that influence health behaviours. Otherwise, health professionals may find themselves trying to cope with symptoms of illness rather than addressing the causes. In short, there is a need to re-contextualise people's health – see health factors in the context of people's lives and communities and repoliticise health – understand that health is linked to forms of social deprivation and cultural norms which require politically and socially aware responses. Current public health responses will be addressed in more detail in Chapter 14.

Summary

- Morbidity and mortality are strongly determined by the socio-economic and cultural contexts of our lives. The social factors of social class, gender and ethnicity are particularly relevant.

- There are four explanations as to why the above social divides are related to health status:
  - Artefact: this suggests that inequalities in health are exaggerated and arise through the way in which data are collected/manipulated.
  - Biological: this suggests that inequalities in health are products of our biology.
  - Cultural/behavioural: this suggests that inequalities in health arise because of how people behave (their lifestyle patterns).
  - Materialist/structuralist: this suggests that inequalities in health arise because the social and physical conditions of our lives affect options for healthy living.

- The artefact argument is a useful reminder to social scientists that there is a continuous need to reflect on and refine measures of social divides such as social class or ethnicity and health status. However, the artefact explanation is widely considered to be a weak explanation, since several different measures confirm the existence of health inequalities.

- The biological argument is also of limited value because it understates social factors in explaining health inequalities.

- The weight of the explanatory value lies within both the cultural/behavioural and materialist/structuralist explanations.
  - In relation to social class, those located higher up the SEG scale tend to adopt more healthy lifestyles and are less subject to health damaging conditions of living such as poverty, hazardous

occupations, poor housing and deprived housing areas and unemployment.

- The closing of the gap between men's and women's health indicates the narrowing of differences in men's and women's lifestyle choices especially in relation to drinking and smoking. This lends support to cultural/behavioural explanations for traditional gender inequalities in health. Materialist/structuralist explanations suggest that greater equality in the socio-economic position of men and women in society, both in the formal labour market and in the home, will further narrow gender inequalities in health.
- In relation to ethnicity, research shows that there tends to be an over-reliance on the assumption that (often 'problematic') health behaviours are uniform or homogeneous within an ethnic group (cultural/behavioural explanations) and an underestimation of the structural issues of poverty and the experiences of immigration and racism (materialist/cultural explanations).

• Highlighting the influence of social factors in relation to health is important because it lifts the veil of assumption that patterns of ill-health that manifest themselves in society are natural, random and inevitable as opposed to phenomena that could be addressed through alleviating social inequalities in society more broadly, and more narrowly through targeted health policies for disadvantaged groups.

Topics for discussion and reflection

1. What can be done to tackle socio-economic inequalities in health?

2. In the context of Ireland emerging as a multi-cultural society, what policies should Ireland adopt to address ethnic inequalities in health?

FIVE

The social determinants of health and illness: a global perspective

While Ireland has long been linked with the wider world though historical emigration practices, it is now more deeply interconnected with processes around the globe than ever before. In this chapter, we consider health in the wider global context at the beginning of the twenty-first century and explore the interaction between global trends in health status and local contexts. We begin by comparing life expectancy rates and causes of death and morbidity in different social locations, to provide a starting point for understanding how health status varies across the globe. The concept of *globalisation* will then be explored, as this is central to comprehending the extent to which the health status of those in distant locations is influenced by and connected with policies and economic systems that ripple across the world. A discussion of the link between poverty and health – already examined in the last chapter in relation to Ireland and industrially developed countries – will be extended to the wider global situation in this chapter. In particular, we will consider how world institutions in health regulation and health normalisation have emerged in recent decades. We will also explore the tensions that have arisen between prominent global organisations, as their fundamental philosophical ideals about how healthcare may be delivered come into conflict with one another as they jostle for position in setting health agendas. Finally we examine the wider dimensions of global environmental health.

Health status across the globe

One useful, albeit indirect, indicator of health status across the globe is to compare **life expectancy** – the number of years of life that a person or group can expect to live – across countries. In Ireland the average life expectancy is 76.7 years, compared for example with a life expectancy of 33.4 in Zimbabwe (United Nations, 2003). The United Nations (UN) has developed qualitative categories on human development for countries across the globe, depending on factors such as life expectancy, education levels and adjusted real income. In areas of high human development (which includes Ireland) the average life expectancy is 77 years compared with countries of low human development with an average life expectancy of just 50.6 years (Shaw et al, 2002). Countries with a low average life expectancy tend to have high rates of infant mortality, although people who survive childhood have a higher life expectancy than the average for that country. In Angola, the mortality rate for children under five years is 260 per 1,000 children in that age group; in Ireland, the corresponding figure is 6 per 1,000 (United Nations, 2003).

Apart from differences in mortality between rich and poor countries across the globe, there are also differences apparent in terms of causes of death. In richer countries, the leading cause of death is circulatory disease, followed by cancers. The majority of deaths in poorer countries fall into the category of 'infectious and parasitic diseases' (Shaw et al, 2002: 90). In the nineteenth and early part of the twentieth century, Western countries also experienced high rates of deaths from infectious diseases (see Chapter 6), prompting commentators to theorise about an *epidemiological transition*, which is the change from high death rates from infectious diseases in a society to high death rates from chronic and degenerative diseases (Wilkinson, 1996). However, Shaw et al propose that the notion of transition may be problematic, as there is an implicit suggestion that all countries are on the same course, and that poorer countries will follow the same trajectory and experience a similar transition over time. Available evidence suggests that this is not occurring (Shaw et al, 2002).

A recent development since the early 1980s has been the emergence of HIV/AIDS across the globe (See Box 5.1).

Box 5.1: *Global trends in HIV/AIDS*

- It is estimated that 34.3 million people world-wide are currently infected with the HIV virus, 95 per cent of whom live in sub-Saharan Africa and the poorer countries of Asia and Latin America (WHOQOL-HIV Group, 2003).
- In the African sub-continent, the rates vary between countries: 33.7 per cent of adults (between 15 and 49 years) in Zimbabwe are infected with the virus, while the equivalent figure for the Democratic Republic of Congo is 4.9 per cent (United Nations, 2003).
- In Botswana at the turn of the millennium, one in every three pregnant women in the 15-24 age group was infected with the HIV virus (United Nations, 2003), potentially leaving thousands of children orphaned. A concern is that HIV can be transmitted from mother to baby via breast milk.

The AIDS crisis is predicted to worsen – Hogg et al (2002) propose that the HIV epidemic, while at an earlier stage, is equally out of control in Russia, India and China, where, they argue, there has not been an effective response to the threat. De Cock et al (2002) root much of the uncontrolled epidemic of HIV/AIDS in sub-Saharan Africa in the notion that too much emphasis has been placed on the human rights element in relation to HIV, that is, on protecting individual privacy and emphasising informed consent when it comes to testing, disclosure and so forth. They propose that a public health approach with an emphasis on targeted testing and follow-up investigation would do much to arrest the outbreak in sub-Saharan Africa.

Health, wealth and poverty

As noted in Chapter 1, a reduction in deaths from infectious diseases in Western countries in the nineteenth and twentieth centuries is believed to have come about through improved nutrition, a better standard of living (McKeown, 1984), and a cleaner environment (Szreter, 1995), with biomedical interventions having a limited input. (These issues will be expanded on in the next chapter.) Epidemiological evidence suggests that infectious diseases are spread more quickly in situations of poverty (Shaw et al, 2002). As Martens notes:

> Poverty is associated with a variety of adverse health effects: poor people have less money to spend on shelter, clean water, and food of sufficient quality and quantity. They have also less access to important services such as medical health services and education—all of which are essential to the attainment of minimal standards of health and well-being (2002: 638).

Martens (2002) outlines the main factors that contribute to low life expectancy in poorer countries. The most significant factor is the lack of access to safe water and sanitation. Martens predicts that international conflict will arise from this water shortage in the future – a number of countries are already in competition with each other for the water supply from the world's biggest rivers. Wars bring with them a further depletion of health through loss of life and normative disruption. A second most important contribution to world-wide poor health is malnutrition. (See Box 5.2.)

An important issue when exploring the relationship between poverty and health status is that the overall wealth of a country is simply one dimension to consider. Once a certain level of wealth – measured as **Gross Domestic Product** per capita – is reached, what matters more in terms of the overall health status of that country is how evenly that wealth is dispersed and shared across the population. Drawing on empirical evidence, Wilkinson (1996) indicated that some countries and states with a modest level of overall wealth have a healthier population overall compared with those countries which have higher levels of wealth, but greater levels of inequality. For example, the USA is the richest country in the world in terms of GDP,

Box 5.2 *World poverty*

- Currently more than a third of the world's population experience a shortage of water (Martens, 2002).

- For the year 2001, just 38 per cent of the population of Angola had sustainable access to an acceptable water source (United Nations, 2003).

- While the numbers of undernourished people in poor countries has decreased in recent years, almost 800 million people do not have a sufficient amount of food, and a further 34 million experience food insecurity (Martens, 2002).

- Education, literacy and income levels are also significant factors associated with health status.

---

but lies twelfth in the world ranking of life expectancy behind poorer countries such as Costa Rica (Kawachi et al, 1999, cited in Miers, 2003). The extent to which wealth is shared across society is therefore very important to the health profile of a population.

A central dimension in how the wealth of a country is socially organised and distributed is the political ideology of those governing the society. On the political right is a doctrine of neo-liberalism where the allocation of a society's resources is based on market forces, with autonomous individuals in competition with one another for resources. By contrast, socialist-type economies on the political left are concerned with regulating the economy so as to moderate the inequalities produced when the market operates freely. They acknowledge that allocating the resources of a society is not best achieved by free trade and the 'free' forces of the market. Markets, socialists assert, are not a fair and equitable way of apportioning resources because some market players have unfair advantages by virtue of their inheritance, privileged headstart through education, absence of disability and so forth. Since the end of the Cold War[9], neo-liberal policies have begun to dominate global markets, and this has important implications for health status across the globe.

Globalisation, neoliberalism and world markets

Part of the problem of sustained poverty for poorer countries is related to the notion of globalisation, and the impact that the practices and policies of richer countries have on poorer countries.

---

9. The Cold War was marked by a state of political and military tension between the former Soviet Union, a socialist state, and the United States of America, a capitalist one. The war symbolically came to an end in the late 1980s, particularly with the destruction of the 'Berlin Wall' in 1989.

Globalisation refers to the manner in which various social contexts across the world have become connected to one another (Giddens, 2001b). In the period before industrialisation, societies tended to be bounded systems, although as Carpenter (2000) has noted, as early as the medieval period diseases were transmitted to different parts of the world via trade routes. In the modern world, however, the sense of connection with, and influence of, circumstances across the globe has intensified greatly, particularly in the past few decades (Appadurai, 2001). Let us trace some economic and political changes associated with globalised late capitalism that have an influence on health across the globe.

In the 1980s, the political ideology of **neoliberal individualism**, advanced by Ronald Reagan in the US and Margaret Thatcher in Britain became dominant across the globe (Carpenter, 2000). The central tenets of this political ideology are that governments would allow free competition to flourish in the market, and reduce regulations that protected vulnerable enterprises. The problem with this is that it allows larger, more powerful organisations to dominate, and squeezes out smaller enterprises that cannot compete with economies of scale. In brief, it represents an ideology of survival of the fittest. The fittest economic organisations tend to be the biggest multinational corporations, and with the political support of richer governments, the power of these large and wealthy organisations against national governments and poorer people has increased.

Proponents of neoliberal economics and globalisation argue that as some developing counties moved in the direction of industrialisation since the 1960s, they have experienced a rise in real per capita income (Mussa, 2003). Mussa argues that, in relation to health and welfare in such countries, globalisation has had a positive impact. Drawing on the UN Human Development Index (HDI), he suggests that there has been an increase in life expectancy (related to improvements in health and medicine) and an increase in literacy levels in countries that have embraced global economic relations. Globalisation and its associated relatively open policies towards international trade, he asserts, bring about stronger rates of economic growth. The official line of the present (2004) Irish coalition government concurs with this positive perspective on globalisation; Charlie McCreevy, as Minister for Finance, stated that Ireland's participation in the International Monetary Fund (IMF) and the World Bank 'underlines our determination to play our part in ensuring economic stability and economic development in the world' (Department of Finance, 2002). We will consider the role of both the International Monetary Fund and the World Bank in relation to global health in greater detail a little further on.

While pro-globalisation economists argue that globalisation has played an important role in the economic success of many countries, others propose that globalisation benefits large private capital investors the most, rather than the poorer economies where they operate (Othman and Kessler, 2000).

As Farmer (2003) notes of neoliberalism, 'this ideology has little to say about social and economic inequalities that distort real economies' (2003: 5). Argentina has recently experienced a health crisis as a consequence of the failure of neoliberal policies imposed upon it by the United States and the IMF (Escudero, 2003). The health crisis arose from the collapse of Argentina's economic and political systems.

In order to understand just how neo-liberal policies mitigate against good health, David Coburn (2000) advanced the ideas of Wilkinson (1996) (referred to earlier in Chapter 4), by focusing on the social context of the relationship between income inequalities and health. He argued that the market-orientated ideologies of individualism (looking after yourself and competing with your neighbour to succeed) undermine social cohesion and a collectivist spirit. The loss of the broader sense of community by this type of self-interest has led to the application of market principles to all areas of human life. Coburn therefore proposes that *'The more market-orientated the society, the higher the social fragmentation and the lower the social cohesion and trust* [emphasis in original]' (2000: 142). Reduced social trust is related to homicide, violent crimes, and an undermining of the welfare state designed to protect those who are vulnerable. Invoking discourses of choice and resistance, Coburn rejects the argument that neo-liberal policies are inevitable and cannot be controlled by domestic governments in the global economy.

Drawing on Isla (1993), Anderson (2000) argues that women are particularly disadvantaged by the spread of neoliberalism, not just through the loss of social services, but also because of exploitative gender relations in the workplace. Isla proposes that multi-national companies endeavour to reduce the costs of production and increase profits by sub-contracting to the unorganised industrial sector, and it is women who are increasingly being squeezed out of the organised industrialised sector to the unorganised sector, with the loss of employee rights.

Farmer (2003) argues that while the US notion of liberalism is often associated with the defence of human rights, it is the distinct minority of the middle class whose rights are being defended. This liberalist political agenda excludes powerless and disadvantaged people. He describes the notion of the right to survive, and links this with social and economic disadvantage as a form of structural violence against humanity. Features of this structural violence, he argues, are not guns and overt forms of violence, but rather the terrorism of money. Wealthy and powerful groups subtly strip those less powerful of social and economic rights, silencing populations and rendering them invisible. Farmer extends the notion of human rights beyond the legal sphere to the domain of health and calls for the development of a new field of human rights medicine and public health. He proposes that the status and prestige already enjoyed by the medical profession can be harnessed by doctors to alleviate the central cause of ill-health – poverty – through human rights medicine.

World markets

Powerful organisations such as the World Bank, the IMF and the World Trade Organisation (WTO), mediated by neo-liberal philosophies and primarily accountable to the USA, are central players in international governance over global economic affairs (Carpenter, 2000). The WTO, a construction of wealthier nations, is attempting to remove restrictions that control the operations of multinationals (Carpenter, 2000). One of its agreements grants multinationals a guaranteed return for patented products, preventing poorer countries from producing cheaper alternatives. This, for example, forces poorer countries to buy expensive medicines because they are not permitted to manufacture their own cheaper alternatives. With regard to drugs for the treatment of HIV/AIDS, a recent agreement was brokered between the Clinton Foundation[10] and a number of companies that produce HIV/AIDS diagnostic tests and drug treatments to make their products available to poorer countries at the lowest available prices (Masango, 2004). Prior to this agreement, the US government had warned that trade sanctions would be imposed against South Africa and Thailand if they themselves manufactured a cheaper product for the treatment of AIDS (Drager, 1999). While this deal enables poorer countries to avail themselves of cut-price drugs, it does not alter the structural arrangement that stops them from producing their own treatments themselves.

World markets also mean that local enterprises cannot compete with powerful multinationals, and workers are forced to work in poor conditions and for meagre salaries. While a new middle-class has emerged as a consequence of globalisation in some poorer countries, who enjoy 'the leftovers from the globalizers' sumptuous banquets' (Othman and Kessler, 2000: 1018), the profits are retained by the companies based in wealthier countries. The overall result is greater impoverishment of the local people, and fewer resources to improve their health. In addition, some economic development in poorer countries involves dirty industries like nuclear reprocessing, and industries seeking 'tax breaks, low wages, and weak health and safety regulations' (Carpenter, 2000: 341). Multinationals are also involved in dumping products that are banned, or falling in demand, onto poorer countries, where consumer protections are less rigorous. In other instances, powdered baby milk substitutes are being promoted by multinationals, diminishing the rate of breastfeeding. It is estimated that 1.5 million infant deaths occur per year (Carpenter, 2000) because of the lack of facilities to sterilise bottles and use boiled water to make up feeds.

While on the one hand the EU provides funding for assistance and the promotion of democratic reform in developing countries (Youngs, 2003), on the other hand, subsidies paid to support farming (including Irish

10. The Clinton Foundation is an organisation established by the former US president, Bill Clinton, with the objective of enabling people in the US and around the world to facilitate global interdependence. Among its aims are to reduce morbidity and mortality caused by HIV/AIDS.

agriculture) by the EU have had a devastating impact on farming in poorer countries beyond the EU, that cannot compete with the subsidised prices. Within their own countries, these poorer farmers are now witnessing cheaper subsidised products replacing their own, as the EU expands its market globally. The WTO, consisting of trade ministers from the wealthier nations, applies its negotiating power in expanding its markets across the globe, and, it has been argued, this squeezes the livelihood from farmers in poorer countries (Pendleton, 2003).

World Bank and poorer countries
Many of the problems that poorer countries are currently experiencing are linked to the fact that they owe vast sums of money to the World Bank as a consequence of recession in the 1970s and 1980s pushing down the prices of primary products, in addition to domestic political problems of coups, civil strife and administrative corruption (Owusu, 2003). The World Bank espouses neoliberal ideologies of economic growth with an emphasis on efficiency in the market place (Owusu, 2003). It has considerable power in directing the policies of poorer countries, and these are often at odds with improving health. Poorer countries have to continue borrowing to cover their debts, thereby reinforcing their dependency status. The World Bank, through its Structural Adjustment Programme, has set out specific conditions for debt repayment, and these curtail the monies available for health and education (Anderson, 2000). The World Bank has, for example, insisted on 'currency devaluation, denationalisation, the ending of food subsidies, wage restraint, and the introduction of user-fees for health and education' (Carpenter, 2000: 344). Other policies that have not improved living standards are the encouragement of growing crops for cash rather than for subsistence (Carpenter, 2000).

Confronted with severe criticism (Carpenter, 2000), the World Bank and IMF did introduce a scheme that allowed poorer countries to access concessional loans, or benefit from debt relief. Countries applying for the scheme are required to submit a Poverty Reduction Strategy Paper (PRSP), and demonstrate that 40 per cent of the debt relief sought will be used to finance the social sector which includes health (Dodd, 2002). However, to avail themselves of the scheme, countries are obliged to sign up for three further years of severe structural belt-tightening, contributing further to poverty levels (Carpenter, 2000). The most recent development has been the adoption of neoliberal policies, long canvassed by the World Bank, as the way forward for Africa by the African leaders' organisation *New Partnership for Africa's Development* (NEPAD) (Owusu, 2003).

Regulating health globally
The World Health Organisation (WHO) is the UN specialised agency for health, with the remit of facilitating for all people of the world 'the highest

possible level of health'. WHO was established after World War II in 1948, when fascism had been defeated, the old European power bases were in crisis, and there was a revival of Enlightenment humanism across the globe (Carpenter, 2000). It was in this 'wave of optimistic universalism' that WHO presented its holistic definition of health as 'a state of complete physical, mental and social well being' (Carpenter, 2000: 338) (See also Chapters 13 and 14). In this famous definition, health was constructed as more than the absence of disease and moved beyond biomedical reductionism. In 1978, WHO produced the Alma Ata Declaration of global health policy, in which specific targets were set to improve health across the world by the year 2000. Kickbusch (2000) notes that this declaration marked the birth of international health policy. While there were international rules on disease control in existence prior to this, these did not have a framework that provided purpose and direction. The Alma Ata Declaration set out norms and the role of the state with regard to health:

> The Alma Ata Declaration ... made it abundantly clear that governments have the responsibility for the health of their people. This was no less than a redefinition of the norms and expectations of the state role with regard to health. States were 'taught' by the WHO that a national health policy was part and parcel of modernization and that the organization would advise countries on how to go about establishing such a policy (Kickbusch, 2000: 981).

Kickbusch notes that outlining the normative expectations for governments was especially important for newly independent countries after the transition from colonial rule.

Central to the radicalised philosophies of WHO in this period was the 'community development' model of pursuing health, that is, a bottom-up approach in which people at the grass roots would be empowered to identify their own health needs, and be active in meeting health goals. Health promotion, primary healthcare, and co-ordination between the various sectors to target social inequalities were central vehicles through which good health was to be achieved (see also Chapters 13 and 14). The approach represented a shift in thinking away from the belief that the benefits of economic growth would trickle down to poorer people (the crumbs of the cake so to speak) to centralising the core needs of the most disadvantaged.

A re-evaluation of the targets set out in 1978 indicates that while the goals of WHO have not been realised, there have been improvements in health across the globe. Infant mortality figures and life expectancy have improved in many countries. However, the emergence of new infectious diseases, most notably HIV/AIDS, and the re-emergence of TB, which is directly associated with poverty, were not anticipated when the health targets were developed. In addition, changes at an economic level since the

1980s, as outlined earlier, have made matters worse in many regards, with vast increases in the number of those in poverty (Carpenter, 2000). The limited impact of WHO's targets for HFA (*Health for All*) need to be understood in the context of the dominance of neoliberal policies espoused by powerful organisations such as the World Bank. WHO has been faced with a constant battle to have its objectives realised in the face of powerful economic and political opposition (Finch, 2000 cited in Carpenter, 2000).

Kickbusch (2000) notes how newly-created independent states were seeking to solve their problems and looked for guidance on how to accommodate to the new global environment. Part of the problem was that a national *Health for All* (WHO, 1985) policy required a well-established infrastructure that poorer countries did not have (Kickbusch, 2000). In addition, the health leaders of such countries were often not linked with the international health community, and had no existing relationship with WHO. What emerged was the involvement of the World Bank in matters of health – its solution was, of course, based on the notion that neoliberal policies would address the economy and health crisis. At the start of the 1980s, for example, as WHO was promoting the development of primary healthcare in rural locations, the World Bank and the IMF demanded that countries in debt should curb these and other public services, and would allow only services tailored to vulnerable groups (Carpenter, 2000).

While WHO and other organisations such as UNICEF have tried to encourage governments to control the activities of multinationals, they are up against wealthier and more powerful organisations such as the WTO and the IMF (Carpenter, 2000). Carpenter uses the example of Guatemala to demonstrate the power of multinationals. In Guatemala, the WHO's Code on Breastmilk Substitutes was incorporated into law in 1983, after which infant mortality rates fell (Finch, 2000, cited in Carpenter, 2000). However, the Guatemalan government was forced to revise the law when the US company Gerber (that manufactures infant formula) threatened to challenge the law through the WTO.

To avoid being marginalised completely, WHO has had to moderate its policies on primary healthcare for all, to a more selective approach focusing on more immediate health needs (Koivusalo and Ollila, 1997). WHO has recently focused on campaigns for oral rehydration therapy and vaccinations (Carpenter, 2000), and has come under criticism for relinquishing its original equity targets (Banerji, 1999). However, as Carpenter (2000: 343) notes:

> The reality is that the World Bank has more resources than UNICEF and WHO to dispense on healthcare programmes, enabling it to enforce its policy preferences.

WHO as an institution of social control?
In spite of recent criticisms of the WHO's shift in orientation, the original

objectives of *Health For All* were well received by those advocating social justice. The movement was, however, criticised by Skrabanek (1994) for representing what he deemed to be an ideology called 'healthism'. Healthism is the pursuit of health, not on an individual basis (which, he proposed, would be acceptable), but by dominant forces in society imposing beliefs and behaviours on the masses of the population, and for the society as a whole. Skrabanek asserted that a societal pursuit of health presented a danger to the autonomy of the individual, and he noted that all totalitarian regimes use the rhetoric of freedom and happiness to appeal to people. Skrabanek (1994) was also critical of the historical shift that occurred in the twentieth century from individuals pursuing health to the 'collective normalisation of behaviour as state policy'. In a hard-hitting statement, he wrote: 'The roads to unfreedom are many. Signposts on one of them bear the inscription 'Health For All' (1994: 11). (For a further critique of healthism see Chapter 14.) Skrabanek was in favour of attempts to alleviate poverty because it is unjust and inhumane rather than for the purpose of pursuing health. In the context of Skrabanek's criticisms, let us explore the regulating role of WHO in the surveillance of health behaviour and in producing particular norms across the globe.

WHO documentation (WHO, 2002) suggests a sense of crusade in cleaning up the age-old vices associated with smoking, alcohol consumption, sexual practices, and dietary intake across the globe. Consider the following message from the Director General of WHO that featured in the *World Health Report* (2002: 3):

> These are dangerous times for the well-being of the world. In many regions, some of the most formidable enemies of health are joining forces with the allies of poverty to impose a double burden of disease and premature deaths on many millions of people. It is time for us to close ranks against this growing threat … . Sometimes, laws, education and persuasion combine to diminish risks, as with health warnings on cigarette packets, and restrictions on the sale of alcohol …

> Too many of us are living dangerously – whether we are aware of that or not. I believe that this *World Health Report* is a wake up call to the global community.

As explicitly stated in the above report, most of the risk factors highlighted in it relate to patterns of living (smoking, alcohol consumption, diet, and exercise), especially to consumption – 'either too little, in the case of the poor, or too much in the case of the better off' (WHO, 2002: 4). It is suggested clearly that 'the world is living dangerously – either because it has little choice, which is often the case among the poor or because it is making the wrong choices in terms of its consumption and its activities' (2002: 9). Clearly, there are moral overtones here, in making value judgements about what health behaviours are right or wrong for those who can afford to choose (see Chapter 14).

From the perspective of some commentators, proposing that those in the world who are overconsuming (a cultural/behavioural practice) should consume less, if it means that that those in poorer countries would receive more resources (a structural shift) makes sound ethical thinking on the basis of the principle of equity or fairness. Social and state regulation to alleviate inequality has been proposed since Marx and is the basis of socialist thinking. In addition, it may be argued that the last thing that poorer countries need is the afflictions of smoking, illicit drug use and alcohol abuse on top of the problems of **absolute poverty**. It might, therefore, be considered appropriate that WHO should step in and urge governments to implement policies to call a halt to these societal health practices, on the grounds of beneficence, or the duty to care. More significantly, with regard to the practice of smoking at least, it has been observed that, as markets in wealtier countries dwindle, major international tobacco corporations are strategically targeting markets in Asia, Africa, and South America for their own financial gains (Lee, 2000), at the expense of the health of the local population. Arguably, what problematises the WHO stance is that its regulatory role extends beyond attempts to redistribute resources so that the world becomes more fair, and indirectly, healthy. Some practices that it is attempting to curb and moderate (such as salt and cholesterol intake) are likely to affect only the individual consumer. Such social modulation and manipulation of cultural practices may be interpreted as an intrusion on civil liberties. At the same time, the notion that individual consumers are responding to multi-million euro marketing of particular lifestyles needs to be considered, and the extent to which individuals should be channeled away from making some choices and propelled towards others is a matter for debate.

WHO's healthist ideology recently formally extended to schools with the launch of the 'Global School Health Initiative' in 1995. Its goal is to increase the number of 'Health-Promoting Schools', that is, schools that are 'constantly strengthening [their] capacity as a setting for living, learning and working' (WHO, 2003: 1). Those critical of the promotion of a healthist ideology might argue that this amounts to an early form of social control and the construction of a disciplinary power over the body through an important agency of socialisation, the school (the notion of disiciplinary power over the body is taken up again in Chapters 7 and 14).

Global environmental health

As globalisation has intensified in recent decades, so too has the concern with global environmental health. Global environmental health has tended to focus on issues of air and water pollution, reducing and disposing safely of the world's waste, and with moderating the drain on the earth's limited energy sources. All of these environmental issues are directly linked with industrialisation (See Box 5.3). Finding ways of production and consumption that do not damage health and/or keep on draining the earth's resources has become a global issue.

Box 5.3 *Global environmental issues*

- The demand for energy around the globe is steadily increasing as living standards rise and world population increases (Wang and Feng, 2003).
- With consumerist lifestyles, energy is purchased to replace labour both in industry and in the domestic sphere.
- Fossil fuels are used to create energy to power industry and homes and the process itself is linked with air pollution and respiratory disorders.
- Oil and natural gas are in limited supply around the globe.

The development of economies based on neo-liberal economics with ideologies of cutting costs and maximising profits has implications for global environmental health. Some countries such as China that have recently experienced new economic growth with the privatisation of industries are suffering the consequences in terms of serious increases in air pollution (Wang and Feng, 2003). In China in 1999, two-thirds of the primary energy consumed was created by the burning of coal. The associated pollution is responsible for 'serious health problems, crop damage and acid rain' (Wang and Feng, 2003). In true neo-liberal style, industries have been found to alter their production process in response to energy price rises (Anker-Nilssen, 2003), rather, it seems, than through any moral conscience about damage to people's health or to the environment.

Since 1972, world leaders have come together on four occasions at mega conferences to consider the issue of sustainable development. The most recent was the UN World Summit on Sustainable Development (WSSD) held in Johannesburg in August 2002. At the conference, concerns were raised about trans-boundary air and water pollution, and targets were drawn up for the disposal of chemical waste (Seyfang, 2003). Seyfang identifies as a limit to such summits the fact that they do not result in new legislation to protect the environment – even international agreements reached at such conferences can be ignored by individual countries as there are no effective sanctions against defaulters. However, such summits have been successful in setting sustainable development agendas internationally (Seyfang, 2003).

Population growth is also important in terms of world health. Fertility rates across the globe have declined sharply in recent years, but the world population will continue to rise in the coming decades (Martens, 2002). This population increase, along with a per capita increase in consumption of energy and materials, impacts upon the economic, social and ecological systems. Put simply, the more people that are on the earth, the more of a drain there will be on the earth's resources, as each person uses and discards the commodities of a lifetime. In addition, extra people require extra (fossil) fuel on the fire to create energy to produce the things that they want, adding to the problem of global warming and climate change. As Firor and Jacobsen (2002: 187-188) note:

> Without reducing dramatically the amount of fossil fuel that each person uses, continued population growth accelerates climate change, as each new person adds more heat trapping substances to the atmosphere.

Local and regional water systems are also placed under extra pressure with population growth.

Summary
- Health processes around the globe are interconnected, and health status is closely linked to political and economic systems.
- Mortality and morbidity rates vary widely across the world, and in many cases the differences in these rates are related to the degree of wealth that a country has. However, it was noted that once a certain level of wealth per capita was reached by a country, of central importance to the health status of citizens then is the extent to which that wealth is dispersed and distributed across the society.
- AIDS has emerged as one of the world's biggest killers, affecting those in poorer countries most.
- The political doctrine of neoliberalism has permeated across the globe, and, according to many critical commentators, this increases the dependency of poorer countries on larger wealthier ones, and erodes the notion of welfare supports for the most vulnerable, with negative consequences for health.
- The global health agenda set by the WHO after World War II was based on human rights, alleviating poverty and empowering those at the grass-roots.
- With the spread of neoliberal policies, particularly since the 1980s, the original WHO ideals have been moderated, and wealthier, more powerful organisations such as the World Bank have begun to engage with setting agendas for the organisation of healthcare.
- Economic development across the globe has had a negative impact on environmental health. The burning of fossil fuels to create energy to power industries is linked with air pollution and concomitant respiratory and other health disorders. Other consequences of air pollution are crop damage, acid rain, and climate changes, all of which diminish health. Disposing of the world's industrial and domestic waste is also a concern of environmental health activists.
- Controlling world population growth has been proposed to limit the problems with environmental health.

Topics for discussion and reflection
1. What changes in policies or practices are needed to make the world a more equal and healthier place for the earth's population?

2. What practical measures might be taken by governments and individuals to address the limitations of the earth's resources?

SIX

Challenges to biomedicine and alternative understandings of health and illness

In industrially developed societies, there is a heroic view of **biomedicine** with an emphasis on dramatic cures and treatments signalling optimism and hope (Tucker, 1997; Taylor, 1997; Petersen, 2001; see also Purvis Cooper and Yukimura, 2002). In Ireland, as in other Western countries, the increase in longevity (long-life) that has occurred over the past 150 years is popularly associated with developments in biomedicine. Statistics for the period 1881-83 indicate that the average lifespan for a person living in the island of Ireland was 49.6 years (CSO, 2004a). As indicated in the last chapter, the average life expectancy for a person living in the Republic of Ireland in the current period is 76.7 years (United Nations, 2003). The situation began to improve at the start of the twentieth century, and this pattern has continued ever since (CSO, 2004a). The dramatic reduction in deaths was due mainly to the reduction in mortality from infectious diseases such as cholera and typhus which ravaged Ireland until the latter half of the 1800s (Robins, 1995). Biomedicine has generally received most of the acclaim for this amelioration in health (McKeown, 1995). Common sense would lead us to credit biomedicine for health improvements (mistakenly, according to some theorists), because if the mortality and morbidity rates are examined in various populations, it is clear that people fare better in developed countries that have a relatively high level of acute high technology services and a relatively high proportion of doctors. These factors would lead one to suppose that biomedicine is highly effective indeed. However, some scholars purport that the historical link between falling death rates and increasing developments in biomedicine is spurious. They argue that the better health outcome for people in industrially-developed countries has less to do with the success of biomedicine and more to do with the fact that physicians 'tend to gather where the climate is healthy, where the water is clean, and where people are employed and can pay for their services' (Illich, 1995: 238).

In this chapter, we explore the work of social theorists who propose that, not only is biomedicine less effective than most people believe, which

106

problematises its revered position, but also that it plays a part in and maintaining collective norms in society. Biomedicine's power relative to complementary and alternative medicine will also be con

The development of biomedicine

In a society, dominant beliefs about how the body works are rooted in the conceptual framework of that society (Marsh et al, 2000). Marsh et al review the changing perception of the world that occurred over the past 200 years (See Chapter 1 on the changes that arose with the advent of the modern period), and relate this to changing beliefs about the workings of the body. They note that before the seventeenth century, the cosmos was believed to be a series of concentric layers, the centre of which was the earth. The next layer was believed to be water, followed by air and then fire, beyond which were the moon and other celestial bodies. The belief was that the elements moved 'naturally' and the natural world was controlled only by the laws of nature rather than the laws of people. In the seventeenth century, thinking began to change and the objective became the control of the natural world by understanding its patterns and regularities. The seventeenth century philosopher Rene Descartes extended the machine metaphor of the world by proposing that there was no essential relationship between the physical world and the sensory experience of it. This way of thinking was extended to the human body, resulting in the human body being likened to a 'machine' and (physical) bodily functions perceived to be separate from the workings of the mind (sensory experiences). Thus the physical body came to be seen as a 'piece of technical equipment to be maintained, serviced and finely tuned for maximum performance' (Marsh et al, 2000: 439). This mechanistic view of the body, and the view that health is the absence of biological abnormality which can be restored through certain treatments, is essentially what biomedicine is. The beliefs within biomedicine about how the body works are different from other and often older types of medicine (Marsh et al, 2000). (See Box 6.1.)

Box 6.1 *Features of the biomedical model*

- Health is explained in biological terms, with central importance given to the body structure (anatomy) and systems (physiology).
- There is an assumption that all causes of disease including mental disorders can be understood in biological terms.
- Disease and illness are explained in relation to specific or multiple aetiology (theory of cause), and the cause and course of disease are identified as they affect parts of the body.
- The notions of science and objectivity are central.
- Health is constructed in mechanical terms whereby all parts of the body are seen to function normally.

Source: Jones (1994)

Biomedicine sells itself by claiming a superior version of knowledge over and above other medicines on the basis that its knowledge is objective and scientific.[11] However, scientific facts are themselves socially constructed, and what constitutes 'diseases' are the outcome of powerful discourses (Bury, 1986). They are created by humans within a particular social and historical context, and develop from an existing socially derived version of reality (Oudshoorn, 1994). As Tucker (1997: 33) notes:

> The construction of 'scientific facts' is not restricted to laboratories somehow hermetically sealed off from the social and political worlds outside them. As the history of the modern pharmaceutical industry demonstrates, laboratory research is in the first instance frequently determined by profit motives rather than by a commitment to the advancement of medical science ... The success of ideas goes beyond the laboratory as when scientists build contacts and alliances with other scientists and interest groups which provide the economic and political support necessary in order for them to obtain the resources necessary for them to carry out their research. Tales of science are also tales of power.

Elites within biomedicine formed alliances with those in political circles and this secured research funding to develop medical schools (see Ehrenreich and English, 1974a).

As biomedicine developed, the concern shifted from viewing disease as affecting the whole person to looking at individual parts of the person. Jones (1994: 420), quoting Foucault (1973), notes that instead of asking 'What is the matter?' physicians began to ask, 'Where does it hurt?' Doctors became interested in the location of disease rather than in how it affected the whole person. However, Armstrong (1995a) cautions against assuming the existence of a golden age of medicine in the past – he asserts that there is no evidence of a golden age in the past except a conviction that it existed.

Physicians' control over individuals expanded through the 'clinical gaze' (Foucault, 1973) (see Chapters 1 and 2). Patient autonomy was lost as the person became the passive recipient of medical attention (Jewson, 1976). With developments in biomedicine, methods of science became central to observing, recording and predicting signs and symptoms (Jones, 1994). As molecular and chemistry-orientated sciences stregthened to become the dominant medical paradigm in the twentieth century, medicine began to make new claims about the body and disease. The fact that this version of how the body worked became widely accepted furnished physicians with a

---

11. Findings from a recent study of people born in Ireland in the late 1920s lends empirical support to the popular perceptions of the efficacy of biomedicine (MacFarlane and Kelleher, 2002). These older participants demonstrated a strong belief in and allegiance to biomedicine, particularly to tablets and antibiotics, which were seen as 'real' treatments, compared to earlier practices used by physicians.

great deal of power. However, the knowledge form developed within biomedicine is but one interpretation of how the body works (this point will be expanded on in a later section).

The rise of hospitals facilitated the growth of clinical medicine in the late eighteenth and nineteenth centuries (Davey and Seale, 2001). It meant that 'patients' could be examined *en masse*, because people with the same symptoms were located within a confined space, and if enough people presented with the same symptoms that deviated from 'normal', a new disease could be created. It was mainly poorer patients who were hospitalised in the nineteenth century; wealthier patients continued to be visited at home by doctors (Jones, 1994). Medical power was consolidated not because of the predictive power of the approach, but because physicians were increasingly perceived as important agents of the state in regulating and controlling the urban masses (Jones, 1994). The Medical Registration Act was passed in 1858, which gave primacy and legal recognition to biomedicine.

Until the second half of the nineteenth century, germs had not yet been discovered, and no clear explanation had emerged as to how infections were spread (Robins, 1995). In the island of Ireland, as elsewhere, a variety of possible theories abounded as to how diseases were transmitted (Robins, 1995). A dominant explanation was the theory of miasma, that is, that disease was caused through contaminated air from a dirty environment (Robins, 1995). A miasma constituted:

> ... an invisible, noxious cloud created by putrid vapours and particles emanating from dead human and animal bodies, rotting waste and vegetation and the stagnant water of swamps (Robins, 1995: 10).

The theory of miasma was the basis for the nineteenth century Public Health Movement in Britain, which was mainly instigated by the reforming middle classes and supported by the state (Jones, 1994). The movement was successful in reducing mortality in spite of its flawed underpinnings. Reforms in personal and public hygiene in Ireland were reportedly slower than in many parts of Britain, perhaps because ordinary people had more immediate concerns of poverty, land reform and the Home Rule (independence) movement (Robins, 1995).

By the end of the nineteenth century, the germ theory presented a major challenge to the theory of miasma. The germ theory originated in microscopic research, and held that each individual disease would have a specific micro-organism present. The theory focused attention on the body of the host rather than the environment, and armed the medical profession with a powerful predictive theory (Jones, 1994). As Jones (1994: 428) notes:

> Germ theory provided the ammunition for a medical attack on personal filth – spitting, lice, scabies, dirty bodies, as well as housekeeping – but

/ided little constructive commentary on the social conditions which
'e such problems widespread in working class districts.

Up until the 1700s, there was a low opinion of doctors among educated
people (Skrabanek, 1994. Indeed, the efficacy of biomedicine was so suspect
that it was not until the start of the 1900s (long after having secured legal
recognition and political alliances) that more benefit than harm was likely
to ensue from visiting a doctor (Skrabanek 1994. As Skrabanek (1994: 23)
noted, biomedical practitioners tended to take the credit for a person's
recovery, when in fact the return to health had more to do with 'luck, nature
or placebo'.

The critique of biomedicine's effectiveness
That medical registration was granted to one group of 'healers' over and
above others may suggest that biomedicine had proven effectiveness in
improving health. However, a number of theorists have asserted that
biomedicine was limited in solving the major health problems of the
nineteenth century (Dubos, 1959; McKeown, 1984, 1985; Illich, 1984;
Cochrane, 1995). While Rene Dubos (1959) acknowledged the preventive
and therapeutic benefits of biomedicine in the early twentieth century, he
was one of the first theorists to highlight the importance of practical public
health improvements in ameliorating health. Later, the social historian
Thomas McKeown (1984, 1995) asserted that, apart from the case of the
smallpox vaccination, biomedicine, either through immunisation or therapy
was likely to have had little impact on mortality from infectious diseases
prior to the twentieth century. He argued that although medical science did
make some contribution, this was very small. Drawing on epidemiological
evidence, McKeown demonstrated that death rates for the major killer
diseases were falling long before biomedicine had discovered 'cures'.

Instead, McKeown proposed that the increase in life expectancy during
the nineteenth and early twentieth centuries came about through nutritional
improvements arising from an increase in living standards. Why did
McKeown favour an explanation based on nutritional improvements rather
than one based on better sanitation and hygiene? He rooted his claims in
two assumptions: (i) public health measures came along too late to account
for the decline in mortality – the momentum was underway (in England and
Wales) 'before' the Public Health Movement wave of reforms at the end of
the last century; (ii) according to the available epidemiological evidence, and
based on aetiology or the causes of disease, sanitation could only potentially
eliminate approximately a quarter of all deaths, while better nutrition could
probably be responsible for double that proportion (McKeown, 1984).
Although McKeown's work was generally well received by the medical
profession (Skrabanek, 1994), details of his interpretations have been
contested. Simon Szreter (1995) argued that McKeown underestimated the

part played by the Public Health Movement in the nineteenth century, and exaggerated the role of nutrition in reducing mortality. Szreter (1995: 194) suggests that McKeown uses the notion of 'standard of living' (and associated nutritional improvements that go with this) very loosely and did not provide a thorough analysis of nutritional improvements during the nineteenth century to support his argument.

In recent years, the notion of medicine as a concrete body of knowledge with predictable outcomes has come to be contested (Carter, 1995). McKee and Clarke (1995) suggest that the concept of doubt in clinical decision making has been understated by both the medical profession and healthcare policy makers. Theorists have highlighted that biomedicine is an inexact science with uncertainties in basic knowledge and techniques (Hatt, 1998; Hyde, 2000). A prominent critic of the effectiveness of biomedicine is Petr Skrabanek, referred to in Chapter 5 in relation to his critique of population-wide health campaigns. In a book entitled *Follies and Fallacies in Medicine* published in 1989, Skrabanek and his co-author McCormick presented an attack on medicine's alleged effectiveness. In addition to highlighting medicine's ineffectiveness, some theorists argue that modern medicine is responsible for doctor-made or iatrogenic diseases (Illich, 1976). Clinical iatrogenesis includes adverse reactions to drugs and vaccines, surgical complications, hospital accidents, and over prescription of drugs such as antibiotics, leading to the production of so-called superbugs. A considerable amount of evidence has accumulated suggesting that patients suffer treatment-induced morbidity (Bedell et al, 1991; Brennan et al, 1991; Leape, 2000). A recent Department of Health (UK) (2001a cited in Johnson, 2004) report in Britain indicates that within the NHS, errors or critical incidents happen in approximately 10 per cent of admissions to hospital; 400 people die or are seriously injured annually by the adverse consequences of medical technology; and 10,000 people report having had serious adverse reactions to drugs.

Medicine as an institution of social control

In spite of medicine's apparent lack of effectiveness in alleviating a number of health problems, and its iatrogenic potential, it has nonetheless become a powerful force in society (Lupton, 1997). Since the 1970s, sociologists have expressed concern about the medicalisation of society, that is, the way in which everyday aspects of life such as death, birth, eating, drinking, sleeping and so on have come under the jurisdiction of medicine. (The issue of *biomedicalisation*, a specific version of medicalisation, will be discussed in Chapter 11.) A glance at the list of recent publications by the British Medical Association (BMA) (BMA, 2002) indicates the number of everyday practices and issues to which medicine claims expertise. Included on the list are publications relating to the use of mobile phones and health; eating disorders and body image; growing up in Britain; cycle helmets; alcohol and young people; biotechnology and weapons; domestic violence; road transport; drugs; and school sex education.

Freidson (1970b) and Zola (1972, 1984) were early observers of how medicine has become a central institution of social control, dictating the norms of society which had previously been strongly influenced by religion and law. Zola argues (1972, 1984) that this increasing power of medicine has come about, not because physicians' political power had increased, but rather because of the medicalisation of everyday life, whereby more and more areas of daily life have come to be associated with health or illness. The medical profession then prescribe what is considered good and evil for individuals and for society as a whole.

Zola (1972, 1984) traces the history of social institutions that held a dominant position of power prior to medicine achieving its power position. In the early Middle Ages, he proposes, Christianity was dominant in Europe and, until the Reformation was well underway, communities were deeply steeped in religion to such an extent that the meaning and values of all relationships were rooted in a religious framework. However, by the seventeenth and eighteenth centuries, the strong influence of religion began to wane in the face of industrialisation, which transformed relationships within and between communities. The French and US constitutions reflected this more secular (non-religious) way of thinking as they developed codes of conduct based on notions of justice, right, duty, franchise, liberty and contract, without reference to religion. Thus, although the religious influence did not disappear completely, the search for meaning and understanding in life began to be sought through law. Zola (1984) notes that in the twentieth century, the experience of two world wars cast doubts over the credibility of law as a task-master. In the Nuremberg trials after WW2, obedience to law and order was not accepted by the court as a reason to commit genocide. Also, with civil disobedience in the 1950s and 1960s, questions arose as to whether there were grounds to break the law. All of this cast doubts on the idea of using law to organise social life, and Zola suggests, left a space for a new authority – medicine – to suggest acceptable social behaviours (norms).

According to Zola (1984), if something can be shown to affect the workings of the body or mind, it can be labelled a medical problem, and fall within the jurisdiction of medicine (see Box 6.2). He uses as examples the previously constructed natural processes of ageing and pregnancy, that have now been turned into medical issues (for a further discussion on the medicalisation of both ageing and childbirth see Chapters 9 and 11 respectively). Because both of these collectively affect the majority of the population, their implications are far-reaching. He also refers to alcoholism and drug addiction, each of which was previously considered to be a human weakness. Zola sees medicine's role in creating the good life and fending off the bad one as the most powerful of all the medicalising processes. He refers to the issue of genetic counselling in which certain characteristics are pre-selected in order to protect the individual and society against 'negative' traits. Zola (1984) cautions against the way in which medicine has come to equate social problems with illness. Individuals have little power to challenge medical labels or diagnosis, and if they do, this may be interpreted by the medical profession as part of their illness.

Box 6.2 *Irving Kenneth Zola on the extension of biomedicine's control in the social realm*

Zola argued that:

- Medicine has attached itself to anything to which the label of illness may be associated, irrespective of whether or not it can deal with it.
- There is increasing emphasis on comprehensive medicine and psychosomatics. Patients now have to reveal symptoms not just of the body, but also of their daily living habits and anxieties. Medicine is increasingly intervening in trying to alter a person's life in relation to working, sleeping, playing and eating. Furthermore, the emphasis on prevention means intervening before a disease even starts.
- There is a growing trend in surgical procedures whereby they are increasingly being conducted to alter the effects of everyday living such as ageing (for sagging breasts, wrinkles, ageing teeth and so forth). Plastic surgery is often conducted, not because people have an organic disease, but because they do not like their appearance.
- There has been an increase in drug prescribing for conditions other than those directly related to organic disease. These include drugs to keep people awake or help them to sleep; to stimulate their appetite or decrease it; to increase their energy levels or reduce them; and to enhance people's memory, intelligence and so on. In other words, medical prescribing has increased for people who might otherwise be described as healthy.

Source: Zola (1984)

Ivan Illich argues that modern medicine has an 'indirect sickening power – a structurally health denying effect' (1984: 134). He suggests that modern medicine has changed pain, illness, and death from a personal challenge to a technical problem, and interferes with human beings' ability to adapt autonomously to their environment (Illich, 1984). Illich (1984: 136) reflects on the time before biomedicine, and admits that individuals found their destiny in a struggle with 'neighbour and nature'. While individuals were on their own in the struggle, the culture to which they belonged provided them with the weapons and rules to get on with things. People did not rely on medicine at the first sign of evil, but rather, drawing on norms within their culture, had to come to terms with pain, sickness and death; these were part of life that had to be dealt with. In this sense, the person's culture provided a mode or forum for suffering. With the advent of medicalisation, Illich (1984: 137) argues, pain impacts on our emotions in a historically new way because pain is now seen to be unnecessary and unbearable – 'meaningless, questionless torture'.

Illich (1976) is also critical of the degree of power that medicine as an elite professional group holds. He accepts medicine's role as a liberal profession using its skills to cure disease or alleviate suffering, but not as a medicalising force (the power of the medical profession is taken up in Chapter 12).

Skrabanek (1994) notes that biomedicine originally developed in a humanist tradition, but in the 1960s and 1970s that shifted to an industrial model governed by financial gain. In the past, he suggests, physicians were 'called in' when their services were required, whereas now they issue invitations to people to come in (this is referred to as anticipatory care). Those who are 'non-compliant' are deemed to be reckless and irresponsible. Skrabanek (1994: 33) problematises anticipatory medicine as follows:

> Anticipatory medicine does not control the identifiable agents of disease, rather it indulges in probabilistic speculations about the future risk of so-called 'multifactorial disorders' ... What anticipatory care means in practice can be seen, for example, in the official guidelines on preventive care for a low-risk, healthy woman between the ages of 20 and 70 ... According to the American College of Physicians, she should visit her doctor annually and have 278 examinations, tests and counselling sessions. Note that this is recommended for a *healthy* woman [emphasis in original].

Skrabanek's central criticism is that medicine extends beyond merely offering advice and education to a form of coercion or social control in relation to health behaviours. This it does through categorising behaviours into those 'approved and disapproved, healthy and unhealthy, prescribed and proscribed, responsible and irresponsible' (1994: 15). Irresponsible behaviours can include not going for regular check-ups, eating the wrong food, or not being physically active. He argues that while the emphasis on lifestyle has a moral tone, its language is presented in mathematical terms, with each factor having a number to quantify risk. The regulating role of biomedicine through health promotion techniques will be explored further in Chapter 14.

In defence of biomedicine

While orthodox proponents of the medicalisation thesis tend to castigate medicine as a repressive and dominating force, Lupton (1997) draws attention to a less negative interpretation of medicalisation. She refers to some of the positive contributions of biomedicine, such as pain relief and recovery, as well as the possible mutuality between doctors and patients. Broom and Woodward (1996), for example, in their study of chronic fatigue syndrome, found that some forms of medicalisation could be productive for sufferers.

The challenge from alternative and complementary medicine (CAM)
Seeking the help of a biomedical practitioner has become so ingrained in people's cultural practices, they do this almost unthinkingly, prompting Engel (1977: 30) to refer to biomedicine as the 'dominant folk model of disease in the Western world'. However, recent decades have seen a growth in alternative medicine in Ireland, Britain (Saks, 1994), and the USA (Yip and Duran, 2001; Newton et al, 2002). An Internet search for CAM therapies in Ireland suggests that there has been a rapid upsurge in the availability of these in recent years. CAM therapies cover a very broad range of philosophies and approaches to healing (see Box 6.3). Across the broad spectrum, some CAM therapies come under much greater criticism from the medical profession than others, and not all CAM therapies pose the same degree of threat to biomedicine. This will be explored in greater detail below.

Box 6.3 *Spectrum of CAM therapies*

A British Department of Health ((2001b) report divides the spectrum of CAM therapies into three groups:

- The principal disciplines of osteopathy, chiropractice, acupuncture, herbal medicine and homeopathy. These share claims to an individual diagnostic approach. Osteopathy and chiropractice are already regulated by Parliamentary Acts in terms of their professional activities and education in Britain.
- Therapies often used to complement biomedicine, but not professing to making diagnoses. These include aromatherapy, massage, counselling, stress therapy, reflexology, meditation and healing.
- Therapies that claim to offer diagnostic information, and are underpinned by philosophical principles rather than scientific ones. There are two sub-groups here: first, the well-established healing systems of Ayurvedic medicine and Chinese medicine, and second, according to a UK Department of Health (2001b) report, 'highly suspect' therapies such as crystal therapy, iridology, radionics, dowsing and kinesiology.

Compared with biomedicine, CAM therapies have very different notions about how the body works (Aakster, 1993) (See Box 6.4 for an outline of the beliefs underpinning acupuncture). These therapies are associated with holism, that is, a recognition of the interrelationship between various parts of a person – the psychological, spiritual, biological and social. This contrasts with beliefs underpinning the biomedical model, which, as indicated earlier, proposes that all disorders can be explained in biological terms, without reference to the influence of a person's subjectivity. Although CAM therapies tend to share the notion that bodily and mental functions are related to one another, their knowledge bases differ from one another (sometimes quite dramatically).

Box 6.4 *Beliefs underpinning acupuncture*

Underpinning acupuncture are the following beliefs:

- The notion that the body possesses twelve meridians through which energy is transported.
- Upon these meridians, it is believed there are about 950 points to which internal organs are linked.
- The treatment of disease is based on inserting small silver needles into these points to manipulate the energy balance.
- The underlying philosophy of acupuncture is the principle of Yin and Yang, or a belief in distinctive yet interdependent poles of a specific kind of life energy.

Source: Aakster, 1993.

A number of suggestions have been proposed to explain the growing popularity of CAMs. Among these are the growth in consumerism and patient-driven changes in values associated with conventional medicine (Saks, 1994; Yip and Duran, 2001). An increasingly discerning public appears to have become sceptical about the efficacy and iatrogenic effects of biomedicine (Schafer et al, 2002), and there is a growing political climate of self-determination (Bakx, 1991). In addition, it has been suggested that patients want more than detached, 'procedurally orientated care' with their healers, and more choice about therapeutic options (Eisenberg, 2002: 221).

Why is alternative medicine eclipsed by orthodox medicine?
Given the reported limitations of biomedicine in solving historical and contemporary health problems, why have alternative medicines been eclipsed by biomedicine? In historical terms, it is relatively recently that biomedicine has come to dominate. As indicated earlier, the rise to power of biomedicine has occurred only since the nineteenth century. Prior to this period, a number of different types of healers competed with one another. Biomedics, or so-called 'regular practitioners', at that time offered treatments such as purging, sweating, bleeding and vomiting. Parallel to these were bone-setters, and those who used touch or herbal preparations, each in competition with the other. 'The great age of quackery' is the term used to refer to this period (Maple, 1992). As indicated earlier, biomedical elites developed strong political support, culminating in the 1858 Medical Registration Act. This emerged after intense parliamentary debates and granted a legitimacy to biomedicine that no other group of healers succeeded in acquiring (Waddington, 1984). It was thus on the basis of political support rather than superior knowledge about the body that biomedicine secured its future as a unified, self-regulating profession.

Over the course of the twentieth century, the state-sponsored health service in the Republic of Ireland has reinforced the professional dominance of biomedicine, with state funding for the service restricted to biomedicine. This situation was echoed in the British NHS until recently. Although, as indicated above, alternative therapies are becoming more prolific in Ireland, the health service continues to support biomedicine over and above the alternatives. Complementary and alternative therapies in Ireland are not covered with a medical card, and are therefore confined to the private market. This puts them in a structurally disadvantaged position, and makes it impossible for them to compete with conventional biomedicine. The situation in Britain is somewhat less restrictive – homeopathic hospitals have been part of the NHS since its inception in 1947, and biomedical doctors can prescribe homeopathic remedies to NHS patients on the basis of their biomedical training (May and Sirur, 1998). A Department of Health document published in 1999 reported that 86 per cent of NHS chronic pain services offer acupuncture.

CAM therapists have made themselves much more visible in recent years, so much so that in 2001 the Minister for Health and Children, Micheál Martin announced the introduction of a system of registration for such therapists (DoHC, 2001a). As a preliminary step in the process, the minister convened a forum in June 2001 to examine and explore the practical issues involved. The Forum reported in 2002 (IPA, 2002) with a 'road map' aimed at addressing an issue raised in the Health Strategy (DoHC, 2001b), namely, the regulation of complementary and alternative therapists (Martin, 2002). Drawing on the discourse of quality and accountability, the report reviewed steps that might be taken in relation to the education of CAM therapists, research development, the protection of the public, and the development of a data base. Self-regulation by CAM therapists themselves was advocated to sustain standards. The report recommended the establishment of a broadly based National Working Group with the remit of progressing the agenda outlined. At the time of writing the deliberations of this Working Group were still in progress.

Likewise in the UK, the government there has been attempting to introduce a system of regulation for CAM practitioners. The results of the first ever Inquiry into Complementary and Alternative Medicine by a Parliamentary Select Committee were published in March 2001 (Department of Health 2001b). It was suggested in the report that any therapy should be able to produce evidence of its efficacy beyond the placebo[12] effect 'under the rigorous conditions that would be required in order to gain wide credence in orthodox Western medicine' (Department of Health 2001b: 6). Sharma (1992b cited in Saks, 1994) noted that the British

12. A placebo is an inactive substance (with no independent effect) administered under the pretence that it has or may contain active ingredients.

government defers to conventional medical elites for perspectives on the safety and efficacy of CAM therapies. The most recent development in Britain brings CAM therapists a step closer to regulation; in March 2004, the British Minister for Health announced plans to regulate complementary therapists and support workers, and published two public consultation papers regarding registration (*Medical News Today*, 2004). At the time of writing, this consultation process is in progress.

The efficacy of CAMs
There are difficulties for some CAM practitioners in relation to proving their worth. First, official funding for research into CAM therapies is very limited. The British Department of Health (2001b) has recommended the setting up of centres of excellence for CAM research, but states that these should be in or linked to medical schools. This harbours the danger of biomedical dominance in research topics and methodologies. A second and related area concerns the use of traditional research methodologies such as randomised controlled trials (RCTs) that are are deemed to be problematic for some alternative treatments (Saks, 1994). RCTs demand that two or more comparison groups are involved in the experiment, receiving either the experimental treatment, the standard treatment or a placebo (used among the control group). Subjects are randomly assigned to the various groups to ensure that individuals in each group are as similar as possible. The idea is that the trial outcome is related to the different interventions (treatments), and not to differences in patient attributes, nor to a placebo effect. However, some CAM treatments, such as homeopathy, are specifically designed for the individual sufferer, which makes the measurement of treatment outcomes across a whole group problematic. In addition, for the bulk of CAMs, engaging the placebo effect is critical because of the perceived relationship between the state of mind and the functioning of the body (Saks, 1994). Critics of the RCT 'gold standard' also argue that RCTs concentrate only on one restricted question – whether a treatment statistically has an effect – ignoring participants' experiences of the intervention and how they give meaning to these interventions (Verhoef et al, 2002).

    In spite of the difficulties with RCTs for CAM therapies, scientific evidence has emerged in recent years to support the efficacy of some treatments. For example, there is scientific support for the notion that CAM therapies are effective in the prevention and treatment of prostate cancer (Yip and Duran, 2001), in improving shoulder problems (Knebl et al, 2002), and that they hold promise in the management of depression (Manber et al, 2002). Double-blind RTCs on the use of CAM therapies for the treatment of asthma have brought mixed results. Some therapies such as homeopathic immunotherapy have been found to have no independent effect on the condition (Lewith et al, 2002), while others such as herbal remedies indicate an independent positive outcome (Urata et al, 2002).

The relationship between orthodox medicine and alternative medicine

Until the mid-1970s, the General Medical Council in Britain imposed an ethical embargo on co-operation between biomedical and CAM practitioners (Fulder and Monro, 1981). Further tension between biomedicine and the alternatives was the openly-expressed contempt for alternative medicine within mainstream medical journals until relatively recently (Saks, 1994). Professional medical organisations have also been dismissive of the benefits of CAM (BMA, 1986; JACM, 1992). A recent BMA report relating to CAM focuses on the safety, efficacy and practice of acupuncture and concludes that for certain conditions, acupuncture seems to be more effective than 'control' interventions (BMA, 2000). Recent accounts within medical journals also suggest a shift from a dismissive attitude within biomedicine towards CAM, to a more open, and in some cases embracing one (Yip and Duran, 2001). There has also been an interest in biomedical students' knowledge of CAM (Murdoch-Eaton and Crombie, 2002). In addition, academics from internationally-renowned institutions such as the Harvard Medical School have proposed that effective CAM therapies be used as standard practice (Eisenberg, 2002).

What this more embracing attitude towards CAM by some biomedical practitioners suggests is a process known as *incorporation* (Saks, 1994). This involves biomedical practitioners themselves offering some CAM therapies alongside their regular biomedical treatments (May and Sirur, 1998). It has been suggested that incorporation may be a self-serving strategy used by the biomedical profession to fend off the competition posed by CAM, while at the same time sustaining the supremacy of biomedicine (see Saks, 1994). An argument implicitly proposed by some sectors of the medical profession in New Zealand about the status of acupuncture was that the acceptance of medical acupuncture (performed by a qualified biomedical doctor) by the profession would limit lay (non-medical) practitioners in encroaching on biomedicine's jurisdiction (Dew, 2000a).

What of the notion that the knowledge base underpinning biomedicine is very different from that of many CAM therapies? Wolpe (1985) suggested that the medical profession redefined the knowledge base of acupuncture so that it would not be at variance with a biomedical framework. This involves the use of neurophysical explanations when using acupuncture (so-called Western acupuncture). Saks (1994) notes that offering biomedical explanations for CAM therapies discourages non-medical acupuncturists whose yin-yang theories may be more difficult for the general population to accept. When the New Zealand Medical Acupuncture Society became affiliated with the New Zealand Medical Association, biomedical acupuncturists portrayed themselves in conventional biomedical journals as dismissing the philosophies of traditional Chinese medicine in their practices (Dew, 2000a). However, Dew (2000a) argues that in medical acupuncture journals, medical acupuncturists displayed views that challenged biomedical views of acupuncture. Dew proposes that, in different contexts medical acupuncturists display different faces and, under the gaze of their sceptical biomedical colleagues, are more restrained in their 'deviant' theories.

While one trend in the relationship between biomedicine and CAM is that of incorporation noted above, a second is the notion of dilution, that is, where CAM therapists attenuate the radicalism of their ideas to gain greater acceptance (see Saks, 1994; Dew, 2000b). This occurred in the case of chiropractice in both Canada (Coburn, 1993a, 1993b), Britain (Saks, 1994) and New Zealand (Dew, 2000b). In these countries, the earlier claims of chiropractice that almost all diseases were related to subluxated vertabrae, and that spinal manipulation impacted on internal organ function were moderated considerably to more modest claims. This de-radicalisation enabled chiropractors to work more easily side-by-side with biomedical practitioners, and allowed their services to be available through publically-funded healthcare systems. Coburn (1993a) refers to this de-radicalisation as medicalisation.

Rather than being alternatives to orthodox medicine, some therapies are seen as complementary to conventional biomedical care (Sharma, 1992a). Information conveyed by The Irish Cancer Society provides a good example of the perceived ancillary role of CAM therapies. While the benefits of biomedicine as the primary treatment for cancer are extolled, the potential of CAM therapies as supplementary treatments, particularly for the psycho-social problems associated with cancer is proposed (Irish Cancer Society, 2002). Saks (1994) has noted that British national surveys demonstrate that CAM therapies are used for a limited range of conditions and to supplement rather than replace biomedical practices. It has also been suggested that the greatest potential for CAM therapies is in the treatment of chronic diseases where biomedicine has been least successful (Saks, 1994).

Saks (1994) notes that in Britain, while some CAM fields such as acupuncture and healing have begun to display a degree of organisational cohesion, on the whole alternative therapists are not a unified group. Because the consultation time between clients and CAM therapists is, on average, considerably more lengthy that with conventional practitioners, CAM therapies are not a cheap alternative (Saks, 1994). Overall, it may be concluded that the threat from CAM to biomedicine continues to remain weak.

The potential for social control by alternative medicine
Coward (1993) suggests that the image of holism associated with CAM presents it as a gentle and natural alternative, almost with religious connotations. However, she cautions against viewing CAM as a benign alternative to the apparent ravages of biomedicine, pointing to its focus on individual will-power and control and therefore its potential to blame individuals for their own ill-health. Coward further suggests that the popular consciousness and cultural obsession about health (akin to

Skrabanek's notion of 'healthism') is fed to some degree by CAM therapies and the notion of commitment to the body, leading to a highly moralistic approach to health. This commitment to the body, she argues, permits people to express their disillusionment with contemporary society. She states (1993: 96):

> To pursue a natural life style and diet is to find yourself on the side of the 'whole', the integrated, balanced and healing forces of nature. Above all, it is to be on the side of the 'healthy'. To ignore natural laws is to side with the fragmented, the inharmonious, with modern 'mass' society, with junk, technology and destruction.

Skrabanek (1994) was also as critical about the regulating and controlling potential of alternative therapies as he was of biomedicine. Recent evidence from research on relations between CAM therapists and their clients conducted in Berlin indicates a significant amount of negotiation and disagreement in such encounters (Frank, 2002).

In an attempt to redress the individualistic connotations of holism, Vincent Tucker (1997) wrote of a broader version of holism that includes the economic and political systems as well as biological and environmental systems. Tucker's construction of holism is based on the notion that health and illness are not merely biological phenomena but are socially produced. This radical or collective holism does not exclude biomedicine, but it also includes environmental campaigns, political action, educational activities and so forth. It engenders not only changes in personal lifestyle, but also collective action to challenge organisations and institutions that act in ways that are detrimental to public health.

Summary
- Biomedicine rose to prominence over the past two centuries and has become a dominant force in contemporary society.
- A number of theorists challenge the idea that biomedicine has been highly effective in increasing life expectancy and fending off illness, instead suggesting that nutritional and environmental improvements account for the increase in longevity over the past century.
- Biomedicine has attained great power in society and people are socialised to have considerable respect for doctors and to have faith in medical knowledge, in spite of the apparently limited effectiveness of many medical treatments.
- Biomedicine is powerful in creating and sustaining societal norms, by regulating how people behave and by watching over them from birth to death.

- Some theorists have suggested that biomedicine has taken over from religion and law in collectively controlling the behaviour of the population.
- While complementary and alternative medicines have become more popular in recent years, and although biomedicine is being increasingly challenged, its legitimacy and cultural dominance remains broadly intact.

Topics for discussion and reflection

1. Do you think that the power of biomedicine will be sustained in the future. If not, what kind of challenges will it confront?
2. To what extent is your life regulated by biomedicine?

Section 3
Experiences of healthcare

SEVEN

The sociology of the body, health
and illness

The purpose of this chapter is to outline some important developments in theoretical thinking about the body in sociology and how these theories are applied to the field of health and illness. From the outset it is important to acknowledge that the sociology of the body is a relatively recent development, which is theoretically rich but short of empirical studies. For this reason, much of the work on the body is theoretically dense in a way that lessens its accessibility for students and practitioners new to the discipline of sociology. In this chapter we will explain why the body has emerged as a current interest in sociological enquires. We will then outline how the body is conceived of from different sociological perspectives and how these theories are applied to health and illness. In particular, we will examine the salience of the body in thinking about experiences of chronic illness, body impairment and experiences of disability, as well as the multiple ways in which medical discourse constructs womanhood in terms of fertility and bodily processes such as menstruation and menopause. The key insights that emerge from these topics of enquiry are that the body can be analysed as a social construct and that our experiences of the body are mediated and shaped by wider social and cultural relations.

The emerging sociological interest in the body

We live in an age where the body is given unprecedented visibility (Terry and Urla, 1995). Consumer culture is saturated with images of the ideal body: the healthy, beautiful and youthful body is the aesthetic ideal of the kind of body we should strive to attain, but this fantasy body for the most part is beyond our reach. Yet, the body is increasingly viewed as a commodity, a thing that is malleable, with body fat that can be extracted, muscles that can be toned and body parts that can be surgically shaped and radically altered. (Shilling, 1994: 5) introduces us to the concept of 'body projects' to capture the idea that in today's society we are encouraged to develop a purposeful relationship to our bodies as part of our self identity This is the idea that we are no longer at the mercy of the limitations of our biological bodies and can partake in transforming them. While the growth in consumerism is associated with new diseases such as anorexia, obesity, heart disease and diabetes, and advertising images are associated with growing bodily angst even amongst children, the cultural significance of the cultivation of a well-toned, fit and muscular body is that it conveys a modern value system of consumer choice, personal autonomy and self-mastery (see Chapter 14 on health-maintenance body projects).

The body has also become a contested terrain and a site of social conflict (Terry and Urla, 1995). New medical technologies such as the engineering of body organs using human cells, cross-species organ transplantation, the creation of transgenic animals as living laboratories for human organs, and genetic and reproductive therapies mean that we not only know the body in new ways, but these technologies also enable interventions that radically alter the biological body itself. The kind of ethical debates that are waged in relation to these technologies (discussed in Chapter 11) are an indication of the modern paradox that the more we know about the biological body and the more we are able to intervene to control and alter our bodies the less certain we are about what the body is (Shilling, 1994). The importance attributed to the body in contemporary culture marks an unprecedented trend in the individualisation of the body, where concern with health and body image is an expression of individual identity, and yet the body has never been so central to political life. Some examples here are heightened public concerns about environmental risks to health; debates about the implications of the new genetics for disability rights; the global trade in body parts from the poorest people to the richest; the global politics of drug therapy distribution most notably in the treatment of HIV in the poorest regions of world that carry the burden of that disease. Opponents of the patenting of human genes collected from indigenous populations in the 'fight against modern diseases' see this development as a threat to bodily integrity, lifestyles, belief systems and biological diversity (Tauli-Corpuz, 2001). These issues are reflected in the concerns of contemporary social movements such as the environmental, feminist, disability, human rights and global public health movements. Hence, in the kind of body projects that we pursue we are constantly faced with the question about which bodies count as valuable in society and what kind of social values drive these projects?

In the nineteenth century, biological explanations were sought for gender and racial differences to prove that certain classes of bodies were biologically inferior (see Chapter 4). The crude science of craniometry, for example, was used to measure brain size and this was taken as scientific proof that women were less intelligent than men, and that black people were inferior to white Europeans (see below). Naturalistic theories (discussed in Chapter 2) have experienced something of a popular renaissance with renewed interest in the discipline of sociobiology since the 1980s (Nelkin and Lindee, 1995). Sociobiologists argue that the dominant forms of social organisation are biologically fixed and human behaviour is genetically determined. In other words the gene is understood as the primary code for patterns of social life. At the turn of the twenty-first century the gene has a particularly persuasive power that extends beyond the realms of health to explanations of human behaviour and cultural differences. Indeed, as Nelkin and Lindee point out, 'the gene appears to be a solid and predictable marker, an unambiguous sign of natural human difference' (1995: 388). In sum, we can see that the body has acquired a new and pervasive presence in social, moral and political life. This is the social context in which sociology has acquired a growing interest in the body.

Sociological approaches to the body

Two dominant perspectives have emerged in the sociological study of the body. The social constructionist perspective argues that the body is socially and historically shaped. In other words, what we understand as the body is the outcome of culturally available meanings and the social practices that surround the body. Some perspectives are more radical than others, for example, as indicated in Chapter 2, postmodernist accounts that deny the biological reality of the body and insist that the body is a *tabula rasa* (blank sheet) that can be inscribed by different cultural meanings and, therefore, always open to different constructions or articulations. A second approach is the phenomenological perspective, which is concerned with embodiment or the lived experience of the body, in other words, how we experience the body in everyday contexts. A third perspective that bridges these two approaches is symbolic interactionism, which emphasises how our bodies are an important resource in how we manage our interactions with others in everyday encounters. While the central question for sociologists is how to explain the link between the social and the biological body, the key challenge that it faces is to develop a theory that avoids both biological determinism (found in naturalistic theories) and social determinism (the idea that the body is merely a social construct). (See Box 7.1.)

The social constructionist perspective

The body as a social construct

This approach to understanding the body is concerned with the way in which bodies are imbued with social meanings and how these meanings change throughout history. So, for example, medical and biological conceptions of the body are shown to be products of a specific history and culture rather than immutable scientific facts. This approach to the body is not concerned with the material body *per se*, but with how the body is culturally represented or socially produced in everyday life. There are different variants of this perspective, different theorists offer different models for understanding the relationship between the biological and the

Box 7.1 *Sociological approaches to the body*

Perspective	Underlying philosophical issues
The social constructionist perspective	The body is socially and historically shaped through culturally available meanings and social practices
The phenomenological perspective	Interest in how individuals experience the body in social contexts
Symbolic interactionism	Interest in how individuals use their bodies to manage interactions with others in everyday encounters

social. One variant of this perspective draws heavily on Foucault. Foucault's work is essentially a political history of the body – how the body became an object of study and a target of specific mechanisms of control and regulation. In his early writings he was concerned with how the body was objectified through the 'gaze' of scientific knowledge and how this knowledge was used to define norms of health and behaviour so that populations could be regulated and individuals disciplined to be docile, useful and productive (also refer to Chapters 2 and 14). In the *Birth of the Clinic* (1973), Foucault shows how in the shift from bedside to hospital medicine by the end of the eighteenth century, which was facilitated by the development of anatomical science, the patient increasingly came to be understood as a body that could be diagnosed with general types of disease. Through the 'clinical gaze' (the technical apparatuses of clinical medicine) the body is understood as an objective physical reality and disease the source of localised pathologies residing in the body.

Foucault did not view the body as a pre-social, organic entity. Instead, he argued that the body is always situated in culture by virtue of the social relations of power and knowledge that surround it. Foucault can be interpreted in a way that suggests that the body has no material relevance outside of the discourses that constitute it, yet social practices and their normalising power have a real material impact on how we experience our bodies. One way of illustrating the value of Foucault's perspective is to consider feminist accounts of the medical construction of the female body (below) and the medicalisation of childbirth (Chapter 11). The difference, however, between Foucault and feminist accounts that engage with this theoretical perspective is that Foucault does not take a political position on the effects that disciplinary power and its discourses have on the real experiences of people (Annandale, 1998). This has led to the charge that social constructionist accounts of the body can lead to relativism and a disembodied approach to sociological enquiry (i.e. disengaged from the everyday experiences of people).

The historically transformed body

Another broad variant within the social constructionist perspective are those approaches that focus on how the social environment impacts on the biological body. The work of Norbert Elias (1978, 1982 [1939]), for example, is concerned with the history of the ways in which our bodies have been 'civilised' and charts the impact of a changing social environment on how we conduct ourselves – for example, how we control our emotions and regulate our physical bodily functions. Unlike Foucault, however, Elias was interested in the way in which biological and social factors interact in the formation of evolutionary processes. For Elias the human body is essentially biological, but the evolution of our biological capacity for language and rational thought has meant that humans are capable of social differentiation and adapt to social change without the necessity for changes in the biological structure of the body (Shilling, 1994). While Elias accepted an underlying genetic component to human behaviour, he rejected the notion that patterns of behaviour were genetically fixed (Williams and Bendelow, 1998).

Elias traces a gradual historical transition from medieval society where there were few social constraints placed on natural bodily functions such as defecating, urinating and spitting, to the emergence of European courtly society in the sixteenth century when new codes of behaviour widened the thresholds of shame and embarrassment governing instinctual drives and bodily functions. New rules of conduct have become such a deep part of our socialisation processes over centuries that they have given rise to a new personality structure and new modes of bodily expression. In the first instance, we have come to view the body in social as opposed to biological terms: the natural functions associated with the body are increasingly hidden from view and the body instead has become the site for expressing who we are through impression management. Secondly, we have come to understand the body as something that can be controlled and we have become socialised not to give immediate expression to our instinctual drives and emotional impulses. Thirdly, the emphasis on body management and self-control has led to what Shilling refers to as 'individualisation of the body and self' (1994: 166). In other words, our learnt capacity to control and manage our bodies has led people to perceive of themselves as separate from others. In Elias's work, civilised order is attained through the gradual historical process of taming bodies – of constraining the natural functions and impulses of the body to conform to social codes of behaviour. In this sense, the human body is transformed into a social body. The intricate etiquette that we are socialised into from early childhood on how to conduct our bodies in relation to others and how to regulate our bodily functions lead us to assume that our bodies follow natural, not social, imperatives.

The body as a carrier of social value

Pierre Bourdieu's work is largely concerned with social class distinction and the way in which the everyday lives of individuals interact with broader social structures in reproducing social inequalities. He develops the concept of 'habitus' to denote how people acquire a world-view and dispositions that are reconcilable to their social position. He describes the habitus as a 'system of dispositions' or 'cognitive and motivating structures' that generate meaningful practices and perceptions in a way that people's lifestyles become second nature to them (Bourdieu, 1977). The habitus is embodied in the sense that how people manage their bodies reveals their social position. So, for example, our social position is revealed by our accent, our facility to 'play the game' in particular social settings, how we dress, how we cultivate our bodily dispositions, what we eat and how we eat, how we talk and what we talk about. It is in this sense that our bodies are carriers of social value and, therefore, distinguish people in terms of their social class position. What is important from the point of view of Bourdieu's work is that the habitus is embodied in such a way that our dispositions appear naturalised rather than consciously acted on, that is, 'something that one is' (Bourdieu, 1990: 73).

Bourdieu's concept of the habitus is developed in his theory of social class inequalities and social power. The social structure is defined by the distribution of capital. The working class not only have less economic capital (income and wealth) but also less cultural capital (valued dispositions, valued cultural goods and educational credentials and skills) and less social capital (valued social networks and social resources). Each form of capital is convertible into other forms of capital and whether a particular form of capital, for example, a certain disposition (as a form of cultural capital) can be converted into another form, such as economic capital or *visa versa*, depends on whether the type of capital is recognised as legitimate or symbolically valued (see Shilling, 1994 for a more extensive discussion).

According to Bourdieu, social classes have distinct relations to their bodies (in the sense that we embody our social position through the system of dispositions made available to us) and bodily orientations carry symbolic value in the way that they operate to distinguish between different social groups. Bourdieu's work has been developed by feminist theorists in order to understand the relationship between class and gender (see for example Reay, 1997; Skeggs, 1997). Later in this chapter we will explore how the concept of the habitus and the idea of the body as a carrier of symbolic value is developed in understanding the social exclusion of people with impairments (Edwards and Imrie, 2003).

The phenomenological perspective: the body as lived experience
When sociologists talk about the material body, they are not only referring to the physical body, but also to the mind and emotions. This idea is captured by the concept of the 'lived body', or human embodiment; in other

words, how we subjectively experience our bodies. This approach to the body is rooted in phenomenology (see Chapter 2) and, in particular, the work of Merleau-Ponty (1962) who dispensed with the Cartesian idea that the mind and body are two separate entities and, instead, characterised them as interfused (Williams and Bendelow, 1998). Whilst sociologists stress that social agency is conscious action, they are often accused of failing to acknowledge that actions are essentially embodied. In other words, our bodies are integral to our actions as well as being shaped by our actions. Within this perspective, the body itself is an expressive medium and our engagement with the world is not only rational but also sensual and emotional.

The phenomenological understanding of the body as 'lived' should not be confused with the naturalistic view that the body is a biologically fixed entity. This sociological approach to the body also calls for an *embodied sociology* as opposed to a *sociology of the body* (Williams and Bendelow, 1998), that is, a sociology that does not theorise about the body in the abstract, but one that connects with and makes visible how individuals experience their bodies. Phenomenological accounts emphasise how conscious experience is always embodied. When applied empirically they have to consider how the cultural, social and historical context in which individuals live their lives shapes bodily perspectives. Because phenomenology emphasises *being* a body (being-in-the world) rather than *having* a body, it challenges both the biomedical notion of the body as an (malfunctioning) object separate from the self and the classical liberal model of the individual where the body is viewed as an appendage to the self over which individuals claim sovereignty in asserting their autonomy (Diprose, 1995).

The interactionist perspective: the body and social action

Between the social constructionist approach and the phenomenological understanding of the body (discussed above) lies the interactionist perspective (see Chapter 2). Following this perspective, Goffman's studies on impression management (1969), stigma and shame ((1968) and how we manage our bodies in public spaces (1963) demonstrate how the smooth flow of everyday encounters, and the integrity of our self-identity and social roles, are maintained through the competence that we exhibit in controlling our bodily expressions. While social actors have a relatively high degree of agency over their bodies, Goffman argues that the meanings that we attribute to each others' bodily performances is determined by 'shared vocabularies of body idiom' (Shilling, 1994: 82, citing Goffmann, 1963: 35) or non-verbal bodily expressions. Bodies give off information all the time in the form of expressions, comportment, gestures, dress, and so forth, that allow us to classify each other's performance, which in turn influences the way we present ourselves to others (Shilling, 1994).

Goffman's work on stigma has been most influential in studies on chronic illness and disability. Stigma can either be 'discreditable' in cases where the source of the stigma can be concealed from others (for example in the management of a colostomy or incontinence) or 'discrediting' where the stigma is publicly visible, for example, a facial disfigurement or speech impediment. In both cases the self is experienced as a 'spoiled identity' and people internalise and experience their difference as a source of inferiority (Goffman, 1963). In this sense, stigma creates problems in the presentation of self. The cultural meanings attached to the body highlight its significance in mediating the relationship between self-identity and social identity (Shilling, 1994). While this perspective offers useful descriptions of the experiences of stigma and shame in the context of understanding how we manage our bodies, it ignores the wider social structures that underlie those experiences.

Application to health and illness
With these theoretical issues in mind, we now turn to a discussion of how these perspectives have been developed in the field of health and medicine. The human body is central to the everyday work of health professionals as the object of medical inquiry and the site of therapeutic interventions. In physical examinations, diagnostic procedures and caring practices, health professionals have to negotiate the most intimate aspects of our bodily existence. Some forms of medical examination and body care are more invasive than others: the objectifying gaze of the medical examination and the sometimes inescapable deprivation of privacy threatens the integrity of the patient as a person. Visual technologies have radically altered the way we encounter the interiors of bodies: high-tech equipment increasingly mediates diagnostic skills and the advent of digital imaging and simulated surgery has made virtual bodies available for medical training (Cartwright, 1995). The body that is the object of medical inquiry is one that appears divorced from the body of the patient. In the following sections we will explore bodily experiences of health and illness, and medical and cultural prescriptions of the normal body from the perspective of disability studies and feminism.

Chronic illness and the lived body
Much of the sociological research on chronic illness is concerned with people's experiences of ill-health. More recently, there has been a shift in the research away from the so-called 'deficit' model of chronicity to explore how people living with chronic conditions experience 'health within illness' (Lindsey, 1996: 466). Studies on the illness experience highlight the uncertainty that people experience when their bodies betray them, the emotional and social impact of a disease or impairment, and the emotional work that is put into managing care regimes, everyday tasks and social

interactions. Chronic illness and impairment, therefore, is not only characterised by biophysical changes or loss but also by 'biographical disruption' (Bury, 1982), 'loss of self' (Charmaz, 1983) or 'social death' (Kleinman, 1988). In chronic illness a person acquires a new status as an individual with a particular condition, which can dominate others' perceptions of him/her and lead to a loss of identity. If the illness or visible disfigurement carries a stigma this leads to a more precarious sense of self, while dependency on others may lead to the loss of social and personal status.

A chronic illness or condition by definition is not curable, nor does it necessarily precipitate death: people live with chronic conditions. Altered biophysical states and disrupted biographies mean that people need to make sense of their past lives in order to create meaning for their present experiences and their future lives. Williams describes this process as a 'reconstructed narrative' where chronically ill people 'reconstitute and repair ruptures between body, self and world by linking up and interpreting different aspects of biography in order to realign present and past and self within society' (1984: 197). Seymour's (1989) study of the experience of people with severe and permanent paralysis explores the relationship between body, self and society by looking at how people rebuild their identities following the catastrophoric and permanent loss of bodily functions. In adjusting to a new body state, the paralysed person is taught strategies to manage the loss of musculosketetal, bladder and bowel control and to adjust to mechanical aids, as well as emotional adjustment to physical loss. The transformation from being a person to a patient and the transition from patient to person as a 'new self' adjusted to a new body state are all part of the process of the reconstruction of 'a healthy self'.

Elias's 'civilised body' (referred to above) is a metaphor that can be used to capture the phenomenon of severe paralysis. As Seymour notes, 'the archaic presence of the body mocks the civilising forces of social constraint' and rehabilitation seeks to re-civilise or resocialise the body so that it may conform to the social imperative of normalcy (1989: 127). However, previous understandings of the body and its relation to the self are radically challenged by the loss of bodily functions and the altered appearance of the body, and patients face formidable barriers in reconstructing a sense of a healthy self and a new body image. When our bodies betray us in chronic disease and infirmity, the dominant social understandings associated with appearance, sexuality, gender and the social roles that become central to our identity can no longer be assumed and there is no escaping the vulnerability of the body. Loss of motor function and sensation, for example, affects sexuality and may impede sexual and reproductive functions depending on the level of paralysis. The expression of sexual pleasure and involvement in intimate relationships are an important aspect of reconstituting a 'healthy self', but sexuality is often denied to people with a disability. Inevitably, definitions of health are transformed for people who go through a trauma or disease that radically alters their bodies. Seymour's study found that people who have developed severe paralysis become much more conscious of maintaining their bodies and health and that many people come to see themselves as healthy again despite permanent bodily loss (1989). Good health, therefore, is not only the absence of disease or infirmity; for people who lose musculosketetal control and control over basic bodily functions, who suffer pain, lethargy or immobility and who have to use prosthetic devices, it is difficult to cultivate the *appearance* of a healthy body (the ideal of a fit, muscular, agile body that can perform with standard feminine or masculine bodily comportment and expression).

Two related concerns emerge from Seymour's work: first, the denial in clinical rehabilitation models of the experience of bodily limitations and, second, how in forging a new sense of self people with severe functional loss are forced to confront dominant social values and structural barriers that impact on embodied experiences. Drawing on a rich field of empirical work on the illness experience (reviewed in Pierret, 2003 and Lawton, 2003), we can see that the extent to which a disease or trauma is more or less disruptive to self and the extent to which a person's biography may be a resource or hindrance to the reconstruction of a healthy self depends on a multiple set of factors. These include the severity of the condition and extent to which an illness or infirmity carries a stigma; the stage in the life course that a person confronts illness or a physical trauma and prior health status; the impact of gender, ethnicity and social class in terms of the cultural norms, belief systems and expectations that give meanings to our lives; the immediate social context of family, friends and social networks, and the resources that the wider social context make available – for example, health policy and organisation of care. In a critical appraisal of the concept of biographical disruption, Williams also notes that for those individuals born with an impairment or congenital condition their 'biographically embodied sense of self [...] have not, in any real or significant sense, shifted' (2003: 103). This observation serves as a reminder that what may appear as a disrupted biography is judged against dominant cultural prescriptions of normality.

Some writers on chronic illness emphasise the alienation of self from the suffering and incapacitated body (Leder, 1990; Williams, 1996). In fighting illness and loss of bodily function there is a sense in which the mind is master over the precarious body, transcending its limits by willing it to live and to develop new capabilities and skills. The cultivation of personal willpower is seen as central to the rehabilitation process captured by the popular notion of 'the triumph of the human spirit' (Seymour, 1989: 89). However, disability theorists argue that this reinforces the notion that disability is a personal tragedy story that must be overcome by the individual (Oliver, 1996). The risk here is that when people fail to surmount their physical limitations they may stand accused 'of a deficient personality, of lack of motivation, or of moral inadequacy' (Seymour, 1989: 130).

Wendell (1996) offers a personal testimony of how when faced with chronic pain and physical difficulty, the desire to take flight from the body involves a new awareness and acceptance of one's altered body. She describes the relationship of consciousness to the body in the following way:

> The onset of illness, disability, or pain destroys the 'absence' of the body to consciousness, ... and forces us to find conscious responses to new, often acute, awareness of our bodies. Thus, the body itself takes us into and then beyond its sufferings and limitations (Wendell, 1996: 178).

Wendell refers to this coping mechanism as a 'strategy of disengagement' or of 'disembodying the self', which involves an identification with the altered body, its limitations and needs rather than a sense of alienation or the denial of bodily loss and suffering (1996: 173-9).

Disability and impairment

In 2003, the European Year of People with Disabilities, Ireland hosted the Special Olympics World Games. This provided the disability movement with the opportunity to spotlight the Dickensian conditions of some of the residential institutions for people with mental and physical disabilities, cutbacks in the provision of residential and respite care and educational supports, and the lack of legislative reform to underpin the citizenship rights of people with disability. The debates that ensued in the Irish media about the rights of people with disabilities challenged the occasion of the Special Olympics as a token cultural representation of difference. The disability movement hoped that the Special Olympics, in highlighting the abilities of people with disabilities, would force wider political visibility of the many social barriers facing people with disabilities and their informal carers. The Special Olympics is also important in challenging the cultural representation of disability and the cultural ideals associated with the athletic body by emphasising the stamina and physicality of the body while at the same time challenging notions of physical normality and the idea that disability is a fixed pathologised state. This international sporting event is part of an emerging disability culture, 'disability pride', which is about people with disabilities re-valuing their own bodily and cognitive attributes. The 'aesthetic oppression' of people with disabilities (Hahn, 1988 cited in Priestly, 2003) involving the exclusion of physical differences from our visual culture and the cultural representations of such differences as a curiosity, hideous or alien and undesirable is compounded by technological advancements in corrective surgery. The growing interest in cosmetic surgery for children with Downs Syndrome, which incidentally has no therapeutic value, is occurring at a time when children with disabilities are increasingly integrated into mainstream society and when disablist attitudes are being challenged by the disability movement (Priestly, 2003).

The normalisation of the appearance of children with intellectual disabilities in this way is telling of the kind of ethical issues that arise in the context of medical technology and the ideological tyranny of bodily perfection so prevalent in consumer culture. The idea that some bodies are more valued than others also arises when we consider that while cosmetic surgery becomes more widely available for children with Downs Syndrome, controversy in Britain has ensued about their disability status in clinical rationing decisions that give lower priority to such children in need of surgical intervention for congenital heart disease (Priestly, 2003).

Dominant definitions of disability view physical, sensory and cognitive impairments as an individualistic and medical problem. An alternative perspective presented by the disability movement and disability studies draws a distinction between impairment as a functional loss or limitation and disability as the social *dis-abling* of people with impairments, leading for example to social barriers and disablist attitudes that limit the social lives of people with impairments. In other words, disability is not the result of impairment but the outcome of social oppression. This alternative framework for understanding disability is known as the social model of disability (Oliver, 1996). The social model falls within the political economy perspective (discussed in Chapter 2) in that it emphasises the importance of the structural barriers of capitalist society in the production of disability. Oliver (1990) argues that in the late eighteenth century people with impairments were seen as unproductive and superfluous to the needs of industrial capitalism. Hence, disabled people were constructed as a burden on society and segregated initially in workhouses and later in residential institutions where they came under the jurisdiction of the medical gaze and dependent on the state.

The emergence of the philosophy of **special needs** coincides with the shift from institutional care and segregation of people with disabilities to the promotion of community care, which emphasises their integration into community life and the education of people in life skills and training for work in the form of sheltered housing, special schools and sheltered workshops. The philosophy of **normalisation** has largely dominated the approach to intellectual disabilities and it emphasises the need to create lifestyles and social roles for people with intellectual disabilities so that they may emulate 'normal' lifestyles and occupy social roles valued in society (Emerson, 2001). However, the concept of normalisation may equally be seen as suspect since the emphasis on conformity to culturally prescribed social roles, behaviours and lifestyles may undermine disabled people and ignore difference (Brown and Smith, 2001). The disability movement emphasises self-determination over the principle of normalisation, and the social model also critiques the philosophy of normalisation for ignoring the structural barriers that impact on the quality of life and social opportunities afforded to people with impairments. Indeed, discourses of normality have a profound impact on the individual and collective identities of disabled people. As Chapter 9 demonstrates, children are subject to a battery of tests and measures for normal childhood development in relation to physical, emotional, cognitive and social development. Hence, what we have come to understand as the normal trajectory of child to adult development is scientifically standardised, which leaves little room for understanding the diversity of human development and positively valuing difference (Priestly, 2003).

In recent years there has been a policy shift towards mainstreaming education, training and employment for people with disabilities. In Ireland, a Supported Employment Programme to encourage employment in the open labour market has been piloted nationally since 1990 (Hanrahan, 2003), and responsibility for employment policy for people with disabilities has been transferred from the Department of Health and Children to the Department of Enterprise, Trade and Employment. This shift reflects growing policy recognition of the social model of disability, which argues that the exclusion of people with impairments from the labour market is part of the historical production of disability (UPIAS, 1976; Oliver, 1990). It also represents a shift away from discourses of paternalism to discourses of social inclusion (Priestly, 2003) spearheaded by the rights-based approach of an increasingly vocal disability movement. Priestly (2003) points out that employment is central to the construction of disability as a dependent social category since ability to work defines the independent status of adults as individuals and their rights as citizens. While the significance of socially valued employment for people with disabilities cannot be denied, it is also important to interrogate dominant constructions of the relationship between work, autonomy, independence and citizenship. Western concepts of personhood and citizenship are tied to idealised notions of independence, competence and autonomy linked to physical and cognitive functioning. As a result, people with disabilities are constructed as dependent in opposition to our Western individualistic model of autonomy (Priestly, 2003). Priestly argues that our discourses of citizenship and social inclusion are centred on this individualistic model and he questions whether claims to citizenship should be narrowly tied to social inclusion through employment (2003).

While the social model emphasises disability as social oppression, it has recently been criticised for ignoring the significance of the body and impairment (Hughes and Paterson, 1997; Paterson and Hughes, 2000). The social model is concerned with how society disables people with impairments rather than on how impairments affect individuals (Oliver, 1992). Paterson and Hughes (2000) argue that the distinction between impairment as a natural biological and, hence, medical category and disability as a social category reproduces the Cartesian binary of opposites (see also Chapter 6 for an account of the mind/body fissure within biomedicine). In assuming that impairment is a natural biological fact, the social model ignores how impairment is socially constructed (the idea that impairment is as much a cultural product as a biological state); and it ignores the embodied experience of disability as a form of social oppression. In theorising disability there is a tension between those accounts that emphasise the everyday lived experience of people with disabilities and those that seek to explain the underlying structural conditions that produce experiences of oppression. How can we account for the social agency of people with disabilities as well as their experiences of oppression? People with disabilities experience myriad forms of oppression that remind them that their impaired bodies are less valued by society – the built environment that bars them from social spaces, policies that exclude them from meaningful social roles and deny them basic citizenship rights, disablist attitudes and images that patronise and infantilise them or deny their existence, and verbal and non-verbal norms of communication that exclude them from meaningful social interaction and, hence, from participating in everyday life. These of course are social barriers that are not part of the perceptual world of non-impaired persons but that profoundly impact on the material and social position of people with disabilities and their embodied experiences of everyday life.

One way of bringing together the different theoretical approaches to the body is to think about the interaction between macro and micro relations of power in producing social meanings about impairment (as a biological failure of ability) and how disability (as social oppression) becomes embodied as a lived experience (Paterson and Hughes, 2000). Edwards and Imrie (2003) develop Bourdieu's theoretical framework (discussed earlier in this chapter) to show how the wider social environment and social relations shape the embodied experiences of people with impairments. They suggest that the concept of habitus is useful in understanding how the experiences of disabled people are tied to valuations of their bodies (as lacking value) and how this, in turn, is linked to broader social structures that reproduce the social inequalities that bear so heavily upon the lives of disabled people. Disabled people are defined by their 'otherness' (something other than normal and, therefore, threatening). Hence, Edwards and Imrie (2003) ask, to what extent are values ascribed to disabled people in areas that dominate their lives such as the fields of medicine and welfare, and how do disabled people manage their bodies in order to seek access to resources (such as social or cultural capital)? What do these processes tell us about the relationship between impairment and disability? Drawing on the testimonies of people with physical and sensory impairments, their study shows that the meaning and experience of impairment is to have a 'less than valuable' or 'less than able' body (2003: 247), that is a body that has less symbolic capital in terms of 'what counts as a legitimate body' (Edwards and Imrie, 2003: 248, quoting Shilling, 1994: 145). These experiences of demeaning valuations stem from medical discourses and professional practices, as well as from everyday encounters in which disabled people are treated as invisible and inferior (Edwards and Imrie, 2003).

Demeaning valuations rooted in medical discourses and practices are not confined to medical constructions of disability. The way in which the female body has been derogated within medical discourses has been the subject of sociological analyses. It is to these that we now turn.

The medical construction of the female body

Over the past few decades, medicine has been criticised by feminist theorists because of the way in which the female body is a site in which gender is constructed in medical discourses (Lupton, 2003). As indicated in Chapters 2 and 4, to propose that gender is something that is constructed is to suggest that it is the product of human thoughts and actions, rather than occurring naturally. By extension, to argue that gender is constructed in medical discourses is to contend that medicine influences how people think and talk about what it means to be female or male. At a societal level, this means that medicine has an input into normative standards about what counts as acceptable social behaviour for males and females and, to some extent at least, impacts upon what masculinity and femininity should be. Sheldon argues that broader constructions of gender have begun to rely increasingly on medical discourses (1997).

The challenge for feminism has been to draw attention to the social processes that represent the female body as inferior and that discriminate against women (Annandale and Clark, 1996). However, feminists themselves are not in agreement as to how to view the female body and bodily experiences (Doyal, 1994; Lupton, 2003; Annandale and Clark, 1996). One school of thought is to celebrate the uniqueness of the female body with its capacity to bear and breastfeed children, in other words, to draw attention to the physical and experiential differences between men and women that have their roots in the body. Other feminist scholars, however, seek to play down differences between women's and men's experiences associated with their bodies because the female body has been differentiated from the male body historically in order to justify female exploitation. That the female body and bodily functions have been used to legitimate injustices against women is a dominant theme within feminism. For example, women's historic exclusion from public and economic realms was based on the fact that women were perceived to be better at domesticity and nurturing, and not very intellectual, decisive or rational. Medical discourses fed this ideology and shaped views about what was considered normal and appropriate female behaviour and what was pathological. Medical science used medico-scientific justification on the basis of biology and anatomy to keep women out of public life (Lupton, 2003).

Ehrenreich and English (1974b) suggest that, traditionally, women have been represented in a derogatory manner within medicine as the 'sick' or 'incomplete' version of males – weaker, unstable, a source of infection and impure. They contend that there are two contradictory ideologies of women in evidence: on the one hand, women are depicted as weak and defective, and on the other, as dangerous and polluting. Birke (2003) notes how women's bodily processes are constructed as aberrations because women's health needs have been defined in relation to male bodies. Even contemporary medical textbooks present the male body as the standard when depicting anatomical features shared by the sexes (Lawrence and Bendixen, 1992). As Lawrence and Bendixen note, this results in medical students having to learn male anatomy first. Aspects of the female body are learnt with reference to the male body and are described as smaller, weaker and less developed than the yardstick of the male body.

Turner (1987) argues that medicine has traditionally viewed the female body as a threat to the moral order and stability of society. It has also been proposed that perceptions of the male and female body have altered historically according to political interests (see Lupton, 2003). Schiebinger (1987) notes how the first portrayal of the female skeleton in Europe in the eighteenth century occurred during a period when efforts were being made to determine women's status in European society. Attention was drawn to specific areas of the body that were to become politically significant. Attempts were made to represent the female body as inherently weak; the female skull was drawn smaller than the male skull in an attempt to depict women's intellectual abilities as deficient. However, during the period of mercantile (early) capitalism when it was in society's interest to promote a population increase, the uterus came to be valued rather than treated with contempt as it had previously been.

In the debates surrounding women's access to university in the second half of the nineteenth century, Harvard professor Edward Clarke blocked women's entry to universities on the grounds that intellectual activity would curtail the transmission of nerve-energy to the reproductive organs, creating over-active cerebration and abnormally feeble digestion (Moscucci, 1990). Masculine intellectual qualities were deemed to be dangerous for women's fertility and capacity for motherhood, insofar as they would undermine her female qualities (Abbott and Wallace, 1990). When women did finally gain entry to higher education[13] 'scientific' evidence was created that allegedly proved that scholarly thought would stop menstruation; since menstruation and potential fertility were central to the construction of womanhood at that time, scholarly women would cease to be women (Bullough and Vought, 1973). On the issue of women studying medicine,

---

13. This occurred in most cases in the late nineteenth and early twentieth century, depending on the programme and university.

various reports in the *Lancet* during the 1860s and 1870s opposed this, proposing that exposure to lectures and dissections on human anatomy and pathology would result in young ladies becoming indelicate (Mort, 2000).

In the nineteenth and early twentieth centuries there was a perception that women were controlled by their uterus and ovaries. Physicians contended that uterine and ovarian malfunctions underpinned almost every female complaint, such as headaches, sore throats, and indigestion (Ehrenreich and English, 1974b). During the 1860s ovariectomy became a key procedure and surgical interventions were performed on normal organs within the female abdomen designed to treat 'typically female mental abnormalities' (Trohler, 1999: 199). The condition of hysteria (the word comes from Greek meaning uterus) in the nineteenth century was linked to the belief that women were governed by their hormones (Lupton, 2003). The first sign of rebelliousness by a woman was interpreted as an indicator of disease. Physicians came to diagnose women who were trying to assert their independence as 'sick', and those pushing for women's rights as hysterical.

Kohler Riessman (1983) suggests that the status of womanhood is tarnished by medical discourses that encourage women and girls to seek medical help for any kind of menstrual problems; the female body is then perceived as a site of frequently occurring illness. The menstrual cycle becomes linked to a negative perception of women as 'unreliable workers, thinkers, and leaders' (Lorber, 1997: 55). Lorber (1997) explored the various medical versions and notions of what is normal and abnormal in relation to the menstrual cycle both in a historical context, and in the current time. She identified a range of interpretations, leading her to conclude that, '[t]he biomedical perspective on the physical, behavioural, and emotional effects of the menstrual cycle is thus a social construction, built out of the values of our time' (Lorber, 1997: 58).

A more recent focus in medical discourses is on menopause which has been associated with a range of symptoms in middle-aged women, even where these symptoms are not age-related (Roberts, 1985). The very manner in which the normal effects of hormonal shifts associated with menopause are medicalised as 'symptoms' signifying pathology has been questioned. Lorber (1997), drawing on Douglas (1966) proposes that menstruation has been superseded by menopause and Pre-Menstrual Syndrome (PMS) as the anti-social momentum needing to be tamed. Both of these conditions are associated with the production of uncontrollable emotions and behaviour.

Finally, Murphy-Lawless refers to the 1994 British Medical Association conference in which the issue of women carrying ovary donor cards was discussed with a view to utilising the creative potential of women following accidental death. She interprets this as the construction of the female body as a repository of ovarian material to be expropriated by technocratic obstetricians. She notes:

> In medical eyes, where the essence of our subjectivity has long been defined as synonymous with our reproductive role, we are not now even the sum of our reproductive parts but merely a source from which they can be 'harvested' ... (Murphy-Lawless, 1998: 28).

Summary

- Contemporary society is marked by a heightened cultural and political visibility of the body. However, at a time when the body has become so visible, there would appear to be less certainty about what the body actually is.
- Sociology challenges the idea that the body can only be understood as a natural, biological entity, and as a discrete and separate entity to the self. However, a bewildering range of theoretical perspectives marks the sociology of the body.
- For some, within what is broadly referred to as the social constructionist approach, the body is always imbued with social meaning, while for others the divisions between mind and body and between the body as nature or culture can only be transcended if the concept of embodiment and, hence, lived experiences of the body are taken into account.
- The relationship between the body, self and society and experiences of embodiment are explored in studies of chronic illness and disability. Both phenomenological and interactionist perspectives focus on how people give meaning to and cope with their changed identity when faced with a chronic illness or impairment.
- The social model of disability challenges the understanding of disability as an individual medical problem and personal tragedy. While the medical model sees disability as the outcome of impairment, the social model argues that disability is caused by the social exclusion and social oppression of people with impairments.
- The social model of disability, however, implies a distinction between impairment (as a biological category) and disability (as a social category). Hence, the social model has been accused of neglecting the embodied experiences of disabled people and the significance of the body as a marker of social position, identity and value.
- The way in which women's bodies are medically constructed reflects and reinforces dominant social and cultural ideas about womanhood and the status of women in society.
- Feminists have questioned the meanings attributed to women's bodies in medical discourses and the material impact of those meanings (and, in particular, the pathologising of the female body) for the way women see and experience their bodies.

Topics for discussion and reflection
1. What kind of body projects do people of your age engage in, and for what reasons?
2. What social barriers and disablist attitutes operate within the culture we live in and how might these be overcome?

EIGHT

The sociology of lay and professional interactions

In this chapter, relations between lay people and professionals will be explored. We begin by considering how people come to be 'patients', and what prompts them to seek the help of health professionals. Popular thinking, rooted in dominant ideologies, suggests that the relationship between patients and health professionals is an equal one based on objective clinical judgements, varying only according to the nature of the pathology identified. However, sociological analyses suggest that clinical pathology itself is far from objective, identifiable, and impartially diagnosable, because the very act of diagnosing, categorising pathologies and intervening with treatments is **socially constructed**. In this sense, diseases, pathologies, and patient categories are products of the social context of healthcare. In this chapter, we will consider the nature of relations between lay people and health workers to determine the extent to which such relations are objective and impartial, or whether they are mediated by a variety of social factors and degrees of power. A number of ways of theorising patient-professional relations have emerged, and these will also be examined. Finally we will consider the manner in which the social divides of gender, socio-economic status, ethnicity and age impact on professional-patient interactions.

The illness experience

Only a fraction of people with symptoms of ill-health actually visit their doctor with the problem (Dunnell and Cartwright, 1972; Scambler et al, 1981). In a UK national survey of general practitioners (GPs) almost a quarter of doctors believed that about half of patients who consulted had complaints so minor that the consultation was unnecessary (Cartwright and Anderson, 1981). At the same time, other research has found that some people delay seeking medical advice for what transpires to be a serious illnesses (Epsom, 1969). Clearly, people appear to make their own assessments of their symptoms, and two people with identical symptoms may make different decisions about seeking help. The decision whether or not to seek help is based on socio-cultural factors. A symptom or set of symptoms considered to be normal or very minor for one person may be interpreted as potentially serious by another person. People make sense of their own experiences in a particular way, through communicating with others. In this sense, individuals are constructing their own social reality (Clarke, 2001). There are no feelings of ill-health out there independent of humans. Illness becomes real in a specific way only to the person who is experiencing it. Thus illness – the subjective experience of bodily discomfort and feelings of pain or unwellness (Field, 1976; Seedhouse, 1986) – is socially constructed.

If illnesses can be interpreted as the individual's subjective experience of his of her own bodily functions or malfunctions, a disease may be characterised as a pathological abnormality or biologically altered state, signified by a particular set of signs and symptoms (Field, 1976; Seedhouse, 1986). While diseases may have some measurable qualities (Seedhouse, 1986), it has also been suggested that they are socially constructed and are the product of medical discourses (Turner, 1987; Foucault, 1973). The latter view suggests that what constitutes a disease reflects dominant modes of thinking in society and relies upon available techniques for examining the human body (Turner, 1987; see also Chapter 7). These techniques are subject to change, as is the medical interpretation or diagnosis of the condition. Biomedical knowledge, like other forms of knowledge, is derived from and reflects its social, cultural and historical context.

Lay and professional interactions

The preponderance of studies on lay and professional interactions focus on doctor-patient relations. This is so because traditionally, in view of medicine's dominant power position, sociological research rendered other occupations almost invisible, considering them only in relation to medicine.

The perspectives proposed in sociological accounts in the 1950s, 60s and 70s tended to highlight the dominance of physicians and, to varying degrees, the passivity of patients. More recent analyses have focused on the *agency* of patients in healthcare encounters, that is, patients' abilities to actively engage with and possibly alter the outcome of the encounter (Ainsworth-Vaughn, 1998; Bensing et al, 2000; Roter, 2000). Roter (2000: 5) refers to this paradigm shift as follows:

> Just as the molecular and chemistry oriented sciences were adopted as the twentieth century medical paradigm, incorporation of the patient's perspective into a relationship-centred medical paradigm has been suggested as appropriate for the twenty-first century. It is the medical dialogue that provides the fundamental vehicle through which the paradigmatic battle of perspectives is waged and the therapeutic relationship is defined.

In exploring the power relationship between doctor and patient, Emanuel and Emanuel (1992) consider three key elements: (i) the party that sets the agenda and goals of the consultation (the doctor, the doctor and patient jointly, or solely the patient); (ii) the manner in which the patient's values are handled (assumed by the physician to be similar to his or her own, collaboratively explored by the patient and the doctor, or unexplored); and (iii) the functional role adopted by the doctor (guardian, advisor, or consultant). A variety of power relations are possible depending on how the various core elements are combined. At one end of the scale is a paternalistic ('for your own good', or 'doctor knows best') style of interaction where the physician dominates in agenda and goal-setting, and in decision making about information and services. The doctor is obliged to act in the patient's best interest, but this action is mediated by an assumption of shared values between each party. The doctor assumes the functional model of guardian. At the other end of the scale is a style of interaction best referred to as consumerist, where the power position of doctor and patient may be juxtaposed. In the consumerist style of encounter, the patient determines the agenda and goals of the visit. A co-operating doctor proffers information and technical services demanded by the patient. The patient's values are accepted by the doctor unquestioningly. The flavour of the exchange would not be dissimilar to a customer purchasing an electrical appliance in a retail outlet. The power lies with the (patient) consumer, who can shop around for a better service if necessary. The doctor is relegated to the role of bio-technical consultant or advisor, with information and services supplied on the basis of patient preferences, professional norms and obligations notwithstanding. These are extremes at two ends of a continuum; clearly, there are various permutations in between. (See also Box 8.1.)

Box 8.1 *Models of doctor-physician interaction*

Salmon (2000) proposes that contemporary approaches to doctor-patient interaction suggests three distinct models, each based on a particular set of assumptions. These models construct the doctor-patient meeting in one of the following ways:

- An encounter between an inexpert (patient) and an expert (physician). (Assumption that the physician knows best.)
- An encounter between equal partners. (Assumption of a non-hierarchical relationship.)
- An encounter where the patient is in the role of consumer seeking (or buying) a service provided by a service-provider (the doctor). (Assumption that the doctor is selling a service.)

Clearly, there has been a shift away from theorising the doctor-patient relationship solely in terms of medical dominance. Newer models for professional behaviour tend to embrace notions of mutuality and equality (Salmon, 2000). These have made their way into policy documents in both Ireland and Britain, with the ideals of consumerism in relation to healthcare encouraged within the health services (Department of Health (Irl), 1992; Department of Health (UK) 1991; Seale, 2001). (For a further discussion of consumerism in relation to shifting healthcare policy, particularly in Ireland, see Chapter 13.) However, models for professional behaviour are merely theoretical constructs and do not necessarily reflect reality. In order to provide insights into the extent to which the elements of various models are experienced in actual patient-professional encounters, it is necessary to explore empirical studies. It is to these that the discussion will now turn.

There is some empirical evidence from Britain to suggest that patients are influencing their doctors' behaviour in the area of drug prescribing (Schwartz et al, 1989; Bradley, 1991). However, these studies have relied on the perspectives of physicians without exploring the patient's position. Britten (2001) notes that it is difficult to determine whether doctors are really pressurised by patients, or whether they attempt to justify poor prescribing decisions on the grounds of patient demands. While there is evidence that doctors believe that they over-prescribe on the basis of patients' expectations (Britten and Ukoumunne, 1997; Cockburn and Pit, 1997), there is also research to suggest that some patients are dissatisfied with what they believe to be excessive prescribing by their doctors (Lupton et al, 1991; Calnan, 1988; Britten, 1996). A recent survey of 250 GPs in Britain found that 80 per cent admitted that they over-prescribed anti-depressants, but their prescribing behaviour was to a large extent attributed to the shortage of therapy and counselling services available (*The Independent*, 30/3/04: 1)

A somewhat contradictory finding in the literature is that although patients are perceived by doctors to make demands for prescriptions, a considerable proportion do not take their prescribed medication (Stimson, 1974; Donovan, 1995). The notion of compliance with medication is an expectation of the medical profession, highlighting their self-perceived status position vis-à-vis the patient and an attitude of 'doctor knows best'. Nonetheless, between 30-50 per cent of patients are non-compliant with doctors' orders, suggesting that patients may exercise a good deal of control over health-related decisions beyond the medical encounter rather than within it (Britten, 2001). While patients may exercise control over their own treatment, Prior (2003: 53) raises questions about lay expertise, drawing on empirical evidence to suggest that because their knowledge is experiential and rarely sufficient to understand technical complexities, 'lay people can be wrong'.

Nonetheless, in spite of the rhetoric about patient-centred strategies for treatment options in general practice, Stevenson et al's (2000) British study found that the dominant pattern was that doctors did not share information with patients, nor did they encourage patients to share information with them. Lack of time was frequently cited by respondents as a reason for the dearth of information-sharing in medical encounters (Stevenson et al, 2000). However, even when information was proffered by patients, this was not acted upon; this mirrors a finding from an earlier study by Tuckett et al (1985). Some theorists have dismissed as impractical, both in terms of time and the unequal knowledge base possessed by each party, the notion that all decisions between physician and patient are shared decisions (Lelie, 2000). However, others have produced empirical evidence to argue that adopting a biopsychosocial perspective rather than a biomedical one is possible in approximately the same amount of encounter time (du Pré, 2000).

Patient-focused studies have found that patients value highly and have a preference for patient-centred medical encounters (Coyle, 1999; Krupat et al, 2000; Mechanic and Meyer, 2000). Coyle (1999) found a sense of dissatisfaction among hospital patients who reported little recognition by health staff of their feelings and sense of humanity. Mechanic and Meyer's (2000) study found that the caring component of the interaction mediated the degree to which patients' deemed doctors to be trustworthy. Patients had a limited basis for judging the worth of a doctor's technical skills, and frequently used aspects of interpersonal competence as indicators of technical competence. At the same time, these patients were aware that a good bedside manner was not always an indication of biophysical assessment and diagnostic abilities (Mechanic and Meyer, 2000).

The notion of increased consumerism has been linked to arguments that the professional status of medicine is in decline or is being de-professionalised (see Chapter 12). The hallmark of a profession is the possession of a unique body of knowledge by a particular group. However, as people become more and more educated about health issues, the knowledge gap between themselves and the professionals declines (Britten, 2001; Hardey, 1999). However, in spite of a better-educated and more articulate public, the extent to which deprofessionalisation has actually occurred, and the power of the medical profession diminished through consumerism, is widely believed to be very limited (Freidson, 1985; Elston, 1991; Gabe et al, 1994; Britten, 2001). Moreover, while the 1970s and 80s witnessed a large increase in the number of patients' associations in Britain and the United States, recent survey research suggests that the degree to which these groups exert an influence over conventional medicine is very limited (Wood, 2000). Wood (2000: 4) attempted to explain the limited degree of patient power found in research into patients' associations as follows:

> The usual explanation offered in the health studies literature focuses on dependency. Patients live in the shadow of doctors' professional power and autonomy, with the culture of 'doctor knows best' resting on the apparent scientific basis and complexity of modern medicine. Patients are largely passive consumers, grateful for the time and expertise of the

health professionals on whom they depend for treatment and therapy to improve their quality of life. This perception of patient dependency on healthcare providers who are accorded high social and political status is found not only in the academic literature but also among patients' association activists ...

In spite of consumer associations' limited power, Wood (2000) concluded that patients' associations did possess real political resources, but did not tend to use them, focusing instead on operating as support rather than campaigning groups. There was, however, evidence that some patients' associations influenced public policy, especially in the fields of mental illness and HIV/AIDS (Wood, 2000). In addition, some consumer movements have adopted an advocacy role. These groups include those lobbying on behalf of people with intellectual disability, the haemophiliac society, and mental health groups. In addition, the gay rights lobby in Ireland has been involved in the hospice movement.

Theoretical perspectives on professional-patient relations
Various theoretical positions have emerged within sociology that attempt to explain the nature of the relationship between doctors and patients. As will become clearer as the remainder of this chapter unfolds, some of these have a heavy focus on medical dominance, while others attempt to uncover patient-power in medical encounters.

The sick role – a functionalist perspective on power relations between lay people and physicians
One of the most dominant approaches to explain interactions between physicians and patients emerged during the 1950s in the work of the American sociologist Talcott Parsons (1951b, 1975), whose work we introduced in Chapter 2. As indicated in Chapter 2, Parsons developed a concept known as 'the sick role' to explain society's expectations of the illness behaviour of individuals. This perspective proposes that illness is 'an inherently undesirable state' (1975: 258), because it interferes with normal social activities (social order), most particularly work-related activities. However, this potentially deviant state may be legitimised and a sick person may be excused from his or her normal social role if that person is committed to recovering as quickly as possible, seeks medical advice if necessary, and is co-operative with that advice (Parsons, 1951b, 1975). Clearly, this suggests a power differential between the physician and patient, with the power vested in the doctor as a legitimate source of authority, who has been 'institutionally certified to be worthy of entrusting responsibility in the field of the care of health' (Parsons 1975: 266). Parsons (1975: 267) also noted the requirement for a good physician to be 'of high intelligence and moral probity' with elaborate formal training. Within Parson's theoretical

perspective, the doctor has the discretion to legitimate a person's sick leave or not. However, Parsons was not claiming that patients were entirely passive and docile in this relationship. Rather, he argued that there are varying degrees to which they participate actively in their own recovery. Nonetheless, Parsons (1975: 271-272) accepted the superiority of the physician in the professional patient relationship:

> ... with respect to the inherent functions of effective care and amelioration of conditions of illness, there must be a built-in institutionalized superiority of the professional roles, grounded in responsibility, competence, and occupational concern ... I fail to see how it is at all possible to eliminate the element of inequality. To go too far in attempting to do so would surely jeopardize the therapeutic benefits of the vast accumulation of medical knowledge and competence which our culture has painfully built up over a very long period.

The acceptance of this kind of power differential is a feature of the theoretical perspective within which Parson's work is located, namely structural functionalism. As indicated in Chapter 2, structural functionalism focuses on the **macro level** of society, and holds that social systems operate as integrated, cohesive and stable social units. Structural functionalism is concerned with how social order is maintained through individuals complying with social norms and conforming to legitimate social roles. The recovery of the sick person is important to restore 'satisfactory functioning in a system of social relationships' (Parsons, 1975: 258). Although, as indicated above, Parsons defends the agency of the patient, the doctor-patient relationship within sick-role theory is not generally regarded as the outcome of conflict, or as a power struggle (Lupton, 2003). Rather, the authority vested in the physician both at the **micro level** of patient encounters, and at the macro level of social respectability, is viewed as desirable to enabling the healing or curing process, and of benefit to the smooth running of society as a whole (Lupton, 2003). Within the structural functionalist position, those in the medical profession are deemed to be worthy holders of such power by virtue of their unique knowledge, their long and extended training and their commitment to altruistic work in serving the community. (See Chapter 12 for a detailed exploration and critique of professional power.)

The political economy perspective on lay-professional interactions
The political economy perspective on professional-patient relations problematises the consensual characterisation of relations between professionals and patients as expounded within the functionalist perspective (Lupton, 2003) (for an introduction to the political economy perspective, see Chapter 2). In view of the dominant position of medicine in healthcare, the perspective focuses predominantly on patient-physician relations, rather

than on relations between patients and other less powerful groups such as nurses. Rather than accepting hierarchical relations between doctors and patients on the basis of doctors' unique knowledge and extended training, political economists suggest that this power imbalance arises from a power struggle between medicine and a number of interest groups jostling with each other for dominance (Lupton, 2003). Thus, according to the political economy perspective, it is not on the basis of its service to society that medicine enjoys dominance and power, but rather for more self-serving reasons of occupational control and monetary gain (see Hyde and Roche-Reid (2004) for a political economy perspective on obstetric practice in Ireland). This perspective not only challenges medicine's apparently altruistic motives in healing the sick, but also links medical practices with a wider system of state and social control. It suggests that medicine's power and dominance is sustained and supported by the state (Navarro, 1986). An example of the way in which this could be said to happen in the Irish healthcare system is the state's sponsorship of private medicine (see Chapter 13).

Within the political economy perspective, it is argued that the state-sponsored medical profession operates to sustain a system of capitalism (Navarro, 1986). With regard to the specific issue of relations between the doctor and patient, how might the nature of these relations serve the interests of capitalism? On the assumption that the relationship between patient and doctor is hierarchical, with the doctor controlling the diagnosis, treatment and social process of the encounter, this relationship has been equated with the that of capitalist and worker (Navarro, 1976). In addition, the focus in medical encounters is on tackling disease at an individual level, thereby concealing the social, occupational and environmental causation of disease that permeates capitalist societies (Navarro, 1980). Put simply, the argument is as follows: In capitalist societies, workers are exploited because they work over and above the real value of their labour-power (Marx, 1867 [1971]). The excess value of their labour power is profit, and this is kept by the capitalist. Because workers come away with less money than the real value of their efforts, they are less likely to be able to create the basic conditions of good health, namely quality food, good housing, and a socially pleasant and stimulating environment. Workers (in many cases) accept the prevailing **ideology** that this is their lot, putting their circumstances down to their own individual failures. Going to the doctor for a cure for ailments, where the focus is on biological aspects of disease, sustains this ideology and detracts from exposing gross inequalities in the system in which the social determinants of good health are not evenly distributed among individuals and groups in society (Navarro, 1976).

Ehrenreich (1978) noted that social processes in the doctor-patient relationship have not generally been considered within the political economy perspective. Other perspectives have been stronger in this regard, namely the critical theory and Foucauldian approaches.

A critical theory perspective on patient-professional interactions
Some theorists have attempted to explain patient-professional interactions
in relation to the perspective of critical theory and in particular the work of
Jürgen Habermas (1984, 1987). (For an introduction to critical theory see
Chapter 3.) Habermas conceptualised two distinct perspectives in
explaining societies, the *system* and the *lifeworld*. The system represents the
realm of society associated with technical-scientific rationality, and is
mediated by power and money. The system requires efficiency and strategic
rationality in its operations (Andersen, 2000). Within the system, the
objectives of individuals are self-serving insofar as the goal is to maximise
the individual pursuit of utility or economic profit. Communication,
communicative reflection, evaluation of relationships and mutual
understanding are diminished (Andersen, 2000). The 'lifeworld', by
contrast, refers to the 'symbolic space' where meaning, solidarity and
personal identity are communicated verbally. It is concerned with the
subjective perspective and is orientated towards understanding. The
lifeworld is, therefore, created and reproduced linguistically, and comprises
culture, the social world and personality (Andersen, 2000). It encompasses
an implicit, pre-reflexive knowledge form of taken-for-granted everyday
assumptions (Habermas, 1984) and constitutes everyday life expressed in
the form of a 'natural attitude' as opposed to a 'scientific attitude' (Mishler,
1984). Applied to medical encounters, technological medicine comprises the
system, and this is manifested in 'the voice of medicine' and an exclusive
concern with bio-medical malfunctioning (Mishler, 1984). What is
problematic about the voice of medicine is its potential to suppress the voice
of the lifeworld, that is, the natural attitude within which the context of
illness is embedded.

Mishler (1984) drew upon Habermas' theory in a study of twenty-five
interactions between doctors and patients in hospitals and private practice
in the USA. In twenty-four out of the twenty-five cases studied, Mishler
identified a doctor-controlled interview with a typical pattern of
communication, whereby an ostensibly coherent and fluent dialogue was
characterised by frequent interruptions by the doctor, a lack of
acknowledgement of responses and unexplained digressions from topics.
Mishler suggested that the outcome of such a consultation style was a loss
of context in understanding the history and course of the problem and its
effects on the patient's everyday life. He argued that a more humane and
effective interaction style on the part of doctors would result from more
listening, asking open-ended questions, substituting technical language with
laypersons' terms (the voice of the lifeworld), and greater power-sharing.
Mishler concluded thay these interactions where the voice of medicine
dominated and suppressed the voice of the lifeworld constitute inhumane
and ineffective medicine.

Mishler's criticisms of medical interactions expressed in such strong
language formed a theoretical backdrop to a later study by Barry, C. A. et
al, 2001.

Barry et al questioned whether ignoring the lifeworld in medical encounters did actually result in less effective medical care, and also whether it undermined the patient as a unique human being. Drawing on data from thirty-five medical consultations in a British context in the late 1990s, they found that 'the voice of the lifeworld' was a feature of about half of all consultations in the study. They constructed four patterns of communication, namely, *strictly medicine, lifeworld blocked, lifeworld ignored* and *mutual lifeworld*. The strictly medicine category was evident in eleven consultations with nine doctors and was characterised by the exclusive use of the voice of medicine by both doctors and patients throughout the consultation. Interestingly, most of the patients in the strictly medicine category were satisfied with the style of communication and according to the researchers, the care and outcome were effective. Barry et al attempt to explain this by virtue of the fact that patients in this category presented without appointments, and with uncomplicated, single acute problems. They also propose as an explanation the possibility that these patients were socialised to expect a biomedical style of consultation with little input from the patient.

Both lifeworld blocked and lifeworld ignored were generally reported to be less than satisfactory by patients. In the former, the patients attempted to introduce aspects of the lifeworld in the dialogue, but these were actively silenced by the doctor. This was reported in eight consultations with seven doctors. Lifeworld ignored referred to situations where patients talked for a considerable amount of the consultation time in the voice of the lifeworld, while the physicians ignored this and confined their language exclusively to biomedical discourse. This occurred in seven encounters involving six doctors.

In the category mutual lifeworld, noted in nine consultations with eight doctors, the voice of the lifeworld dominated the consultation and was used heavily by both parties. In this style of interaction, patients often presented with psychological problems, and were long standing patients. These consultations were characterised by a sense of equality. They took longer to complete, and involved doctors speaking in the natural language of the everyday, listening without interruption, and using humour. Barry, C. A. et al (2001) note that specific communication styles were not exclusive to individual doctors. For example, some doctors whose consultation style was conceptualised as mutual lifeworld in one consultation were found to rely heavily on biomedical discourse in other consultations. The authors conclude that consultation styles by individual doctors are context-specific and far from fixed and stable.

A Foucauldian perspective on professional-patient relations
The theoretical perspective developed by Michel Foucault provides further insights into relations between professionals and patients. (See Chapters 1 and 2 for an introduction to Foucault's work, and Chapter 7 for an account

of Foucault's ideas on the body.) Foucault used the discipline of medicine as an example in his attempt to elucidate the relationship between knowledge and power at a broader societal level. For Foucault, power is not something that individuals or groups possess, but rather something that reveals itself in the course of interactions, and has a somewhat fluid rather than absolute nature (Foucault, 1994). This makes the notion of medical dominance problematic within Foucauldian thinking.

Even though there is usually no direct coercion involved in relations between patients and professionals, Foucault's analysis exposes the potential that medicine has in objectifying the body and in rendering human subjects docile. Lupton (1994: 112) highlights the voluntary characteristic of patient-professional relations as follows:

> Both the doctor and the patient ... subscribe to the belief of the importance of medical testing, constant monitoring and invasive or embarrassing investigative procedures in the interests of the patient. Explicit coercion is generally not involved; the patient voluntarily gives up the body to the doctor's or nurse's gaze because that is what people are socialised to expect.

Foucault (1973) explored the power that biomedicine held in defining bodies as deviant or normal and as needing control or being controlled. As indicated in earlier chapters, the practice of scrutinising the body though various scientific measures was coined the 'clinical gaze' by Foucault. It resulted in doctors having greater control over patients, who in turn became passive recipients of care.

The clinical gaze resulting in the surveillance of the body has been extended to surveillance of the workings of the mind with the more recent shift to holistic care within nursing and medicine (Armstrong, 1983a; Porter, 1997; May, 1992). Social, psychological and spiritual care have now come within the jurisdiction of healthcare workers, and arguably add another dimension to the socially controlling potential of medicine (Zola, 1972). This Foucauldian criticism of medicine's extended functions is clearly at variance with the Habermasian one presented earlier (Porter, 1997). While there is deep suspicion within Foucauldian thinking of the potential of holistic care to control all aspects of the mind and body, within Habermasian thinking holistic care is viewed as a positive attempt to encompass communicative value-rationality and mutual understanding into relationships between health professionals and patients (Porter, 1997).

The mediation of social divides on patient-professional interactions

As well as the pervasive effects of gender on healthcare encounters, there is evidence that patient-professional encounters are also influenced by a patient's sex, class, ethnicity, and age. (For a broader perspective on the impact of these social divides on health see Chapter 4.) Van Ryn and Burke

(2000) suggest that doctors may be particularly prone to using stereotypes, in view of their time pressures and the need to manage complex tasks in a brief time period. Stereotyping occurs in the processing of large quantities of complex information whereupon judgements are made about categories of people, and these evaluations are then generalised to all individuals within a particular category (Klopf, 1991).

Impact of gender on healthcare encounters

Prior to the 1970s, gender in professional encounters was not the focus of research (Miles, 1991). There was a belief that the medical encounter was an objective, detached, asexual one, focusing solely on the impartial facts of clinical pathology, and unaffected by the patient's socio-demographic characteristics. Since the 1970s, feminist sociologists have attempted to highlight that, like class and race (see the next sections), gender has a pervasive effect in healthcare interactions. This body of research has demonstrated that normative constructions of female behaviour, femininity and the female body impact upon healthcare encounters. In particular, the construction of women as docile, passive, submissive and unintelligent has been found to mediate interactions between women and health professionals. Feminist critics of medicine generally perceive the medical profession as an elite, patriarchal institution that sustains gender inequalities through its everyday practices.

Chesler's (1972) classic study of psychiatric practices noted that psychiatry regulated the production of masculinity and femininity and that categories of normality were created. For example, an acceptance of passivity and dependency was perceived as normal behaviour for women. Psychiatric labels were applied to women who rejected the female role, or demonstrated ambivalence about it. Lesbianism and promiscuity were treated as pathologies within psychiatry. (See also Chapter 10 on mental health and illness.) Macintyre (1977) observed that in general practice, physicians used their personal value judgements (consistent with wider social values) to assess single pregnant women's situation, and made a medical decision based upon this. Single pregnant women who presented were constructed by GPs as either 'normal as married' (that is, in a stable relationship), 'nice girl[s] who made a mistake' (one partner, and therefore not sexually promiscuous), or 'bad or promiscuous girl[s]'. Those in the last category were more likely to be refused an abortion. This demonstrates that expectations about proper female behaviour were being reinforced by medicine and physicians were not making objective decisions. In a later analysis, Macintyre (1991) focused on how 'normal reproduction' was socially constructed in medicine. The idea of maternal instinct (a contentious concept) is based on the notion that women have an instinctive drive to bear children. However, post-natal experiences of depression were perceived as normal for married women, but considered to be related to ambivalence about the baby for single women. The contradiction here is that while women are meant to have maternal instinct (although this has been strongly contested by some feminists), a biological phenomenon, responses to motherhood (such as depression) were associated with the women's civil or social status. Indeed, Macintyre found that in some instances, women's own definition of their circumstances were seen to be secondary to what medical professionals diagnosed as their real situation. Hyde's (1997) Dublin study noted that during medical encounters with single women, the pregnancy was often immediately framed as problematic. Physicians frequently introduced the notion of adoption as an option, and pressurised some single women to consult with the social worker. Some participants in the study were questioned by obstetricians about their arrangements for childcare or capacity to mother.

Oakley's (1980, 1995) classic study of women's experiences of obstetric practice found that women's own knowledge about their pregnancies was often discounted by obstetricians. She noted an attitude of 'doctor knows best', and medicalisation of the pregnancy, with large numbers of healthy pregnant women being subjected to a range of medical and pharmacological techniques as routine. (The theme of the medicalisation of childbirth is taken up again in Chapter 11.)

There is also evidence that the treatment that female patients receive differs from that offered to men. For example, an analysis of US data between 1981 and 1985 demonstrated that a female having renal dialysis had just 70 per cent of the chance of an equivalent male to secure a transplant (Held et al, 1988). Women in the 46-60 age group had just half the chance. The AMA Council on Ethical and Judicial Affairs concluded that the main reason appeared to be the relatively low value assigned to women's contribution to society relative to that of men (AMA Council on Ethical and Judicial Affairs cited in Doyal, 1994). Drawing on US data, Tobin et al (1987) found that men were six times more likely to be given diagnostic catheterisation than women presenting with the same symptoms. More recent studies have found a continued gender bias with women with comparable symptoms to men being less likely to receive cardiac diagnostic tests and interventions (Steingart et al 1991; Di Cecco et al, 2002; Burnstein et al, 2003). Similar findings were observed in the South West Thames Region of the UK, with males being 60 per cent more likely than females with the same clinical condition to be offered coronary artery bypass surgery or angioplasty (Petticrew et al, 1993).

There is now a growing number of studies to indicate that female doctors interact differently with patients than do male doctors (Langwell, 1982; Preston-Whyte et al, 1983; Cypress, 1984;). These studies generally suggest that female doctors spend more time with their patients than do male doctors, and that they also engage with patients to a greater extent in partnership building.

Impact of socio-economic status on healthcare interactions

Health professionals are located in the higher socio-economic groups (SEGs), and are likely to hold middle-class values about health and health behaviour that may be at variance with those of patients from lower SEGs. Since the 1970s, British studies on doctor-patient encounters have identified differences in how doctors interact with patients from various SEGs. It was noted that doctors spend less time with their working-class patients, and that such patients asked fewer questions and received fewer explanations (Cartwright and O'Brien, 1976; Tuckett et al, 1985).

More recent research supports the notion that socio-economic status influences doctors' perceptions of patients. An Irish-based study conducted at a GP surgery in Bray, County Wicklow, compared the diagnostic techniques employed for private patients compared to public patients, all of whom had coronary heart disease. Seventy-seven per cent of the private patients compared with 25 per cent of public patients had had angiograms[14]. In addition, all apart from one of the private patients had had an exercise electrocardiogram, while 15 of the public patients had not been offered this procedure (McManus, 2001, cited in Wren, 2003). In a US study by van Ryn and Burke (2000) of post-angiogram encounters between doctors and patients, findings indicated that patients in lower SEGs were rated more negatively than their middle-class counterparts on personality characteristics (such as lack of self-control and irrationality) and intelligence levels. Compared to patients in higher SEGs, patients in lower SEGs:

> ... were rated as less likely to be compliant with cardiac rehabilitation, less likely to desire a physically active lifestyle, less likely to have significant career demands, less likely to have responsibility for a care of a family member and more likely to be judged to be at risk for inadequate social support (van Ryn and Burke, 2000: 821).

Impact of ethnicity on healthcare interactions

Does racism permeate the delivery of healthcare, albeit unconsciously in some cases? In relation to the UK situation, Smaje (1995) notes the difficulty of linking specific poor practices in health services directly to racism, when they may actually be associated with clients' low socio-economic status or may be standard practice for all. Without comparing the treatment that people from ethnic minorities experience compared to the indigenous population when using the health service, it is difficult to determine the independent effect of racism. However, drawing on McNaught (1987), Dyson and Smaje (2001: 54) identify a number of possible effects of racism within the health services that include:

---

14. An angiogram is a diagnostic test used in the diagnosis of coronary artery disease.

... inaccuracies in patient reception and handling; consultations with poor or no explanations or stereotyping of the patient; pressure to consent to treatment on the basis of inadequate explanation; perceptions of the minority ethnic client as less 'intelligent' or a 'bad' patient ...

Culley (2001) refers to a number of UK studies that found negative attitudes among health professionals towards members of minority ethnic groups in a range of healthcare settings (Ahmad et al, 1991; Pharoah, 1995; Bowler, 1993; Hayes, 1995; Fernando, 1991; Bhugra and Bahl, 1999; Douglas, 1995; Ahmad, 2000; Ahmad and Atkin, 1996). One such study (Bowler, 1993) found that midwives in an English hospital considered Asian patients to be un-intelligent, non-compliant, mis-users of the health service, over-emotional, poor at tolerating pain, and demanding. Coyle (1999) found that eighteen out of the twenty-one non-white people that she studied felt that they were being stereotyped by health staff, and women from ethnic minority groups believed that their intelligence had been undermined in such encounters. Similarly, van Ryn and Burke (2000) found that, even when sex, age, income and education were controlled, doctors rated black patients as less intelligent than white patients. Black patients were also perceived to be at greater risk of noncompliance with their medical regimes (van Ryn and Burke, 2000).

In one of the few Irish studies concerning the maternity care experiences of refugee and asylum seeking women (referred to earlier in Chapter 4), Kennedy and Murphy-Lawless (2000) make little reference to direct episodes of racism experienced by study participants from health staff. However, language and communication problems were reported.

Studies within Britain have highlighted structural problems with the services provided to ethnic minority groups, such as the shortage of female doctors (preferred by Asian women) and the limited number of interpreters and advocates (Chapple, 1998; Chan, 2000). Gerrish (1999) found that the public health nursing service provision was much greater in GP group practices serving a predominantly white population compared to an inner city GP practice with a larger ethnic minority population. The basis for the deployment of public health nurses in this case seemed to be based on institutional decisions.

Evidence from an emergency room study (Hunt et al, 1988) in the United States provides further evidence that racism mediates medical encounters. Hunt et al investigated sixty consecutive medical records of teenage patients admitted through casualty with acute abdominal pain. The patients were categorised according to ethnic group and socio-economic status and this information was cross-matched with whether a sexual history had been obtained. Findings demonstrated that a far higher number of black and Hispanic young women had had sexual histories taken than had white middle-class adolescent girls. The author concluded that a sensitivity to delicate questions was restricted to the white middle-class girls.

Racism in healthcare is not confined to episodes of racism towards patients emanating from professionals. There are reports of racism by patients directed at healthcare staff from ethnic minority groups (including doctors), and indeed of racism between patients themselves (Gunaratnam, 2001). Both Hughes (1988) and Porter (1993) found examples of racism in relations between professionals themselves. Furthermore, in September 2001, the BMA was found guilty of racial discrimination for failing to support the case of a surgeon from an ethnic minority group who had been rejected for promotion. The surgeon was awarded £815,000 Stg in damages by an employment tribunal; the BMA lost an appeal taken in March 2004 (*The Independent*, 30/03/04: 32).

Impact of age on healthcare interactions
Very little research has been conducted on the mediating effects of age in patient-professional encounters, signifying the invisibility of older people in society (see the sociology of ageing in Chapter 9). In one of the few studies where the impact of age was analysed, Coyle (1999) noted that older women reported that doctors dismissed their feelings of pain and discomfort as age-related, and failed to make a diagnosis of the problem. In relation to styles of interactions, it has been found that older patients tend to have a preference for doctor-led interactions (Johnson et al, 1995; Irish, 1997). A number of studies have found that older patients remain passive in medical encounters in order to avoid being viewed as challenging or disrespectful (Beisecker and Beisecker, 1990; Breemhaar et al, 1990; Blanchard et al, 1988). Beisecker (1988) noted a tendency among older patients to perceive the doctor as an authority figure and they usually allowed the physician to control the amount of information they needed.

Summary
- At a conceptual level, a shift has occurred within sociological scholarship from constructing the physician as a powerful and dominant social actor in health encounters, to considering the potential for patients to influence such encounters.
- Discourses of consumerism have now entered the rhetoric of patient-professional encounters.
- Empirical evidence varies, with some studies suggesting that patients do indeed influence the process and outcome of health interactions, while others suggest that their influence is more marked beyond the encounter than within it.
- Evidence suggests that patients value the caring dimension and mutuality of encounters with professionals.
- Overall, the extent to which the power of the medical professional has been reduced through consumerism is widely believed to be very limited.

- In sociological literature, diverse theoretical positions (functionalism, political economy, critical theory, and a Foucauldian approach) have been used to explain the nature of patient-professional encounters, offering alternative interpretations into how patient-professional encounters may be understood.
- Studies focusing on particular patient categories and particular social divides (based on gender, socio-economic status, ethnicity and age) have found that, far from being objective and impartial, patient-professional encounters are influenced by these categories and divides.

Topics for discussion and reflection
1. What style of encounter do you consider to be the most appropriate between health professionals and patients?
2. In your opinion has lay expertise gone too far in the current climate of healthcare?

NINE

Sociology of the lifecycle: childhood, ageing, dying and death

In contemporary Irish society, and elsewhere in the Western world, we refer to various stages of the lifecycle as childhood, teenage years, adulthood, middle age and old age. Specific meanings and expectations are attached to these categories which vary historically and across cultures (Jones, 1994). In this sense, these categories are socially constructed – there is no natural script for what these phases mean; rather, human beings develop and redefine meanings associated with different parts of the lifecycle as societies change and new norms emerge. In this chapter, we consider phases of the lifespan in relation to childhood, ageing, dying and death. It will become clear as the chapter unfolds that all of these stages have been influenced by the notion of **modernity,** that is, the transition from a traditional society to an industrially developed one, with associated changes in people's values and attitudes. (See Chapter 1 for an introduction to the concept of modernity.) The meaning and experiences of parts of a person's life continue to change and are shaped to varying degrees by contemporary discourses in a period of **late modernity.** We will begin by exploring the infant's first introduction to the social world through the process of socialisation, and how societal norms influence the experiences of childhood. Discourses on the family will then be explored with particular reference to health issues. We move through the lifecycle to consider how ageing, particularly old age, is constructed in contemporary societies, and more specifically in Ireland. Finally, we discuss dominant and competing discourses on the issue of death and dying.

Socialisation
A key theme in sociology is the concept of *socialisation* which refers to the process whereby an individual learns the norms, values and roles approved by the society in which they live. Individuals learn to adopt the norms and customs of everyday social interaction of the culture in such a way that they do not feel they are being brain-washed (Marsh et al, 2000). In the process of socialisation, the expectations and approved ways of behaving become

absorbed unconsciously. As Marsh (2000: 29) notes, 'the requirements, rules and standards of a society become part of their own identity, motives and desires so imperceptibly that they are experienced as natural and unique although they are clearly social and uniform'.

Almost thirty years ago, Berger and Berger (1976) clearly described aspects of the socialisation of the infant that help us to understand the process more clearly. They describe how many of the infant's early experiences are *not* social but physical or non-social, for example the experiences of hunger, heat, cold, being stung by a bee, and so forth. Nonetheless, they note that from the very start the infant interacts with other human beings, some of whom become very important to him.[15] Of critical importance is the fact that the non-social aspects of the infant's experiences are 'mediated and modified by others' (1976: 17), for example the baby's hunger (a non-social experience) can only be alleviated by the intervention of another (a social interaction). How often and at what times a baby will be fed is directed by the parent and, in this way, the latter is creating the pattern through which the child experiences the world. As Berger and Berger (1976: 57) suggest, the child's physical needs adjust to the time set by the adult. They state:

> ... society not only imposes its patterns upon the infant's behaviour but reaches inside him to organise the functions of his stomach. The same observation pertains to excretion, to sleeping and to other physiological processes that are endemic to the organism.

Berger and Berger focus on the role of the mother in the socialisation process, reflecting the highly gendered division of labour in the 1970s when they produced their ideas. They illucidate how the mother's childrearing practices are part of the broader pattern of the society in which she lives (the norm of childrearing in that culture). There are many choices she could make about infant feeding, responding to crying, toilet training and so forth. The way that she responds, they note, has been learnt within her own culture, that is from wider social practices. (We know that childrearing practices vary over time and across SEGs and cultures, for example the practice of smacking children was widespread up to relatively recently.) Berger and Berger (1976: 58) refer to the norm of infant care as an 'invisible collective entity', rather than the mother acting alone, unaffected by the parenting practices around her. Whatever methods the parent uses, they suggest, these are experienced in very absolute ways by the child because the adult holds greater power in the situation, and because the child is not aware of alternatives (Berger and Berger, 1976).

---

15. Berger and Berger (1976) refer to the child as a male, reflecting unconscious sexism within sociology in the 1970s.

There is evidence that the socialisation process is different for girls and boys, and that children learn gender-approved behaviour from the world around them. The images that children receive from story books about their place in the world, for example, were the subject of a classic US study in the 1970s (Weitzman et al, 1972). Weitzman et al found that the messages that these storybooks send out are that for girls attention and praise may be gained for physical attractiveness, while boys are approved for their achievements and cleverness. Women's status was defined in terms of their relationship to men – they were the *wives* of important men, but were not presented as being important in their own right, reinforcing traditional sex role stereotypes. In the current period, while books produced for children tend to be more gender balanced, traditional favourites continue to be widely available. The theme of poor attractive girl with feminine characteristics and talents meeting a wealthy prince or king who transforms her life presents a particular gendered pathway to small boys and girls.

More recent sociological theory challenges earlier perspectives in sociology that children are almost entirely acted upon and are passive objects being processed, as earlier notions of socialisation suggested. Instead it has been proposed that a child can actively resist, collaborate and to some degree shape his or her world (Corsaro, 1997).

The impact of modernity on the construction of childhood

Before the period of industrialisation,[16] the concept of childhood had little meaning, as children worked beside their parents (Aries, 1973). The role of children changed dramatically with the growth of capitalism and industrialisation; the spacial separation of home and work meant that the child's role changed from that of worker to dependent, with parents expected to provide food, clothing and shelter (Thane, 1982). According to Kennedy (2001), evidence suggests that in the past children in Ireland were exploited for their labour. In was not until the nineteenth century that minimum protection for children was enacted. However, as Kennedy notes, while an idealised notion of childhood began to surface in the late 1800s among privileged groups, children continued to work for their parents until long after this period. Ireland's late industrialisation meant that even by 1961, more people were employed in agriculture than in industry, with implications for the role of children. In 1964, almost two-thirds of sixteen year olds in Ireland were no longer in full-time education; children, both boys and girls, were an important source of labour, especially on family farms (Kennedy, 2001).

---

16. The transition to industrialisation occurred approximately 200 years ago in Britain and is bound up with the notion of modernity. It was not until the 1960s that Ireland experienced its first wave of industrialisation. (See Chapters 1 and 2 for an account of the project of modernity.)

The notion of the teenage years illustrates the socially constructed notion of phases in the lifecycle. Until the 1970s in Ireland, it was common for children to leave school at fourteen years and to enter paid employment, or work on the family farm (Kennedy, 2001). A normative practice was that these young people would forfeit a large portion of their earnings to support the family (Kennedy, 2001). With the extension of compulsory schooling, and changes in society more widely, the dependency years have been extended, and children are now seen as a financial drain rather than an asset during the teenage years. The societal expectation of young people going out to work and providing financial support for their families also appears to have changed. In the current period, the notion of teenage years conjures up images of self-centred, demanding youths who expect immediate gratification. New cultural values include 'the quest for hedonism, an obsessive concern with the Self, and immediate gratification' (Delanty, 1999: 54).

Children's rights, healthist ideologies and the regulation of childhood

The notion of protecting children's **labour power** from being exploited even by their own parents is bound up with changing perceptions of the role of children in society and the emergence of a discourse on children's rights. The UN Convention on the Rights of the Child, comprising a Bill of Rights for all children was ratified by Ireland in 1992 (DoHC, 1999a). The advent of a discourse advocating rights for children is generally viewed as a positive development. However, as Irish society has changed, particularly with industrialisation and post-industrialisation, the capacity of the state to regulate childhood has increased. Compulsory schooling, mandated by the state, has had a considerable influence in how childhood is experienced. The daily routine of classroom life, a dominant feature of contemporary childhood, is very different from the daily routine of working for or beside one's parents.

Associated with the discourse of children's rights is the notion of child protection, and child surveillance. Both child protection and child surveillance denote the extension of a regulating and socially controlling role over children that extends beyond parental powers, although it is acknowledged that the parents still have the primary responsibility for their children (DoHC, 2001b). Under the Childcare Act (1991), health boards have a statutory duty to promote the welfare of children under the age of eighteen who are not receiving an adequate standard of care and protection (DoHC, 1999a). Child protection and child surveillance have to a large extent been associated with a healthist ideology.[17] Indeed, that the formerly

---

17. As indicated in Chapter 5, healthism refers to the pursuit of health through the practice of imposing on the society as a whole the dominant beliefs of the powerful as to how people (in this case parents and children) should conduct themselves.

entitled 'Department of Health' amended its name to the 'Department of Health and Children' in 1997 bears witness to the degree to which childhood has become medicalised and mediated by healthism. Child care services, family support initiatives, and even socially-challenging behaviour come under the auspices of the Department of Health and Children (DoHC, 2001b: 71). Health professionals are acknowledged to have a major role in child protection, with a remit to 'promote the welfare of children through health promotion and health *surveillance* programmes' (emphasis added) (DoHC 1999a: 52).

The regulating influence of health professionals is evident throughout the years of childhood – the public health nurse's post-natal visit, the six-week medical check-up of the infant, and subsequent developmental checks at particular stages. The child's physical, psychological, social, linguistic and toileting behaviours and home environment are collectively normalised, and any aberrations are noted, investigated and often referred to other health experts in an effort to re-align the deviation with cultural expectations. Socially acceptable childrearing practices have changed historically. For example, Berger and Berger (1976) refer to studies that describe highly punitive measures used to toilet train children in the USA in the 1960s which included the use of enemas by parents to regulate the toddler's bowel action according to the routines of the adult world. Such a practice in contemporary society would be highly likely to involve social and health services, as it is no longer seen as acceptable. Similarly, as indicated earlier, the practice of smacking children, which was widely endorsed until the very recent period, is now generally discouraged by child care and health experts. Indeed, 'use of excessive force in handling' comes under the definition of child physical abuse (DoHC, 1999a: 32).

Throughout the school years, contemporary measures to subtly regulate children's behaviour are facilitated by the social and personal health education programmes which present ideas about aspects of a healthy lifestyle (DoHC, 2001b). It was noted in the recent *Health Strategy* (DoHC, 2001b: 30) that many adults and children 'did not adhere to the national healthy eating guidelines', insinuating a degree of deviance associated with non-compliance. In addition, reference is made to the notion of children as 'active' participants (DoHC, 2001b: 136). While this recognises the agency of children and accords with contemporary ways of constructing the contribution of children (Corsaro, 1997), it also assigns them to a share of responsibility 'in shaping their own health and well-being' (DoHC, 2001b: 136).

Parenting is also influenced by a regulating healthism. Parents are regularly confronted with messages, mainly from the medical profession, to immunise their children against common childhood diseases, with routine reminders and normative expectations that children should be immunised. The recent Irish government's *Health Strategy* (DoHC, 2001b: 65) proposed that 'national minimum standards and targets for immunisation uptake, surveillance and screening will be drawn up'. Some 'lay' groups, such as the Cork-based Hope organisation have aired doubts about the validity of medical knowledge around vaccines, in spite of medical evidence indicating that vaccines are safe (Taylor et al, 2002)[18]. Such groups are sceptical about the objectivity of research into the safety and efficacy of vaccines on the grounds that these medicines are produced by pharmaceutical companies who have a vested interest in promoting them, and provide a lucrative income for medical professionals who administer them.

Changes in the family associated with modernity

Ireland did not experience an industrial revolution as happened in the eighteenth and nineteenth centuries in other Western societies (see Chapter 1), and did not begin to experience changes in family life associated with industrialisation until the last fifty years, with the first wave of modernisation. Since the 1930s, family life in Ireland has undergone rapid change over a short period that took much longer in other countries (Fahey, 1995; Kennedy, 2001; see also Corcoran and Pellion, 2002), with a proliferation of family types in the very recent period (See Box 9.1). Economic changes are perceived to be central to changes in the family, because the conventional wisdom within sociology is that economic changes bring with them changes in political thinking and in the values that people hold, and these affect how people relate to one another.

Within sociology, constructions of the family have been crudely divided into two types: the pre-industrial family and the modern family. The pre-industrial family is generally believed to have been close-knit, and extended to include wider kin such as grandparents. Religious values were deemed to have been central in regulating conduct between individuals. People worked on the land, and while inheritance of property was a concern for property-owning groups, for all classes the family operated as an economic unit and depended on producing its own goods and services (Bilton et al, 1996). In pre-industrial society, home and workplace were often merged, with childrearing groups cross-cutting production groups. The modern family, on the other hand, has been described as nuclear consisting only of parents and their children, with roles within the family organised along gendered lines (breadwinner father and nurturing mother) (Parsons, 1951b).

18. In 1998, the debate about the safety of immunisations intensified after the publication of an article by Wakefield et al (1998) in *The Lancet*, suggesting a link between the MMR vaccine and autism. In 2004, the debate took a new twist when it was alleged that there was a conflict of interest in Wakefield et al's research that had not been declared to the editors of *The Lancet* at the time of submission of the article (Horton, 2004). Ten of Wakefield's original research colleagues retracted their earlier scientific conclusions (Murch et al, 2004) while Wakefield and a minority of his colleagues defended their position and integrity (Wakefield et al, 2004).

Box 9.1 *Major changes in the structure of families in Ireland with the process of modernisation.*

- A reduction in family size and birth rate. The birth rate fell from 21.4 in 1950 to 13.5 (per 1,000 in the population) for the years 1994 and 1995 (CSO, 2003b). However, there has since been an upward trend to 15.4 for the year 2002 (CSO, 2003b). In 2003, Total Period Fertility Rate[19] for Ireland was 1.89 (CIA World Factbook, 2004) compared to 2.96 in 1982. However, Ireland continues to have the highest fertility rate among countries in the EU (International Reform Monitor, 2004).[20] Contraception has been legally available in Ireland for married people since 1979, and for single people (with age restrictions) since 1985.

- In the 1950s Ireland had the lowest marriage rate in Europe and very high celibacy rates. The high rates of non-marriage started around 1900 and continued until the late 1950s (Breen et al, 1990).

- An increase in the marriage rate began in the 1960s and peaked in the mid 1970s. In 1950, the marriage rate (per 1,000 in the population) was 5.4. For 1972, 1973, and 1974, it was 7.4. The marriage rate began to fall thereafter to 4.4 by 1997. In 1999 there was an increase in the marriage rate to 4.9, and to 5.1 by 2002 (CSO, 2003b). While the marriage rate in Ireland was among the lowest in the EU in 1990, the falling marriage rate in other European countries since then has put Irish marriage rates on a par with those of many other European countries such as Austria, Luxemburg and Switzerland (World Statistics, 2004).

- In the earlier part of the twentieth century, the average age at marriage for both men and women in Ireland was higher than that in the rest of Europe. Age at marriage fell in mid-1970s and has been rising ever since. The more recent rise in age at which people are marrying is echoed across every member state of the EU. In 1992, age at first marriage for women was considerably higher in Ireland than the European average (26.3 as compared with 24.5) with only Denmark, Sweden and Finland having a higher average age at marriage (O'Connor, 1998). The most recent national figures available are for the year 1996, when the average age at marriage for men was recorded as 30.2 years, and for women 28.4 years (CSO, 2003b).

- There has been an increase in lone-headed families, and especially in non-marital childbearing. By 2002, 31 per cent of births were non-marital compared to 1.5 per cent in 1960 and 2.6 per cent in 1970 (CSO, 2003b).

- There has been a change in female employment patterns with a large increase in the number of women in the labour force, and more recently, married women in the labour force. In 1971, just 28 per cent of Irish women participated in the labour force (CSO, 1997 cited in O'Connor 1998). By 2002 the figure had increased to almost 49 per cent (CSO, 2003a). This is close to the European average.

- There has been an increase in marital breakdown. According to the 2002 Census data, 133,800 people were recorded as being either separated or divorced, an increase from 87,800 in 1996 (CSO, 2004b).

Until the last quarter of the twentieth century, the Catholic Church in Ireland was a major regulatory source in people's lives. Religious beliefs and reverence to church leaders operated as social control mechanisms over the number of children a person had, their sexual practices, their dietary norms (fasting and abstinence were governed around a church calendar), and matters of the mind such as self-control, contrition and conscience. Lust, anger, sloth and so forth were constructed as deadly sins and human weaknesses, and regulated by religious power. In recent decades these human characteristics have come under the control of medicine, and one is now more likely to be referred to a physician than to a priest for problems relating to any of these 'sins'. The last quarter of the twentieth century has witnessed the decreasing influence of the church in state policies in Ireland, and an increasingly influential medical profession in regulating areas of life that previously fell within the jurisdiction of the church. This regulating influence has already been referred to above in relation to how parents raise their children.

Prior to the increase in state control over childcare in the nineteenth and twentieth centuries, families were deemed to be almost exclusively responsible for their children's health and wellbeing. Indeed, included among the traditional roles of the family was that the family would maintain the health of its members. Since the 1960s, the notion of family as an analytical category has been deconstructed by feminist sociologists who have proposed that it is not the family *per se* that maintains the health of family members, but rather women within families. This health work of women is unpaid, invisible and undervalued (Oakley, 1974). Finch and Groves (1983) drew attention to the unpaid labour of women caring for chronically ill or handicapped family members and dependent older relatives. In the case of very poorly paid home helps in Ireland, who care mainly for (unrelated) older people in the latters' home, almost all are women (O'Donovan, 1997). The ideal home help according to health boards in Ireland, is a 'capable mature woman [with] some experiences of caring and whose interest in the work is not determined primarily by the level of pay' (Lundström and McKeown, 1994: 156). This conception of the ideal carer perpetuates the ideology of traditional gender roles with exploitative consequences for women (O'Donovan, 1997).

In addition to the invisible caring work undertaken by women for sick, dependent relatives or those with special needs, feminists argue that routine

19. The TPFR is derived from the age-specific fertility rates in the current year. It represents the projected number of children a woman would have if she experienced age-specific fertility rates while progressing from age 15-49 years. A value of 2.1 is generally considered to be the level at which the population would replace itself in the long run, ignoring migration (CSO, 1999).

20. This pertains to comparisons among countries of the EU before the Union expanded in May 2004.

women's work in the home is unpaid, undervalued, unjust and creates economic dependency (Moller Okin, 1989; Walby, 1990). Recent research from Ireland suggests that women continue to undertake the bulk of childcare and domestic tasks (Kiely, 1995; Rubery et al, 1995; Eurobarometer, 1997; Fine-Davis and Clarke, 2002). It has been difficult to observe historical trends in the Irish context because the use of differing methodologies make comparisons over time problematic. However, a comparative analysis of the domestic division of labour in Britain between 1975 and 1997 has shown that while men have increased their engagement in domestic tasks over that period, the outcome remains unequal (Sullivan, 2000). Men in manual/clerical class households who were historically most traditional had also improved their contribution to cooking and cleaning tasks (see Box 9.2).

Box 9.2 *Changes in the domestic division of labour in Britain over two decades.*

Sullivan (2000) summarised the main changes in the domestic division of labour between 1975 and 1997 as follows:

- a reduction in gender inequality in the performance of some traditionally female tasks
- an increase in the proportional time that men from lower SEGs contribute which makes their contribution almost on a par with men in higher SEGs
- a considerable increase in more egalitarian couples, particularly where both partners are in full-time paid employment.

However, overall, in spite of these improvements, women still undertook several times more housework than men.

Old age

Ireland has an increasing number of older people in its population (see Box 9.3).

Box 9.3 *The older population in Ireland*

- Estimates suggest that in 2001, 11.2 per cent of the population of the Republic of Ireland were aged 65 and over (National Council on Ageing and Older People, 2004).
- It is projected that this figure will rise significantly over the next ten years to over 14 per cent of the general population by the year 2011, while the overall population in the country is expected to stabilise (National Council on Ageing and Older People, 2004).

The notion of old age, like childhood, is a socially and culturally shifting construct (Jones, 1994). In other words, the norms associated with being older vary over time and in different socio-cultural contexts, and the nature of ageing is influenced by how societies perceive ageing (Edmondson, 1997). There are societal age-based expectations about how older people ought to behave and present themselves. The popular term 'mutton dressed as lamb', for example, is used to describe older people (usually women) who deviate from normative age-appropriate standards of dress. Age-appropriate housing in the form of retirement homes or sheltered housing for older people is now a feature of contemporary Irish society, a phenomenon unheard of prior to industrialisation.

The notion of compulsory retirement, a central feature of industrially developed societies, is seen to be problematic in that it suddenly excises people out of the **public realm** of employment and forces them to live on income levels below – and sometimes very much below – those of the actively employed population (Layte, 2001). This situation reflects the low value and diminished power of older people in industrially developed societies. While retirement is actually welcomed by many older people, a recent survey in Ireland suggested that approximately 70 per cent of 55-69 year olds currently in employment favoured a more gradual system of withdrawal from the workforce (Fahey and Russell, 2001). The state welfare system of industrially developed societies has also been subject to criticism. It has been suggested that state policies developed in the nineteenth and twentieth centuries framed the notion of 'old age' as a social problem (Macintyre, 1977). Prior to the introduction of the old age pension in 1908 in Ireland and the UK (Edmondson, 1997), older people worked until they succumbed to poor health and entered the workhouse or sought parish relief, or until their savings were sufficient to sustain them until death (Jones, 1994). While the old age pension protects older people from absolute poverty, the construction of old age as a financial burden emerged strongly during the 1970s following the economic fallout of the oil crisis (Walker, 1999).

The fluctuating meaning of old age within a society may be seen in discourses of ageing embedded in official texts, even within a relatively brief historical period. The economic needs of a society appear to have influenced historical constructs of ageing. In Ireland from the mid-1970s to the mid-1990s, negative attitudes about older people, or ageism, in the labour force abounded (Murphy, 2001). The expulsion of older workers from the workforce through redundancy or early retirement was commonplace during this period (Murphy, 2001). However, by the mid-1990s, in a climate of labour shortages, the emphasis shifted to integrating older people into the economic realm. A statement from Tom Kitt (Kitt 2001: 10), then Minister for Labour, Trade and Consumer Affairs, made at a conference aimed at addressing employment and retirement among the over fifty-fives, implicitly suggests that drawing on the economic resources of the older population is a last resort:

> To date, policies have focussed on increasing participation in the workforce, reducing unemployment and increasing immigration. Given the limited scope to tap further into these sources, and the continued need to tackle labour and skills shortages, the government has given consideration to increasing the participation of older people in the workplace ... From an economic viewpoint, the issue of retaining people in the workforce longer becomes significant – a reversal of the situation that prevailed in the past when early retirement was encouraged in order to create employment for younger people.

Concessions made to older people in the form of special offers, discounts, travel passes and so forth, may also be considered ageist – they demonstrate to some extent the acceptance of a less than adequate income for older people (see Jones, 1994). Although many older people welcome these, they also serve to construct older people as poor and dependent (Jones, 1994). However, there are many diverse sub-groups of older people across Europe, some of whom are relatively wealthy, while others are relatively disadvantaged (Edmondson, 1997; Walker, 1999).

Walker (1999) notes that older people in most European countries were excluded from political participation since the post-war period. However, in recent years there has been a move towards greater political participation among older people, although, on the whole, political activism among older people has been marginal.

Positive ageing

Recent sociological accounts of old age have focused on the body as a source of analysis (Featherstone and Hepworth, 1991; Chaney, 1995; Featherstone and Wernick, 1995; Hepworth, 1995). These suggest that negative societal constructions of the declining body and visible bodily changes have problematised the older population as a whole (Katz, 1996). A dominant perspective in contemporary Western societies is to try to resist the appearance of old age as much as possible – clearly, youth is associated with beauty, and ageing is seen as something negative (see Hepworth, 1995).

Hepworth (1995) argues that since old age is viewed as a social problem, society discourages or even punishes deviant types of ageing, that is, ageing that is self-indulgent or that succumbs to social dependency, unless this dependency is perceived to be really necessary. The alternative to deviant ageing is positive ageing – that is, the pursuit of an independent and individual lifestyle in older years. Society encourages and approves of this style of ageing (Hepworth, 1995). Associated with the notion of positive ageing, a knowledge base on health promotion for older people has developed in recent years (Bernard, 2000). Arguably, this has all the potential for social regulation and control of older people that permeates society more generally through the ideology of the *Health for All* movement (see Skrabanek, 1994 and Chapter 14).

Hepworth (1995) problematises the notion of positive ageing, and conceptualises it as a social control mechanism that reduces the burden of ageing for society as a whole by putting the responsibility firmly back to the individual. Hepworth draws on the work of Rory Williams (1990) to demonstrate that some older people believe they have a moral responsibility to fend off late old age for as long as possible, and to be as active as possible for as long as possible after retirement. Participants in Williams' research could only justify restricting their activity and social interactions when serious ill-health struck, and 'it became legitimate to abandon the struggle against the ageing process when it was perceived that there was nothing in this world left to do' (1990: 180). This resistance model of ageing was also found in a study by Jerrome (1992) among older people in South East England. Respondents believed they had an obligation to be content, make the most of things, and maintain sensible routines in spite of their circumstances. Among the main objectives of a recent Irish conference on ageing and health promotion was to explore how older people '... can take a lead role in improving and maintaining their own health' (National Council on Ageing and Older People, 1999: 5) by among other things, changing their lifestyles and health behaviour. While the conference objectives also echoed the discourse of rights, autonomy, and participation, the focus on individual behavioural changes were clear, with references to lifestyle modifications in exercise and nutrition, and the acquisition of individual and personal skills in preparation for retirement.

Hepworth (1995: 187) notes that professionals have attempted to transform old age into an extension of middle age culminating in a 'quick and painless exit'. They do this, he argues, by reconstructing the problems associated with old age (for example, disability and confusion) into evidence of clinical pathology (such as Alzheimer's disease). In this sense, the source of fear is not biological ageing, but rather illness and disease. Thus, ageing itself is reconstructed as positively normal, and the biological deviations (disease) as the thing to be feared. Hepworth notes that the emphasis on positive ageing may further marginalise dependent older people. He concludes: '[t]he chief characteristic of prescriptions for positive ageing should be an ironic acceptance of the natural ending of one's life' (1995: 190), and he questions the notion of showing hostility towards physical demise.

The discourse of 'active' ageing is evident in the stated concerns of official groups such as the Expert Group on Future Skills Needs, Forfás, and the National Council on Ageing and Older People (Loftus, 2001).

Theories of ageing

A number of sociological theories have been used to understand ageing. Broadly, these theories tend to fall into two main perspectives, consensus functionalist theories and conflict theories (Jones, 1994). (See Chapter 2 for an introduction to sociological theories.)

Consensus functionalist theories

Consensus functionalist theories view society as an integrated whole comprising structures that interlink closely with each other. There is a covert acceptance of social control mechanisms to regulate society, so that individuals and groups slot in and function in harmony with one another. The approach has been criticised for tacitly accepting inequalities and injustices for the sake of the smooth running of the society as a whole.

Two theoretical positions are associated with the consensus functionalist perspective insofar as they focus on the individual older person slotting into the existing social structure. These are (a) disengagement theory and (b) role and activity theory.

(a) Disengagement theory

This theory was initially formulated by Cumming and Henry (1961). Commencing in the 1950s, a group of healthy older people were followed over a number of years to observe the changes that occurred as they got older (Fennell et al, 1988). The set of findings that emerged were subsequently integrated into a theory called 'disengagement theory'. The central premise of the theory is that the older person disengages from social activities in preparation for death (Victor, 1994). The key assumption was that as a person ages, 'ego energy' diminishes, and the individual becomes more and more self-preoccupied and increasingly less influenced by social mores and therefore he or she disengages from social activities (Fennell et al, 1988). The underlying belief is that because the timing of death is unpredictable, it would be socially disruptive if people died while strongly engaged in social and work activities. The disengagement is seen as both natural and inevitable (Fennell et al, 1988) or a 'the quiet closing of the doors' (Jones, 1994: 350). Cumming and Henry (1961) summarise the process as follows:

> Aging is an inevitable mutual withdrawal or disengagement resulting in decreased interaction between the ageing person and others in the social system he belongs to. The process may be initiated by the individual or by others in the situation. The aged person may withdraw more markedly from some social classes of people while remaining relatively close to others. His withdrawal may be accompanied from the outset by an increased preoccupation with himself; certain institutions in society may make the withdrawal easy for him. When the ageing process is complete

the equilibrium which existed in middle life between the individual and his society has given way to a new equilibrium characterised by a greater distance and an altered type of relationship.

Disengagement is seen to begin for men at the point of retirement and for women at widowhood (Fennell et al, 1988). Because retirement is more abrupt than the loss of the domestic role, ageing is considered to be more problematic for men (Victor, 1994). There was a great deal of criticism levied at disengagement theory when it emerged (Fennell et al, 1988; Victor, 1994). It was viewed as legitimating the social exclusion of older people and could be used to avoid dealing with the problems facing older people (Fennell et al, 1988; Victor, 1994). Although it was accepted by many that some older people do disengage, some critics believed that this was more to do with the physical and social difficulties they faced rather than a natural and voluntary process (Fennell et al, 1988). Disengagement theory is part of the functionalist group of theories because disengagement is viewed as functional or useful in preventing disruption to the smooth functioning of society. It therefore ensures the transfer of power from old to young with minimum disruption (Victor, 1994).

(b) Role and activity theory
This theory focuses on the loss of valued social roles that older people experience, particularly for men in paid employment. From retirement onwards, older men were seen to be in a particularly functionless position, cut off from the socially valued world of paid employment. Retirement was seen as a crisis point, resulting in depression and social isolation from mainstream functioning society (Jones, 1994). To countermand the problems of being redundant after retirement, emphasis was placed on the need to pursue new activities. The emphasis on activity was developed by Havighurst (1963) who contended that successful ageing was rooted in the person engaging in the activities of middle age for as long as possible. The contention was that if certain pursuits had to be terminated, then new ones should replace them (Victor, 1994). Successful ageing according to this theory is about extending middle age pursuits into old age.

Empirical support for this theory is limited (see Victor, 1994). As Jones (1994) notes, social, financial and physical decline makes it difficult for some activities to be continued into older years. Structural and economic realities restrict the choices available to older people (Jones, 1994). Again, although quite the opposite to disengagement theory, the solution to the problem is rooted in the individual rather than in society, and this is what brings it under the consensus functionalist banner. In other words, what is being proposed is that if older people pursued new activities, the crisis of retirement would be addressed, and existing social structures would not need to be altered.

Conflict theories

Conflict theories are concerned with the way in which dependency in old age is socially constructed, that is, is *socially* rather than naturally designed. Conflict theorists propose that the maintenance of social order happens because dominant social groups persuade or force more vulnerable groups into accepting an unjust social arrangement (Jones, 1994). Unlike functionalist theories that root solutions to the problems of ageing in individual behaviour, conflict theories are critical of the way in which modern industrial societies are organised. That people are forced to retire at a specific age, that they are then forced to live on welfare benefits, and that they are very poorly valued, are seen as problems that societies need to address rather than focusing on individual older people for solutions. Conflict theorists associate the perception of older people as burdens and unproductive members of society with the economic and ideological crises of the welfare state (Jones, 1994).

Conflict theorists further suggest that divisions of class, race, and gender cross-cut the experience of old age and strongly impact upon it. They propose that political and cultural processes mediate older people's experiences of ageing. Poverty and exclusion in older years, for example, are not viewed by conflict theorists as natural but rather as something that arise from the way in which social and economic policies are designed. The welfare state, it is argued, has created a structured dependency, that is, it has created a dependent status through restricting access to a wide range of resources, in particular income (Bond et al, 1993). Older workers have been marginalised and pushed out of the workforce and subsequently become dependent. An Irish study found that people's satisfaction with retirement was linked to their financial position and health status (Fahey and Russell, 2001). Because older women are less likely to have occupational pensions compared to older men, they are affected to a greater degree (Bardasi et al, 2002). Women in Ireland are over-represented among the poorest sub-groups of older people, particularly rural older women whose participation in insurable employment was low in the past (Layte, 2001). In addition, farmers did not participate in the social insurance system until recently (Layte, 2001). Conflict theorists also acknowledge that there is a great deal of diversity among older people in terms of their levels of independence (Jones, 1994).

While conflict theorists tend to highlight the structural disadvantages faced by older people, Wray (2003) proposes that within social gerontology the effects of structural disadvantage have been overstated. She asserts that there has been a failure to consider the diverse individual and collective strategies that older women employ to sustain agency and control in later years. She argues that social gerontology is steeped in Western values and ideals about ageing. In her study of older women from a variety of ethnic backgrounds, she found that participants were active in a number of ways that sustained their social networks, a sense of agency that was not negated by material and structural conditions.

For an account of the way in which age mediates encounters between professionals and lay people, see Chapter 8.

Death and dying

The social organisation of death and dying varies across cultures and historical periods. In spite of a rich folklore about traditional death rituals within Ireland that apparently were widespread until the 1960s, almost no sociological analyses have been published about cultural practices around death in contemporary Irish society (very late twentieth/early twenty-first centuries).

A key perspective within sociology is that, since the early part of the twentieth century, death is no longer acknowledged in dominant discourses of industrially-developed societies (Walter et al, 1995). The view is that normative collective cultural practices and rituals surrounding death and dying have become obsolete (Aries, 1981, 1985). Much of the debate about the silencing of death in public discourses centres on the view that in late or high modernity people do not have the same sense of meaning in their lives, or ontological security that existed before industrialisation (Giddens, 1990, 1991; Mellor, 1993; Mellor and Shilling, 1993). Traditional religious beliefs operated as a binding force in pre-industrialised societies and offered a degree of certainty about life and the afterlife at a transpersonal level (Mellor, 1993). In the context of late modernity, individuals are challenged to continually reflect on their meanings and values, creating doubt and the need for continual revisions in thinking (Giddens, 1990). As Mellor (1993) argues, while this can be an empowering experience for individuals insofar as it liberates them from the repressive aspects of religion, it exacerbates the threatening dimension of death because of the absence of a communally-accepted framework to contain an individual's death-related anxiety. It has been suggested that discussion about and avowal of death has become silent in the **public realm** or space; death within mainstream society has become relegated to the personal or **private realm** or domestic sphere, or alternatively, hidden away in hospitals.

Philippe Aries (1981), a prominent sociological commentator on this topic, has proposed that across Europe the transition from death as a publicly acknowledged, communal affair across society generally changed after World War I. He claimed that a public discourse acknowledging death is forbidden in modern society because of the high value placed by twentieth century culture on happiness and romantic love. However, Aries did note that in the USA social scientists were encouraging the public to be expressive about death. Similarly, Gorer (1955), argued that since WWI, funeral rituals are minimal. He suggested that a society that is silent about death becomes obsessed about horror events, war films and disasters. Gorer argued that death has replaced sex as one of society's major taboos. Norbert Elias (1985) admired Aries' historical account of changing perceptions of death, but criticised Aries view of death in earlier times as being calm and serene. Elias suggests that on the contrary, death in an earlier epoch could have been painful and agonising. However, he does acknowledge that death and dying are now rarely observed. Mellor (1993) argues that there is an apparent contradiction between both the presence and absence of death in contemporary societies. With the recent increase in academic and popular writings on death and dying, he suggests that death can hardly be considered a taboo subject now.

Although much sociological writing on death and dying proposes that in modern societies death is denied, arguments to the contrary have also been presented. Drawing on the accounts of people who described the end of life of someone known to them, Seale (1995a, 1995b) argued that death was not always the meaningless event that it is often depicted, but rather highly meaningful in contemporary modern societies. The source of meaning was the dying person's self-awareness of the dying process during which he or she was accompanied psychologically by loved ones in the journey towards death. In his study, both the dying person and significant others engaged emotionally in this journey (Seale, 1995b). Seale acknowledged that not all deaths follow this pattern, especially the deaths of very old people, mentally confused people, and those who die suddenly.

Walter et al (1995) challenge the 'public absence of death' thesis by suggesting that the mass media bring images of death to the public gaze at a level never experienced historically. They further assert that so engaged in articulating the emotional dimension of deaths are the media, that they actually play a role in monitoring and determining what is a normal or acceptable response to death in a particular context.

The bureaucratisation of death and dying: death and dying in hospitals and hospices

In the premodern period, patterns of death and dying were integrated into the hub of everyday social life (Moller, 1996: 24). Moller (1996: 24) notes that rituals involving the community and the holding of ceremonies were associated with death and dying:

> Premodern societies tamed death through ritual and fellowship, whereas modern societies hide it from public view through a bureaucratic and technological system of care for the dying.

Bureaucracy is a way of organising human activities through specialisation, rationalisation, expert and specialised knowledge, knowledge secretly protected, and depersonalisation. Bureaucracy eliminates personal and emotional aspects in its daily functioning. Moller argues that as well as bureaucratic organisation, US society also holds science and technology in high regard, and organises death and dying around these notions. Moller (1996) suggests that two things occur: (i) dying is located in specialised institutions such as hospitals, nursing homes and hospices and (ii) formal caretakers of the dying take over death/dying care.

In a study of deaths in Belfast, Prior (1989) analysed the range of state agents and agencies involved in the bureaucratic process. Included among the state agents and agencies are the 'general practitioner, the registrar of deaths, the pathologist, the coroner and possibly the police (1989:199)'. He refers to the Consumers Association booklet entitled 'What to do when someone dies,' and its advice on how to deal with a death such as:

> ... formal rules for establishing death, registering death, disposing of the dead, acquiring documents, utilising documents and establishing legal rights to property, pensions and the like (Prior, 1989: 199).

Prior (1989) also acknowledges the private realm of death occupied by the grieving family, and suggests that in Belfast, at least, a broader community response is also in evidence.

A recent interesting development offering a different perspective on the notion that death has been taken over and managed by the medical profession is the emergence of the requested death movement (McInerney, 2000). This essentially concerns the legalisation of euthanasia and doctor-assisted suicide, and has become an international social movement (McInerney, 2000). The movement has had considerable success in some Western societies such as in Australia's Northern Territory, where a physician is legally authorised to comply with a person's request for assisted death (McInerney, 2000). In Europe, the Netherlands is the only country where a restricted form of euthanasia is legal when performed by a medical practitioner, who is obliged to adhere to ten official guidelines and conditions (Smartt, 2000). That doctors are the only ones permitted to assist with suicides in countries with legalised systems of assisted suicide reinforces the power of the medical profession, and adds substance to the argument that physicians have replaced God in relation to end-of-life decisions.

Is death denied in healthcare institutions?

In developed countries, an increasing proportion of people die in hospitals (Seale, 2000). There is evidence that invasive medical treatment is given to seriously ill patients very shortly before they die, even in the face of very poor prognosis (Faber-Langendoen, 1992, 1996; Ahronheim et al, 1996; Seymour, 2000). Seymour (2000) suggests that in relation to deaths in intensive care units (ICUs) at least, this occurs because in the highly technical climate of the ICU the natural and artificial aspects of life and death become blurred. She notes that intensive care reflects the modern preoccupation with the mastery of disease and the eradication of untimely death.

How communication about impending death and dying is organised in hospitals also gives us insight into whether death in industrially-developed societies is denied. Generally these studies provide contradictory accounts on the issue. Some studies indicate that giving patients information about their poor prognosis is to a large extent actively impeded in communication between hospital staff and dying people (Glaser and Strauss, 1965; Knight and Field, 1981; Costello, 2001). By contrast, other research has found that there is an openness to death and dying in clinical contexts (Field, 1995). Earlier research on awareness contexts (Glaser and Strauss, 1965), that is, on how information between professionals and dying patients is managed, has been criticised for its focus on the exchange of medical knowledge without analysing the emotional processing of such information by patients (Timmermans, 1994; Mamo, 1999). Put simply, giving patients information about their condition and prognosis says little about how emotions interact with knowledge – how much of this information is blocked out or incorporated by the patient at various times and stages of the illness. Both Timmermans' (1994) and Mamo's (1999) works reflect the development of the sociology of emotions, that is, undertaking sociological analyses of how people respond emotionally to events or information and how they manage their emotions. Mamo (1999) noted that even where the patient and family were made aware of the former's impending death, the emotions that ensued were complex, unpredictable, and 'messy'.

Does medicalisation of death facilitate its denial? Evidence suggests that it depends on the location in which death and dying occur. Moller (1996: 41) notes that the hospice philosophy has among its aims: 'maximising the control of pain, providing fellowship for the dying person, promoting maximum independence for the dying person and his or her family, and providing support systems for the staff so that they can continue to offer compassionate care to the terminally ill'. However, few studies have been conducted on hospice care to see if these ideals are being met.

The few hospice studies conducted provide some insights into the degree of openness associated with death and dying. Based on her Dublin study of hospice patients, McDonnell (1989) found that just over half of respondents (twenty-six of fifty) seemed unaware that they were being transferred to a hospice from a hospital. Many respondents reported not having been consulted about the decision, or were under the impression that they were being transferred to either a hospital, nursing home, convalescent home or rehabilitation centre. In addition, many did not appear to be aware of the aims of the hospice (McDonnell, 1989). Mazer's (1993) Scottish study exploring the experiences of people dying in a hospice highlights the complex issues in the debate about whether or not death is denied. While Mazer demonstrated that death at the hospice was concealed, she acknowledged that the process of dying was visible to others at the hospice. However, visible dying was restricted to comatose and peaceful dying. On the other hand, dying people who released smells (as happens with certain kinds of cancer) or made excessive noise were often placed in side-rooms. This suggests a fracturing in the degree to which dying was open and visible, with openness confined to more presentable images of dying. Lawton's (1998) British study offers further sociological commentary on the role of hospices. Based on participant observation in a hospice, Lawton (1998) argues that hospices do not screen and cloister all types of dying that are experienced across societies; rather they seclude from wider society a particular kind of death and category of dying patient that societies find most offensive and disgusting. These are cancer patients, whose disease frequently results in the surface of the body to break down and release fluids and matter normally contained within the body. She refers to this as the unbounded body of a disintegrating patient. The seclusion of this type of patient reflects the Western intolerance of dirt and decay.

Summary

- Modernity has strongly influenced changes that have occurred at various phases of the lifecycle. Childhood, ageing, dying and death are all strongly influenced by changes that occurred in the transition from traditional to modern society, and these changes continue apace in a period of late modernity.

- There is an increasing influence of medical regulation, and the notion of healthism more generally, in the course of the lifecycle from conception through to death itself.

- Family structure and processes have changed considerably in Ireland over the past fifty years. There has been a marked increase in non-marital childbearing, and in marital breakdown. Family size has fallen, and there has been an increase in the number of women in paid employment.

- With the process of modernisation, the concept of childhood has shifted from one where older children were expected to contribute to the family income, to a situation where children are economically dependent for a much longer period of time.

- Critics suggest that the way in which modern societies are organised marginalises older people, contructing them as unproductive burdens on society.

- Currently, there is no consensus among theorists as to whether or not death and dying are absent in public discourses of societies at the stage of late modernity. Death may be a fairly open issue in the media, yet people are restricted from witnessing death and dying first-hand.

- Some healthcare institutions have more open policies on acknowledging death and dying in the current period, yet evidence suggests that openness to death and dying, even in hospices, is not straightforward. The extent to which there is an openness to death and dying is not fixed but shifting and appears to depend on the social context.

Topics for discussion and reflection
1. How would you evaluate the impact of modernisation on the family?
2. Do modern societies really deny death?

TEN

Mental health and illness

In this chapter, the range of issues that impact on our understanding of mental health and illness will be examined. We begin with the definitional problem of mental illness and outline the different and, sometimes, competing models and perspectives that prevail in a clinical and therapeutic context. We then outline the main sociological approaches to the study of mental illness. These perspectives are further explored by examining the explanations they offer of the relationship between mental illness and social class and gender. The remainder of the chapter is concerned with the shift from institutional to community care as the hallmark of contemporary mental health services, which has led to changes in the definition and scope of mental disorder; here we outline the main explanations offered for this shift. We then examine this shift in the context of the history of mental health services in Ireland and contemporary trends in health service policy and provision. Despite the movement to community care, the mental health services continue to be dominated by the biomedical model, and while psychiatry has become more eclectic, its therapeutic approach is still strongly biased towards drug-based treatments. In the closing section, the ethics and politics of mental healthcare from the point of view of mental health users, social policy and the dominance of the psychiatric profession and the pharmacological model are explored.

Defining mental illness: different models and perspectives
Mental illness is a complex, ill-defined and contested field. The reason for this is that there are vastly different ways of speaking about mental illness and the meanings associated with mental illness vary historically and culturally, and expert definitions differ between explanatory models and disciplinary perspectives. Categories of mental disorder are usually distinguished between **mental handicap, behavioural disorders** and **mental illness.** Evidence of an underlying bodily disease or biological causation is far from conclusive for the latter two categories of disorder. Disorders such as schizophrenia that tend to run in families are thought to have a genetic origin. Schizophrenia like depression, however, is a generic name applied to a wide group of symptoms and there is little understanding of how genetic factors interact with environmental conditions. More recently, the search for

an organic basis to psychotic and depressive disorders has focused on neuro-chemical imbalances and genetic dispositions. However, the evidence is inconclusive and contentious. The key difficulty in this kind of medical research is the problem of distinguishing between cause and effect: do physically altered states trigger psychological disturbances or does emotional distress produce biochemical changes in the brain? If these problems are intrinsically genetic, which if proven would lend greater scientific support to the biochemical hypothesis, research has yet yielded little in terms of understanding the multiple causal pathways leading to certain conditions.

In terms of understanding what constitutes mental illness and its underlying causes, a broad distinction can be drawn between biological, psychological and sociological theories. The biomedical model, which dominates psychiatry, understands mental illness as a clinical condition associated with an underlying biological disorder. The dominant propositions of psychiatry may be summarised in the following way.

- Psychiatric illness is akin to physical illness.
- Psychotic, depressive and neurotic illnesses along with other so-called minor disorders are biologically or genetically caused or involve some level of biochemical brain dysfunction.
- The environment or certain aspects of the environment (such as the emotional dynamics in a family) are important in understanding the situational context of the patient, but are secondary to our understanding and treatment of mental illness.
- Pharmacological treatments are effective and future developments in treatment and prevention lie with the biological sciences, in particular genetic and molecular science.
- The success of pharmacological drugs is direct evidence that affective and psychological problems are caused by brain chemistry most probably linked to genetic dispositions (Kendell, 1996).

These propositions lend themselves to a certain way of conceptualising and responding to psychological distress and disorder, which sees the problem as internal to the individual's biochemical and genetic makeup and, hence, the individual is viewed as the most appropriate site of intervention and physical therapies seen as the first-line treatment (Kaplan, 2000).

The psychological explanation of the causes of mental illness focuses on the internal mental processes that result from the interaction of the individual and his or her social environment. The dominant schools within the psychological model of mental illness include psychoanalysis, developmental psychodynamics and cognitive therapy. The dominant psychological framework is concerned with normal personality development and focuses particularly on the formative years of early childhood development and family dynamics. The role of the therapist in the case of psychoanalysis and psychodynamics is to uncover unconscious conflicts and, in the case of cognitive therapy, to identify distorted patterns of perception that lead to inappropriate behaviour. In the case of behavioural modification, the therapeutic focus is on changing the rewards that inadvertently maintain patterns of problematic behaviour, whereas cognitive behavioural therapy focuses on changing negative cognitions (Dallos, 1996).

Sociological perspectives

As we outlined above, what constitutes mental health/illness is premised on different explanatory models and assumptions. Just as the experts are divided about mental health and illness, sociology also adopts very different perspectives. Here we will outline four key sociological perspectives relevant to the study of mental illness: social structuralism, social constructionism, labelling theory, and feminism.

Social structuralist perspective

Like physical illnesses, empirical evidence demonstrates that there is a steep social gradient for most categories of mental illness. Research also suggests a strong correlation between physical ill health and mental illness linked to socio-economic position, which Gomm refers to as the 'unholy triangle' (1996: 113). A recent report on inequalities in health in Ireland found a marked social gradient across all socio-economic groups for all psychiatric conditions. The report notes that what is most marked about the psychiatric database is that the proportion where the socio-economic status is unknown is greater that any other health based data set. In addition, the Standard Discharge Ratio is five times higher for this group compared to professional social groups for all major categories of psychiatric illness (Barry, J. et al. 2001). While we know little about this unknown category other than that it has the worst mental health index of all social groups, we can speculate that this group is most likely to consist of the unemployed and non-employed, including the old and retired, those who are chronically ill and the homeless – generally those who have been set adrift from the labour market and social networks.

While mental illness may well lead to low social class position for some, by virtue of the fact that people with a chronic mental disorder such as schizophrenia have a very tenuous hold on life opportunities, it is doubtful that this can account fully for mental health differentials across social classes. The structuralist or social causation approach argues that structural inequalities have a powerful impact on our sense of well-being. People in lower social classes have lower socio-economic status and the environmental and social circumstances of their lives expose them to a range of stressors over which they have little control. These stressors are structurally embedded or a feature of structural inequalities, for example, lack of access to employment or limited employment opportunities, low incomes, poor living accommodation and under-resourced community environments. Financial stressors associated with poverty and low-income have a powerful impact on psychological and social well-being, and compound the problems of stressful life events. While money and power cannot offset all potentially stressful situations, limited resources mean limited choices, limited personal control and hence limited solutions for dealing with everyday stresses.

An ESRI study, *Unemployment, Poverty and Psychological Distress* (Whelan et al, 1991), examines the effect of unemployment on mental health with reference to social conditions such as social class, lifestyle and income and how the relationship between these factors and mental health is mediated by access to personal and social resources. Based on the General Household Questionnaire (GHQ) measure of psychological distress, the study conservatively estimates that over one sixth of its national sample (or 17 per cent of the population) could be classified as suffering from a non-psychotic mental illness. In this survey, 23 per cent in the unskilled manual class reported above the threshold score for clinically significant psychiatric distress compared to 8 per cent in the professional and managerial class. Furthermore, those in the unskilled manual class have psychological distress scores that are almost three times higher than those of the professional and managerial class. The study also shows that the differences in mental health scores is not only between those in the higher and lower social classes, but there is a marked gradient across the social classes with the clearest divide between the non-manual and manual classes. For those living below the poverty line, the cumulative effect of material disadvantage increases vulnerability to mental distress/disorder to a 1 in 3 chance.

This study supports the hypothesis that social support networks, both in terms of emotional and instrumental support (access to information, influence or money), act as a buffer against the negative effects of stress to the extent that economic stress on mental health is stronger where social supports are weak (Whelan et al, 1991). While social support mediates the impact of psychological distress, it cannot be viewed as an independent variable in explaining class differences in mental health. The authors of this study conclude:

At low levels of deprivation those lacking support are more likely to be distressed but the strongest effects come when deprivation is high. Correspondingly, primary deprivation has a clear effect when support is present but is most damaging in situations where support is absent. While the pattern of interaction means that the effect of one factor is dependent on the other, overall primary life-style deprivation is clearly the most important factor, followed by emotional support and finally instrumental support (1991: 120).

The main finding of the study is that exposure to unemployment and poverty rather than differential vulnerability is the major factor accounting for mental distress, explained in terms of the 'grinding experiences of day-to-day poverty' (Whelan et al, 1991).

Social constructionism
Whereas social structuralist perspectives generally accept the classification of mental disorders based on psychiatric diagnoses (Pilgrim and Rogers, 1993), a social constructionist perspective broadly argues that realities are socially constructed. This means, for example, that our understanding of mental illness is historically and culturally variant, reflecting social values and processes that emerge over time and become culturally and institutionally embedded in public attitudes and professional norms. Social constructionism, therefore, is not concerned with the question of what is a more valid account or adequate description of reality, but rather why certain meanings of reality become established as fact, are taken for granted, or take on the appearance of a natural order or authority. This approach has opened up medical claims to sociological enquiry. It does this by showing how medical knowledge is influenced by and in turn shapes dominant social thought. For example, clinical definitions of mental illness are bound up with socially accepted definitions of what constitutes normal and deviant behaviour. Furthermore, the scientific status of claims is bound up with the social, economic and political order, which determines the scope of professional claims. While the medical model is dominant in explaining mental illness as individual pathologies with an underlying biogenetic or biophysical dysfunction, very few mental illnesses and disorders have a proven biological basis. Within psychiatric classificatory systems there is considerable definitional latitude, both in terms of the classification of disorders and apparently objective diagnostic processes. While there are numerous categories of disorder and hundreds of specific diagnostic categories, mental illness is largely defined as deviant behaviour whether or not its causes are attributed to behavioural, psychological or biological dysfunction (Tussig et al, 1999).

Sociologists observe that more and more deviant behaviour is subject to a process of medicalisation. As indicated in Chapter 6, what this means is that deviant behaviour, once defined as sinful, immoral or even criminal and subject to social control by religious and penal institutions, has increasingly come under the jurisdiction of medicine and is treated as a health problem. This process owes more to social and cultural factors than a process of scientific discovery. There is also the reverse process of de-medicalisation, which again is better explained by social and cultural factors than scientific evidence. For example, homosexuality was removed from the Diagnostic and Statistic Manual (DSM) as a mental illness in 1980 in the context of growing pressure from the Gay Rights Movement. In the same year the DSM added post-traumatic stress disorder as a diagnostic category following growing politicisation of the psychological stress caused by war. In 1984, the American Psychiatric Association was asked to include a diagnostic category of 'self-defeating personality disorder', whereby behavioural patterns such as involvement in successive abusive relationships or avoiding success by for example turning down job promotions would be interpreted as illness behaviour. This request was subsequently turned down on the basis that such a diagnostic category was likely to be culturally biased with respect to the social roles of women and cultural assumptions about gender that could ascribe to women moral culpability with respect to abusive and violent relationships (Tussig et al, 1999 citing Kass et al, 1989 and Scott, 1990).

Labelling theory
The basic premise of this theory is that the categories deviant and normal are not objective referents with fixed meanings, but emerge from a process of moral appraisal in which the deviant label is conferred upon the behaviour and actions of others. This theory owes its philosophical roots to symbolic interactionism (see Chapter 2). Within this perspective, deviance is not an intrinsic or innate property of the individual but emerges from the process of interaction between people when meanings are conferred upon the behaviour and actions of others. In other words, deviance is the product of socially generated meaning.

Labelling theorists are concerned with explaining the social process by which certain behaviours are defined as deviant. Thomas Scheff's work (1966) (referred to earlier in Chapter 2) was the first systematic articulation of the application of labelling theory to mental illness. What is of interest to Scheff is not the original cause of the behaviour, which may be biological, psychological or social in nature, but how the behaviour is labelled and how cultural stereotypes operate at the level of social interactions in a way that amplifies deviant behaviour (Clarke, 2001; Tussig et al, 1999). He argues that there is a certain kind of violating behaviour that is more susceptible to the label of mental illness. Drawing on the work of Goffman in particular, Scheff (1984) asserts that there are certain types of social conventions that appear so natural in everyday encounters that they are unspoken. He refers to these social norms as 'residual rules', in other words rules that are implicit but nonetheless necessary in maintaining social interactions. When somebody regularly violates residual rules, their behaviour is incomprehensible; so we may describe it as odd, bizarre or even frightening. Behaviour that is understood as deviant but for which we have no ready category is assigned to the category of mental illness.

Residual rules are broken all the time, but these rule-breaking instances are more usually normalised or temporary. According to Scheff (1966), certain contingencies are at work in determining whether residual rule-breaking is labelled deviant or not. In terms of broad categories, these include the nature of the rule-breaking, its severity and visibility, the status of the rule-breaker and the social distance between the rule-breaker and the agents of social control, as well as the cultural resources available to a community for understanding deviant behaviour and making available non-deviant roles. Scheff argues that once behaviour is categorised as mental illness the person is labelled as mentally ill. The label is subsequently internalised by the person through the process of stereotyping that occurs in social interactions. Since stereotypes are stigmatising, the mental illness label serves to exclude people from social life. Because people are most likely to be at their most vulnerable when they are labelled mentally ill, they are more likely to accept the label. In addition, Scheff maintains that a system of reward and punishment keeps the individual in the role of the mentally ill. Individuals who attempt to resist the label are punished, whereas those who accept the label are rewarded for the insight that they show in acknowledging the condition of their disorder. As a result, the individual internalises his or her status as mentally ill and develops an identity that is consistent with the stereotype of the label. The most controversial aspect of Scheff's theory is that once labelled, the individual is set on the path of a 'deviant career' by behaving in ways that confirm the stereotypical expectations of the label (Scheff, 1984, 65-74). In other words, the individual's sense of self becomes intimately bound up with the stereotype of what they ought to be.

Central to Scheff's theory of the labelling process is the idea that once certain types of deviant behaviour are medicalised (that is, deemed amenable to treatment) psychiatry acts as an institution of social control over such behaviours. Labelling theorists maintain that the process of medicalisation, which is underpinned by the cultural authority of psychiatry and its social function of control, actually creates mental illness. Medicalisation and social control are core themes in the sociology of health and illness (see Chapter 6). The power of definition establishes medicine as a powerful institution of social control, and the medicalisation of deviance as illness extends the scope of health professionals to define, regulate and monitor deviant behaviour.

Labelling theory provides important insights into the stigma of mental illness, and the distinct possibilities that exist for negative labels to amplify and compound the conditions of mental illness when an individual is excluded from alternative social roles. Prior (1997), for example, notes that the professional narratives that constitute a patient's case notes and the label assigned to a patient will determine future health encounters even when none of the symptoms of the condition are present. The labelling perspective continues to be relevant for those who challenge dominant discourses and the assumptions made about people with a mental illness, especially beliefs that are understood to contribute to a stigmatised identity and a disadvantaged social status.

Feminist perspectives

Socio-epidemiological research suggests that gender is an important variable in the prevalence and type of mental illness suffered by men and women. Women dominate in certain diagnostic categories, in particular affective psychoses, depression and neurotic disorders. Men, on the other hand, show a slight predominance in the schizophrenia category and are more than twice as likely to be treated for alcohol psychoses and alcoholism than women (Pilgrim and Rogers, 1999). While women report more distress, men are more likely to be committed – a trend that is common across Western societies. Suicide is the second most common cause of death for men in the 15-24 age group in Ireland (Cleary, 1997 citing the Department of Health (Irl), 1996). Contrary to trends elsewhere, men have historically been over represented in the public psychiatric hospital system in Ireland, although women dominate in community-based statistics and in the private psychiatric hospital system (Cleary, 1997).

The 'feminisation of madness' thesis put forward by feminist theorists is based on the empirical observation that for much of the nineteenth and twentieth centuries women in the US, Europe and Britain were over represented in asylums and mental hospitals. Feminists link this with the regulatory role of the asylum and psychiatric systems in the patriarchal control over women's sexuality and the dominance of a male medical profession with considerable social power in defining and policing the boundaries between normality and deviance (Chesler, 1972). From the mid-nineteenth century, women's sexuality became the focus of psychiatric discourse and a host of female specific disorders were directly linked to the threat that women's sexuality posed both for society and for themselves. Female maladies included hysteria, erotomania, ovriomania and nymphomania (Groneman, 1995) – organic disorders associated with women's 'excessive' sexuality and weakness of character. Feminist scholars point out that these disorders reflected dominant cultural and social attitudes to women and even the most minor transgressions of social codes of marriage, domesticity, motherhood and sexual passivity were interpreted as forms of madness. While biological theories of female disorders gave way to psychological theories that located disorder in the female psyche in the early part of twentieth century, feminists insist that these new theories continued to position women as 'Other' and to define normal behaviour within the narrow social roles assigned to women (Ussher, 1991).

Social roles are assumed to have a significant impact on the mental health of men and women. Research shows that women whose social role is restricted to marriage and motherhood have a higher risk of depression. Furthermore, the loss of a maternal role for women whose social role has largely been defined by motherhood increases the risk of depression in middle years. For women in restricted social roles with few outlets for social activities, few possibilities for developing meaningful friendships and other sources of social validation, the risk of depression is higher if their personal relationships do not provide them with emotional support. Men tend to have more social outlets than women and wider social roles from which to draw validation for their lives.

Whilst marriage appears to have a stronger protective impact for the psychological well-being of men, women's dependency status within marriage makes them more vulnerable to psychological distress, often by virtue of their social isolation, the limitations of their social roles and the negative impact of routine, monotonous work that is under-valued and unpaid. The ESRI study (discussed above) found that married women report the highest levels of mental distress, and that women on home duties report significantly more and higher levels of distress than both men and women who are employed (Whelan et al, 1991). The extended social roles of work outside the home serve women better in psychological terms. The study found that less than 10 per cent of employed married women in the study had an above the threshold score for psychological distress compared to 25 per cent who were unemployed and 20 per cent on home duties (Whelan et al, 1991). However, it also found that women who work outside the home have higher psychological distress scores than employed men. The authors of the study conclude that it is not clear from the data whether this can be explained by differences in work situations or because of the conflicting situation that women find themselves in negotiating domestic, care and paid work roles (Whelan et al, 1991).

The now classic study by Broverman et al (1970) illustrates how dominant notions of masculinity and femininity are internalised by mental health professionals and form part of the framework of diagnostic evaluations. It shows how the normative ideal of what constitutes a psychologically healthy adult with which health professionals work conforms to a masculine stereotype, whereas descriptions of the psychologically unhealthy adult fits the stereotype of femininity (that is, 'more submissive, less independent, more easily influenced, less aggressive, less competitive, more excitable in minor crises, more emotional, more conceited, and less objective') (Broverman et al, 1970 cited in Cockerham, 2000: 170). This suggests that women whose behaviour is closely identified with conventional notions of femininity may risk being defined as psychologically unstable, or conversely, women who deviate from conventional feminine behaviour may also risk such labels. Busfield (1982) also found that the description of certain diagnostic categories are gender specific in the way that they conform to dominant notions of feminine behaviour.

Gender stereotypes also impact on perceptions and evaluations of men's behaviour. So, for example, psychotic behaviour by men is perceived as more dangerous than when diagnosed in women (Cockerham, 2000). Cleary (1997) notes, for example, that men are significantly over represented in the Irish judicial psychiatric system accounting for 84 per cent of admissions in 1995. Psychiatrically ill men are more likely to be labelled criminally deviant and a threat to others and sentenced to secure psychiatric units, whereas women are more usually perceived a threat to themselves and directed to the soft end of the psychiatric services (Burns, 1992). Given that the most significant difference in the psychiatric admission rates between men and women is that women are more likely to be admitted for depressive disorders and men for alcohol dependency, this might suggest that these diagnostic categories reflect culturally acceptable labels for men and women experiencing similar kinds of distress (Cleary, 1997). The over-prescribing of minor tranquillisers for women is often cited as an example of how women are subject to social control and how the medicalisation of women's problems may in turn mask the social causes of their distress (Pilgrim and Rogers, 1993).

The shift from institutional to community care

The most significant change in the delivery of mental health services to have occurred in western societies is the shift from institutional care to community care. In the 1950s and 1960s growing concern was publicly expressed about the conditions of large public mental hospitals. In 1948, Albert Duetsch publicly exposed the dehumanising conditions of US state mental hospitals and the neglect and ill treatment of patients in *Shame of States* (Tussig, 1999). These criticisms were echoed in Erving Goffman's *Asylum* (1961), which used the concept **total institutionalisation** to capture the negative and counter-therapeutic effect of institutional confinement on patients. The critique of mental hospitals as total institutions began to permeate psychiatric ideology. For example, in Britain, the psychiatrist Russell Barton (1959) coined the phrase 'institutional neurosis' to describe the negative psychological effects of institutionalism. In the 1960s the anti-psychiatry movement became associated with the work of the radical psychiatrists Szasz (1961) and Laing (1960). While the work of the professional dissenters was not a critique of institutionalisation *per se*, it challenged the legitimacy of the institution of psychiatry as a regulatory agent of social control and rejected outright the orthodoxy of psychiatric theories and treatments. In political terms, the anti-psychiatry movement provided an ideological platform for the emergence of mental health survivor groups in the 1970s, which continued to highlight the abysmal conditions of psychiatric institutions and the abuse of human rights (Campbell, 1996).

Changes in definition and scope of mental disorder

By the 1940s mental illness was redefined in the context of the realisation that there were more people living in the community suffering from mental distress than in mental hospitals. In the effort to sustain recruitment for

World War II, populations were subject to large-scale physical and psychological screening. This revealed that there was far more debilitating psychological distress in the general population than previously assumed. The detailed medical surveillance of soldiers in the battlefield also led to growing interest in the role of environmental stressors in causing psychological distress and this initiated further medical interest in the prevalence of milder depressive and neurotic conditions associated with 'problems of living' in the wider population (Tussig et al, 1999). The expansion of identifiable disorder required a new response to the treatment of distress amongst a potentially sizable population. The fact that people with untreated psychotic symptoms were living in their communities suggested that there might be a valid alternative to institutional-based treatment and the discovery of such a high prevalence of mental disorder and distress in the community challenged the rationale of the segregation function of the mental hospital system (Prior, 1993).

The revolution in psychotropic drugs

The most frequently cited explanation for the shift from hospital to community-based treatment is the revolution in pharmacology in the 1950s, especially the discovery of major tranquillisers that facilitated the treatment of psychotic disorders outside of the hospital system. The discovery of new psychotropic drugs, however, cannot fully account for the trend towards community care. The movement away from institutionalised care had already begun a decade previously in the US and Britain and this pattern of discharge was not accelerated by the widespread use of psychotropic drugs. Indeed, in a number of European countries the share of psychiatric beds increased in the decades when major tranquillisers were increasingly widespread (Pilgrim and Rogers, 1993). However, the popularity and widespread use of psychotropic drugs inevitably was an important factor in the medical belief that mental disorder could be treated effectively in the community and that the shift to community care would not undermine the jurisdiction of psychiatry in the treatment of mental illness. The causal link drawn between the revolution in psychotropic drugs and deinstitution-alisation is propagated as a myth that equates 'miracle' drugs with the emptying of hospitals and the return of patients to normal lives in the community.

Economic rationalisation

By the 1950s, growing political concern was being expressed about the fiscal burden of maintaining large-scale public mental hospitals. In addition, there was growing public concern about the conditions of these institutions, reform of which would have enormously increased the costs of institution-based care. The fact that community care became operationalised through a policy of running down the large mental hospitals, without adequate community provision, was an indication that community care was embraced as a policy of economic rationalisation by welfare states (Pilgrim and Rogers, 1993).

Changes in psychiatric discourse and practice
Prior (1993) argues that the above explanations of the change from institutional to community-based care do not offer a full picture of the reasons for this shift. Furthermore, he argues that the growing disenchantment with institutional care for the mentally ill was an effect and not a cause of changing perceptions of psychiatric illness. Instead, Prior argues that institutionalism was challenged from within and that this was linked to changes in the target and scope of psychiatric interventions. Prior takes four major sites of psychiatric practice, namely, the hospital, the patient, the community and family, which he sees as central to modern psychiatry and examines how each of these sites is represented and understood in professional practice. He further explores how changes in the representation of these sites reflect changes in the object and scope of psychiatric practice and, hence, changes in the professional understanding of mental illness. While each of the factors discussed above are important, Prior argues that on their own they would have had little impact except for the fact that psychiatric practices were already beginning to change. These changes may be summarised in the following way.

During the first half of the twentieth-century psychiatrists began to lose their monopolistic control over the definition and treatment of mental illness as they confronted competing professional claims. In the 1920s, we begin to see a shift away from the asylum and custodial care and the emergence of the mental hospital as a place of treatment marked by open-door policies on some wards. As more serious, untreated mental disorder was discovered amongst the general public, mental illness became normalised. While the 1930s was seen as a revolutionary and visionary period for psychiatry through the development of physical treatments, concern with social relationships and the social environment as therapeutic agents was also beginning to impact on psychiatric discourse. While psychoanalysis was to have a marginal impact on psychiatry, psychological theories broadened the scope of psychiatry to assess the social and behavioural properties of the individual patient (Prior, 1993). Prior also notes that changes in the division of labour within the mental health profession broadened the definition and understanding of mental disorder. As new therapeutic spaces opened up outside of the mental hospitals, especially child guidance clinics, new autonomous forms of professional practice developed such as psychotherapy, family and behavioural therapy and, hence, new objects of psychiatry that contributed to changing the understanding of mental illness.

Prior (1993) argues that the idea of the mental hospital as a therapeutic environment did much to revolutionise nursing practice. The therapeutic role of the psychiatric nurse did not fully develop, however, until the 1960s-70s when new models of nursing set the goal of the discipline in terms of the psychosocial dimensions of care. The distinction between the physical and social properties of the patient initially became the fundamental basis by which the professional division of labour in the psychiatric health system was organised (Prior, 1993). Consequently, different understandings of mental illness and how it should be organised and responded to emerged through the occupational division of knowledge on which it was based. By the 1960s, a rationale was being articulated for bringing these distinct knowledge bases into a multidisciplinary approach to mental illness.

Mental health in Ireland
For much of the eighteenth century those who were classified as lunatics were imprisoned along with other categories of deviants, including beggars, prostitutes and the infirm or incarcerated, in workhouses and houses of industry, and subject to the most brutalising regimes of coercion, restraint and cruelty (Robins, 1986). In Ireland, as elsewhere, this policy of confinement was largely a response to the wide-scale problem of pauperism. By the late eighteenth century, reformers were beginning to express concern about the depraved and squalid conditions of these institutions, the mixing of the insane, pauper and criminal inmates and the potential threat of the spread of disease to the general population. The establishment of a district lunatic asylum system in the first half of the nineteenth century was part of a new social programme for the development of regimes that were expected to perform a more positive function in improving the moral worth of individuals and their usefulness to society. This regime change reflected a shift from a predominantly religious worldview that understood madness as a form of demonic possession to the emergence of new scientific disciplines such as psychiatry and medicine that established insanity as a scientific category and form of illness. The design of the new asylums with open wards and open exercise yards reflected the shift away from the principles of penal correction and restraint to the principle of moral treatment (Robins, 1986). However, patients admitted into the asylum system were so admitted on the basis of legislative provision and, hence, they were categorised as 'dangerous lunatics' and continued to be viewed as in-mates. The over-crowded conditions of the asylums made moral treatment based on the principle of individualised care a moot point. By the turn of the twentieth century, asylums were still operating within the terms of nineteenth century poor relief and as centres of custodial care under the autocratic power of medical superintendents (Walsh, 1997). Lay managers of public asylums began to be replaced by 'asylum doctors' from the 1940s, which paved the way for the establishment of psychiatry as a specialism within medicine (Finnane, 1981). Under the Local Government Act of 1925,

lunatic asylums were renamed mental hospitals although the provision of care continued to be largely dependent on un-trained attendants (Walsh, 1997). The training of attendants in mental nursing, which began in the 1890s and resulted in their formal recognition under the Nurses Registration Act (1919) (Finnane, 1981), was significant in terms of turning mental hospitals into training centres that in turn required the management of hospitals to provide programmes of care within their institutions. As Finnane notes that 'with the training movement came the first sustained effort to routinise the management of the insane under a medical model' (1983: 81). However, the shift over to professionally trained staff was slow and was not consolidated until the 1960s (Walsh, 1997).

The most significant policy change in the first decades of the Irish state was the introduction of the Mental Treatment Act 1945, which replaced the asylum admission law of 1867. The key provisions of the Act were the introduction of the category of voluntary patient, which had come into law in Britain in 1930, and the appointment of an Inspector of Mental Hospitals. Walsh (1997) notes that by the end of 1947, 376 admissions for public mental hospitals out of a total of 3,700 were voluntary. In the same year, 304 patients were voluntary out of a total of 17,791 residents in district and auxiliary mental hospitals. While the 1945 Act was to reflect the transformation from the asylum system of custodial care to a modern psychiatric system based on the principles of therapeutic care, it did little to alter the situation of those already admitted, many of whom were institutionalised for social as opposed to medical reasons and whose admission was on a par with a life sentence. Mental hospitals continued to serve a regulatory role for a wide range of social problems including poverty and homelessness, and as a place of incarceration for the mentally handicapped and, more generally, social misfits well into the second half of the twentieth century. In 1963, 41 per cent of patients were resident for eighteen years or more and 11 per cent had spent over twenty-eight years as residents (Robins, 1986), and no less than 16 per cent were mentally handicapped (Walsh, 1997). The living conditions of these patients were sub-standard with some wards housing over a hundred patients (Walsh, 1997). Despite the revolution in psychotropic drugs in the 1950s, physical treatments such as lobotomy, insulin coma therapy and ECT in vogue in the 1930s continued to be widely, if not indiscriminately, used. While the clinical efficacy of these treatments and their scientific bases have been under dispute, there is little doubt that their routine use was an efficient means of creating docile patients that easily fitted into the routine of large mental hospitals. Walsh (1997: 130), for example, comments that 'it was not uncommon for fifty to sixty patients to be on the ECT lists on treatment days' in the larger mental hospitals in Ireland in the 1960s.

The decline of the mental hospital
The mental hospital population had peaked by 1958; by the early 1960s

more patients were being treated as out-patients than were admitted to hospitals and the balance had shifted to voluntary in-patient admission. However, by this time it had become apparent that the Irish psychiatric system was over subscribed: relative to the size of its population Ireland had the highest population resident in psychiatric hospitals, with 7.3 psychiatric beds per 1,000 of the population (Robins, 1986). Moreover, the economy of large hospitals required high admission rates (Walsh, 1997) and, in turn, large hospitals had become important to the local economy of communities. While Ireland had maintained a system of large-scale mental hospitals that displayed a strong continuity with the asylum system, elsewhere mental healthcare was moving into another era. The move to community care in Britain was facilitated by the expansion of state welfare provisions (Busfield, 1996). In Ireland, the late development of the welfare state was a significant factor in the retention of the mental hospital system and the policy of institutionalisation for so long. As long as a residual poor relief system existed, it was difficult to reform the mental hospital system. In 1961 a Commission of Inquiry on Mental Illness was established. Its report, which was published in 1966, recommended a policy shift from institutionalised, custodial care to community-based treatment and the establishment of smaller psychiatric units in general hospitals. This new philosophical orientation to treatment was given an economic rationale in the context of growing political concern about the fiscal burden of maintaining unviable large-scale institutions.

Change in the mental health services over the coming decades was sporadic and fragmented. Contrary to the forecast of the Commission the number of psychiatric beds in 1981 was approximately twice the projected 8,000 and the mental hospital was far from redundant (Walsh, 1997). The report *Planning for the Future* (1984) became the new blueprint for the development of a comprehensive, integrated community model of care. A central recommendation of the report was the need for the provision of residential and day care, and the development of rehabilitation facilities to support the deinstitutionalisation of long-stay patients. The new strategy was to consist of three parallel actions: short-stay psychiatric inpatient units in general hospitals, continuing care residential beds, and community-based accommodation (including day hospitals and day centres) (Walsh, 1997).

The *Green Paper on Mental Health* (Department of Health (Irl), 1992b) outlined a commitment to the creation of new legislation to provide explicit legal protection for people suffering from mental illness, in line with international civil rights. The main legal shortcomings of the 1947 Act are the wide grounds on which a person can be detained; that persons categorised as of unsound mind can be detained indefinitely; and the lack of provision for independent review of detention orders or automatic reviews of long-term detentions. The Mental Health (Amendment) Act, 2001 substantially overhauls the legislation governing involuntary detention. It widens the powers of the Inspector of Mental Health Services; provides for the establishment of tribunals to review detention decisions; created the independent Mental Health Commission to oversee the detention review process, and the implementation of the statutory framework for the development of psychiatric services. The new legislation came into effect in 2003 with the establishment of the Mental Health Commission; however, its full implementation will be slow given the considerable cost implications of the extensive review process.

By the early 1990s, comprehensive psychiatric services were still not the norm, and while hospital admission rates were steadily declining they remained high by international standards. By the mid-1990s community-based mental health centres were beginning to replace hospital-based services. Since 1986, the trend has been to phase out large psychiatric hospitals and within a decade sixteen psychiatric units were operating in general hospitals (Walsh, 1997) with a further eighteen acute units under development (DoHC, 2001b). Throughout the 1990s, the numbers of patients in psychiatric hospitals continued to decline. Walsh (1997) observes that this is mainly due to mortality among long-stay patients: of those remaining in 1996, over 50 per cent were over the age of sixty-five and a third were seventy-five or over. Walsh argues that these trends suggest that by the end of the first decade of the twenty-first century a population of long-stay psychiatric patients will cease to exist.

Community care reassessed

The plight of those patients who have suffered under the legacy of the policy of long-term institutionalisation has never been systematically addressed in a community-focused policy. The vision under the new policy was that community services would be expanded; older long-stay patients rehabilitated and assimilated into their communities; the conditions for maintaining mental hospitals would no longer pertain; services for the acutely ill would be incorporated into general hospitals and the public stigma of mental illness would subside. The scaling down of psychiatric hospitals is tied in policy terms to the provision of acute psychiatric wards in general hospitals. The community care model is, therefore, largely conceived in terms of serving the needs of those with an acute mental disorder whose condition can be monitored through medication and who are responsive to low-key and short-term interventions, while the needs of those with chronic mental illness are not appropriately met. A symptom of this is the problem of a revolving door in acute wards with the majority of patients discharged only to be re-admitted within a short time. Furthermore, the resources put into the community care model are mainly targeted at acute mental health problems, which leave many gaps in the services for those suffering with chronic mental illness, as well as gaps in the geriatric psychiatric services.

Busfield (1986) identifies a two-tier mental health service under the community care model in Britain. The upper tier consists of community mental health services including acute psychiatric units in general hospitals, short-stay beds in psychiatric hospitals, primary care services and outpatient services. This sector caters for acute mental illness and is targeted at 'a largely new population as far as public mental health services are concerned, with a higher proportion of younger adults, women and middle classes than those dealt with formerly by state funded mental health services' (Busfield, 1986: 351-2). The second tier continues to be attached to the old mental hospitals where patients are more likely to be old, male and working class. In Ireland we are beginning to see a similar trend. For example, Walsh (1997) predicts that one of the impacts of phasing out public psychiatric hospitals and the provision of community-based services is that public psychiatric services are now more likely to be taken up by those who would have traditionally used private services. A two-tier health service implies a difference in resources and quality of service. In the process of phasing out psychiatric hospitals and targeting funding at acute services, the conditions of long-stay hospitals (and, hence, the conditions of patients) have deteriorated (*Report of the Inspector of Mental Hospitals*, 1998). Moreover, the care of long-stay patients is more indicative of regimes intent on creating docile patients than the impulses associated with reform of the mental health services. The *Report of the Inspector of Mental Hospitals* (DoHC, 1998) observes that long-stay patients are frequently on very high dosages of drugs that are not adequately reviewed and that the apparent increased number of sudden deaths in psychiatric hospitals may be attributed to such practices.

The lack of resources put into community residential facilities is not the only problem facing those with a chronic mental illness; communities continue to protest against residential treatment facilities and housing projects. One of the barriers to community care is the association between mental illness and criminal violence – a view that is sustained by negative media stereotypes. The ethos of community care is also undermined by a public perception that vulnerable patients are victims of an inadequate mental health system. Under the current National Health Strategy, a specialised mental health service is planned for mentally disturbed patients through the establishment of psychiatric intensive care units (PICUs) in each of the health boards (DoHC, 2001b: 145). This parallel policy underwrites the community care policy in at least three ways. Firstly, the policy is framed by the community care ethos that has facilitated the medicalisation of disturbed persons as opposed to their criminalisation. Secondly, the language of security is supplanted by language of care. Thirdly, it addresses the perception that community care does not adequately protect either the public or vulnerable patients. More fundamentally perhaps, the need for PICUs arises from the closure of large-scale psychiatric hospitals where disturbed behaviour could be more easily managed than in acute psychiatric units in general hospitals.

The *Commission of Inquiry on Mental Health* (1961) was highly critical of the inappropriate treatment of children in institutional settings designed for adults. However, child and adolescent mental health services remain underdeveloped despite the growing pressure for such services. The long-standing professional consensus in this area of mental health is that services should be based on multi-disciplinary, community-based teams offering a range of therapeutic and social supports. Under the *National Development Plan* (2000-2006), five child and adolescent inpatient psychiatric units are to be developed. While community services are currently playing catch-up, adolescents as young as sixteen and seventeen continue to enter the adult psychiatric system where psychological and counselling inputs remain marginal to the dominant drug-based therapies.

The shift to smaller institutional settings in the community does not necessarily have a clearly defined therapeutic value and a shift in the site of care does not automatically entail a shift in the therapeutic approach. Despite the ethos of multidisciplinarity, the dominance of the psychiatric profession and the powerful belief in psychotropic and anti-depressive drugs has meant that the community services are largely clinical in their therapeutic approach. The *Report of the Inspector of Mental Hospitals* (DoHC, 1998) observes that many mental health services do not have multidisciplinary teams. For example, the report notes that in one health board operating four mental health services there was no social worker attached to those services. The report also notes the paucity, if non-existence, of psychological services within the mental health system. Within a community care model, psychological services provide an important gateway for patients to access appropriate social services and the gap in this service means that patients are largely dependent on drug-based regimes. At hospital and ward level, therapeutic inputs from non-medical professions are overshadowed by psychiatry and drug-based treatments, which amounts to a very pale version of multidisciplinarity. Despite the shift to community care, the biomedical model largely supplants a socio-therapeutic model of care. This raises pressing ethical and political questions about the way mental health services will be shaped in the future.

The ethics and politics of mental healthcare

The field of mental health is fraught with pressing ethical and political questions. The psychiatric services, which dominate the mental health field, continue to serve a regulatory function in detaining persons against their will. This gives extraordinary power to psychiatrists to sanction treatment interventions and suspend an individual's liberty. The vulnerability of emotionally distressed and psychologically disturbed persons is amplified by the legal powers invested in psychiatrists to determine whether a person is competent to make decisions for him/herself or not. While this represents one pole of the psychiatric services, mental health patients in general experience professional power in a more sharply discriminating way

(Pilgrim and Rogers, 1993). The psychiatric services remain a stronghold of paternalistic medicine and the ethical principle of informed consent is precariously held in balance against professional norms, which demand that patients show insight into their condition by accepting their diagnostic label and complying with treatment regimes. While there is a degree of consensus among mental health professionals about the description of diagnostic categories, there is considerable dispute about the causes of psychological distress or disorder and the efficacy of different treatment modalities. Given this uncertainty, coupled with the fact that psychiatric assessments are essentially based on interpretations of behaviour, there is considerable scope for professionals to exercise subjective judgements. While psychiatrists accept that this is an essential feature of their work (Webb, 2000), they are reluctant to negotiate treatment strategies with patients. As a result, patients and their caregivers or families are rendered voiceless and alienated from treatment rationales that have a significant bearing on the quality of their everyday lives. Pilgrim and Rogers argue that psychiatrists 'are less willing than physicians to discuss diagnosis and rationale for treatment with their patients' (1993: 111).

While health policy has come to place a greater emphasis on consumer satisfaction and consumer choice, in line with policy initiatives on accountability and quality assurance (see Chapter 13), mental health services have lagged behind this trend. Consumerism implies that users have access to a range of services, yet public mental health patients rely on psychiatric services where alternative therapeutic options are either non-existent or marginal. In addition, the marginal social position in general of people with mental health problems effectively means that this client group has little buying power, and it is nonsensical to apply the term consumer to involuntary patients whose client status is undermined by legal sanctions (Pilgrim and Rogers, 1993). In light of the conditions and neglectful regimes of some wards and secure units in psychiatric hospitals under 'run-down' policies, the term 'survivor' adopted by the mental health movement appears a more apt description of the status of some mental health users. However, the hold that consumer ideology now has over health policy has meant that service providers are now expected to consider the views of mental health patients not only in relation to individual care plans but also with respect to service planning and policy development.

Mental health advocacy
Internationally, the main political impetus for involving mental health patients in decision-making processes has come from the mental health user and survivor movements. The survivor movement, in particular, has emerged from and given voice to patient dissatisfaction and disaffection. Mental health advocacy is not based on a unified programme of action, but is made up of diverse groups engaged in different levels of activities. For

example, in Ireland AWARE is a nationally organised self-help support group for people affected by depression. The focus of its advocacy work is to work in close partnership with mental health professionals, supporting research into biological and genetic causes of depression, the efficacy of medication therapies, patients' knowledge and practices; and also to support public education campaigns to address the stigma of mental illness. Another prominent group, the Mental Health Association of Ireland is entirely led by professionals (Speed, 2002). The Cork Advocacy Network (CAN) is an example of a group that is more actively involved in the legal and political advocacy of the rights of people suffering from psychological distress. This group was launched at a public meeting in January 2001 attended by more than six hundred people under the campaign title, *Is there another way?* The main focus of this group is to advocate for direct user involvement in mental health policy, to politically campaign for greater openness and accountability within the mental health system, and to develop an advocacy system within the mental health services so that patients may have a legal right to nominate an advocate to speak on their behalf. As part of its campaign for consumer choice, it has become a voice for the wider availability of alternative therapies and community and domiciliary services based on a socio-therapeutic – as opposed to the medical or drug-based model of care – and the development of a holistic residential therapeutic community. The *National Health Strategy* gives specific attention to the mental health advocacy model as a way of facilitating mental health users' participation in decision making about their care and treatment, of representing the concerns of users to service providers, and as a model for challenging public and professional attitudes to mental health problems (DoHC, 2001b). While the state has taken a more active role in formalising its relationship to voluntary organisations working with people with physical and learning disabilities in recent years, its support for the participation of mental health users in policy development and for informal, peer-support networks and alternative therapeutic options will be indicative of any shift away from the idea of 'care in the community' to 'care by the community' (Clarke, 2001: 185). However, as Speed (2002) notes, most mental health groups in Ireland subscribe to the biomedical model and are professionally led, while the mental health agenda is largely determined by top-down government policy.

Controversial treatments

While psychiatry dominates the mental health field, it remains a controversial mode of treatment. A long-standing criticism of psychiatric treatments is that drug-based therapies only alleviate symptoms in the short term and do not address the underlying causes of emotional and psychological distress. While many patients undoubtedly find drug-based therapies beneficial to manage their everyday lives, the main source of user disaffection is that drug-based therapies are used as a substitute for 'talk therapies' and more resource intensive forms of social support (Pilgrim and Rogers, 1993). Since the 1980s there has been growing professional and public concern about the iatrogenic effects of anti-psychotic drugs or neuroleptics, as well as minor tranquillisers and the prescribing practices of psychiatrists and GPs (Glenmullen, 2000; Lynch, 2001; Breggin, 1993; Breggin and Breggin, 1995). These debates have largely centred on the safety of drug-based therapies and the reluctance of pharmaceutical companies, regulatory agencies and medical practitioners to acknowledge and monitor their risks, in particular the addictive and physically disfiguring and disabling side-effects of long-term use. More recently, criticism has centred on the increase in the use of SSRIs (serotonin selective reuptake inhibitors), better known under the popular trade name of Prozac[21], which was aggressively marketed in the 1990s as a 'mood brightener' for the 'worried well' and 'socially inhibited' (Kramer, 1993).

Since Prozac was heralded as a cosmetic psychopharmacology by the psychiatrist Peter Kramer (1993), the way has been opened up to view personality structures and human temperament as amenable to treatment. The medicalisation of everyday problems greatly expands the market for serontonin booster drugs heralded as risk-free and non-addictive alternatives to the more traditional class of anti-depressants. In the short history of these drugs, concerns have already arisen that half a million children in the USA have been prescribed these drugs (Glenmullen, 2000). Despite the uncertainties about the causal relationship between affective disorders and biochemical brain dysfunction, and the uncertainty about how drugs achieve their therapeutic affect, the hard-hitting marketing of SSRIs broadens the range of problems likely to come under the orbit of psychiatry and points the future towards the dominance of pharmacological interventions and traditional drug-based psychiatry. While psychiatry conceives of mental health in narrow clinical terms and views alternative socio-therapeutic interventions as ancillary to drug-based interventions, the pressing political question is whether social policy should be guided by this view. While psychiatry's allegiance to the biomedical model and cutting-edge medical science is important to its professional power base (see Chapters 6 and 12), the influence that psychiatry has over the mental health field has social and political implications for how we understand and respond to complex human problems.

One of the key political tasks concerning the future of mental healthcare will be the development of a public health policy to monitor the long-term side effects of anti-psychotic drugs and minor tranquillisers, including the new serotonin booster family of drugs. On the one hand, there is growing professional concern about the neurological damage and dependency caused by long-term use of neuroleptics and tranquillisers, including the newer SSRI drugs widely prescribed for affective and so-called minor disorders.

21. Other well known brand names include Paxil in the USA and Seroxat in Europe.

These drugs have been linked to psychotic and suicidal behaviour and the neurological disorder tardive dyskinesia associated with anti-psychotic drugs (Glenmullen, 2000; Lynch, 2001). On the other hand, there is growing consumer resistance to paternalistic medicine that fails to fully inform patients of the potential risks associated with long-term use and professional resistance to alternative and comprehensive non-drug based therapeutic options. From a political and ethical perspective on public health, these concerns have focused public attention on the role of multinational pharmaceutical companies in the aggressive marketing of drugs, and the control they exercise over clinical trials and public information on neurotoxicity and the aetiological effects of the long-term use of drugs.

Summary

- Mental illness is a contested concept in the sense that different therapeutic approaches are based on different explanations of the causes of mental distress.
- Psychiatry dominates the field of mental health and while its practices have become more eclectic it remains firmly wedded to the biomedical model and drug-based therapies.
- Sociology shows how mental illness is socially patterned, which suggests the importance of the social environment to mental well-being.
- There is considerable convergence between social constructionist, labelling and feminist theories. All of these approaches are concerned with tracing the discourses of insanity and mental illness through the history of psychiatric practices and societal responses to moral, political and social transgressions.
- The history of the mental health services in Ireland demonstrates the legacy of the asylum as an institution of social control.
- In the shift from institutional to community care the definition and scope of mental illness has greatly expanded.
- While the community care model may be lauded as a progressive change, its implementation in Ireland has been exceedingly slow and incremental, and the implementation of its vision needs to be critically readdressed.
- In the changeover to a community-based mental health model, the consumer demand for multidisciplinary approaches and alternative treatment modalities threaten to weaken the dominance of psychiatry.
- While psychiatry is expected to become part of a multidisciplinary and integrated network of community-based services, the basis of its future alliance with medicine lies with developments in genetic and molecular science in explaining and treating an ever-widening range of complex behaviour seen in terms of biogenetic dysfunction.
- The future of the mental health field remains fraught with ethical and political concerns, some of which were explored in this chapter.

Topics for discussion and reflection
1. Which of the explanations for mental illness presented in this chapter do you find to be the most convincing?
2. What factors do you believe have had the strongest impact impeding the move to community care in the realm of mental health?

ELEVEN

Science and technology in healthcare

Since the discovery of the structure of DNA in the 1950s, research into the association between genetics and disease has begun to redefine the development of medical science and technology. Developments in molecular biology and genetics are set on radically transforming medicine in the twenty-first century. The Human Genome Project (HGP), which is described by Conrad and Gabe as the 'largest biological research enterprise in history' (1999: 505) was launched in 1990 as an international, public research initiative to map the sequence of the human genome with the purpose of identifying the genetic bases of diseases. The HGP is seen to represent the dawn of new era for medicine in understanding the fundamental causes of disease, opening up new avenues for the prevention and cure of even the most intractable diseases. The speculative benefits of these technologies in curing diseases or in overcoming infertility and eliminating genetic disorders in future children are subject to debate because, in extending the boundaries of medical science to manipulate biological processes, they threaten to outstrip our moral understanding of the human body and raise the spectre of eugenic thinking.

We will begin by outlining the framework of the Sociology of Science and Technology (SST) for analysing how science and technology are socially shaped, that is how and why particular technologies develop the way they do. Here we will consider the formation of a 'bio-industrial complex', which sees the powerful interests of science and capital merging through new institutional arrangements, which have global implications for health. Moving from economic power to cultural power, we will complete our theoretical framework by considering the shift from *medicalisation* (Zola, 1972), where more and more aspects of life come to be constructed as medical problems, to *biomedicalisation* (Clarke et al, 2003), where science and technology promise to radically transform the face of clinical practice and the way we understand the body, health and disease. In the following sections, we take a closer look at these issues by exploring the social context of the technologies of childbirth, New Reproductive Technologies (NRT), reproductive genetics, human cloning technologies and gene therapy.

Sociology of science and technology

The Sociology of Science and Technology (SST) is a field of sociology which is concerned with the way scientific knowledge is constructed and how technology is socially shaped. SST, as Lohan and Faulkner (2004) point out, is based on a critique of two popularly held views or myths of science and technology. The first of these is that science and technology are value neutral enterprises that only become invested with values in the way society interprets knowledge and makes use of technologies. The second of these myths is that technology is deterministic, in the sense that technological innovations follow an 'innate technical logic' (Martin, 1999: 519). This implies that technology has its own 'internal dynamics' (Bijker, 1995: 281), that can affect society in pre-determined ways. In this popular framing, science and technology are autonomous forces that drive social change and society finds itself in the position of playing catch up to techno-scientific changes by designing ethical and regulatory frameworks for the appropriate use and control of new technologies. SST, by contrast, argues that technologies are never value-free in origin but are rather the outcome of complex social, as well as technical, processes, and that the effects of technologies in society are contingent upon further socio-technical negotiations over their use over time.

The two dominant theories within the SST framework are the social construction of technology model (SCOT) (Bijker, 1995; Martin, 1999) and actor-network theory (ANT) (Callon, 1986; Martin, 1999). Although each of these theories takes a distinct approach they generally raise three important questions. First, how are scientific facts and technological artefacts produced – for example, who are the key actors, what interests do they represent and how are different, if not competing, interests and visions negotiated? The second major question is how are the validity of scientific claims and the use values of novel technologies promoted, marketed and legitimised in order to enrol the support of policy makers, the public and potential users, as well as mobilising resources? The third major question is how are scientific facts and technological artefacts (re)interpreted and used in everyday life – for example, in the healthcare setting, the domestic environment or the work place? In other words, SST is concerned with the way in which technical, social, economic and political processes (socio-technical relations) shape technology and the scientific knowledge claims that underpin their use value. Technology is seen as the outcome of *heterogeneous* relations (Law, 1987) between the technical and the social or as 'socio-technical ensembles' (Bijker, 1995). The case studies that are found in SST research demonstrate how scientific knowledge and technologies are socially shaped in the negotiations between diverse actors such as scientists, engineers, clinicians, venture capitalists, policy makers, the public and users. So, rather than assuming that techno-scientific changes follow a linear deterministic path, SST studies focus on the role of negotiation and controversy, competing interests and visions, disruption and resistance, and the alignment and realignment of key actors, practices and discourses in shaping technology, as well as the unintended consequences that result from technological changes.

The bio-industrial complex

So far, we have not discussed the role of power in shaping scientific knowledge and its technological applications. In the socio-technical networks that develop to support technological innovations, some social groups are more powerful than others, and recognising the differential power afforded to different social groups and interests is a first step in understanding how science and technology are socially shaped (Cunningham-Burley and Boulton, 2000). It is now widely expected that the commercialisation of biological material from plants, animals and humans will drive economic development in the twenty-first century. From a political economy perspective, the relationship between medicine and capitalism is important in understanding the social power of medicine. The term medical-industrial complex was coined in the 1970s in the USA to describe the privatisation of medicine and the alignment between medical professional power and capitalism through private insurance schemes (Ehrenreich and Ehrenreich, 1971 cited in Clarke et al, 2003: 167). Today, we can talk about an emerging bio-industrial complex, which refers to the privatisation of genetic research, the alliance between academic research and multi-national corporations and the commodification of biotechnological products and services. Furthermore, the bio-industrial complex has global reach in terms of both economic power and in the social impact of biomedical conglomerates on the provision of healthcare by nation states.

Life forms have become commodities that can be engineered, patented and a source of profit for private interests (Clarke et al, 2003). Most striking in this respect is the use of publicly funded research under the HGP by private biotechnology companies who seek monopoly patenting over the commercial products developed, for example the patenting of the genetic marker for breast cancer, BRCA1 by Myriad Genetics (discussed in Chapter 2). Monopoly patenting of human genetic material in the hands of a relatively small but powerful multinational biotech and pharmaceutical industry has direct consequences for healthcare research and services both in terms of cost and access to the new technologies. The current merger between giant chemical, pharmaceutical and biotech enterprises demonstrates the emergence of an elite group of multinational conglomerates that control health, agricultural and food markets, and for whom the patenting of life forms and biological processes is a key asset (Shand, 2001).

The consolidation of the bio-industrial complex whose global reach is supported by the WTO and the World Bank changes the institutional structure of science and technology. The strategic alliances between academic and publicly funded research and the profit-driven biotechnology industry raises questions about the efficacy and reliability of research that is profit driven, and the constraints of new institutional arrangements on the production of knowledge and technological innovation, and the impact that this has on public trust in the institutions of science, technology and medicine. For example, will health research and the distribution of health resources be dictated by stock markets? The powerful alliance between the institutions of science and medicine, whose privileged status is based on the cultural authority of knowledge expertise, the state, which controls public research, and the biotechnology industry that wields considerable economic power, exerts considerable influence on shaping future research agendas and on how the social impact of genetic science and new technologies are understood.

From medicalisation to biomedicalisation

In Chapter 6 we have explored medicalisation as the process through which more and more aspects of everyday life have come under the jurisdiction of medicine. Clarke et al (2003) argue that this process has intensified with the rapid development of techno-scientific innovations over the last number of decades, and they refer to this process as biomedicalisation. This historical change is marked by a shift in focus. Whereas in the past, science and technology were concerned with controlling and harnessing external nature, today they are concerned with harnessing and altering biological life forms or internal nature (Clarke et al, 2003). Molecular biology and genetic science have not only altered the way that we understand human and non-human life forms, but have also opened up the possibility of radically transforming them. For example, molecular genetics not only offers new explanations for understanding diseases but it also offers the promise of altering disease processes by intervening in bodies at the level of genes, molecules and proteins – and, herein, lies the idea of genetically programming life itself. In line with the theoretical framework of SST (above), this historical shift is not explained by the idea that these changes are driven by technologies alone (the idea of technological determinism). After all, there is nothing certain about the direction and shape that technologies take; rather technologies are contingent on human action and, hence, are socially shaped. As Clarke et al note, 'sciences and technologies are made by people *and* things working together', or in a more sociological formulation 'human action and technoscience are *co-constititutive*' (2003: 166, emphases in original).

Much of the debate on molecular genetics, or so-called new genetics, centres on their potential social impact. Long before the technological capabilities that we know today, the ideas of creating and sustaining human life outside of the womb and of manipulating biological heredity to control human populations had captured the imagination of scientists and social reformers. Francis Galton coined the term eugenics in 1883 to describe how the management of human reproduction through selective breeding could be used to eliminate those considered socially undesirable or morally unfit. Eugenics, therefore, became associated with 'improving the quality of the human race through the manipulation of its biological heredity' (Kevles, 1992: 4, cited in Cunningham and Boulton, 2000: 174). Following the atrocities of Nazi Germany during World War II, eugenics lost its scientific authority and became associated with bad science. Today, genetics is popularised by media-led stories about the claims of scientists to have discovered genes for a diverse range of complex human traits, emotions and behaviours, including a gene for aggression, alcoholism, homosexuality, intelligence (Pilnick, 2002) and obesity, as well genes for a range of psychiatric disorders including manic depression and schizophrenia (Conrad and Gabe, 1999). Some commentators see this line of thinking as a new form of biological determinism that promotes the idea that the gene itself is a tool for understanding the complexity of social life and human behaviours. While geneticists distance themselves from many of the more spurious claims concerning behavioural genetics that are popularised by the pseudo-science of sociobiology, these claims, nonetheless, remind us of the rhetorical power of genetic discourse to promote dominant cultural notions of normality. As Pilnick observes, 'all the traits [under research] are to a greater or lesser extent socially stigmatised or may be seen as socially problematic in some way, which perhaps raises more profound ethical questions about why this research is being carried out at all' (2002: 56).

It is widely expected that molecular genetics will impact on how healthcare is organised in the future, as well as having considerable impact on individuals themselves (Cunningham and Boulton, 2000). As the focus of genetics shifts from relatively rare hereditary diseases to more and more commonly acquired diseases and even to behavioural traits, and from a focus on actual risk of a disease to the use of genetics as a form of predictive testing to determine the probability of genetic risk or susceptibility, genetics become part of the surveillance apparatus of medicine. Surveillance medicine (Armstrong, 1995) does not focus on disease *per se*, but on the risk of disease and illness (see Chapter 14 for further elaboration). Population-based DNA databases linked to medical records are already underway in some countries such as Iceland and Britain (see Pilnick, 2002). This represents a major change in the social organisation of biomedicine and shifts the focus from individuals and families with a known risk factor to the wider surveillance of populations. Genetic screening and testing technologies have become part of a risk-conscious society, which reinforces our dependency on the authority of medicine. At the same time, the uncertain nature of genetic knowledge of risk may undermine trust in medical authority (Pilnick, 2002). Genetic screening and testing do not necessarily remove the uncertainty associated with the risk of a genetic disease. For example, Cunningham and Boulton (2000: 179) cite two studies that show that women with a family history of breast cancer who refused genetic testing perceived that irrespective of a test result they would always see themselves at risk and opt for regular breast screening (Julian-Reynier et al, 1996; Lerman et al, 1995). For individuals with a family history of Huntington's Disease (HD) for which there is no effective treatment, uncertainty as to their risk status may be perceived as less of a psychological cost than knowing that they would develop the disease and pass the disease to their children (Quaid and Morris, 1993 cited in Cunningham and Boulton, 2000: 180).

The emphasis on individual choice (both in terms of the idea that people may voluntarily choose genetic testing and screening and that genetic information broadens choices for individuals) would appear to safeguard against the eugenic implications of genetic screening and testing. However, Cunningham and Boulton note that 'a language of individual rights masks strong cultural pressures to make particular decisions, and to hold individuals responsible for their own health and for the genetic health of their offspring' (2000: 180-1). As we note in Chapter 14, there is a strong cultural imperative for individuals to take responsibility for their own health, and genetics appeals to and is shaped by this cultural imperative of health, as well as giving a 'powerful new legitimisation' to the ideology of individualism (Pilnick, 2002: 191; Peterson and Bunton, 2002). Predictive genetics, which is concerned with an individual's genetic disposition to developing a disease in the future, and the current research focus on seeking genetic causes for a wide range of diseases and behaviours, downplay the significance of the environment in determining health inequalities, so that 'good health' becomes a matter of 'good genes' (Pilnick, 2002: 191). To locate disease within the body at the level of cells and genetic mutations shifts the focus away from environmental concerns such as industrial pollutants, the presence of toxic chemicals in our water, food and air, and the structural conditions of poverty (Rothman, 2001; Petersen and Bunton, 2002).

Medicalisation: a case study of childbirth

Social norms around childbearing changed dramatically in the nineteenth and twentieth centuries in Ireland and in other western societies with the introduction and routine use of medical technologies in pregnancy and childbirth. The widespread use of such technologies arose as the normative location of childbirth moved from home to hospital, and the birthing process came to be managed by obstetricians rather than midwives. There is a common sense belief that the reduction in deaths of mothers and infants over the past fifty years or so is directly related to developments in obstetric medicine. This is used to justify the confinement of all women to hospital for the births of their babies, and to standardise pregnancies and births using technological interventions. A glance at figures for maternal and **perinatal mortality** rates would lead one to conclude that there is indeed some substance to the claims that obstetric science has contributed significantly to health gain for expectant mothers and infants. In 1955, a third of births in Ireland took place at home; by 1999, 99.5 per cent took place in hospital (Kennedy, 2001). Over this period, maternal mortality has fallen from 70 per 100,000 in 1955 to 3 per 100,000 in 2001 (CSO, 2004c). However, the belief that obstetric science is responsible for the bulk of this decline has been strongly contested (Tew, 1998; O' Connor, 1995; Murphy-Lawless, 1998).

Central to changes in the process of childbirth over the past two centuries have been two interrelated factors: (i) the interoccupational relationship between midwives and physicians (the displacement of midwives as central carers); and (ii) the development of the science of obstetrics, which reduces women to reproductive machines needing intervention for efficient functioning (Donnison, 1977; Ryan, 1997). Until around 1800, the event of childbirth was a female centred affair. Female midwives assisted the woman giving birth, and female friends and relatives attended and supported. A repertoire of skills was transmitted from one generation to the next (Lupton, 2003). These midwives used traditional medicines such as herbs that had been empirically tested for effectiveness (Oakley, 1993). Traditional midwifery was linked with witchcraft, which was used to undermine midwives in the struggle between themselves and the emerging male dominated medical profession during the eighteenth century (Lupton, 2003; Ryan, 1997).

The term obstetrician, coming from the Latin translation 'to stand before', was coined in 1828 by an English physician (Lupton, 1994: 148). The use of forceps from the late eighteenth century 'gave these men the edge over female midwives who were adept at the manual delivery of babies', as custom dictated that traditional midwives were not allowed to use instruments as an accepted aspect of their practice (Lupton, 2003:158). Throughout the nineteenth century, debates ensued about the exclusion of women from obstetrics and medical training (Lupton, 2003). When obstetricians had successfully colonised childbirth, midwives responded by developing their own professionalising strategies through registration (1902 in Ireland and Britain) (Ryan, 1997). However, they became an ancillary workforce, operating under the control of medicine (Ryan, 1997).

Challenges to the science of obstetrics
Since the 1970s criticisms have been directed at obstetric science from a number of quarters – feminists, childbirth and women's health activists, academic sociologists and from within anthropology and history (Murphy-Lawless, 1998). In addition, in countries across the Western world, midwives in the 'new midwifery' movement are calling for a revision to the medical model of childbirth as the normative framework for all births in

Western countries. Criticisms of obstetric practices have been directed at two interrelated issues: the apparent lack of effectiveness of medical interventions and the role obstetric medicine plays in controlling women. Mediating these two issues is a debate about the appropriate level of technical overlay required at the location of births.

Criticisms of the effectiveness of obstetric practices
There is widespread consensus among critics that medico-technological intervention in pregnancy and childbirth is necessary in a small proportion of cases. However, the concern is that many obstetric interventions that may be appropriate for certain pathological conditions for a fraction of childbearing mothers, can do more harm than good when imposed on a population of healthy expectant mothers (Tew, 1998). A number of sources concur that the lowest rates of maternal (Loudon 1997; Johanson et al, 2002) and perinatal mortality (Tew, 1998) occur in countries, districts and areas where maternity services are provided predominantly or exclusively by trained midwives with low levels of technological mediation. In the 1860s, at a time when obstetricians were establishing their control over childbirth, deaths in Lying-In hospitals in Dublin actually exceeded those at home, even where many of these homes were 'completely wretched and ill-ventilated' (Phelan, 1867 cited in Murphy-Lawless, 1998:141). Ironically, the use of forceps was responsible for many deaths from puerperal fever in these institutions during this historical period, although there is evidence that alternative explanations were offered by obstetricians at the time (Murphy-Lawless, 1988). Records of home versus hospital birth for the 1920s and 1930s in Dublin continued to favour home as a safer place for birth (Ryan, 1997).

Cecily Begley's (1997) review of current medical research relating to labour and childbirth indicates that many technological interventions and routine practices are not even supported by conventional obstetric research. These interventions include episiotomy, artificial induction of labour and continuous foetal monitoring. Studies demonstrate that episiotomies have little effect on the length of second stage labour (Sleep et al, 1984), do not prevent lacerations (Begley, 1988), and result in a loss of perineal muscle performance after birth (Fleming et al, 2003). Induction of labour can trigger many other interventions (Tew, 1998). The increased pain can lead to use of anaesthesia and mobility is restricted by the application of a foetal monitor, increasing the risk of postpartum haemorrhage and postpartum infection. The risks to the baby from interventions are a reduced oxygen supply and increased distress, depression of the respiratory system by the absorption of sedative drugs given to the mother, and injury from instrumental or operative delivery (see Begley, 1997). It is argued that births are sometimes induced so that the timing of the birth is convenient for obstetricians (MacFarlane, 1978). The practice of foetal monitoring in labour also appears to have adverse effects – one study found that those experiencing foetal monitoring were a third more likely to have deliveries involving forceps, vacuum or Caesarian section, with no difference in perinatal mortality rates (Grant, 1989 cited in Begley, 1997).

Tew's (1998) explanation for the reduction in maternal and perinatal mortality rates in the past fifty years is the improved health of populations associated with better nutrition. She argues that even though nutritional standards had been improving towards the end of the nineteenth century, maternal mortality remained high until the 1930s in Britain because childbearing women had inherited their body and pelvic structure from an earlier less well nourished generation (Tew, 1998).

The control of women by obstetric practices
Associated with the critique of obstetric practices for using unnecesssary technological interventions is the argument that these result in the regulation and social control of the birthing woman. At a broad level, obstetric control over childbirth is held to be an expression of patriarchial control that creates a helplessness among women, socialising them to believe that they cannot give birth without technological assistance, the latter being controlled by men. One school of feminist thought contends that the capacity of the female body to bear and breastfeed children is a source of empowerment for women and something to be celebrated, and that male regulation of childbirth forcefully undermines this. Ann Oakley (1980), in her classic study exploring women's transition to motherhood in the 1970s, highlighted the way in which the medical model of childbirth disempowers childbearing women and sustains the ideology that women are uncontrollably trapped by their reproductive systems.

The modern maternity hospital has been likened to a factory, with reproduction being treated as a form of production (Martin, 1989; Begley, 1997). To illustrate this, Begley summarises the 'active management of labour' plan invented by Professor O'Driscoll at the National Maternity Hospital, Dublin, and later exported across the world (Ryan, 1997). All patients are processed through the plan regardless of their preferences or physiology, which involves the artificial rupturing of membranes after one hour since the diagnosis of labour, and the administration of intraveneous oxytocin at a standard rate if dilation has not accelerated meanwhile. The plan according to its instigator, has since its introduction, reduced the unit cost of production and permitted staff to be deployed in the labour ward, demonstrating economic motives for its use (O'Driscoll and Meagher 1980, cited in Begley, 1997). This has led Begley to argue that the active management approach to birth amounts to an industrial or economic model of care.

Active management of labour is used in 73 per cent percent of maternity units in Ireland (Irish Association for the Improvement of Maternity Services, 1995), and exemplifies a technocratic rationality oriented to processing as many women as possible in the minimum time. Murphy-

Lawless (1998) argues that state approval of the active management of labour is fostered through a system that produces normality and epitomises efficiency. Obstetricians hold a retrospective notion on normality, arguing that childbirth may only be viewed as normal in hindsight (Murphy-Lawless, 1998), creating patients out of all pregnant women, and extending the market to the whole of the childbearing population.

Davis-Floyd (1994) noted that for some women technocratic control was experienced as highly valued and empowering. However, it has also been argued that satisfaction with the obstetric experience may arise because of an uncritical belief in obstetric expertise, in which both obstetrician and patient 'adopt the voice of medicine' (Campbell and Porter, 1997:353). In this sense, women are duped by dominant discourses and act in complicity with **patriarchy.**

The place of birth – high and low technology locations
The safety of the infant and the notion of risk has been central in competing discourses about the degree of technological overlay deemed necessary at the location of childbirth. (For a further discussion of the way in which the concept of risk has come to permeate health work more generally, see Chapter 14.) As McAdam-O'Connell (1998) notes, different perspectives on childbirth are each linked to a body of knowledge that frames knowledge about childbirth in a specific way. Proponents of (low technology) home birth suggest that there is little compelling evidence that hospital births are safer than home births for the vast majority of women (Wagner, 1994; O'Connor, 1995, 2001; Campbell and MacFarlane, 1995; Tew, 1998; Goulet et al, 2001). The Netherlands has the highest proportion of home births among Western countries, and even where known risks are accounted for, births attended at home by midwives have been found to be safer than deliveries by obstetricians in hospitals (Tew, 1998). In Britain, while the relatively small number of home births obviates the possibility of a randomised control trial to measure outcome, Campbell and MacFarlane (1995) undertook various data base searches of existing evidence regarding the safety of home births versus hospital births. They concluded that there was no evidence that it was safer for all women to give birth in hospitals. Tew (1998) also conducted a retrospective analysis of the British Births Survey from 1970, using the same risk scores used by the survey researchers. Apart from women at very high risk, births at home or in a general practitioner unit were found to be safer than those in hospital.

In the Irish Department of Health's (1995) policy document on women's health, home births are forthrightly discouraged because of the belief that 'the newborn child is at greater risk in the home than in a well-staffed maternity unit' (1995:36). Murphy-Lawless (1998) proposes that, throughout its development, the obstetric profession has used claims of safety and the notion of risk to retain control over both women and midwives. Obstetricians have constructed 'every aspect of pregnancy and birth in terms of risk in a mistaken attempt to cover all possible eventualities ... and in this sense the entire female body has become risk-laden as the possibilities for something going wrong proliferate' (Murphy-Lawless, 1998: 21-2).

This risk notion has enabled obstetricians to sustain their monopoly of control over the maternity services and over midwives (Murphy-Lawless, 1998). Funding necessary for midwife-led units must be sought from the state, whose officials are influenced by the 'what if' theory of obstetrics (Murphy-Lawless, 1998). It has been argued that obstetricians' tendency to over-use technology arises from defensive medicine, that is, a perceived or actual threat of legal action, and there is evidence that this is indeed the case (Bassett et al, 2000). However Bassett et al (2000) argue that defensive medicine is not simply a consequence of the effect of law on medicine, but rather involves the complementary impact that medicine and law have upon one another. As Bassett et al (2000: 534) note:

Medicine and law cooperate most directly in developing explicit and implicit clinical standards. These standards comprise strictly ordered routines and expectations adopted by adept practitioners consciously and even semi-consciously, and they are passed on through formal and informal training using oral traditions and written medical texts.

In the 1940s in Ireland, the high mortality rate in childbirth, spuriously attributed to home births and unskilled birth attendants, effected changes in public policy that led to the setting up of obstetric-led maternity units and hospitals around the country (Murphy-Lawless, 1998), allowing free hospitalisation in many cases (Robins, 2000). This lends support to a political economy perspective, linking medical practice to state-sponsored capitalism (Hyde and Roche-Reid, 2004; Narvarro 1976, 1986; see also Chapter 2 for an introduction to the political economy perspective). In Ireland, obstetrics is a lucrative business where state-employed midwives care for obstetrician's private patients (O'Connor, 2001).

Efforts to demonise home births have come to the fore in Ireland in recent years. In one case in 1996, a senior obstetrician raised a formal complaint against an independent domiciliary midwife, Ann Ó Ceallaigh, in relation to her judgement about the timing of transferring a woman in labour to hospital. The obstetrician believed that Ms Ó Ceallaigh had acted too late and he made a complaint to An Bord Altranais about the matter. Ó Ceallaigh defended her clinical judgement and neither the mother nor baby involved suffered adversely; indeed, the mother involved actually wrote to the obstetrician requesting that the complaint be dropped. A court action ensued in which An Bord Altranais sought to have Ó Ceallaigh removed from the register of midwives. International experts supported Ó Ceallaigh's decisions and she won her case in the Supreme Court in March 2000 (Ó Ceallaigh, 2000).

Since the publication of *Developing a Policy for Women's Health* (Department of Health (Irl), 1995), policy documents have tended to be less dismissive about home births (Department of Health (Irl), 1997a). This suggested that the social model of childbirth might be gaining strength until it suffered a blow in 2003, which we will consider below. In response to The Maternity and Infant Care Review Group, the Department of Health (Irl, 1997a) recommended the establishment and evaluation of pilot programmes by the regional health boards. These programmes include the provision of a birthing location in the home but with emergency support if required, and a scheme to allow for continuity of care by the same midwife from the pre-natal period right through to the post-natal period. An Expert Group on Domiciliary Births was established in Ireland in 1997. In Britain, the contention that home births are not unsafe for women has been acknowledged in policy documents since 1993 (Department of Health (UK), 1993). In Northern Ireland, special public funds have been made available to develop projects such as midwife-led care and team midwifery (Pollock and Daly, 1998). In addition, a number of isolated obstetricians across Europe have lent their voices to criticisms of medicalising childbirth for all women, but they remain minority voices, particularly in Ireland (Murphy-Lawless, 1998).

The most recent setback for the homebirth movement arose on the 5 November 2003 when the Supreme Court ruled that health boards had no statutory obligation to provide for home births under the 1970 Health Act. The home birth pilot programme had already come under threat in a number of health boards and the three main maternity hospitals in Dublin had withdrawn routine antenatal ultrasound and blood testing from those considering a homebirth (Bourke, 2004). In addition, two leading obstetricians in Ireland had published an article in August 2003 which claimed that one in seventy home births resulted in the unnecessary death of a baby (McKenna and Mathews, 2003); the scientific credibility of their findings has been contested by the sociologist Marie O'Connor (O'Connor, 2004).

New reproductive technologies (NRT): a case study of IVF in Ireland
In this case study we will not rehearse the ethical, moral and legal questions that emerge in debates about NRT (see Dooley et al, 2003); instead we follow the SST framework, to understand how NRT are socially constructed and the socio-technical networks that have developed to support the clinical application of these technologies. We will specifically look at the history of *in vitro* fertilisation (IVF) in Ireland as it changed from a controversial experimental procedure that was framed by the moral controversy of abortion in the early 1980s to a therapeutic practice for the treatment of infertility (McDonnell, 2001). NRT refers to a number of treatment options that are available to those who are diagnosed with fertility problems, but

which are not necessarily limited to those who are unable to conceive. Following the birth of the world's first test-tube baby, Louise Brown, in Britain in 1978 the idea of 'assisted reproduction' has changed from being a highly controversial issue to an acceptable therapeutic practice for the treatment of infertility.

The technique of IVF involves the stimulation of the ovaries' follicles using high dosages of fertility drugs, the retrieval of eggs and their fertilisation outside of the woman's body, and the implantation of the resulting embryo. The conventional case of IVF involves the gametes (sperm and eggs) of the infertile couple who intend to rear the prospective child, while complex IVF cases involve gamete and embryo donation. A distinction is now also drawn between traditional surrogacy where a surrogate is inseminated with the sperm of the commissioning man and host surrogacy where the embryo of the commissioning couple is carried by the surrogate mother or where a donated egg may be used. NRT, therefore, make it possible to divide reproduction into genetic motherhood, gestational motherhood and social motherhood.

Since reproduction can be divided into discreet components involving three separate people – the genetic mother, the gestational mother and the social mother – the problem arises as to how to adjudicate between competing claims with respect to the rights of prospective parents and children? For example, in the cases of embryo and egg donation or surrogacy, what significance should we attach to the biological connections? Furthermore, as science and medicine gain unprecedented access to the biological processes of reproduction, to what extent do the values of commodification, propriety, markets, and supply and demand begin to dominate how we think about human reproduction? While IVF has been conceded as a right of childless couples and has become part of routine medical practice, infertility therapeutics combined with advances in genetic science constantly push at value boundaries. For example, in the following section we will discuss the complex issues that arise when medically assisted conception is combined with genetic testing in the case of pre-implantation diagnosis (PID).

The early development of IVF: from prohibition to a cautious ethical consensus

In the context of a predominantly Catholic medical ethos, IVF generated the same moral problem as abortion in regard to the sanctity of life and the theological principle that human life begins at conception. Following press leakages that Professor Robbie Harrison had introduced IVF at St. James Hospital in 1985, a moratorium on IVF became official medical policy until early 1987 in the absence of any public debate (*Irish Medical Times*, 34(1), 1 January 2000). During this period a cautious consensus had been established within the medical profession that IVF was an acceptable treatment for about 5 per cent of married couples, where the woman had damaged or blocked fallopian tubes (*Guide to Ethical Conduct and Behaviour and to Fitness to Practice*, 1989). Ethical acceptance was created by further prohibiting research on fertilised ova and embryos and the storage or freezing of spare embryos created in the process of IVF. This had the effect of avoiding the adversarial politics that continued to mark the abortion issue in the mid-1980s and over which the medical profession was deeply divided.

This strategy is in contrast to the public debate in Britain following the publication of the Warnock Committee Report (1984) on the ethics of medically assisted reproduction and embryo research, which eventually led to the passing of the Human Fertilisation and Embryology Act and the establishment of a licensing authority (1990) to oversee clinical practice and research (Mulkay, 1997). By the time the Irish Medical Council had issued its 1994 ethical guidelines, the medical criteria for IVF were expanded from the select case of tubal damage or blockage to include cases of male infertility and unexplained infertility. This was largely because conventional treatments were seen as ineffective in the treatment of infertility and the Human Assisted Reproduction Institute (HARI) unit at the Rotunda Hospital, which pioneered IVF in Ireland, was claiming to have 'one of the most successful take-home baby rates in the world', (*Irish Medical Times*, 27(47), 19 November 1993). While Artificial Insemination by Donor (AID) was never ethically prohibited, there was a *de facto* ban within hospital-based fertility services, and the use of donor gametes in IVF was explicitly prohibited.

Breaking the silence
Following the public launch in December 1995 of an infertility patient advocacy group, the National Infertility Support and Information Group (NISIG), the experience of those faced with involuntary childlessness began to attract media attention. These personal narratives told the story of women on the treadmill of treatments as they went from one consultant to another, often repeating the same diagnostic tests and treatments, and stories of women travelling to Belfast and clinics in Britain to avail of IVF with donor sperm and embryo freezing, without adequate follow-up medical care in their own jurisdiction. The public visibility given to these personal narratives helped to construct the need for infertility services and highlighted the role of the expert patient seeking medical advice and services outside of the regulatory and ethical jurisdiction of their own country.

On the 24 October 1996, an RTÉ *Prime Time* programme took up an adversarial role on what it termed the official silence on IVF practices in Ireland. This programme highlighted the lack of public debate in Ireland on the ethical, social and legal implications of IVF practices, and the plight of those faced with the problem of infertility. The debate in the programme centred on the status of the embryo and the ethical prohibition on embryo freezing in Ireland. In lifting the veil of silence on IVF practices in Ireland, the programme probed into the practice of disposing of spare embryos produced in IVF. As it stood, ethical guidelines required that all embryos should be replaced in the woman's body with an optimal of three embryos per treatment cycle. The programme revealed that because of ethical restrictions on the freezing of embryos, spare embryos produced in IVF procedures were effectively disposed of by replacing them in the woman's cervix, where there was no possibility that they would implant. The programme questioned this practice and went on to discuss the therapeutic value of embryo freezing in reducing the risks of Ovarian Hyper Stimulation associated with each hormonally induced cycle of egg retrieval, as well as the risk of multiple pregnancies. For those within the medical profession who hold to the moral principle that life begins at conception or fertilisation, a conflict arises between what is technically feasible and what is morally permissible. For those doctors associated with a pro-life position, embryo freezing represented the slippery slope towards the commodification of human life and the liberalisation of attitudes towards infertility treatments.

In the midst of this controversy, the Rotunda hospital introduced embryo freezing and published its own ethical protocol for the storage and subsequent use or disposal of spare embryos, ahead of revised Medical Council guidelines in 1998, which subsequently did not refer to embryo freezing. As a way of publicly distancing therapeutic practices from the abortion question and the moral question of the status of the embryo, the Rotunda referred to embryo freezing as zygote freezing. For those who hold a pro-life position, the technical distinction between zygote and embryo is merely a question of semantics obscuring the moral questions central to the debate on NRT. However, a number of subtle shifts in the rhetoric of IVF show how moral problems are transposed into technical problems as technologies develop and therapeutic rationales expand, and how this in turn reshapes the moral landscape of technology itself.

Towards the regulation of NRT
The arrival of private fertility clinics in the late 1990s expanded the socio-technical network to support NRT. Both Dr Brinsden of Bourne Hall and Dr. Tony Walsh, medical director of the J. Marion Sims Clinic, became public advocates of the need for legislation in the field of assisted reproduction. In February 1999, Dr. Mary Henry introduced a Private Member's Bill in the Senate on the Regulation of Assisted Human Reproduction. While the Bill was defeated, it pushed the government to agree that there was a need for legislation. The Irish medical establishment, however, appeared much more circumspect about the external regulation of the profession. In anticipation of future legislation governing the field of assisted reproduction, the Institute of Obstetricians and Gynaecologists set up a Sub-Committee on Assisted Reproduction in June 1996 and published a report in May 1999. The majority opinion of the Assisted Reproduction

Sub-Committee of the Institute accepted that legislation was necessary to safeguard future developments in infertility therapeutics. However, we can glean from the sub-committee's report the lines of tension that legislation and external regulation raise. Any external regulation is likely to be perceived as a threat to professional autonomy, which in the area of assisted reproduction not only concerns clinical decisions but also power over social criteria concerning access to treatment, for example in relation to martial status, sexuality and reputed suitability as a parent. Some clinicians feared that legislation would liberalise access to NRT; for example, Professor Bonnar, while chairperson of the Institute of Obstetricians and Gynaecologists, expressed the fear that any future legislation would give single women and lesbians the right to access AID (*Irish Medical Times*, 34(11), 10 March 2000). Others feared that restrictive legislation would impinge upon clinical judgements and scientific developments.

The report favoured the establishment of a voluntary licensing authority that would eventually be placed on a statutory footing. Such an interim measure ensures that medical standards and ethics remain within the jurisdiction of the regulatory bodies of the profession, while ensuring that those involved in infertility therapeutics will be involved in the framing of any future legislation. In its report, there was unanimous agreement about the therapeutic value of embryo freezing and majority support for the donation of spare embryos on a non-commercial basis with the consent of the donating couple. The report, however, draws a technical distinction between freezing at the pronuclear stage of embryo cellular development or at the zygote stage, while the term embryo freezing is entirely omitted. This is testimony to the moral unease generated by any possibility of reactivating an abortion type controversy on the status of the 'unborn'. The technical distinction between embryo and zygote, which is based on stages of cellular development, and the distinction between zygote and pronucleus based on the principle of syngamy or genetic uniqueness, effectively serve to obscure the moral issues over which the medical profession is politically divided. In February 2000, the government set up a Commission on Assisted Human Reproduction to establish policy proposals for future legislation. This commission brings together a network of key actors representing the scientific, medical, legal, ethical and patient perspectives.

McDonnell's case study (2001) identifies a number of key shifts that occurred as IVF moved from being a highly controversial issue to a clinically valuable technology. Firstly, infertility was defined as a disease and IVF was indicated as an appropriate treatment for a very limited number of infertility cases involving married couples only. Secondly, the medical criteria for IVF were extended to include unexplained infertility and male infertility. The formation of a national patient advocacy group brought IVF into the public domain and highlighted the ethical restrictions imposed on infertility treatments in Ireland. The ethical ban on the use of donor sperm in IVF procedures and restricted access to married couples was only lifted in 1998.

The next major transition was marked by a key media event, which highlighted the clinical practice of disposing of spare embryos by placing them in the patient's cervix. This served as an occasion to publicly debate the therapeutic value of embryo freezing and the need for legislation in the area of assisted reproduction. The HARI unit at the Rotunda Hospital introduced embryo freezing in the absence of Medical Council guidelines or legislative regulation. However, by using the term zygote freezing it effectively distanced clinical practice from the moral discourse of abortion.

The arrival of private infertility clinics to Ireland in the late 1990s widened the possibility that egg and embryo donation would become part of the private market in infertility treatments. These private clinics are part of a widening socio-technical network, and they are the most vocal supporters amongst the medical profession of legislation to regulate NRT. Subsequently, all the key actors have been enrolled into the process of considering future legislation. The Institute of Obstetricians and Gynaecologists published a report by its sub-committee on assisted reproduction in an attempt to establish a framework for professional consensus in anticipation of the legislative regulation of NRT. The work of the government established Commission on Assisted Reproduction is primarily to create a dialogue amongst experts in order to offer public assurance on current medical and scientific practices and build consensus on the need for legislation on a broad range of issues from assisted reproduction and embryo freezing to reproductive genetics and embryo research.

However, at the time of writing, the commission's much anticipated report has yet to be published. Two of the key issues facing the commission, which inevitably have led to the delay in the publication of its report and the low public visibility given to its work, are (a) the problem it has in negotiating between the competing visions and claims of experts, which reflect wider public divisions and (b) whether in managing these conflicts and setting the terms of a public debate on future legislation, the commission can distance NRT, genetics, gene therapy and embryo research from the emotively and morally charged issue of abortion.

Reproductive genetics
In Ireland, where abortion is not available as an option to women who test positively for foetal abnormality, the rationale for providing prenatal screening and genetic testing (such as chorionic villus and amniocentesis for Downs Syndrome) is that women will be prepared for the birth of a disabled child. In Britain, the debate has been quite different and critics argue that the only real option opened up by providing women with foetal diagnostic information is the termination of a pregnancy (Pilnick, 2003). A 1980 survey of 323 obstetricians in Britain found that three quarters of them required women who sought to undergo chorionic villus or amniocentesis to agree to an abortion if diagnosed positive for a foetal abnormality (Farrant,

1985 cited in Pilnick, 2003). The contrasting cases of Ireland and Britain highlight the social context in which individual women's choices are constrained. In the age of risk assessment, the question arises whether individuals who refuse to take up prenatal screening and testing will be held morally culpable if they have disabled children (Pilnick, 2002). Much of the rationale for providing prenatal and genetic screening and testing is that it empowers women by broadening their reproductive options. However, it must also be recognised that risk assessment is based on the probability of risk, which itself creates uncertainty. The choices that women now confront to achieve motherhood are fraught with anxieties. For example, a genetic screening test does not ease anxiety about the possibility of having a disabled child; it simply establishes whether an individual is high or low risk. The possibilities for reproductive genetics are extended by embryo pre-implantation diagnosis, for example the Human Fertilisation and Embryology Authority (HFEA) in Britain allows embryos to be genetically screened before implantation in IVF procedures where a couple already has a severely handicapped child and feels unable to cope with another (Dingwall, 2002). Whereas, pre-fertilisation genetic screening allows an individual to be tested in the absence or otherwise of a risk indicator for genetic disorders that they do not wish to pass on to their prospective offspring.

Generally a distinction is drawn between *diagnostic* and *predictive* genetic testing. Diagnostic testing is carried out when a patient shows symptoms of a disease (symptomatic) and genetic tests are used to confirm diagnosis for the management and treatment of a disease. Predictive tests are more commonly associated with reproductive genetics 'in the sense that that they are used to provide information about the likelihood of genetic disorders in future children' (Pilnick, 2002: 80). Complex ethical issues arise for the individual who is concerned that she is a carrier of a genetic disorder or susceptibility trait for late onset diseases that may be passed on to her offspring, as well as for society. For example, in the absence of a cure a person's life may be blighted by the social stigma attached to a particular condition or by a sense of fatalism or, indeed, direct discrimination in relation to work and insurance. Genetic information about an individual also has consequences for other members of a family. The question therefore arises whether it is incumbent on the individual to disclose information about her own genetic status to other family members, who are now known to be carriers or potential carriers of affected genes or are potentially affected by hereditary diseases. Furthermore, to what extent does patient confidentiality apply where an individual is unwilling to consent to disclosure to third parties? Third party disclosure of an individual's genetic status also has implications for health and life insurance and opens up the possibility of discrimination in the workplace.

Let us look at one scenario that illustrates the complex legal, social and ethical issues at the heart of the debate on reproductive genetics. In October

2000, the international media covered the case of an American baby, Adam Nash, who was born as a result of IVF and PID to ensure that he did not have the rare and life threatening bone-marrow deficiency disease, Fanconi Anaemia. While PID is ethically and legally permissible in many countries on the therapeutic grounds of a life-threatening hereditary disease, this case was different because baby Nash was also a donor of transplant cells for his sister Molly who is afflicted by the rare disease. This case illustrates how developments in reproductive genetics extend the therapeutic criteria for embryo pre-selection (using PID) from cases of rare life-threatening hereditary diseases to pre-selection for donor compatibility in the case of a sick sibling; however we may also see a further change in therapeutic criteria from cases such as sex-linked hereditary diseases to the risk of less serious conditions and diseases or genetic predispositions for adult onset diseases. After all, genetic science has broadened its focus from rare inherited disorders and **monogenic disorders** such as Huntington's disease (HD) and cystic fibrosis (CF) to more common and complex **polygenic disorders** where more than one gene is involved, and multifactorial diseases that are seen to have a genetic component but where there are also strong indicators for environmental risk factors such as in the case of cancers, heart disease and diabetes. There is also an increasing focus on behavioural traits and behavioural disorders such as depression, schizophrenia and alcoholism.

Reproductive versus therapeutic cloning
One issue that has not yet been considered in the discussion of reproductive genetics is the question of human cloning. Cloning is one application of genetic engineering involving the creation of a genetic copy of an organism. A clone has only one genetic parent and cloning occurs by removing the nucleus of an egg and replacing it with the nucleus of an adult donor cell (see Pilnick, 2002). There are two different applications of human cloning, namely *therapeutic cloning* and *reproductive cloning*.

Therapeutic cloning involves the cloning of human stem cells for organ and tissue transplantation, which would be genetically identical to the transplant recipient and, therefore, unlikely to be rejected by the recipient's body (Pilnick, 2002). It is also viewed as cutting-edge research into disease processes, the ageing process and the development of new drugs. In therapeutic cloning, a further distinction is made between the use of stem cells from an embryo and stem cells from an adult's body. While the use of adult stem cells is generally seen as ethically acceptable for research and therapeutic purposes, embryonic stem cell research is seen as far more problematic because it involves the creation of embryos or the use of spare embryos from IVF procedures for the culturing of cells and tissues and their subsequent disposal.

Reproductive cloning involves the creation of an embryo from a single donor organism, as opposed to combining male and female sex cells, so that the genotype of the embryo will be an identical copy of the genotype of the donor organism. In other words, a cloned embryo has only one genetic parent as in the case of the cloned adult sheep Dolly.

The difference between therapeutic cloning using embryonic stem cells and reproductive cloning is the distinction between creating clones for therapeutic purposes and creating cloned human beings. Reproductive cloning is generally viewed as morally abhorrent because it is seen as unnatural and a commodification of human life, and it captures public fears about the power of science to pursue a eugenic agenda.

At the time of writing (November 2003), the UN Human Rights Committee is debating a global ban on human cloning. The main issue in this debate is whether to ban outright all forms of embryo cloning, which the majority of countries including Ireland support, or to permit the cloning of embryos for research purposes (therapeutic cloning) while outlawing human reproductive cloning. At this time, the European Council is set to debate a European Commission proposal to lift the current EU funding moratorium on stem-cell research from surplus embryos arising from IVF treatments (reported to be supported by the Irish Government, *Irish Times*, 6 November 2003). While Ireland has no statutory framework for regulating human cloning, the question arises whether countries that adopt a restrictive approach to human cloning and embryo research should subsequently seek to benefit from such research. Ireland has been extremely slow in responding to the issues raised by new genetic technologies, whether in respect to research, clinical applications, or the substantive issues that arise in relation to health policy, insurance policy and discrimination in the workplace, and there has been a clear absence of public debate. European policy on genetic technologies follows a human rights approach. The European Convention on Human Rights and Biomedicine (1996) emphasises that the right to informed consent and the right to private life should inform genetic screening and testing. It also rules against the use of sex selection in IVF procedures except in the case of serious hereditary sex-related diseases. While Article 18 of the Convention accepts research on embryo *in vitro* (where states have enacted regulatory legislation, such as in Britain), it explicitly rules against the creation of embryos for research purposes. Following the announcement to the world's media of the birth of Dolly, the EU Parliamentary Assembly called for an additional protocol to the Convention to explicitly ban human cloning. In the USA, human cloning has been the subject of a ban on federal research since 1997, while private research continues into human cloning and embryonic stem cell research. Ireland, Germany and Britain have not signed the European Convention of Human Rights and Biomedicine. While Germany explicitly bans embryo research for commercial purposes and any manipulation of germ cells (MacKellar, 1997), in Britain embryo research, including stem-cell research from embryos donated through IVF treatments and cloned embryos, is regulated under license from the HEFA (Pilnick, 2002). It would appear that Ireland's constitutional reference to the 'right to life of the unborn' is interpreted as an implicit prohibition on embryo research, although Article

40.3.3 has never been contested in relation to the new genetics or the status of the embryo in infertility treatments.

The development of gene therapy
While gene therapy remains essentially experimental, it is heralded as the new therapeutics of the twenty-first century. Martin (1999), for example, shows that since the mid-1990s in the USA there has been a rapid expansion in genetic clinical trials for a wide range of diseases and conditions. Martin traces the way in which gene therapy has changed our conception of common acquired diseases and how this, in turn, has shaped the technology of gene therapy. The development of recombinant DNA technology in the 1970s opened up the possibility that disease processes could be genetically altered. Martin points out that in the 1960s two competing visions of genetic engineering dominated research programmes. The first was a neo-eugenic vision, which advocated the genetic modification of future generations by transferring genes into sperm or eggs, the so-called reproductive or **germ cells**. The second vision was directed at the genetic modification of **somatic cells** (or non-reproductive cells) to treat disease processes in individual patients (somatic therapy) and, therefore, was more closely associated with clinical medicine rather than the eugenic vision of genetic programming.

In response to public fears about genetic engineering throughout the 1970s, the US government established an enquiry into gene therapy, which drew an ethical distinction between gene therapy and somatic therapy. According to Martin this distinction played a key role in establishing the legitimacy of somatic gene therapy 'as little more than a conventional medical intervention'; and, in strengthening the association between genetic technology and therapy, it distanced the technology from the discredited science of eugenics (1999: 523). A moratorium on gene cell research was an important part of the process to gain public trust in science, and the establishment of a regulatory framework for clinical research in genetics under the auspices of the National Institutes of Health Recombinant Advisory Committee (RAC) was part of the process of building a national consensus on the social value of genetics amongst the public. The composition of RAC was dominated by scientists and clinicians, who played a key role in the framing of the issues of genetic science, but it also included representatives of other key social groups, such as lawyers, policy makers and lay persons 'whose support had to be enrolled' (Martin, 1999: 523). Initially, ethical support was only granted for clinical trials on life threatening genetic diseases for which there was no alternative cure. Furthermore, ethical approval was only granted for *ex-vivo* somatic therapy, where cells would be removed from the patient's body before being genetically modified and then transferred to the patient as opposed to the direct injection of genes into the patient, known as *in-vivo* therapy (Martin, 1999).

In the mid-1980s gene therapy remained controversial; research was focused on rare genetic diseases caused by single gene defects; and the clinical application of this research faced serious technical difficulties transferring genes into blood stem cells; furthermore, there was little clinical interest in genetic research (Martin, 1999). In 1989, the world's first human clinical trial using gene transfer began for the treatment of leukaemia. Martin shows how this trail was made possible through the ethical consensus established by the RAC regulatory framework, the link between science and clinical practice and, most importantly, the link between research and the emerging biopharmaceutical industry that provided the venture capital. A socio-technical network of all the key actors had been put in place to ensure scientific, clinical, social, political and economic resources for the development of somatic gene therapy. This marked the beginning of a shift in the focus of research away from classical gene therapy (that focused on very rare diseases caused by a single gene defect) to the big disease of cancer. Martin notes that by 1996 over 70 per cent of clinical trials for gene therapy were in the field of cancer (1999). Medical centres in the US were re-structured to build new collaborative networks between molecular biologists and clinicians and many formed gene therapy companies to attract venture capital to access manufacturing resources, or collaborated directly with the biotechnology industry to commercially develop gene therapy. The collaboration between public research and private industry was supported by US government policy to encourage industrial competitiveness.

The focus on cancer, which already had extensive networks to support research and experimental medical practice, attracted scientific, clinical, social and commercial interest. A major factor that contributed to the development of gene therapy was that cancer was increasingly described in genetic terms (Martin, 1999). Understanding how genetic mutations occur in cells may provide an understanding of cancer, but this is not the same as saying that cancer is a genetic disorder. However, as Martin goes on to note, 'for the advocates of gene therapy, if a diagnosis could be made in molecular terms, then it might also be possible to intervene therapeutically at this level using gene transfer' (1999: 528). Furthermore, research into gene sequencing had identified a number of tumour suppressor genes, which contributed to the redefinition of cancer as a genetic disease (Martin, 1999).

Once acquired diseases, other than inherited conditions, could be described in terms of molecular genetics, the idea of genetically modifying a patient's own cells to secrete the missing protein using cell implants for the treatment of diabetes, chronic heart conditions and Alzheimer's disease became the subject of research. However, Martin notes that cell implants proved technically difficult and, therefore, gene therapy shifted its focus to *in vivo* therapies. Like conventional drugs, 'gene therapies would be designed to act over relatively short periods of time rather than providing a permanent cure, would be mass-produced and administered by conventional means such as simple injection' (Martin, 1999: 531). This form of gene therapy was more commercially exploitable and this shift of focus coincided with the interest of the pharmaceutical industry in gene therapy. As Martin notes 'a major reason for this interest was that the construction of gene therapy as a drug fitted easily into the dominant pharmaceutical product paradigm and was much more attractive to large firms than therapies based on classical gene therapy or *ex vivo* cell implants' (1999: 531). He also points out that while cell-implant research did not attract the kind of support necessary to establish long-lasting socio-technical networks, it did nonetheless open up the possibility of applying genetic therapy to a wide range of major chronic conditions and, hence, paved the way for commercial interest in genetic drug-based therapies.

In this case study Martin shows how gene therapy technology, the process of building socio-technical networks to support the technology and the redefinition of common acquired diseases as genetic conditions, 'mutually shaped each other' (1999: 534). In building socio-technical frameworks to enrol support from a range of different social groups for scientific and clinical research, common acquired diseases were redefined as genetic and this reconceptualisation led to the reshaping of the technology itself. This effectively meant that the definition of a genetic disease also changed from describing an inherited disorder based on a single gene to describing diseases and all biological functions in terms of cellular processes and the regulation and management of genes (Martin, 1999). The emergence of the biotechnology industry in the USA in the 1980s to exploit the profitability of genetic research and the merger of the biotechnology and pharmaceutical industries in the 1990s increased the influence of economic markets on the direction of research and the shape of technology. This was a major factor in the transformation of gene therapy from 'being a largely surgical procedure for the treatment of rare inherited disorders to a novel form of drug therapy for cancer and other acquired diseases' (Martin, 1999: 534).

Summary
- The Sociology of Science and Technology shows how scientific ideas and technological innovations are shaped by the social context in which they develop.
- Feminists argue that the routine use of medical technologies in pregnancy and childbirth has led to the over-medicalisation of women's bodies.
- Men's monopoly of technologies in the formation of gynaecology and obstetrics as male professions led to the professional marginalisation of midwives and women's knowledge.
- While individual choices and reproductive decisions are seemingly expanded through the new genetics and NRT, social scientists have begun to question the social impact of these new technologies.

- The development of molecular biology and genetic science is set to transform medicine, along with our understanding of health, disease and the body itself.
- The new genetics have redefined the scope and scale of medical intervention. For example, the field of genetic screening and diagnostics has extended its focus from families at risk of relatively rare inherited serious conditions and diseases to whole populations at risk of common and more complex multifactorial conditions and behaviours, which are increasingly defined in genetic terms.
- Developments in therapeutic cloning and embryo stem-cell research have raised social expectations that significant cures and therapies for intractable diseases and more efficient drugs are on the horizon. However, at the same time, these technologies are shot through with profound uncertainties about the ethical landscape of future health interventions.
- Given the complex legal, ethical and social issues raised by new technologies, there is a pressing need for greater public involvement in debates about the future of research and the application of medical technologies.

Topics for discussion and reflection
1. Should societies attempt to curtail the development of NRTs and new genetics, and if so, on what basis?
2. Why do so many women opt to have their babies in hospitals?

Section 4
The social context
of healthcare

TWELVE

Interprofessional relations: the healthcare division of labour

Virtually all of the sociological analyses that have emerged in recent years on the healthcare division of labour have focused on medicine and nursing.[22] However, the issues that have surfaced in terms of relativities of power, medical dominance, and autonomy are also increasingly issues for other paramedical occupations such as physiotherapy, occupational therapy, radiography (diagnostic imaging), and dietetics as each expands its educational focus and knowledge base. Given that almost all of the theoretical debates and empirical studies of the healthcare division of labour in sociological literature has concentrated on nursing and medicine, in this chapter we focus on relations between these two occupations. Specifically, we consider the role of gender in this division of labour. In the later part of the chapter, the professional power of doctors and nurses is considered, and the relative power of each examined. Finally, we discuss relations between nurses and doctors in the clinical context. Specifically, we ask: Who makes the decisions in relation to the treatment of patients? How much decision-making freedom do nurses actually have, and is the level of freedom in a clinical context made clear in a concrete and formal way?

Gender and the healthcare division of labour

Historical constructions of gender have impacted strongly on the knowledge base, training and work practices of both nursing and medicine (Wicks, 1998). Let us trace the historical developments of nursing and biomedicine in order to better understand this gendered division of labour.

In the pre-Nightingale period (before the mid-1800s), hospital nurses had a poor reputation as drunks, prostitutes and thieves (Ehrenreich and English, 1974a). It has been suggested that this poor reputation was overstated, and that nursing reforms were well underway before the

22 There have been isolated studies on the division of labour between nurses and carers (see, for example, Allen, 2002 and Daykin and Clarke, 2000).

much-publicised visit of Florence Nightingale and her colleagues to the Crimean war. In addition, recent accounts suggest that, in the nineteenth century, Irish nursing religious orders in particular had a central role to play in providing the 'prototype for what was to follow'. (Nelson, 1997: 6; see also Connell Meehan, 2003). The development of nursing as an occupation for women in the late nineteenth century came at an opportune time historically for Irish women. Post-famine Ireland had few opportunities for them, since the chances of marrying a farmer (one of the few options for women) dried up for many, with family farms no longer being sub-divided (Luddy, 1995; Bourke, 1993; Rhodes, 1992). With large numbers of women being forced to emigrate due to a lack of economic opportunities (Fitzpatrick, 1986, cited in Preston, 1998), both nursing and teaching became popular choices for Irish women (Preston, 1998). The expansion of religious orders in the nineteenth century also had an influence on Irish nursing; towards the end of the century nursing became associated with female religious commitment and the nursing service was headed by nuns in many hospitals (Luddy, 1995).

The social class background of women entering nursing in Ireland in the nineteenth century has been a matter of dispute among theorists. Preston (1998) maintains that most of the foot soldiers were from working-class backgrounds, who would otherwise have emigrated, or opted for factory or domestic work. Drawing on archival evidence from Dublin hospitals, Fealy (2001), on the other hand, proposes that the requirement that nurse probationers pay a fee to enter nursing and be fairly well educated suggests that it was upper and middle-class women who entered nursing. Robins (2000: 11) also noted that training schools in Ireland attempted to attract nurse probationers who were 'of good stock, of high moral standards and of unblemished character' (Robins, 2000: 11). Similarly in the UK, although the 'Nightingale' nurse was perceived to be a product of Victorian oppression where the outlets for single upper and middle-class women were highly limited (Ehrenreich and English, 1974a), it has been noted that a diversity of women from varying class backgrounds entered nursing (Miers, 2000). Irrespective of which social class nurses were really drawn, what was powerful was the image of the ideal nurse as the ideal woman (Maggs, 1980), and according to Preston (1998), upper-class nurse reformers set about training recruits to fit this image.

In the preface to Florence Nightingale's (1860) classic work *Notes on Nursing: What It Is and What It Is Not* she wrote:

> Every woman, or at least almost every woman ... has at one time or another ... charge of the personal health of somebody, whether child or invalid – in other words – every woman is a nurse.

The idealised version of the nurse was a single, ladylike woman, clean, gentle, and quiet (Brockbank, 1970), with experience in cooking, needlework and household management (Miers, 2000). Quoting exerts from a series of articles entitled 'The lady nurses of the Irish hospitals' that featured in the popular women's magazine *The Lady of the House* in the 1890s, Fealy describes the gendered world of nurses in Dublin in the 1890s. Even in their free time, nurses at Jervis Street Hospital were expected 'to assist in plain sewing or other duties required of them' (Fealy, 2001: 9), and similarly, nurses at St Vincent's Hospital were expected to '...willingly assist in needlework' (2001: 10).

Gender is a central issue of concern for nursing in view of the type of work that women have historically undertaken, and also because of the manner in which that work was conducted (Wicks, 1998). With regard to the type of work, historically nurses have engaged in nurturing, caring, and service-type labour that was socially approved work for women. The scientific, objective, decision-making type tasks of physicians were associated with the male domain while nursing work was associated with female traits – emotionality, subjectivity, and nurturing (Gamarnikow, 1978). The manner in which the work was conducted was also highly gendered, with nurses formally taking orders from physicians, and medical work taking precedence over nursing work. As Ehrenreich and English (1974a) suggest, the Victorian nurse pledged obedience to the physician as the Victorian wife did to her husband. Indeed, it has been noted that nurse reformers were unanimous in their contention that the good nurse should *unquestioningly* obey the doctor (Preston, 1998: 100). From the beginning of modern nursing, nurse training was framed and defined by medical practice, with the nurse's role subordinate to the dominant medical model (Hart, 2004).

Before feminist analyses of the nurse-physician relationship, the division of labour in healthcare was not questioned (Wicks, 1998). On the contrary, it was seen as essential to the smooth functioning of health work, or the complementary roles of men and women (Wicks, 1998). Wicks (1998: 4) notes that:

When feminist theory arrived on the scene in the 1970s, it shone like a beacon onto the nurse/doctor relationship and illuminated the unequal and often exploitative power relations which underpinned the ostensibly complementary gender dimension of the division of labour. It raised vital questions such as who gives the orders and who takes them, who does the stimulating work and who does the drudge work, and who gets paid more and who gets paid less ... .

These analyses challenged the essentialist notion of caring, that is, that women are biologically programmed to nurture and care (see Chapter 2 for an account of essentialism or biological determinism). Writers such as Gamarnikow (1978) were among the first to assert that the sexual division of labour was not pre-designed as part of the natural order, but rather a relationship that was socially constructed to serve the interests of a patriarchal (male dominated) society. In other words, critics suggest that it was not because of a natural disposition that women joined the ranks of nursing and engaged in caring work, but rather, that aspects of the society that they lived in promoted a caring role for them. The 'good' nurse was perceived to be akin to a good woman. Propelling women towards a caring role through social approval simultaneously restrained them in occupying positions that required them to be in authority.

The nature of work undertaken by nurses has been analysed as 'emotional' labour, and questions have been raised about the way in which caring work is poorly valued compared to 'scientific' work (James, 1989). While nurse theorists have attempted to assert the value and centrality of caring in nursing (Benner, 1984; Watson, 1985), the problem is more broadly related to the invisibility of caring (Oakley, 1998). Although caring is apparently central to nursing, its relatively low status compared to technical aspects of nursing was in evidence during the 1999 nurses' strike in Ireland. An analysis of press coverage of the strike in the *Irish Times* found that both health professionals and the general public referred more frequently to the technical skills of nurses than to their caring role (Clarke and O'Neill, 2001).

Nursing socialisation

A number of studies have explored the process by which lay citizens become nurses, and the messages that they receive during their educational process (Melia, 1987; Treacy, 1987; Bradby, 1990). Professional socialisation concerns the process by which the culture of a profession is acquired, and the values, attitudes, and practices specific to that profession are learned (Gray and Smith, 1999).

Historically, in the apprenticeship system of training, student nurses were part of the work force, learning as they worked under the supervision of qualified staff and were given considerable responsibility for patient care (Crotty, 1993; Hyde and Treacy, 1999). The move from apprenticeship training to a higher education has effected a fundamental change for student nurses in the granting of conventional student status (Wilson, 1989; Hyde and Brady, 2002). It was intended that nurses educated to a higher level would create a new nurse who would be a 'thinking practitioner', someone who would reflect upon and critically analyse how knowledge might inform practice (Slevin 1995; see also O'Connor et al, 2003).

Studies conducted before the advent of Project 2000 (late 1980s) in the UK (Melia, 1987; Bradby, 1990) and the attainment of supernumerary status for student nurses in Ireland (mid-1990s) (Treacy, 1987, 1989) found that student nurses quickly became subjected to regimental norms of the hospital at the expense of their own self-development and educational needs. Melia's (1987) in-depth interviews with forty nursing students in Scotland found that some students tried to fit into their slots unquestioningly. They concerned themselves with adapting to the situation in which they currently found themselves, rather than acquiring the skills necessary for the role that they would eventually be required to perform as staff nurses (which was different to what they did as students). Students accepted the existing situation in a passive manner so as not to jeopardise their chances of registration. They simply focused on getting through their training, and forfeited long-term goals. Bradby's (1990) UK study noted that a subtle degradation process may occur during socialisation, of which neither the student nor the organisation is necessarily conscious. This process results in the individual's loss of identity, and conformity with organisational norms. During the socialisation process, student nurses began to value being part of the ward team more than the quality of patient care they delivered – patients began to be view in a more detached way.

Treacy (1987), in an Irish study, identified a hidden curriculum in the three nurse training locations studied in the early 1980s. She argued that powerlessness, uncertainty, mortification, and depersonalisation dominated the student nurses' experiences. The outcome of this socialisation process was that students complied and conformed and used existing structures and routines to survive. She noted that life in the hospital training school was akin to that in a '**total institution**'. A total institution was described by Goffman (1961) as a residential area where a large number of people experience complete control over their lives and are cut off from wider society for a period of time – examples include prisons, monastic settlements and boarding schools. Treacy proposed that the school of nursing *resembled* a total institution, yet was different insofar as student nurses did enjoy freedoms beyond the nursing school. Student nurses experienced low status, felt they were under surveillance and worked within a disciplinary hierarchical structure. The service needs of the organisation took precedence over the educational and personal needs of students.

In a later paper, Treacy (1989) focused on the gender aspect of the socialisation process, arguing that during the nurse training programme, *positive* female traits that might enhance the nurse's role were disapproved, while *negative* female traits were promoted. Caring qualities such as empathy and emotionality were discouraged, yet passivity and submissiveness were approved. 'Ladylike behaviour' was encouraged, including the notion of not thinking for oneself. The wearing of jeans or trousers was forbidden in classrooms, with a sameness imposed across the board. The way in which knowledge was presented also sent subtle messages to students – the timetable was inflexible with little or no time for reflection, and knowledge was presented in a hierarchical manner indicating to the student that he or she had nothing to contribute. Other messages that were reinforced during the student's training related to the relatively low status of nursing compared to medicine. Nursing work stopped during the physician's rounds to convenience medical work above nursing work.

In her Irish study of the socialisation of midwives who started their training in 1995, Begley (1997, 1999a, 1999b, 1999c, 2001) noted that students were taught to manage all patients in a routine and regulatory way, and in the education process many essential midwifery skills were not taught thoroughly. Participants in Begley's study learnt to be obedient, but were not well prepared to function as autonomous practitioners in the midwife role (Begley, 1997).

Since these socialisation studies, the education system has changed in Ireland (see a later section in this chapter) and the UK, so that students are no longer employed as part of the work force, but rather are supernumerary (over and above the agreed workforce numbers). Little research is available on the socialisation experiences of student nurses under the new systems of education. However, Gray and Smith's (1999) longitudinal qualitative study of Project 2000 students demonstrated the critical role of the mentor in the socialisation of student nurses. The researchers noted that for some students, decision making based on intuition was experienced at the end of the second year, while other students did not develop intuition at all during the programme. By the final stage of their educational preparation, increasing confidence, and for most a readiness to embrace the role of staff nurse, was noted. In a further UK study (in the Project 2000 era) Girot (2000) found that there was no significant difference in the critical thinking skills of graduate nurses compared to non-graduate practitioners. However, with regard to clinical decision making, graduate nurses fared better than their non-graduate counterparts (Girot, 2000).

Boychuk Duchscher (2000) draws on the work of Habermas in proposing future nursing curricula that redress the problems of traditional programmes. She writes of the oppressive nature of the traditional nursing curriculum in socialising student nurses and advocates the unveiling of the 'illegitimate and hidden curricula through open and honest communication' (2000:459) – in other words, exposing the ideology that has kept masses of student nurses oppressed. Boychuk Duchscher (2000) suggests that students may be liberated from the objectification and depersonalisation inherent in past curricula by revising curricula to include dialogue and dialectical thinking.

Professional power and medicine

In conventional sociology, the power of doctors over and above lay people and occupations allied to medicine was captured in medicine's possession of a number of traits that made it a 'true' profession. Various characteristics of a profession have been identified (Carr-Saunders and Wilson, 1933; Freidson, 1970b; Jones, 1994; Clarke, 2001) and these are summarised in Box 12.1.

Box 12.1: *Traits of a profession*

- The possession of a body of knowledge underlying and informing the practice of the profession.
- The possession of a code of ethics (accepted rules) regulating practice.
- The control of entry to the profession, through rigorous entry criteria, examinations, training and so on, and an extensive socialisation into the profession.
- Professional authority over the lay person by having expert knowledge.
- Having a confidential relationship with the client.
- Members strongly affiliating with fellow-members, and subscribing to behaviours that sustain respectibility/superiority.
- Altruism and a concern with the wider interests of the community rather than with self-interest.

Associated with the possession of these traits are a high income, power, status and the ability to attract high-quality candidates (Goode, 1960). Although the boundaries of what occupations qualify for professional status are nebulous (Etzioni, 1998), medicine was traditionally viewed as the prototype of the professions. The status and autonomy that medicine had attained allowed doctors to control the substance and performance of their work, with little interference or competition from outside bodies. Furthermore, medicine's monopoly over the diagnosis and treatment of illness granted it a dominant position in the clinical division of labour. As Freidson (1970b) argued, its freedom to self-regulate allowed it to control and monitor the work of others in the healthcare division of labour, making it a dominant profession. According to Freidson, professions were more concerned with serving themselves and consolidating their own power base, rather than serving their patients.

Max Weber (1948) identified the way in which some occupations have risen to dominance by developing strategies such as an extended formal education that are designed to exclude. The term *social closure* is used to refer to mechanisms deliberately employed to create boundaries around a social group. Drawing on the work of Weberian scholars, Porter (1999) notes how medicine strengthened its exclusionary tactics by securing state legitimacy – only those individuals approved by the state could practise medicine. Medicine then attained and maintained market control over its services. The monopoly medicine enjoys over diagnosis and treatment allows it to subsequently control occupations allied to it.

Medicine – a profession in decline?
In recent years, sociologists have analysed the apparently declining power of the medical profession. Let us consider some of the theoretical positions advanced by theorists before exploring to what extent they provide explanatory power in the case of the medical profession in Ireland. We will then turn our attention briefly to the situation in Britain.

Questions about the power and autonomy of medicine have arisen in the wake of increasing **bureaucratisation** in the health services, an increase in consumerism among members of the public and a series of medical scandals (Annandale, 1998; Morrall, 2001; Britten 2001). A sociological explanation for the challenges to medicine's power due to increasing bureaucratisation is the notion of proletarianisation. Proletarianisation is related to the word proletarian which means worker in the context of capitalism. The proletatian sells his or her labour power for a wage to the capitalist or owner of the **means of production** (Marx and Engels, 1848). In relation to the declining power of medicine, the argument is that doctors are generally no longer free to sell their services in an autonomous way as they did in the nineteenth century. Rather, with increasing incorporation into complex state-sponsored systems of care in a period of advanced capitalism, they are increasingly subjected to state regulation and control (Oppenheimer, 1973; McKinlay and Stoeckle, 1988). In this sense, with the move from self-employed to employee status, doctors are selling their labour power in the market, akin to other workers, in return for a wage (McKinlay and Stoeckle, 1988). The theory of proletarianisation as related to the circumstances of contemporary doctors has, for obvious reasons, not been widely accepted (Annandale, 1998). Most people see doctors as wealthy and powerful, an image at variance with that of a proletarian who is normally considered to be exploited and powerless to control his or her working conditions (Marx, 1867).

An alternative theoretical perspective to explain changes in the power and status of professions is that of deprofessionalisation. Deprofessionalisation refers to the process over time whereby professions lose their monopoly over knowledge, their autonomy, the public's respect, and authority over their clients (Haug, 1973). Haug (1973) suggests that the growth in consumerism and an increasingly educated public have facilitated professional decline. The proliferation of medical knowledge in recent years has made it difficult for doctors to sustain expertise in all areas of medicine, exposing them to the possibility of clients having greater knowledge in some areas. The public's access to the Internet and data systems further threatens medicine's once unchallenged knowledge base (Annandale, 1998; Morrall, 2001).

Let us consider the extent to which the medical profession in Ireland fairs in relation to the threat of proletarianisation and deprofessionalisation in view of both recent changes in the health services and a more discerning public.

The medical profession in Ireland

To what extent has Freidson's notion of autonomy to control the nature and performance of work been preserved among the medical profession in Ireland? Barrington (1987) has analysed the relationship between the medical profession and the Irish state from 1900-1970, and observed that towards the latter part of this period, escalating costs in medical treatment and a climate of social inclusion for all, regardless of one's means, spelled the demise of the predominantly private arrangements between doctors, patients and hospitals that had prevailed earlier. This private arrangement had allowed the medical profession to control its own fees and work practices. She noted that in spite of earlier bitter opposition during the 1940s and 1950s to state interference, the medical profession appeared resigned to working in a publicly funded and planned health service by 1970.

However, lest it be misconstrued that the medical profession in Ireland has been proletarianised, with increasing state control over its work, it should be noted that medical co-operation in the public health service has emerged from compromises with the state that have worked in the medical profession's favour. These compromises have allowed doctors working in the public sector to enjoy high salaries, to continue their private practices, and to have a high degree of involvement in the administration of the health service (see Chapter 13). Indeed the *Report of the Commission on Health Funding* (Government of Ireland, 1989) rejected the argument for restricting or excluding consultants employed in the public sector from practising on a private basis. The rationale for this stance was that talented consultants would confine their business exclusively to the private sector and be lost to the public service. In this sense, the medical profession in Ireland had succeeded in attempts to resist incorporation and regulation by the state.

The medical profession in Ireland has considerably more power than in Britain (which we will explore a little further on) in relation to its autonomy for financial gain within the private sector. While in Britain consultants enjoying a state salary by working in the public sector must confine their work in the private sector to 10 per cent of their earnings, no such restrictions apply to consultants in Ireland (Wren, 2003) (for a more detailed account of consultants' contracts, see Chapter 13). A central problem has been the successive failure of goverments in Ireland to impose a monitoring system over the private work undertaken by consultants enjoying state salaries with pension rights. While, at the time of writing, consultants working in the public health system are expected to dedicate thirty-three hours per week to the care of public patients, there is no insistence on this under the terms of their contract. They may delegate the care of public patients to more junior doctors (Wren, 2003).

Ninty-one percent of consultants in Ireland work in the public and private sectors, yet all of the evidence suggests that private patients get priority treatment. Since, in the private sector, consultants get paid per patient treated, and a flat salary for all public patients treated, it has been proposed that many are acting out of self-interest based on financial gain rather than on the basis of clinical need (Wren, 2003). In this sense, although resisting state regulation may enhance professional autonomy, one of the traits referred to earlier, it also serves to undermine another of the traditional features of a profession – altruism and serving the interrests of the community rather than being self-serving.

The threat of consumerism to professional dominance in Ireland
Challenges have arisen for the medical profession in Ireland in recent years that potentially threaten its professional power, such as the rise in consumerism among the public, and questions and scandals about the clinical judgement of doctors. These relate to the deprofessionalising theory advanced by Haug (1973) (referred to earlier).

Evidence of a rise in consumerism among the Irish public may be gauged by the dramatic increase in litigation cases taken against members of the medical profession in recent years. It was reported in 1999 that the rate of medical litigation in Ireland had reached crisis point, and that doctors in Ireland were three times more likely to be sued than their counterparts in Britain (*Irish Times*, 02/10/99). Speaking on the issue of medical negligence, a professor of legal medicine, Professor Denis Cusack, noted that 'a more fundamental and worrying cost is the continuing disintegration, if not destruction, of that most basic aspect of healthcare, the relationship based on trust between doctors and their patients' (*Irish Times*, 20/04/01).

The practices of obstetricians and gynaecologists in Ireland have also evinced outcries from various groups for a greater degree of accountability and monitoring by those outside the profession. Groups such as the Patients' Association, The European Institute of Women's Health in Dublin, and the Irish Childbirth Trust have all criticised the closed shop operations of the medical profession, the lack of external objective controls, and the lack of transparency and information (*Irish Times*, 15/12/98).

Recent scandals have also had the potential to damage the public's trust in the medical profession. In 1997, a three-month tribunal was held in which the Irish Blood Transfusion Service Board's (BTSB) decisions that resulted in 1,000-2,000 women in the state being infected with hepatitis C was investigated (Department of Health (Irl), 1997b). Senior members of the medical profession were implicated in 'wrongful acts', 'failures' and 'inadequacies' (Department of Health (Irl), 1997b). A further tribunal of enquiry reported in September 2002 concerning decisions made by the BTSB during the 1980s that resulted in haemophiliacs being infected by the HIV virus. A further judicial inquiry and compensation tribunal was sought in relation to allegations that a consultant obstetrician performed unnecessary hysterectomies on women following Caesarean sections. The consultant's name was subsequently removed from the Medical Register, and his former employer, the North Eastern Health Board, reported that it had amended its rules to improve checks and regularly scrutinise consultants' surgical records (*Irish Times*, 23/07/01). Further discrediting information was exposed in relation to the medical profession in recent years when it was revealed that the practice of retaining human organs, as happened in the UK, also occurred in Ireland. After the scandal broke, organ donations in Ireland fell significantly (*Irish Times*, 03/03/00, 29/03/01).

In spite of these recent challenges, the medical profession in Ireland can hardly be said to be a profession in decline, in the same way, for example, that the powers of the Catholic Church have diminished. It may be concluded that while some aspects of their professional status have been challenged in recent years, they have, nonetheless, managed to sustain a great deal of power and status.

The medical profession in Britain
The introduction of general management into the NHS since the 1980s spelled a shift in the administration of the service by civil servants and clinicians to its administration by outside agents, placing bureaucratic constraints on the medical profession's authority (see Harrison and Dowswell, 2002). In the 1990s, the autonomy of the medical profession in the UK has been further shaken by legislation that attempted to limit the clinical freedom of doctors and make them accountable for expenditure (Annandale, 1998). This was part of the Conservative government's move towards a market economy by making publicly-funded healthcare cost-effective, and creating a quasi-market or **internal market** in healthcare (Clarke, 2001). Competition and tight managerial controls were required in the process which involved the separation of purchasing and providing functions within healthcare. The main purchasers under this new arrangement were health authorities who shopped around for the best deal for the populations they served. NHS Trusts were set up and could tender for contracts in various health authorities (Clarke, 2001). What these changes meant for doctors in Britain was increasing managerial control emanating from the state (Morrall, 2001).

While the notion of the internal market came into being in the lifetime of a Conservative government, the Labour government that came to power in 1997 has continued the notion of accountability, through the concept of clinical governance (Department of Health (UK), 1997a). This demands that the standard of service to be given to health consumers is set out, and both the NHS and practitioners, including doctors, are held accountable for the quality of the service (Morrall, 2001). GP and consultant contracts require doctors to provide job plans outlining their day-to-day work, and the Audit Commission has recommended that trusts oversee the completion and monitoring of these plans (Annandale, 1998). British legislation since the 1990s now means that doctors deemed to be performing their job poorly can have penalties imposed; in the past such censure was confined to severe malpractice such as having caused injury, or having abused or killed a patient (Medical (Professional Performance) Act, 1995). The most recent develoment is the introduction of performance indicators to monitor clinical care in general practice which 'could augur a significant erosion of medical autonomy, since assessment of work performance is no longer the doctor's sole prerogative' (Exworthy et al, 2003: 1493). Recent NHS reforms have also advocated a shift from a consultant-led to a consultant-delivered system of healthcare (Department of Health (UK), 2000).

At the same time as these controls appear to be tightening, doctors are increasingly occupying dual roles as physicians and managers within the NHS, so that doctors themselves can control and regulate the work of their peers and subordinates, and fend off interference from outside (Annandale, 1998). Recent moves within the NHS also suggest that doctors are to be more heavily represented on the NHS Management Board (Morrall, 2001). This notion of *countervailing pressures* to which medicine is exposed has been proposed by Freidson, in his revisiting of the concept of profession (Freidson, 1994). Drawing on Freidson, Annandale (1998) argues that recent changes affecting the medical profession in Britain suggest that some moves appear to undermine the professional powers of medicine, while others serve to enhance it. Identified among the challenges to medicine are changes in management structures, nursing, alternative medicine, lawyers, the media, and patients' organisations (Gabe et al, 1994). Armstrong (2002) identifies a recourse to evidence-based medicine as a possible way for the medical profession to cry off the imposition of external controls – by adhering to scientifically-proven interventions across categories of patients. However, this he proposes would serve to undermine the autonomy of individual practitioners to provide individually tailored patient-centred care and subject them to a new type of technicality that (ironically) elites within their own ranks are promoting.

Overall, most commentators seem to agree that while the professional autonomy of medicine is being challenged within Britain, the medical profession still remains a very strong and powerful elite (Hunter, 1994; Annandale, 1998; Morrall, 2001).

As in Ireland, in recent years in the UK the public's respect for the medical profession suffered a blow in the face of a series of scandals that called into question the integrity of the profession (Morrall, 2001). Drawing on a review by Cartner-Morley (1998), Morrall (2001) outlines a series of medical scandals that were reported in British newspapers over a period of one month. A plethora of examples of medical oversights and professional misconduct were featured during that month. Further doubts were cast over the credibility of doctors in 1999, when a GP, Dr Harold Shipman, was charged with murdering fifteen of his patients. Like Ireland, Britain has also experienced scandal in relation to the unauthorised retention of body parts following death. The paternalistic attitude of doctors has been the subject of public horror following revelations that over 100,000 organ and body parts of former patients had been retained by hospitals throughout England without the permission of the next-of-kin (*Irish Times*, 31/01/01).

Professional power and nursing

Etzioni (1998: 175) referred to nursing as a semi-profession, by which she meant:

> ... their [semi-professions] training is shorter, their status is less legitimated, their right to privileged communication less established, there is less of a specialised body of knowledge, they have less autonomy from supervision or societal control than 'the' professions.

Freidson (1970a) referred to health workers employed alongside medical personnel as paraprofessional, working ultimately under the control of medicine. However, nursing has struggled to attain professional power on a par with medicine. Witz (1992) proposes that nursing elites in Britain have invoked a dual closure strategy in attempting to professionalise. One dimension of the dual closure strategy has been for nursing elites to resist domination from medicine in carving out a territory for nursing, while on the other, to control and regulate entry. However, the whole notion of whether nursing ought to become a profession has been questioned (Oakley, 1998; Davies, 1995). The debate has centred around whether professionalising actually improves patient care, or whether it simply gives more power to the occupational group (in this case nursing).

Although nurse theorists do not all share the same aims for nursing with regard to professional status and the concomitant power base that traditionally go with it (Porter, 1995), there is a specific set of features that have emerged in recent years which are collectively referred to as 'new nursing' (Salvage, 1990). New nursing represents a departure from some of the philosophies and practices set down in the preceding period and encompasses specific approaches to nursing work. The origins of the knowledge base that constitutes new nursing lie mainly in the work of nurse theorists in the USA who are endeavouring to create an identifiable body of nursing knowledge (which is the hallmark of a profession).

Central to the notion of new nursing is an emphasis on caring, communication, and subjective aspects of the experience of illness (Jones, 1994); partnership with patients and clients accomplished through primary nursing (a named nurse assigned to a patient and accountable for his or her care); and a process approach to care, where care is individualised and planned around specific problems or potential problems (that is, through using the nursing process) (Salvage, 1990; Porter, 1995). The first stage of the nursing process ends with the identification of the patient's problems, or what some theorists refer to as 'nursing diagnosis', that is, the identification of functional problems a patient has that are amenable to nursing interventions. The notion of nursing diagnosis is considered central to the notion of professionalisation, because it represents the identification of a knowledge base which only a registered nurse by virtue of her training and registration has control over. These new nursing concepts are still in the course of being developed. Nonetheless, the theoretical basis of new nursing is not about creating sub-doctors out of nurses, but rather to deepen nursing's commitment to total patient care. New nursing, therefore, is not about developing nursing as a technocratic activity in response to technical developments in medicine, but rather an attempt to construct a separate knowledge base for nursing, with nurturing (caring and communicating) as a central theme (Watson, 1979, 1985; Benner and Wrubel, 1989).

It is interesting that the knowledge base that nursing is attempting to develop has been associated with a feminine cultural form of knowledge (Porter, 1998b). Some theorists believe that this provides the best opportunity to enhance the power of nursing and offer better patient care (see Porter, 1998b). Others are sceptical and believe that elites are more concerned with the former – consolidating nursing's power. Davies (1995) suggests that professionalising may not be the best thing for nursing as professionalising is a masculine enterprise mediated by objectivity, rationality and depersonalisation. Bolton (2001: 93) notes that the move towards a professional identity means that nurses 'have to present the detached, but caring, face of the professional carer'.

Davies' argument against conventional professionalisation centres on a critique of masculinity as a cultural form. She uses the notions of masculinity and femininity, not as biological distinctions but rather as 'immensely powerful cultural ideas about the sexes' (Davies, 1998: 191). She notes (1998: 192-2) that:

> [m]asculinity … means being detached and calmly evaluating the opinions, being strictly in control of self and, indeed, of others. For if the world is populated by other masculine selves, each with its individual project, then there is little room for shared enthusiams or co-operative activity. The logic of masculinity's project (not necessarily the project of individual men …) has to be able to control relations with others in a world that is otherwise bleak in its competitiveness.

Davies goes on to argue that the ideal of bounded masculinity underlies organisational culture. The embodiment of the 'all-knowing, distant and detached' professional, she suggests, is in the guise of the medical consultant paying a fleeting visit to 'his' patients, with nursing as 'a necessary adjunct to professionalism'. Instead, she advocates a new professionalism relevant to contemporary healthcare, a professionalism that supersedes a masculine ideal and is gender neutral, transcending both masculinity and femininity. This new professionalism would comprise reflective practice, supported practice with collective responsibility and the engagement of the professional.

The notion of gender is strongly interrelated with the issue of professional power, because the knowledge base that nursing is attempting to develop is strongly associated with female characteristics (caring, communication, and nurturing). As Gordon (1991) notes, a critical affirmation of the value of nursing is rooted in defending the importance of emotional labour. The recognition of nursing as an equal occupation to medicine is rooted in the acknowledgement that female attributes are on an equal footing to male attributes, and that feminine tasks performed by nurses are of equal worth to the masculine work of doctors (Gordon, 1991).

Miers (2000) notes that while recent changes in Britain may facilitate a more autonomous role within healthcare for nurses, developments within the nursing profession continue to be impeded by labour force requirements of the health service. Nurses' pay and conditions are dictated predominantly by the government rather than by the profession (Miers, 2000).

Nursing and the professionalising project in Ireland

To what extent has nursing in Ireland become more professional? Although the characteristics of a profession depicted in trait theory have been criticised for their self-serving motives (Davies, 1995), one means of gauging the progress nursing has made towards becoming a profession is to assess where it stands in relation to these traits. In particular, how nursing in Ireland has fared in relation to the traits of self-regulation, control of entry and educational standards, and the development of a separate body of knowledge will be explored.

The registration, control and education of nurses in Ireland is under the auspices of An Bord Altranais (The Nursing Board). An Bord Altranais has the powers to discipline its members, and indeed to remove them from the register of nurses.

Many of the issues and concerns around nursing's aspiration towards professional status have been articulated in the *Report of the Commission on Nursing* (Government of Ireland, 1998). The commission was initially set up following a Labour Court recommendation to address industrial unrest and retention problems within the ranks of nursing. Problems considered by the commission included the structural and working conditions of nurses, grading structures, training and educational issues, promotional opportunities and the changing role of the nurse in an evolving healthcare context. Indeed, these issues that dog nursing might be interpreted as frustrations of an occupational group who were subjected to a high degree of control in the workplace, with poor promotional prospects, little recognition and paltry remuneration relative to the degrees of responsibility which they were expected to hold. While the implementation of the commission's recommendations was too tardy to halt the first ever national nurses' strike (in 1999), since then changes have been initiated to meet the commission's recommendations, and are monitored by a Monitoring Committee at the Nursing Policy Division of the Department of Health and Children. In addition, a National Council for the Professional

Development of Nursing and Midwifery was set up to oversee developments in specialist nursing and continuing education for nurses

Among the changes recommended by the Commission on Nursing and currently being implemented are the transfer of nursing education to third level and the introduction of clinical career pathways. Until 2000, individual hospitals approved as training schools by An Bord Altranais were free to select suitably qualified entrants to nursing through an interview process. This changed in 2001, when applicants to nursing were selected through the Central Applications Office along with all other third level students. Although arguably this move resulted in the relinquishing of a degree of control over who might be selected, it is also linked with the increasing professionalisation of nursing by developing a third level education. Increasing professionalisation is also evidenced by the increase in the preparation programme from three to four years, and an increase in the basic level of qualification from diploma to degree level that commenced in 2002 on a nationwide basis.[23] Clinical career pathways are currently being developed in the form of specialist or advanced roles so that those nurses who wish to stay in clinical practice do not have to abscond to nursing education or management in order to get promoted. At the time of writing, a number of advanced practice posts have been approved in Ireland by the National Council for the Professional Development of Nursing and Midwifery. These posts demand extended education, to a minimum of master's level in the case of advanced practice roles. This extended training suggests an increasing professionalism among nurses in Ireland. However, the notion of advanced roles for nurses, encompassing limited prescribing powers, while lifting the status of nursing, may well facilitate rather than threaten the medical profession in a climate of reducing junior doctors' working hours (see Hughes, 2002).

With regard to the creation of a separate body of knowledge, nursing in Ireland has generally relied upon nursing knowledge created elsewhere. Research funding for nursing has been problematic (Treacy and Hyde, 1999), reflecting its marginal status relative to medicine. This situation is improving, however, with research fellowships for doctoral nursing students available from the Health Research Board since 1999. Also, the Department of Health and Children published a research strategy for nursing and midwifery in 2001, outlining proposals for developing nursing research in Ireland (DoHC, 2003a). Nonetheless, a separate body of nursing theory continues to remain underdeveloped, and represents the single most difficult challenge for those aspiring to full professional status for nurses. A further and arguably more complex challenge for nursing lies in articulating in clinical practice whatever separate body of knowledge it has developed; this issue will be explored further in the next section.

---

23. Prior to this, a National Implementation Committee was established in 2001 with the remit of implementing the 4 year, pre-registration nursing degree.

Empirical studies on relations between doctors and nurses in clinical settings

There is no published sociological research available on the nurse-physician relationship in the Republic of Ireland. However, studies conducted elsewhere are informative in terms of where the balance of power lies between the two occupations in clinical settings. It was noted earlier that traditionally medicine's monopoly over diagnosis and treatment of illness provided it with power to dominate other occupations in the division of labour. As Porter (1999: 102) (citing Johnson 1973) notes, 'Because all actions stem from diagnosis and subsequent prescription, the diagnostician enjoys a unique position of authority in relation to both clients and allied occupations'. Whether and/or in what circumstances medicine actually dominates nursing in clinical settings will be considered in exploring existing empirical studies.

Prior to the 1960s, there was little research available anywhere on the nurse-physician relationship. However, the conventional wisdom on the status of the relationship was the emphasis on obedience, loyalty and handmaiden status on the part of the nurse (Porter, 1991). The general view was that a gendered division of labour existed with nurses exhibiting 'unproblematic subordination', that is, nurses accepting subordinate roles without conflict (Porter, 1991). Empirical research since the 1960s has cast doubt on the notion of unproblematic subordination as the dominant way that nurses interact with doctors. The first of these studies was Stein's (1998[1967]) classic (albeit empirically limited) US study of a telephone conversation between a nurse and a doctor, from which an interaction called the 'doctor-nurse game' was derived. This is described as follows:

> The cardinal rule of the game is that open disagreement between the players must be avoided at all costs. Thus, the nurse can communicate her recommendations without appearing to be making a recommendation statement. The physician, in requesting a recommendation from a nurse, must do so without appearing to be asking for it (Stein, 1998[1967:261]).

The game required the nurse to conceal her knowledge, skills and information and present herself as deferential. It was not until the 1980s that further evidence suggested that nurses' interactions with doctors involved more than the so-called doctor-nurse game (Hughes, 1988).

Hughes (1988) studied nurses' and physicians' interactions in a hospital casualty department in the United Kingdom. He observed that a good deal of responsibility for processing and triaging patients rested with nursing staff. The latter's work often bordered on areas of decision making for which doctors were legally responsible. Hughes found that nurses reprimanded junior doctors for such factors as not responding to calls when requested, leaving patients waiting, or being late on duty. While sometimes recommendations were made subtly by nurses, akin to the doctor-nurse game, Hughes noted that for a good deal of the time nurses were assertive. Although nurses might acknowledge the physician's clinical authority, they nonetheless gave advice in a number of aspects of departmental practice in a direct manner. Less frequently, senior nurses candidly criticised the work of junior doctors, and took control of the matter in hand themselves. A number of factors cross-cut nurses' power in Hughes' study. These included the large number of admissions to the casualty department, the rapid turnover of doctors compared to nurses, and the number of overseas doctors (particularly form the Indian sub-continent) who were not familiar with the social cues presented by patients and relied on local nurses to read these. Overall, Hughes' study demonstrated that while nurses possessed more open control over decision making than the doctor-nurse game allowed, it was informal influence. In this sense, nurses exercised control over matters that might be considered to be within the jurisdiction of medicine rather than nursing and over which medical personnel could reclaim their authority at any time.

Stein and his colleagues (referred to above) revisited the doctor-nurse game in an article published in 1990. They noted that since the original study, a number of important changes had occurred, namely a reduced public esteem for physicians, an increase in females joining the ranks of medicine, and an increasingly recognised value of nursing in a climate of nurse shortages. The development of nurse practitioner roles has also had an impact. Stein et al (1990) noted that nurses had, for the most part, stopped playing the game and were consciously attempting to change nursing and nurses' relationships with others in the healthcare system. The researchers again produced a single interaction incident as empirical evidence of changes in the nurse-patient relationship. However, Prowse and Allen (2002) found manifestations of Stein's doctor-nurse in their recent British study of interactions between medical and nursing staff in a post-anaesthesia care unit. They observed that nurses were often more knowledgeable than inexperienced medical staff and, sensitive not to offend them, the nurses prompted and guided doctors towards the most important aspects of the patient's clinical condition.

Porter's (1991) participant observation study of nurse-physician relations in an Intensive Care Unit (ICU) in Belfast provides further insights on relations between nursing and medicine, particularly with regard to clinical decision making. Porter (1999: 100) noted that formal power 'involves nurses making decisions about care that are independent of medical power'. However, Porter (1991) found that nursing theory did not inform nursing decisions, forcing him to conclude that formal decision making had little impact compared to the informal mechanisms used by nurses (see Box 12.2).

In a later paper based on the same study, Porter (1995) expands on a critical issue in the nursing-medical relationship, notably its impact on the under-utilisation of nursing theory in the ICU. This occurred partly because

Box 12.2 *Relative strength of decision-making strategies observed among nurses in Porter's (1991) ICU study*

- *Unproblematic subordination* (nurses' unquestioning obedience to medical orders) was used to a very limited degree, as incidences where medical orders were given without an explanation were uncommon. This type of interaction occurred only in encounters with medical consultants.
- *Informal covert decision making* (a pretence of unproblematic subordination as occurred in the doctor-nurse game) was also used infrequently because physicians were usually prepared to acknowledge the input of the nurse.
- *Informal overt decision making* (open involvement of nurses in decision making, but without formal backing of the nursing process, with medicine having the formal power to re-assert its authority) on the part of nurses was quite common. This was especially so among senior nurses who argued their cases even where there was contestation by doctors. In some interactions, the physician appeared to be in the subordinate role! Various degrees of assertiveness by nurses were in evidence.
- *Formal overt decision making* (decisions based on nursing theory and the nursing process). Porter found little evidence of this type of decision making.

of the intense medical overlay in the ICU, whereby many nursing decisions were in fact made by medical personnel. For example, nurses were using the Roper, Logan, Tierney model of nursing and an activity of daily living such as patient's nutrition was decided by physicians. Porter (1995) noted that nurses spent a considerable amount of time attending to the writing of the nursing process, but actually did not use it in decision making. He noted that, instead of guiding nursing decisions, the nursing process 'had been incorporated into the existing network of power relations with the minimum of disruption' (1995: 31). Porter (1995) argues that the lack of success nursing theory has had in being incorporated into nursing practice is because of the lack of attention theorists have given to social structure. New nursing, he argues, has not taken on board the significance of nursing's interrelationships with other elements of the occupational structure, particularly medical dominance. In the ICU, for example, the introduction of nursing diagnosis was superseded by physicians' capacity to over-rule nursing decisions and by the dominance of biomedicine.

In a British study by Walby and Greenwell (1994), nurses and doctors were found to be mutually dependent on one another so that the work of each could be conducted more efficiently. The authors noted that the boundaries of care and treatment were often nebulous, particularly in relation to areas where nurses have a high degree of expertise such as in wound management. In spite of nurses' command over wound care interventions, a physician's prescription was still required for particular treatments. Walby and Greenwell (1994) found that senior nurses contested the decisions of junior doctors, and many conflicts were noted in this relationship. However, nurses accepted the authority of consultants and senior physicians. In addition, nurses were critical of the fact that doctors would not listen to them in matters relating to patients. Walby and Greenwell (1994) reported that physicians were likely to accept nurses taking on more extended medical duties, provided that the doctors could continue to control these skills.

Based on interviews conducted with nurses in Swedish hospitals, Svensson (1996) presented a fairly positive perspective on the impact of nurses' knowledge on interactions between physicians and nurses. He noted that a new knowledge context of healthcare had emerged, particularly because of an increase in chronic illness, which demanded an understanding of *social* aspects of patients. Nurses had greater access to this domain, and, he contended, this strengthened their position vis-à-vis medicine. In addition, he argued that nurses' continuous presence in the clinical area provided them with a more comprehensive picture of patients, which medical personnel needed to draw upon to make medical diagnosis. He noted a degree of **negotiatiated order** in relations between between nurses and physicians. The notion of nurses' knowledge was used in a much more general sense by Svensson compared with Porter's analysis, and was not directly linked to a body of nursing theory. Snelgrove and Hughes' (2002) British study noted that while nurses provided an idealised image of teamwork when interviewed, they produced very few actual examples of decision making that could be constructed as a joint endeavour with their medical colleagues. Rather, joint decision-making appeared to be confined to discharge planning and the social realm of care.

In a more recent UK study, against a background of managers encouraging nurses to expand the scope of their practice to include junior doctors' work, Allen (1997: 505) observed 'minimal inter-occupational negotiation and little explicit conflict' between nurses and physicians. This contrasted with Svensson's (1996) finding of negotiated order in clinical sites. Allen found that although nurses reported that their priority was nursing care, and that when busy other work would be negotiated with medical staff, she nonetheless observed that nurses did physician-devolved work irrespective of other pressures. Nurses were more likely to be permanent than medical staff, which allowed them some degree of influence. Allen (1997, 2001) found that doctors relied on nurses for guidelines about local protocols, and had considerable influence over clinical decisions. Furthermore, while nurses questioned junior doctors' prescriptions, the former were rarely questioned by the latter. Rather, nurses' knowledge and skills were overtly acknowledged by doctors. For nurses, their capacity to engage in 'medical work' increased their autonomy, enhanced patient care and avoided interpersonal tension. However, in spite of the extended input of nurses, doctors still enjoyed higher status. Allen's study broadly supports the findings of Hughes (1988) and Porter (1991) insofar as nurses were found to be assertive in decision making vis-à-vis junior medical staff, yet their influence was not officially legitimated.

In an altogether different perspective from Porter's (1991) focus on whether and/or how nursing knowledge was used in decision making, Manias and Street (2001) abandoned the notion of identifying a separate body of nursing knowledge in their study of decision making between physicians and nurses in an Australian ICU. Instead, the researchers focused on 'the process of contextualising knowledge' (2001: 130). This is underpinned by the notion that different ways of knowing are possible regarding the same problem. This means that the same body of knowledge could be used differently by different groups, depending on the occupational experiences of each group. Manias and Street noted that, in the interplay between nurses and physicians, some aspects of nursing knowledge (a combination of scientific/technical/medical knowledge forms and practical and experiential knowledge drawn from various sources) were acknowledged by medical personnel, while others were ignored. They also observed that while there was a tendency for junior doctors to draw upon nurses' knowledge to surmount challenges in an unfamiliar territory, nurses rarely relied on junior doctors' knowledge. Characteristics of the doctor-nurse game and a process they call 'staging' were also identified in the relationship between nurses and junior doctors. Staging referred to a practice whereby nurses controlled the amount and type of knowledge they revealed to junior doctors about patients in order to steer the latter towards a decision that the nurses favoured. Manias and Street's work elucidates the complex input and influence that nurses have in decision making about patient care. However, while the authors noted an informal recognition of this contribution a good deal of the time, they did not problematise the fact that the physician's last word or signature obviated official avowal of the nursing input.

Before concluding, let us return to the issue of gender which, it was noted earlier, has historically had a central role to play in the relations between nurses and physicians. With more women entering medicine, is there evidence that female doctors interact differently with nurses than do their male counterparts? Walby and Greenwell (1994) noted that there were few differences between male and female physicians in their encounters with nurses in day-to-day activities. They argued that the occupational socialisation process had a stronger influence on female doctors than their initial gender cultural socialisation. However, they strongly attest to the impact of gender on the relationship in terms of the structural position of doctors and nurses in issues such as pay and conditions, the nature of the work done by each group, and their relative status and prestige. By contrast, Porter (1998b) noted that while the gender of the nurse had little impact in encounters with physicians (male nurses did not display greater authority that female nurses), there were differences noted according to the gender of the doctor. Female physicians were found to be more egalitarian and polite in their interactions with nurses. Both Porter (1998b) and Walby and Greenwell (1994) observed that female physicians were more likely to clean up clinical waste after procedures compared to their male counterparts. Porter (1998b) noted, however, that nurses in his study were actively attempting to assert themselves against subordination. Wicks (1998) came to a similar conclusion arguing that while theories of patriarchy and medical dominance are useful, nurses' active role in re-defining nursing must not be underestimated.

When the literature base on relations between nursing and medicine is drawn together, it is clear that a number of dominant themes emerge. Most studies suggest that contemporary nurses display varying degrees of assertiveness in their dealings with physicians depending, to a large extent, on the seniority of the physician, and the circumstances in which the interactions take place. Nurses seem to have little difficulty asserting themselves in interactions with junior doctors (Allen, 1997; Porter, 1991; Walby and Greenwell, 1994; Hughes, 1988; Manias and Street, 2001). However, a number of studies suggest that even senior nurses accept the authority of consultants (Porter, 1991; Walby and Greenwell, 1994). In an equal situation, senior members of each occupation would interact as equals. Furthermore, the status of nurses' decision-making capacity appears to be highly fragile, and subject to collapse in the face of medical dominance because the purely nursing component of patient care, over which nurses might legitimately have control, is not always clearly separated from medical aspects of care.

Of concern for nurse theorists must be under-utilisation of nursing theory in clinical decision making and the extent to which nursing's position in relation to medicine impacts on this (Porter, 1995). There seems to be an assumption that once nurses themselves are educated in new nursing theories and research, and the traditional nursing hierarchy is overthrown, then nursing theory will slot itself in side by side with medicine in clinical areas. However, such a view does not account for the complex relationship that nursing has with medicine and the extent to which this relationship affects the articulation of nursing theory in clinical decision making. As Davies (1995: 181) notes in relation to health service planning in the United Kingdom, nursing has been treated as 'an adjunct to the "real" business of medical care', with nurses not being allowed the space to undertake 'the real business of nursing at all'. Indeed, as recently as 1998, a letter published in *The Lancet* advocating the reinstatement of the traditional hierarchical nurse-physician relationship was followed by an outburst of support from both nurses and doctors (Kitson, 2001). This epitomises the vulnerability of the new nursing agenda.

The informal decision making that nurses enjoy vis-à-vis physicians is, to a large extent, based in situational factors that arise by virtue of nurses' more stable position within the organisation, rather than through a status acquired as a result of their education and registration. This stable position allows nurses to see the bigger picture in relation to both the patient and the workings of the organisation, compared to the transient position of most junior doctors. As indicated earlier, nurses were most assertive in the face of inexperienced doctors, who were more likely to be temporary and unfamiliar with ward policies and local protocols (Hughes, 1988; Porter, 1991; Allen, 1997; Manias and Street, 2001). The high degree of exposure of nurses to the same patients compared to doctors' more fractured exposure provided the former with a degree of power, because doctors relied on nurses' more comprehensive knowledge when making diagnosis (Walby and Greenwell, 1994; Svensson, 1996).

Nursing has come a long way in striving to attain equality with medicine. Further challenges lie ahead with the development of advanced nurse practitioner roles, where the boundaries between nursing and medicine legitimately overlap to a greater degree than before (Cox, 2001). While efforts at formalising nurses' decision making seem to hinge on identifying a separate body of knowledge which is jurisdictionally nursing knowledge, the structural dimension of medical dominance remains a major obstacle to the articulation of such knowledge. The notion of contextualising knowledge, and recognising the complementary and equally valuable contributions of both nursing and medicine to patient care without slicing up knowledge forms between the occupations, offers an attractive alternative. However, it does not eliminate the fundamental problem nursing experiences in relating to medicine – a lack of formal recognition of its contribution.

Summary

- From the outset of modern nursing, the work of physicians and nurses was highly gendered and related historically to socially approved work for men and women.
- The relative status and societal value of medicine and nursing reflects widespread societal perceptions of scientific versus caring work, with medical work enjoying a higher status.
- The traditional system of nursing education prepared nurses to be deferential workers who fitted in with the organisational system.
- Medicine has traditionally been considered the prototype of professions, while nursing is striving to achieve professional recognition.
- Recent societal changes have posed challenges to medicine's freedom and autonomy. In Ireland, while medicine has had to negotiate with the state to maintain its power position, it continues to exert a great deal of influence. In the UK, major bureaucratic reforms occurring since the 1980s have had a greater regulatory influence over medicine than has happened in Ireland.
- Recent scandals and public dissatisfaction, both in Ireland and the UK, have the potential to undermine some of medicine's professional power.

- There is evidence that nursing is becoming more professional, with qualifications awarded at a higher educational level and a more extended training period for specialist and advanced clinical posts. Empirical studies suggest that while some nurses do enjoy a considerable degree of freedom in clinical decision making, their power is largely *informal*.
- The blurring of the boundaries between nursing and medical work places nurses in a vulnerable position should physicians, who occupy the dominant position historically, wish to re-assert their authority.

Topics for discussion and reflection
1. To what extent do you believe that the power of the medical profession in Ireland has been eroded over the past thirty years?
2. Are the recent changes in nursing education in Ireland, the move to the third level sector, a positive step?

THIRTEEN

Healthcare systems and health policy in Ireland

In this chapter we trace the development of the Irish healthcare system and examine current health policy reform. We begin the chapter by outlining the key transformations that have occurred in understandings of health and healthcare provision. Next, a general overview of the Irish healthcare system is given, outlining the historical dynamics that gave shape to the distinct institutional features of the system. In this section, we follow the key policy and legislative phases in the transformation of health services from a system based primarily on charitable and private medicine to a state-controlled and publicly financed system of healthcare. While public health is funded directly from general taxation, the Irish healthcare system is characterised by a mix of public and private provision. We will outline how this system operates at the level of patient entitlement and identify the key institutional features that underpin the private-public model of care. We will also assess a two-tier health system as a structural feature of the public-private mix. We will review the reorientation of health policy since the mid-1980s, and specifically address three important elements in terms of the future of health policy and healthcare: equity, the structural reform of primary care and health consumerism.

Transformations in health and healthcare
Nettleton (1995) outlines the key transformations that have occurred in our understanding of and response to health issues. These changes include a shift in the burden of disease from acute, life-threatening diseases to chronic, long-standing debilitating forms of illness that are considered more amenable to preventative strategies than curative medicine; a corresponding shift away from the hospital to community care and a parallel shift in emphasis from the view that patients are passive to the view that patients are discerning customers. Concomitant with these general transformations, a key policy shift has been the movement away from a delivery or producer-led system dominated by health professionals to a demand or consumer-led system. (For a discussion of the concept of consumerism in the context of lay-professional relations see Chapter 8).

Since the 1970s, international health policy has shifted the emphasis away from the biomedical definition of health and illness as the absence of disease to an understanding of health as a resource affecting physical, mental and social well-being (see Chapter 14). There are a number of factors that account for this shift. By the 1950s, mortality gains achieved throughout the first half of the twentieth century were beginning to level off in most Western countries, and with a general decline in birth rates and increased longevity chronic illness and disability were emerging as the principle threats to population health. These epidemiological shifts in the burden of disease in Western societies led to governments devising policies on disease prevention and health promotion, which led to a shift in focus from the elimination of disease to health maintenance. By the early 1980s, Western governments were confronted by the growing cost of medical technology and increasing demands on public health services that were dominated by hospital care. The key challenge facing Western societies was to balance rising consumer demands on health services and the rising cost of healthcare with changing population health needs. The main policy direction that took hold, albeit through different strategies, was to cap the cost of care by controlling the utilisation of the more technological and labour intensive aspects of the health services where medical dominance prevailed. This led to a shift in emphasis from hospital-based specialised treatments to community provision, which was regarded as a key site for the implementation of preventative and health promotional strategies.

Prior to the economic crisis of the late 1970s, governments invested heavily in the supply side of health provision. This policy became increasingly untenable from an economic point of view and, moreover, the investment in meeting universal needs did not have the expected return of improved health for all. This led to a shift away from a delivery or producer-led system dominated by health professionals to a demand and consumer-led system. Put simply, this means a shift from the policy concern for more services to a consumer concern for better outcomes. The push towards health consumerism comes from two fronts. On the one hand, the consumer health movement demands wider public consultation on the development of appropriate health policy, reflecting a shift away from the notion that patients are simply passive recipients of medical care. At the same time, the experience of patients is increasingly seen as important to the evaluation of health needs and the delivery of effective services and, in this sense, consumers have become important allies to health managers in challenging professional power and the producer-dominated health system.

The development of the Irish healthcare system: an historical overview
Following the foundation of the state in 1922, responsibility for health fell to the Department of Local Government and Public Health, which oversaw a basic public health system consisting of county and workhouse infirmaries

and a dispensary medical service established in the latter decades of the eighteenth century and developed under the Poor Law (1838) (Barrington, 1987). Over the next four decades the state played a growing role in the organisation and financing of healthcare, leading to significant changes in healthcare policy.

The voluntary hospital sector and the state
In historical terms, a defining feature of the Irish healthcare system is the role of voluntary hospitals, which developed in the eighteenth and nineteenth centuries under the auspices of philanthropic organisations and religious orders. The importance of the voluntary hospitals grew as hospitals were transformed from providing medical relief to the poor into clinical training centres in the nineteenth century. While voluntary hospitals received an annual grant from the state, they were independent of statutory authority and their income was largely generated through charitable funds. Visiting doctors were not directly remunerated but had access to income provided through medical tuition and private practice through their association with reputable hospitals (O'Ferrall, 2000). By the late 1920s the rising cost of advancements in medical technology meant that the capacity of the voluntary hospitals to provide medical services for the poor became dependent on funds generated by the provision of private beds (Barrington, 1987). The encroachment of the state into the voluntary health sector coincided with the gradual expansion of state responsibility for health services between the late 1920s and the 1950s. The voluntary hospitals have over time become increasingly dependent on public sector finance. The main lines of tension and conflict to emerge in the development of the hospital system have centred on the vulnerability of the voluntary sector to fiscal policy, and the threat that state control poses to the autonomy of the independent hospital boards and their specific ethos.

Expanding public healthcare: 1940s-50s
The expansion of public healthcare, which was consolidated through legislative reform under the Health Acts of 1947 and 1953, brought the state into direct conflict with the Catholic hierarchy and the Irish medical profession, which together formed a strong political alliance against what they perceived as the dawning of socialised medicine in Ireland (Barrington, 1987; O'Ferrall, 2000). The political compromises the state reached with these key interest groups during this defining period in the history of healthcare accounts for important features of the current health services. At the time of the publication of the Beveridge Report (1942) in Britain, which laid the foundation for the establishment of the National Health Service (NHS) in 1948, the Irish government appeared intent on developing a free national health service.

By the time the 1947 Health Bill was drafted the original blueprint for a free national health service had been diluted. The Irish Medical Association

(IMA) was opposed to the provision of a free comprehensive health service, which was a threat to the vested interests of private practice and to the professional autonomy enjoyed by Irish doctors. The voluntary hospital consultants were particularly forceful in their opposition. In their case the extension of state responsibility not only potentially threatened private practice but also their control over clinical teaching. The Catholic hierarchy was opposed to state provision of welfare and perceived the expansion of state responsibility for health as an encroachment on the Catholic social principle of subsidiarity, which emphasised the role of voluntarism through self-regulatory professional organisations like the medical profession. An expanded public health system was seen as a threat to the Church's authority and influence over health, education and social services.

The most controversial aspect of the Health Bill was the proposed provision of free health services to all mothers and their children up to the age of sixteen. This aspect of the Bill was reformulated by Dr Noel Browne (then Minister for Health) as the Mother and Child Scheme (1950), which was opposed by the IMA because of the threat it posed to private general practice. The Catholic hierarchy opposed the Mother and Child Scheme on the basis that it contravened the rights of the family to provide for the needs of children and the right of the church to educate on sexual morality. The church feared that state control over medical services for women would include education and information on contraception and abortion. Medical and church opposition to the Mother and Child Scheme was fuelled by the knowledge that the Health Bill conceived the scheme as a first step towards widening the scope of public health provision (Barrington, 1987). This was a direct threat to private practice and to the control that the Catholic Church had over voluntary hospitals and the appointment of Catholic doctors. After the passing of the 1947 Health Act, the Mother and Child Scheme faced further opposition and by the time its provisions came into effect under the 1953 Act it had been greatly modified.

A number of substantial political compromises reached with the medical profession and Catholic hierarchy shaped the 1953 Health Act. While free hospital care was extended to 85 per cent of the population, covering lower and middle-income groups, this was at the expense of the development of primary care. The proposed expansion of GP services was curtailed and the proposal to provide a comprehensive and free health service to children under the age of sixteen was abandoned. In addition, the Act instituted payment for consultants treating public patients in voluntary hospitals while allowing them to retain their rights to private practice within the voluntary hospitals, while consultants working in the county hospitals were permitted to engage in private practice outside of public hospitals. As part of the negotiations on the implementation of the Act, the government agreed to the establishment of voluntary health insurance advocated by the IMA, which saw the expansion of a free hospital service as a threat to the private income of hospital doctors. The Voluntary Health Insurance Board (VHI) was established as a statutory, non-profit insurance scheme controlled by the Minister for Health in 1957 (Barrington, 1987), which effectively secured the continuing supply of fee-paying patients for hospital consultants.

Structural reform and administrative efficiency: 1960s-70s
This period marks another distinct phase in the development of health policy. The expansion of public health provision led to soaring costs, and by the 1960s there was growing political opposition to financing health services from local rates (Barrington, 1987). In preparation for the state becoming the sole financer of health services, the government commissioned a white paper, *The Health Services and their Future Development* (Department of Health (Irl), 1966), to address the financing and administration of the health system. The white paper, which was the blueprint for the 1970 Health Act, put the case for a comprehensive and free national health service firmly off the political agenda and, instead, the focus was on the structural reorganisation of the health services and administrative efficiency (McKevitt, 1990). The 1970 Act replaced the dispensary system established in 1851 under the Poor Law with the General Medical Service Scheme (GMS), which allowed public patients to choose their doctor. An independent body, Comhairle na nOspidéal, was established to regulate the appointment of hospital consultants, and the administration of health services by local authorities was replaced by a structure of eight regional health boards.

Much of the context of the 1970 Health Act is explained by Barrington (1987) in terms of the power bloc formed by the Catholic hierarchy and the medical profession in their opposition to a universal health service in the 1940s and 1950s. The ideological conflicts over state involvement in health cemented the interests of moral authority, professional autonomy and private practice. In mustering support for a publicly financed and state controlled healthcare system, a number of key concessions were encoded in the 1970 Act. Local authorities were willing to relinquish control of increasingly expensive health services on the basis that state funds were to relieve and eventually replace local rates. To ensure democratic accountability, a provision was made for local public representatives to be in the majority on the new regional health boards. The GMS scheme that replaced the dispensary system where doctors were salaried employees was accompanied by a fee for service agreement whereby doctors received a fee for each public patient visit. This was replaced by a capitation payment system in 1989, whereby doctors receive an annual payment for each GMS patient. The 1970 Act, therefore, laid the foundation for general practice to develop as a private system of care. The right to private practice was also protected for consultants in voluntary hospitals, and health boards were given the power to make provision for private and semi-private patients in public hospitals in line with the dual system in place in voluntary hospitals. The independence of the voluntary hospital sector, despite its increasing reliance on public funding, was protected and the sector continued to have autonomy over administrative decisions and the employment of staff (Wren, 2003).

These concessions were intended to take politics out of health, but they left the state in a relatively weak position from which to challenge professional interests (Barrington, 1987; McKevitt, 1990). Catholic Church control of voluntary hospitals and the influence it exercised in health board hospitals, medical schools and in the training of nurses meant that it retained considerable authority over medical ethics, the organisation of health services and the development of health policy (Barrington, 1987). Following the Second Vatican Council (1962-1965), the Catholic Church adopted a more liberal stance on state intervention in the provision of health services to tackle health inequalities. However, it became increasingly active in lobbying for legislative protection of Catholic social morals against the introduction of contraception and abortion (Wren, 2003)

The policy of retrenchment: 1980s
By the late 1970s, health services in Ireland were overwhelmingly financed through direct taxation. The response in Ireland as elsewhere to the world economic crisis was to cut back the public sector, and in the period 1979–1986 spending cuts were implemented across the health services, including the closure of hospitals. In 1987, the opposition party's (Fianna Fáil) general election campaign included the billboard slogan, 'Health cuts hurt the old, the sick and the handicapped' (Wren, 2003: 74). However, in government the party introduced a policy of cutting overall health expenditure to half of the EU average per capita public spending, with the consequence that wards and hospitals were closed, hospital charges were introduced for non-GMS patients and there was an embargo on health service recruitment (Wren, 2003). While the conditions of economic recession are frequently cited as the reason for the health cutbacks, McKevitt (1990) argues that the problem was largely exacerbated by the failure of the state to develop clear policy objectives underpinned by a legislative framework to guide policy decisions on the huge public investment in health undertaken during the structural reorganisation of health services in the early 1970s. The health cutbacks were publicly seen as a blunt administrative tool and health once again became a political issue (McKevitt, 1990). The far-reaching consequences of the cumulative effect of the health cutbacks for public health, which carried the burden of the cutbacks while state subsidises for private health increased, continue to dominate healthcare debates today about the public/private divide in health service provision.

A mixed health economy

The key policy phases and legislative changes described above have shaped a health service model whose defining characteristic is a public-private mix. In historical terms, one of the key features of the development of health services has been the concession of the right to the members of a powerful medical interest group to remain as independent contractors and to allow consultants to combine public and private practice. The public-private mix refers to two parallel systems of healthcare service that cut across primary medical care and hospital services. In Ireland, general practice is a 'private enterprise' with the vast majority of people paying out of pocket for each and every visit to a GP (Wren, 2003), while the state pays GPs in the form of a capitation fee for approximately 30 per cent of the population who have access to a free service. Hospital services, on the other hand, are free to everyone irrespective of their GMS status, but private health insurance allows those who can afford it to access private care. In this section we will examine how this model of health operates at the level of entitlement and its institutional and structural features.

Medical entitlement

The percentage of the population entitled to a medical card based on means tested eligibility has fallen from 37.4 per cent in 1986 to 30 per cent in 2001, despite the extension of the GMS to all those over seventy in 2001 (NESF, April 2000). The main reason given for this fall off is the failure of successive governments to raise the narrow income threshold for eligibility. Wren estimates that the burden of the personal cost of a single visit to a family doctor is the equivalent of 'one-third of the weekly income of an individual earning just above the threshold for a medical card' (2003: 204). In addition to the GMS, various drug subsidy schemes operate for certain categories of patients with chronic and disabling conditions, who may also receive discretionary medical cards in cases of undue hardship. Under the 1991 Health (Amendment) Act, free public hospital care was extended as a basic right to everyone, subject to certain nominal charges for non-GMS patients (Quinn, 1999). Since the 1980s, the demand for private health insurance (PHI) has greatly increased to its current uptake by 45 per cent of the population (Watson and Williams, 2001). The monopoly of the VHI was challenged by an EU directive and BUPA entered the Irish market in 1997; the Health Insurance Acts (1994, 2001) are intended to regulate market competition. Under the Act, the key regulatory principles are **community rating**, open enrolment, life-long coverage and **risk equalisation**, which has yet to become fully operationalised (O'Sullivan and Butler, 2002). PHI is attractive to patients and insurers because it is highly subsidised: in addition to tax relief on private insurance, private patients and their insurers are not charged the full economic cost of treatment in public hospitals.

Institutional features

The institutional features of the private-public mix within the hospital system include the provision of supplementary private insurance, private beds in public hospitals and common contracts, which allow public hospital consultants to combine private practice on a fee-for-service basis with their public practice. The model of the public-private mix, where private health insurance is supplementary and runs parallel to health benefits covered by the universal public system, is also common in other European countries, such as Britain, Portugal, Norway, Sweden and Finland (NESF, April 2001). What makes Ireland peculiar is the large and expanding percentage of the population covered by PHI for hospital-based treatment and the extent to which the public sector subsidises private healthcare (NESF, April 2001). The common contract, which came into force in 1981, allows for state salaries to be paid to consultants working in voluntary hospitals, while they retain their right to income from private patients. Under the terms of this contract, salaried consultants working in public hospitals who previously had limited rights to private practice were allowed to engage in unlimited private practice on a fee-for-service basis. Since 1991, the common contract operates under two categories: Category 1 confines private practice to within public hospitals and, Category 2 allows public salaried consultants to also practice in private hospitals. Under the terms of the revised common contract, consultants forfeit 10 to 15 per cent of their basic salary in return for unlimited private practice (NESF, April 2002). Wren (2003) points out that one of the most extraordinary features of the common contract is that the commitment of consultants to public patients for their salaried hours is left unmonitored. Consultants have traditionally resisted health management monitoring as a threat to clinical autonomy. The full-time, public-only contract introduced for consultants who wished to work exclusively within the public system in 1991 was short-lived because it contradicted state policy of ring-fencing 20 per cent of beds in public hospitals for private patients. (See also Chapter 12 on professional power within medicine.)

A two-tier health system

The internal market created by the above public-private mix is described structurally as a two-tier health system (NESF, April 2002). This structural feature of hospital services and general practice is associated with systemic inequalities within healthcare. Within hospital services, the two-tier system is associated with the common contract, which creates an economic incentive for consultants to dedicate a greater proportion of their time to private patients compared to public patients (Watson and Williams, 2001; Wiley, 2000) and the model of supplementary health insurance that buys certain patients speedier access and, presumably, a better quality service (NESF, April 2002). The rising demand for PHI since the 1980s is associated with public perceptions of an increasingly inadequate public health sector indicated by the waiting-list crisis. Without state subsidies, however, there would be few incentives for patients to take out private insurance since this in effect would mean patients paying twice for services through insurance subscriptions and direct taxation. This would indicate that, relative to service provision, the demand for PHI is actively created through health policy and a sustained political commitment to attractive public subsidies for private care. PHI not only offers patients more consumer power with respect to choice of services, but also faster access to services and the promise of a higher quality service.

The equity implications of the public-private mix have been subject to various policy reviews. The *Report of the Commission on Health Funding* (Department of Health (Irl), 1989) did not view the public-private mix as a necessary source of inequity and it accepted the rationale that private health insurance provides those with the ability to pay speedier access to certain treatments and treatments not available in the public sector. The commission, however, pointed out that equity is dependent on comprehensive publicly funded health services and that timely access to necessary treatment should not be dependent on private insurance (1989). In order to operationalise this policy objective, the commission recommended the adoption of a common waiting list for public and private patients in public hospitals, the elimination of tax relief on health insurance and the recovery of full costs for public hospital beds occupied by private patients.

A key policy challenge is the strong and widespread public perception that preferential treatment is given to private patients within public hospitals. The NESF report notes that 'it is generally recognised that consultants play a more direct role in the treatment of their private patients in public hospitals than in that of their public patients' (April 2002: 27). A BUPA Ireland/ESRI national survey found that almost 90 per cent of the public perceive that speed of access to hospital care is dependent on the status of patients as public or private (Watson and Williams, 2001). An analysis of the waiting list issue by Kinsella (2001) confirms that this perception reflects the reality for some categories of public patients in accessing necessary surgery. The BUPA Ireland/ESRI survey also reports that fewer than half of the respondents gave a positive rating to the quality of care in the public health system, while four out of five respondents rated the overall quality of care in the private sector as positive. Nearly two thirds of those surveyed believed that quality of care is better in the private sector; however, for both the insured and the non-insured surveyed, access to timely treatment was given as the main attraction of PHI rather than concerns about the quality of care available in the public sector (Watson and Williams, 2001).

The white paper on Private Health Insurance (DoHC, 1999b) revisited the implications of the public-private mix for equity of access. The white paper identified the shortcomings of the public-private mix, including the following: the below-cost charging for pay-beds in public hospitals; the economic incentive for consultants to spend more time with private patients; the lack of quality of service for public patients who depend on low-paid junior doctors in training, and the potential for the expansion of PHI to impact negatively on the equity of the public health system. While private patients are personally cared for by consultants, public patients are given consultant led care. This usually means care by junior doctors under the supervision of consultants. Different policy solutions have been offered in response to the inequities that the system has fostered, particularly in the acute hospital sector, which we will revisit later in this chapter. The principle of providing universal hospital and consultant care is undermined by active state policies on subsidised private healthcare and the common contract in support of a private market in health, while the failure of the state to systematically review access criteria in terms of the efficacy of public expenditure and the failure to introduce a common waiting-list undercuts the principle operationally.

Wren (2003) documents how the hybrid payment structure for GPs creates multiple tiers within primary care. An unpublished study conducted by the Department of Community Health and General Practice, Trinity College Dublin, in 1997 found that there were three times fewer GPs in working-class areas of Dublin with high concentrations of medical card holders than in middle-class areas (cited in Wren, 2003). Since the annual capitation payment for a public patient is more or less the equivalent of the charge for a single visit to a GP, there is a strong economic incentive for GPs to be biased towards locating their services in wealthier areas. Wren (2003) also notes that when medical care eligibility was extended to those over seventy, the capitation payment for treating higher income, newly eligible patients was far in excess of the payment for treating lower income, formerly eligible patients. As Wren concludes:

> GPs in middle-class areas were thus compensated for the extension of free GP care to their elderly patients, while the more sparsely scattered GPs in working-class areas must continue to treat their elderly patients for as little as one fifth the payment (2003: 208).

Since general practice is the first point of contact a patient has with the health services, the cost of accessing this service is seen as a major barrier to patients seeking preventative care and early treatment. This has wide implications for individual health and the burden on hospital care. We will return to the implications of a multi-tiered primary care structure in considering the proposed reform of the sector.

A changing policy context
In this section we will review the reorientation of health policy since the publication of the policy statement *Health: the Wider Dimensions*

(Department of Health (Irl), 1986) in response to the WHO health strategy, *Targets for Health for All* (1985). Following the 1970 Health Act, no major structural changes had taken place in the delivery and management of the health services for over twenty years. From the mid-1980s the main thrust of health policy reform has been based on the need to rationalise and fundamentally reorganise hospital services, and to restructure the administration of the health services. In the 1980s the main concern of health policy was to contain costs, while the main thrust of reforms from the mid-1990s has been guided by the principles of efficiency, effectiveness, quality of care and equity. These principles are about ensuring that health services are efficiently run by giving value for money, that they are effective in providing for people's health needs and that people can access treatment depending on medical need and not factors such as ability to pay.

Laying the foundations for policy change
The WHO 'health for all' philosophy advocated a preventative, community-based model of health (see Chapter 14) and the Department of Health policy statement (1986) embraced this strategy, emphasising multi-sectoral planning, community care and health promotion. The key political issue highlighted by the policy statement was the failure of sustained public investment in health services to improve the overall health status of the population. However, just when the WHO strategy was diverting the future of health policy away from hospital and treatment based care, the political landscape in Ireland was dominated by hospital politics precipitated by public hospital closures and health spending cuts. Any shift towards the implementation of the radical change in health policy envisaged by the WHO strategy would have required significant administrative and structural changes, as well as economic restructuring and resource investment. Given the pressure to contain public expenditure in health, it is not surprising that the new policy statement was seen as cost rationalisation by another name (McKevitt, 1990).

The *Report of the Commission on Health Funding* (Department of Health (Irl), 1989) (discussed earlier) became the blueprint for future policy change. The commission concluded that the central problem for the health service was not how it was funded, but how it was administered. The issues highlighted by the report have been reiterated in subsequent policy reviews. These issues include: the considerable confusion and cross-over between on the one hand, the executive function and national decision making, and on the other hand, the day-to-day management and local decision making about services; the lack of evaluation about the efficacy, efficiency and quality of health services; the absence of accountability; the failure to integrate services; the lack of a formal framework for ensuring that the health services provided by statutory and voluntary agencies are complementary; and the inadequate representation of the views of patients regarding healthcare appropriate to their needs (O'Hara, 1998). The commission also recommended that the health board structure be replaced by a Health Services Executive Authority because of the power of veto that local politicians had in deciding the implementation of national health policy at regional level. The idea of a Health Service Executive forms the core of the new administrative structure recommended by the latest policy review undertaken by the Department of Health and Children, known as the *Prospectus Report* (DoHC, 2003b).

The reorientation of health policy

The reorientation of health policy in the early 1990s was based on the perceived need to create a more rational approach to the planning, organisation and delivery of health services. The emphasis of the Health Strategy, *Shaping a Healthier Future* (Department of Health (Irl), 1994), was on creating greater efficiency and effectiveness by changing the structure of how health services were managed and delivered. Clearer lines of responsibility were sought between the Department of Health and Children and the health boards. The executive function of the Department of Health and Children, which involves national policy development and strategic planning, was to be separated from the day-to-day management of the health services, by devolving responsibility to the health boards (O'Hara, 1998; Wiley, 2001). The delegation of responsibility requires health boards and service providers to be more accountable to the central authority of the Department of Health and Children. Under the terms of the Health (Amendment) Act, 1996, known as the Accountability Legislation, service planning and service contract agreements are adopted as core accountability mechanisms. Health boards must now submit detailed service plans on an annual basis to the Department of Health and Children. While in the past voluntary agencies were directly funded from the Department of Health and Children, they must now enter into direct service agreements with the regional authorities.

The Accountability legislation institutionalises a clear distinction between commissioning health agencies (the health boards as funders) and service providers (publicly owned hospital and public voluntary hospitals). The commissioning/provider split is seen in policy terms as a mechanism for ensuring greater accountability and integration of public health services, rather than creating a quasi-market based on competition between providers for public funds in the way the NHS in Britain is currently organised (see Annandale, 1998). Public health services in Ireland have not been subject to the same level of free market principles as in Britain, and the new accountability mechanisms, it may be argued, strengthen central government control over health services and the efficient use of funding. However, the decentralisation of funding decisions may also serve to shift the burden of cost containment to local health authorities and public voluntary hospitals. O'Ferrall (2002) argues that competitive tendering for public funds under the new restructuring and service contract arrangements may not only transfer the responsibility of cost-rationing to the voluntary sector, but also threaten the ethos of voluntarism and patient advocacy within the sector. On the issue of cost containment, Wren notes that the impact of the more recent health spending cuts on local service provision are popularly seen as 'a failure of health board management' (2003: 196).

Equity

Reducing health status inequalities is understood as an important public good and the cornerstone of public health policy. Despite improved access to health services, increased quality of healthcare and expenditure, health inequalities appear to be an intractable problem. As Chapter 4 demonstrates, current realities of the unequal distribution of health status are sobering. The principle of equity is promoted as a central policy issue in both the 1994 and 2001 health strategies. The intent of the equity (or fairness) principle is that people obtain adequate and effective healthcare based on medical need (health status) rather than ability to pay. While the importance of equity should not be undermined, sociologists point out that improvements in access to healthcare and improved rates of health service utilisation are not the most important determinant of health status (Layte and Nolan in Wiley, 2001; see also Chapter 6 on the importance of living standards and the environment on health status). The importance of equity, however, cannot be downplayed because differential access to and quality of care remain pressing problems.

The waiting list crisis

The public waiting list for hospital treatment is a barometer for assessing current policy reform against the criterion of equity. By the time of the publication of the Health Strategy (DoHC, 2001b) the waiting list crisis was threatening to undermine the credibility of the public hospital system. The Waiting List Initiative (WLI) introduced in June 1993 to tackle the backlog of patients waiting for necessary, if not urgent, treatment had done little to alleviate the problem. The NESF (April, 2002) analysis of the waiting list problem up to 2001 shows that hospital waiting lists continued to increase, as did the waiting time for treatments. The Health Strategy (DoHC, 2001b) has aims to reduce the waiting time for public patients for elective treatments with the commitment that by the year 2004 no public patient who has seen a hospital consultant will spend more than three months on the waiting list for treatment. This target is to be met by a number of strategies, including the addition of 3,000 new acute beds over ten years, which will be designated specifically for public patients. However, not all of these beds will be allocated to the public sector.

In addition to the proposed establishment of a National Hospital Agency to oversee the strategic development of the acute hospital system, a National Treatment Purchase Fund (TPF) has been established as an interim measure to purchase private treatment for public patients who are on a hospital waiting list for more than three months, until the targeted waiting time is met in 2004 (DoHC, 2001b). Lest the system of purchasing private treatment for public patients be seen as a perverse incentive for consultants and hospitals to maintain long waiting lists, it has been agreed with private providers that the majority of patients treated under the terms of the fund will not be treated privately by their public consultant (*Irish Times*, 11 July 2002). However, tensions emerged between hospital consultants and the Department of Health and Children over the terms of the TPF. Consultants in the Mater Hospital publicly argued that funding should be directed towards treating public patients in public hospitals (*Irish Times*, 5 July 2002). The slow up-take of private treatment under the TPF led the Department of Health and Children to accuse consultants of failing to cooperate with the scheme. In an effort to side-step consultants' control of waiting lists, the Department in 2003 launched a public advertising campaign on the TPF and gave GPs direct referral responsibility for purchasing private treatment for public patients on the waiting list (Wren, 2003).

In addition to various efficiency measures to facilitate the target waiting time, it was proposed that private admissions for elective treatment in public hospitals be suspended if hospitals failed to meet their targets for public patients (DoHC, 2001b). While this provided an incentive for providers to treat public patients on a more equitable basis, it failed to address the underlying structural basis of the inequity of a two-tier system and sidestepped the issue of a common waiting list, which would encode the principle of equity in terms of medical need (NESF, April 2001). An important oversight in the administrative reform of the waiting list is the failure of the Health Strategy to address the substantial differences in waiting times for first consultant appointments between public and private patients (NESF, April 2002). Official waiting lists are not indicative of the number of patients awaiting treatment, since those patients who are waiting to see a specialist after a GP referral are not counted on the waiting list. For some specialities, the waiting time to see a consultant within the public system can be years, as opposed to weeks or months in the case of private patients.

Renegotiating the common contract
While the 1994 Health Strategy reiterated the state's commitment to 'maintaining the position of private practice within the well established public/private mix' (Department of Health (Irl), 1994), the current Health Strategy recognises that the public-private mix in the public hospital system is an integral part of the problem of inequity (DoHC, 2001b). It proposes that newly contracted public hospital consultants will work exclusively for public patients for a specific period before they can take on private patients, in the interests of improving equity. However, the Health Strategy leaves in

place the private bed designation scheme within the public hospital system as an alternative strategy to introducing a common waiting list. The very tentative way that it approaches the renegotiation of the consultant's contract, which is underpinned by the principle that public consultants have a right to private practice, suggests that consultants continue to operate as a powerful elite in setting the agenda for health services. Individual consultants and the Irish Hospital Consultants Association (IHCA) waged a public relations campaign in the media during the more recent 2003 health spending crisis about the unfair representation of the profession as an obstacle to a more equitable hospital system. Also, the IHCA has remained publicly neutral on the need for a common waiting list and has maintained its traditional stance against a mandatory public-only contract for newly appointed public consultants (Wren, 2003).

Reform of the primary care sector
While health has traditionally been dominated by the hospital sector, primary healthcare has remained structurally underdeveloped and fragmented. The proposed reform of primary care – *Primary Care: A New Direction* (DoHC, 2001c) – under the National Health Strategy is an attempt to shift the bias in Irish healthcare away from costly, hospital treatment to low-cost, community-based preventative care. The main barriers to the development of a comprehensive primary care system identified by the Primary Care Strategy (PCS) include the lack of infrastructure to facilitate the integration of services that are currently fragmented with some aspects seriously underdeveloped; the domination of primary care by medical treatment services and the limited availability of allied professional groups; and the lack of clear eligibility criteria for a wide range of primary care services (DoHC, 2001c).

Restructuring primary care
The PCS promises a more equitable, accessible and integrated range of services that are more responsive to individual needs. These services will be community based with the added value of sustaining and enhancing the individual's social networks within his or her local community. Central to this policy vision is the fusion of health and social care by integrating services through the development of up to 1,000 inter-disciplinary primary care teams. Primary care teams will serve local geographic populations of between 3,000 and 7,000. The primary care teams will consist of GPs (with patients enrolling with a single GP in the care team), along with administrative personnel, other health professionals such as nurses, community midwives, physiotherapists and occupational therapists, as well as social workers, healthcare assistants and home helps. Each team will be further networked to a range of other primary care professionals to provide services for the enrolled populations of the primary care team, including

'speech and language therapists, community pharmacists, dieticians, community welfare officers, dentists, chiropodists and psychologists' (DoHC, 2001c). In order to integrate hospital care and primary care, patients will be given a package of care tailored to individual needs. Following the *Hanly Report* (The National Task Force on Medical Staffing, DoHC 2003c), it is envisaged that a fully developed primary care system will enable patients to access diagnostic and treatment facilities at local health clinics in areas where local acute hospital care is no longer available.

A radical vision?
Despite the use of the strong and persuasive rhetoric of 'sustainable health' and 'social development' (DoHC, 2001c:7) that frames the PCS as a radical vision for developing public health on the WHO principle that health is a fundamental human right, the principle of universal access to a comprehensive primary healthcare service is glaringly absent from the strategy. According to Wren (2003), the working group charged with the early draft of the PCS argued that universal eligibility for primary care was a necessary prerequisite to developing a preventative health strategy, since the cost of primary care is a major barrier to patients seeking preventative care and early treatment. However, by the time the PCS was published, the principle of universal access was replaced by a political promise to improve access for those on low income. Therefore, the commitment to addressing health inequalities and improving access to primary care services was made subject to budgetary constraints and, under the 2002 Budget, medical card eligibility was not extended.

In its radical vision, the PCS poses a potential challenge to the professional autonomy of GPs and their status as independent contractors. The sources of this challenge are both economic and ideological, and are further complicated by the traditional underdevelopment of primary care and the public/private mix in general practice. We have seen that within organised medicine there is a strong ideological resistance to the provision of universal, free access to general practice. At the same time, there is strong criticism of the failure of successive governments to invest in primary care. While doctors have traditionally dominated the healthcare division of labour (see Chapter 12), the PCS envisages an extended role for other occupational groups in delivering a social model of health. Moreover, once a patient is enrolled with a primary care team, he or she may self-refer within the team (Wren, 2003). Some doctors will view this as a diminution of their traditional care role in the diagnosis and treatment of illness and of their power of referral, which is tied to the doctor's status and income.

The policy review undertaken by Deloitte and Touche (2001) notes that one of the key structural problems in integrating general practice into a community based primary care strategy is the self-employed status of GPs and the extent of private practice. This leads Wren (2003) to conclude that the provision of an integrated and comprehensive primary care system is dependent on universal eligibility across the range of primary care services, including general practice. Wren's (2003) analysis suggests that the profession's traditional opposition to a state-funded GP service has waned somewhat since the publication of the PCS. She also points out that the changing occupational interests of GPs may well break down the traditional consensus that supports the status quo of the private-public mix of payment. The cost of private modernised practice that is equipped and staffed to meet changing health needs is already threatening single-handed general practices, particularly in rural areas. Furthermore, as more women enter general practice, the traditional culture of working long hours to build up a practice single-handed may appear less attractive (Wren, 2003).

The health consumer

One of the key transformations to have occurred in health policy since the publication of *Health: the Wider Dimensions* (Department of Health (Irl), 1986) is the shift in emphasis away from paternalism to consumerism. Patients are no longer viewed as passive recipients of care, but as customers who have needs and expectations that the health services should strive to meet (McAuliffe, 1998). Here, we consider how the concept of consumer choice informs health policy (for a discussion of consumerism, see also Chapter 8).

Principles of consumerism

In the 2001 Health Strategy, consumerism is articulated as central to the realisation of the goal of delivering care that is appropriate and responsive to health needs. Under the objectives and actions specified for the operationalisation of this goal, consumerism has come to mean the following: providing adequate information to patients and improving staff communication skills and attitudes to customers; reducing waiting times for treatment, and providing appropriate care in appropriate environments; expanding and improving the standard of services; developing a statutory framework for customer complaints; ensuring the quality of services by taking the views of customers into account (by carrying out patient satisfaction surveys and needs assessments) to assist in quality control and service planning; developing public education initiatives on health policy and democratising health by establishing consumer panels (DoHC, 2001b). Within the scope of these objectives and actions we can identify the core principles of consumerism described by Epstein (1990) – information, access, choice, redress and consumer representation (cited in McAuliffe, 1998: 292).

Types of consumer participation

There are different levels of consumer participation ranging from non-participation to token participation, to direct participation. Each level in turn may involve different orders of decision making, from an individual's involvement in decisions about their treatment or decisions about service provision to the collective involvement of citizens in decisions about policy (White, 2000). There are different techniques for involving consumers in decisions about healthcare. These range from needs assessment and patient satisfaction surveys to public consultation processes, such as that carried out in drawing up a national policy on women's health (Department of Health (Irl), 1995), to more direct models of local participation such as consumer panels or advisory committees like the Women's Health Advisory Committees that were established to oversee the implementation of the National Strategy on Women's Health (DoHC, 1997) in the health boards.

Policy support for consumer involvement
Since the 1980s, Western governments have enthusiastically embraced consumer and community participation in the health domain. Policy support of the new consumerism is explained by the rise of free market values, where public services are increasingly modelled on the idealisation of the private sector as responsive, flexible and demand-led (McKevitt, 1998). Administrative support for incorporating the patient's perspective into healthcare decision making is driven by health service management's concern to monitor contract and service agreements. Evidence-based research is increasingly viewed as a managerial tool to shift decisional authority away from the tacit control that consultants have over hospital resources to a more explicit form of rationing based on patient needs assessments and patient satisfaction surveys. Social movement support for wider citizen participation in decision-making – for example, the Disability Rights Movement, environmental groups, women and Traveller groups – reflect the need for public input in determining which values should decide policy priorities. In the literature on consumer and community participation in the health field, a distinction is drawn between consumerist and democratic models of citizen participation (White, 2000). The consumerist model is based on the sovereign individual who exercises choices and shops around for health services, in much the same way as a person goes about buying any consumer item. Within this model the needs and preferences of consumers are translated into markets (McAuliffe, 1998), and through purchasing power consumers ensure that a range of relevant services are available at a reasonable price. This model is based on market principles and individualism. In the democratic model, citizens are seen as capable of forming social alliances around consumer power and acting collectively in articulating needs, deciding questions of value and demanding rights. Active citizenship is about creating the conditions and spaces where ordinary citizens can enter public debate and dialogue about policy issues that affect them as patients, carers and prospective consumers.

Translating lay voices into health action
Consumerism implies a shift in the balance of power from providers to

consumers (McAuliffe, 1998). Therefore, as a measure of the effective role of consumer participation in decision-making processes sociologists ask whether any transfer of power occurs. Both White's (2000) and Annandale's (1998) reviews of the research literature suggest that the evidence is stacked against any effective role for consumers. Based on an extensive review of evaluation studies on consumer and community participation in health, White (2000) shows that health professionals have considerable power over the outcome of such processes and greater influence in the setting of priorities. This observation leads White to conclude that 'lay participation is not about empowering consumers and communities or about turning them into decision makers, but rather, it is about empowering existing decision makers' (2000: 475). There are considerable political and administrative risks involved in extending the decision making process to consumers. The policy priorities supported through consumer advocacy may increase demands on existing services and resources and oppose cost-containment or imperil the general thrust of policy and legislative reform (White, 2000). A historical and current example of this includes local opposition to the closure of general hospitals and the scaling down of services provided by county hospitals.

Given the political risk involved in fostering public debate through consumer consultation on policy decisions, why do governments continue to invest in the ideal of consumer-citizen participation? White's (2000) analysis of this question is based on a case study of a public consultation process undertaken by the US state of Oregon to determine public values in deciding cost rationing priorities in the health services (Coast, 1996). He concludes that the political risk involved is weighted against the legitimacy that the consultation process bestows on administrative decision making. Rather than empowering consumers, public consultation empowers administrators by 'reducing the uncertainty of public response and cooperation, by increasing administrators' confidence in the actions they take, and by alleviating authorities of sole responsibility for delicate decisions' (White 2000: 476). This leads White to conclude:

> Lay participation in health-care decision making is, to a significant extent, less an investment than a transaction cost of administrative legitimacy and risk management ... . Lay participation as it is preached and practised is clearly about administrative and political efficiency, not democracy, consumer empowerment, or community control. It derives its value principally from its role as an administrative strategy (2000: 477).

Despite the persuasive and powerful rhetoric of consumer empowerment, it is important to question the values that give meaning to the new consumerism and the interests that determine its limits and possibilities for democratising health.

Summary

- A number of key shifts in focus have occurred in our understanding of and response to health. These include a shift from acute to chronic illness, a change in emphasis from disease to health, from hospital-based treatment to community care, from cure to prevention, and from a producer-led to a consumer-led system of healthcare.
- By the late 1970s, Ireland like other Western countries was facing the encroachment of an unregulated global economy that threatened to undermine the welfare state. This exacerbated the challenges emerging from the rising cost of medical technology and increasing demand for health services.
- Since the foundation of the Irish state, health services have been transformed from a system based on charitable and private medicine to increasing state control over the management and financing of an extended public health system.
- In the process of establishing a national public health system, political compromises with a powerful medical elite that was unwilling to be controlled by the state, and with the Catholic Church that exercised considerable influence over medical training and the provision of health through the voluntary hospital sector, undermined the universalist principles of equity, free access and comprehensive health cover.
- The public-private mix has become an entrenched policy direction despite long-standing debates on the implications of the system for equity of access and provision.
- Private specialised care is largely dependent on consultants who are salaried employees of the public sector, while general practice is largely a private enterprise with GPs acting as private contractors, which in turn has structural implications for the development of a comprehensive primary care strategy.
- Private health insurance not only offers patients more consumer power with respect to choice of services, but also faster access to services and the promise of a higher quality of service.
- The waiting-list crisis has created much public contention about the preferential treatment of patients with private insurance or, more simply, ability to pay for consultant and hospital care.
- The problems identified in policy reviews in the 1980s associated with a two-tier structure remain unresolved as the health services face into the twenty-first century.
- The main thrust behind recent policy reviews and health strategies is to create a more rational, and hence, efficient, effective, fair and accountable organisational structure.
- A consumer-led health policy is seen as the route to greater accountability, transparency and choice in the delivery of healthcare. However, consumerism can have different meanings in terms of the political interests and ideologies that drive health policy.

Topics for discussion and reflection
1. What do you see as the central problems with the health services in Ireland?
2. How might these main problems be addressed?

FOURTEEN:

New public health and
health promotion

The purpose of this chapter is to trace the emergence of health promotion as a priority strategy of contemporary health policy. A key sociological task in this regard is to show how society's current preoccupation with health reflects wider socio-economic and cultural changes. We will begin by characterising what has come to be known as the 'New Public Health' (NPH) and the policy context of health promotion. We then map out the terrain of the sociology of health promotion, which covers a number of themes including the body and consumer culture, risk society, surveillance and the self-care ethic. This is followed by an overview of the main sociological critiques that have emerged in response to health promotion as a public health strategy, namely structuralist, surveillance and lifestyle critiques. We next explore the health promotional strategies of community health, HIV/AIDS prevention and breast cancer screening. Finally, we highlight some dilemmas and tensions within health promotion, which the discussion illuminates.

The emergence of the New Public Health paradigm

Ashton and Seymour (1993) periodise the historical development of public health into four phases. The first phase emerged in the context of large scale demographic shifts in Western populations that accompanied industrialisation in the eighteenth and early nineteenth centuries and the movement of people from rural areas into sprawling urban centres that harboured abject poverty and diseases. The early public health movement was mainly concerned with containing the spread of contagious diseases, through public sanitation programmes and improving the social conditions of the urban poor. This coincided with the consolidation of modern states and government concern for maintaining social order in the face of the social chaos wrought by rapid industrialisation and urbanisation. Concern for the health of populations was intimately bound up with the economic imperative of the emerging capitalist system and the need for a productive and, hence, healthy work force. This led to the development of new systems of administration to monitor and regulate the health of the population as a whole, through the detailed observation and recording of disease patterns, mortality, marriage and birth rates and the gathering of data on personal behaviours to establish norms to govern sexuality and moral fitness. Public health became associated with the political goal of maintaining social order and the economic goal of productivity. Interventions included the control of public spaces through sanitation, public hygiene and housing and the regulation of prostitution.

By the latter half of the nineteenth century, the development of germ theory and clinical medicine led to the emergence of a more individualistic approach to health (see Chapter 6). During this second phase, social reform led to the emergence of a rudimentary form of state welfare and public health strategies began to shift their focus away from the social environment to personal behaviours and the domestic environment, with the aim of improving the morals and conduct of the poor. Physicians were given a greater role in the monitoring and policing of health, and the development of a dispensary system (under the Poor Law Relief Act, 1851 in Ireland) widened the scope of medical examination to observe and regulate health in the interests of public welfare. The dominance of the biomedical model was consolidated during the next phase (the third phase), which Ashton and Seymour (1993) date to the 1930s. This phase is described as the therapeutic era, marking the period when clinical medicine began to dominate the health services through the development of teaching hospitals and when public health became an ancillary activity to hospital-based medicine. During this phase, the emphasis of public health shifted from moral regulation to educating the public on how the principles of medical science could be applied to personal health (Lupton, 1995). From the 1970s a fourth phase in public health began to take shape, which sought to fuse environmental measures with personal health maintenance strategies in order to tackle chronic illness and health inequalities that continue to persist in wealthy, developed countries. Ashton and Seymour (1993) describe this phase as the New Public Health (NPH).

The ascendancy of health promotion
Against the background of the emergence of chronic and degenerative illness as the major threat to population health, and the escalating cost and demand on health services in the 1970s, health promotion was embraced as a key policy in many Western countries. The WHO Constitution (1946) defines health in terms of the trinity of physical, mental and social wellbeing, which broadens the definition of health beyond its negative biomedical meaning (see Chapters 5 and 13). As indicated in Chapter 5, *The Alma Ata Declaration* (1978) declared health a fundamental social right and put it at the centre of global and national economic and social policies. Following this, *Health for All by the Year 2000* (WHO, 1985) and the *Ottawa Charter for Health Promotion* (WHO, 1986) set out the principles

and actions by which health promotion could be comprehensively realised in tackling fundamental socio-economic inequalities. The main principles are summarised in Box 14.1.

Box 14.1 WHO *health promotion strategies*

> • Health promotion is a population approach concerned with the context of everyday life, rather than concerned wholly with people at risk from specific diseases.
> • It is concerned primarily with the social, economic and environmental determinants of health.
> • Its approach is multi-disciplinary and inter-sectoral.
> • It is dependent on effective public participation.
> • Primary healthcare has a central role to play in health promotion.

Sources: WHO, 1984; Parish, 1995

The key action domains for realising the WHO principles for enhancing health are: 'building healthy policy, creating supportive environments, strengthening community action, developing personal skills and reorienting health services' (Kelly and Charlton, 1995: 80).

The WHO philosophy provides a conceptual framework for defining health promotion as a public health practice, in contrast to the biomedical approach. Contrary to health promotional strategies that emphasise individual choice over lifestyle at the expense of wider environmental concerns, the WHO model stresses that the structural patterns available in a given society determine the kind of lifestyles available to individuals and groups (EDU, WHO, 1993: 229). Within this model, health is not simply defined by what is amenable to clinical interventions, but rather is intimately bound up with macro socio-economic policies that impact on equality, work, education, transport, housing and the environment. Essentially, the WHO health promotional message is that people must be *enabled* to lead healthy lives.

The sociology of health promotion
Sociology provides different interpretative frameworks for understanding the social context that has generated a new political and moral agenda for health. Here we will examine some of the sociological themes that help us to understand how the prevailing orthodoxies of public health and health promotion take hold.

The body and consumer culture
Today's society is dominated by the twin ideologies of individualism and consumerism, which are marked by the growing importance of the body as a site for the cultivation of self in the form of lifestyle choices (see Chapter 7). When sociologists examine lifestyle they look at patterns of consumption

and the meanings we attach to different commodities and lifestyle practices as a way of expressing the self and social identity. While health-related consumption has long been associated with middle-class dispositions, health and body maintenance have increasingly become part of a wider and all-embracing consumer culture (Bunton and Burrows, 1995). Health is increasingly viewed as a commodity – something that can be branded, marketed and purchased in the form of services and goods that offer us control over our lives and our bodies: private health insurance, fitness programmes, cosmetic surgery, anti-ageing products, diet, vitamins and body therapies, and so forth. While health promotion seeks to influence consumption patterns through the notion of healthy lifestyles, at the same time it is deeply implicated in consumer culture (the so-called health and lifestyle industry), which constantly blurs the distinction between the healthy body and the body beautiful.

Is it that the less we are able to find collective ways to give expression to our expectations, the more insecure we feel as individuals, and the more likely that we will retreat to our own bodies as a way of exerting control over our lives? Shilling observes:

> Investing in the body provides people with a means of self-expression and a way of potentially feeling good and increasing the control they have over their bodies. If one feels unable to exert control over an increasingly complex society, at least one can have some effect on the size, shape and appearance of one's body (1993: 7)

The ascendancy of consumer culture and the body as a project of self (or as a means of self-expression) is further explained by an unprecedented social consciousness of risk.

Risk society
The sociologist Ulrick Beck (1992) coined the phrase risk society to capture the notion that late modern society is characterised by a widespread and heightened awareness of risk. This sense of apprehension emerges out of a perception of a runaway world – a world that appears to be out of control and where the future itself is uncertain. This awareness has made us more reflexive about the double-edged nature of technological and scientific progress. In today's society we are increasingly aware of risks, in particular the environmental risks associated with technological and industrial policy and the lifestyle risks associated with consumer capitalism – in other words, risks of our own making. In public health discourse, risks are divided between environmental hazards that are external to the individual and therefore assumed to be largely outside of individual control, and lifestyle risks that are assumed to lie within the control of the individual (Lupton, 1995).

In the *Tyranny of Health*, Michael Fitzpatrick (2001) argues that a flurry of health scares since the 1980s have fostered moral panic and public anxiety about health risks. The AIDS panic has been the most intensive of these scares, which also include cot death, melanoma, the pill-scare, Bovine Spongiform Encephalopathy (BSE), the human form of mad cow disease, Creuzfeldt Jakob Disease (CJD), the MMR-autism scare, the MRSA or superbug scare and, more recently, Severe Acute Respiratory Syndrome (SARS). There are also heightened concerns about the environmental risks of food contaminated by growth hormones and antibiotics, water and air pollution, nuclear radiation, toxic waste, and so forth. These scares are magnified by their scope and impact. Fitzpatrick argues that the diseases at the heart of major health scares are terrifying in their consequences because they are difficult to treat and, in most cases, the risks are difficult if not impossible to quantify. They have a bearing on everyday, taken-for-granted activities. The indeterminacy of risks associated with these activities and competing expert claims about the nature of health scares further serves to inflate public anxieties (Fitzpatrick, 2001).

In public health, risk is viewed as a technical concept that relates to the measurement of the probability of disease and its statistical distribution amongst population groups. In public health promotion, knowledge about susceptibility to risk is understood as a key motivating factor for individuals to change their behaviour (Lupton, 1995). As more and more aspects of our lives are defined as risky, health promotion becomes a major influence over our daily lives. While not everyone will heed the advice of public health promotion, few will be unaware of what is the official line on healthy living (Fitzpatrick, 2001). Where once the notion of sin was widely used to moralise about dangers in a society, this is now being replaced by the concept of risk. Moreover, risk is individualised: it is the responsibility of the individual to avoid negative health behaviours to protect themselves not only for their own sake but also for the 'greater good of society' (Lupton, 1995: 89-90).

Surveillance and the self-care ethic
This perspective draws principally on Foucault's twin concepts of disciplinary power and 'technologies of self', and his theory of governmentality. As discussed elsewhere, Foucault's work concerns the emergence of a new form of social power that marks modern society, which he refers to as disciplinary power (Chapters 2 and 7). For Foucault, disciplinary power is exercised across multiple sites and institutions, from the school to the factory, from the clinic to the penal system, from the family to social agencies – all of which are concerned with producing norms on how we should conduct ourselves. This network of surveillance, however, is most effective as a form of power that appears benign or, at least does not weigh down too heavily on us as we go about our daily lives. This form of social power works in two ways. On the one hand, it serves the interest of

public welfare in the form of social programmes to increase productivity, expand education, develop the economy and raise levels of public health and morality (Foucault, 1979). On the other hand, it operates through technologies of self that enable individuals to become self-governing in producing a sense of a normalised self through, for example, maintaining a sense of personal good health (Foucault, 1985, 1986).

Foucault's theory of governmentality shows how the structure of power relations that is involved in the regulation of populations is not so much state-centred, but diffused throughout society in the form of expert knowledge systems and their institutions. In this sense, experts are an important part of the process of government. Governmentality is an effective tool of the liberal state in the sense that populations are more effectively regulated through processes of normalisation as opposed to direct state coercion. Indeed, as Nettleton (1997) notes, if governments are to achieve health in the modern liberal state, then this also has to be an individual goal that can be autonomously acted upon. The role of expertise in this process is two-fold: (i) it develops and refines techniques for the management and regulation of populations through the systematic recording and accumulation of data, which is used to produce 'truths' about human behaviour in categories, classifications, statistics and discourses about what constitutes normal behaviour; (ii) it dispenses this knowledge in a way that individuals can make use of, in the form of self-knowledge (Foucault, 1990 [1978-86:3 volumes]). To put this another way: the objectifying gaze associated with the production of knowledge about human conduct achieves its power of normalisation in the way that it is transformed into a subjectifying or a self-directing gaze through various social practices and norms associated with self-surveillance.

So how are these ideas applied to public health and health promotion? In following Foucault, Nettleton (1997) points out that health is both a political and personal imperative and that contemporary discourse of risk is linked to an ever-expanding network of health surveillance. Armstrong (1983b, 1993, 1995b) captures the process in the concept of surveillance medicine, where more and more aspects of our lives are scrutinised for risky behaviours that may give rise to future health problems. At the heart of surveillance medicine is the notion that health is a question of personal behaviour – behaviour that can always be modified in a way that not only benefits the individual but also society. Armstrong (1993) describes how, in the course of the twentieth century, a regime of total health emerged in the form of new surveillance mechanisms for the monitoring of population health. This coincided with a change in both the object and scope of medicine from a focus on the body as the site of disease and an emphasis on the elimination of disease to the extension of the power of the medical gaze throughout the social body and to an emphasis on health maintenance. A number of important features of this new regime are worthy of note in this respect. Firstly, surveillance is extended from those who are ill to those who are at risk of potential illness. In other words, all members of a society become subject to health surveillance. Secondly, medicine is transformed from a biomedical to a biopsychosocial practice and a new ideology of health emerges, which Armstrong defines as a total regime of health. Armstrong explains: 'the patient is now constituted as a psychosocial being whose every movement and gesture is monitored, evaluated and recorded by a medical machine based on a new ideology of health' (1993: 65). Thirdly, the healthy self comes to symbolise the ideal of an ethical self, suggesting a new relationship to our bodies, which may be interpreted to mean that disease is a product of self-neglect and, hence, a failure of self (Hughes, 2000).

Sociological critiques of health promotion

Here, we identify three broad sociological appraisals of health promotion. Each presents a critique of its ideological bases in exploring the implications of health promotional policies and practices.

Structuralist critiques

Within the political economy of health perspective, structuralist critiques essentially argue that health promotional practices fail to take account of the material conditions of people's lives and the structural basis of ill-health (see Chapter 4). These critiques challenge the assumption that variations in population health can be explained by the distribution of negative health behaviours, and while health promotional strategies may alter individuals' behaviour there is little evidence to suggest that they have altered the distribution of health status amongst social groups (Layte and Nolan, 2001). As we discussed earlier, the WHO vision for health is to develop health proofing for economic and social policy. What this means is that socio-economic policies that cover such diverse areas as transport, waste, energy consumption, agriculture, the organisation of production and consumption, as well as policies that relate to the economic distribution of resources and opportunities such as education, employment, and so forth, are understood as partly health policies by virtue of the way that they reproduce (or potentially reduce) the conditions of unhealthy lives.

As a signatory to the *Ottawa Charter*, Ireland has signed up to the ethical vision of the WHO principles for placing health promotion at the centre of socio-economic policies. The replacement of the Health Education Bureau with the Health Promotion Unit in 1987 represented a shift away from viewing health promotion solely in terms of health education programmes and clinical prevention strategies to an approach that required multi-disciplinary inputs and inter-sectoral actions coordinated through strategic planning. Since the publication of the first health promotional strategy, *Making the Healthier Choice the Easier Choice* (Department of Health (Irl), 1995) and the passing of the Health (Amendment) Act, 1996, Health

Promotion Departments have been established in all health boards, and a plethora of initiatives covering various issues such as workplace health, youth at risk and healthy ageing and public awareness campaigns on alcohol, smoking, exercise and diet have been developed, as well as a National Alcohol Policy and Cardiovascular Health Strategy. While health policy increasingly recognises that personal health behaviours are influenced by the social and economic environments in which people live and work, the solutions that it profiles in health promotional strategies is to persuade individuals to adopt healthier behaviours. For example, in discussing strategies for positive mental health, the *National Health Promotional Strategy* (DoHC, 2000a) draws our attention to individually focused lifestyle factors by referring to data produced by SLÁN (National Survey on Lifestyle, Attitudes and Nutrition). Here it states: 'The majority of respondents from both genders ranked "less stress" as the top requirement for better health, followed by more willpower, a change in weight, more money and less time in smoky places' (DoHC, 2000a: 53). The effect of conceptualising mental health as the problem of individual lifestyle and willpower is to depoliticise the economic and social conditions that are largely beyond an individual's control and which may put people at risk of mental illness. It is interesting to note that the data represented here on lay health beliefs accords with dominant health promotional messages, which undercuts sociological insights into the complexity of lay health beliefs and values (see Chapter 8).

Structural perspectives are also critical of the rhetoric of empowerment adopted by community health promotion. While the WHO initiatives endorse community action principles in the development of health promotional strategies, policy expressed through such concepts as community development and community empowerment can have very different meanings and implications depending on where the impetus for these developments come from (Farrant, 1997). Social exclusion policies have for the most part abandoned macro-economic and social change programmes and, instead, concentrate on policies aimed at individuals in socially marginalised communities, for example stress management and counselling for the unemployed, and parenting skills and smoking cessation programmes for low-income and poor women (Fitzpatrick, 2001). Wainright (1996, cited in Fitzpatrick, 2001) argues that these interventions, far from empowering the socially excluded, simply serve to help people adapt to conditions of inequality and reinforces the idea that social action is unlikely to alter the material circumstances of people's lives. The community model of health promotion is further discussed below.

Surveillance critiques
Nettleton and Bunton (1995) use the term surveillance critiques to refer to sociological analyses that view health promotion as a new form of social control. As the definition of health expands and more aspects of our lives

become medicalised (see Chapter 6), the scope of health promotional strategies expands across a range of sites from the clinic to the community, the school, workplace and leisure areas comprising an ever expanding network of surveillance. Across these various sites a new code of personal behaviour is being championed and normalised (Fitzpatrick, 2001). For example, in the workplace concerns for health have gone beyond the more traditional concern with occupational health to encompass the personal lives of workers including fitness assessment and screening for recreational drug use (Fitzpatrick, 2001). The question arises as to how far should corporate control over the personal lives of workers be extended? Should it, for example, include HIV testing or genetic testing for disease susceptibility, and to what extent could occupational health be used to screen out undesirable workers (Lupton, 1995)? Furthermore, corporate control over the lives of workers shifts the focus away from occupational hazards and, while workers are well aware of these hazards, they may have little choice about levels of exposure. Poorer workers are at the greatest risk of occupational hazards and the risk of losing a wage may be greater than the risk of exposure (Lupton, 1995, citing Nelkin and Brown, 1984).

The role of health professionals is also being transformed by health policies that take health promotion as their central tenet. Doctors are increasingly expected to have an intimate knowledge of their patients' lifestyles and personal behaviours: doctors frequently keep computerised lifestyle data on patients and are expected to actively promote routine check-ups and screening (Fitzpatrick, 2001). The central paradox of the NPH is that the wider our definition of health (that is, the closer that definition comes to a psycho-social model as opposed to the traditional biomedical definition of health as the absence of disease), the greater the opportunities for the state to intervene into more and more areas of personal life under the auspices of health promotion (see Chapter 6). However, this kind of power is neither experienced directly or coercively, but is diffused across different sites of interventions that promote the social imperative of healthy lives – a worthy aim that seems above questioning.

Holistic models of care where health professionals are expected to negotiate with and empower patients by gaining insights into their subjective experiences of illness are promoted as preferable to the paternalistic model characteristic of biomedical practice. This model may be applied to the imparting of health promotion to empower patients to take ownership over health practices and behaviours that may be detrimental to their health and to encourage personal lifestyle changes. Here we can think about a range of self-surveillance techniques from regular medical check-ups to vigilant observational practices, counting calories and alcohol units, from diagnostic-predictive screening to self-examination where we learn to adopt a medical relationship with our bodies as a form of self-empowerment and self-knowledge. However, as Nettleton and Bunton (1995: 47) note, 'a more authoritarian health regime may be easier to challenge, ignore or reject than a supporting, caring one that sets an agenda for our lifestyles'. Fitzpatrick (2001: 10) argues that far from empowering patients, those who succumb to diseases associated primarily with lifestyle behaviours are viewed as morally culpable, while resources are increasingly targeted at the 'worried well' – encouraging otherwise healthy people to subject themselves to a battery of expensive tests and screening protocols – the effect of which produces much anxiety and high levels of medical intervention that have yet to be proven valuable as preventative techniques.

Another issue is the extent to which health promotion is emerging as a regime of surveillance that radically alters power relations in a way that masks a more insidious form of power. Fitzpatrick (2001) is a strong advocate of this critique. His thesis centres on the observation that increased state regulation over the personal life of the individual has occurred at a point in history when the welfare state is in decline and public services are increasingly susceptible to privatisation. However, this power is not seen as coercive because it is justified in the name of health of both the individual and the population. He argues that once the state becomes the central sponsor of health promotion, these initiatives acquire wider political and ideological significance in which health ceases to become the central concern. Essentially, health becomes a means of widening the jurisdiction of the state over the personal lives of individuals (Fitzpatrick, 2001). Scambler (2002: 129-30) also makes this point, arguing that in the context of the emergence of neo-liberal ideology (where economic and social policies are reoriented towards a private market economy) the concept of risk 'has been expropriated to serve the ends of surveillance through the political promotion of technologies of the self'.

Lifestyle critiques
Both consumer oriented and public health promotional messages focus on those aspects of lifestyle that imply choice at the individual level, hence the focus on diet, fitness and the consumption of alcohol and smoking over environmental risks that are outside of the control of the individual (Davison et al, 1997; Nettleton, 1997). Health promotional strategies have largely been driven by the notion that public ignorance of the harmful effects of negative health behaviours leads to unhealthy lifestyles. This idea has been somewhat modified by concerns about the role of culture in influencing lifestyle, in particular the fatalistic culture often associated with working class and minority ethnic groups, and the risk culture associated with youth sub-cultural groups or gay sub-culture. These are the groups most likely to be identified as high risk, yet who are least likely to be receptive to health promotional messages. Health promotional practices have come under criticism for perpetuating fatalistic stereotypes, of assuming that behaviours associated with lifestyle are a question of personal choice and of delimiting lifestyle as the only sphere over which individuals can exercise control (Davison et al, 1997).

While health promotional professionals are encouraged to adopt culturally sensitive strategies as a means of not appearing to talk down to the intended recipients of health promotional messages, less attention is given to the way in which health promotional practice endorses a dominant form of subjectivity based on the notions of self-discipline, deferred gratification and the commitment of time and resources to the accomplishment of an individualised self – values that concur with middle class dispositions and lifestyles. While the philosophy of health promotion is moving away from the individual approach premised on behaviour-base prevention, Lupton (1995) argues that in practice the emphasis remains at the level of lifestyle. Indeed, as Nettleton and Bunton (1995) point out, health promotion is largely driven by the ideology of individualism.

While self-surveillance as a technology of health promotion may be viewed in positive terms as self-empowerment, the rational-choice theory underlying the dominant health promotional message that 'healthy choices are the rational choice' (Thorogood, 1992) implies a level of paternalism that runs counter to the idea of empowerment. The privileging of rationality prompts the sociologist to ask whose knowledge claims are presented as rational and what versions of subjectivity are encoded in the idea of the rational? For example, if health promotional messages impose a version of subjectivity that privileges self-control and self-mastery over the body and a positive mental attitude, the self-policing of our bodies that may never attain this ideal may well provoke guilt, anxiety, fatalism and self-repulsion and invite moral rebuke for ill-health (Lupton, 1995; Frankenberg, 1992; Crawford, 1994). Health that can be chosen represents a moral value system that privileges the healthy as rational agents who not only have choices but are capable of making the right choice or healthy choice (Nettleton, 1997: 322, citing Greco, 1993).

In health promotion discourse, lifestyle choices are presented as prescriptions for living (Hughes, 2000). Such prescriptions centre on risk as the dominant motif and are premised on the expectation that individuals will adjust their individual behaviour on the basis of an aggregate or statistical likelihood of risk (Davison and Smith, 1995). While lifestyles choices carry a highly publicised risk (Hughes, 2000), the way in which people construct lifestyle in their everyday lives may not necessarily accord health with the same priority as health promoters or subscribe to the health needs assumed by the risk-lifestyle agenda (Backett et al, 1994).

Health promotional strategies

Community development for health
Community development for health is seen to promote a social model of health, which recognises that the primary determinants of health are social, economic and environmental factors. The community model of health

promotion is premised on the principles of community participation, equality, and partnership between voluntary groups and statutory agencies with a view to enhancing opportunities for community advocacy in determining health needs and appropriate forms of action (Amos, 2002). Community development owes its origins to the radical social movements of the 1960s, which emphasised collective political action to effect social change. This model of grass-roots activism challenges the power structures that determine health experiences, including medical dominance over health and state policies on the distribution of resources and power in society. One of the aims of the *National Health Promotion Strategy* (DoHC, 2000a) is to incorporate community development into health promotional strategies. The first major initiative 'building healthy communities' (2003) to support marginalised communities to address poverty and health inequalities in Ireland has been undertaken by the Combat Poverty Agency and is currently funding thirteen community based projects.

A number of recurrent themes emerge in critical assessments of community development models of health promotion that distinguish between what Amos (2000) defines as 'capacity building for social control' and 'capacity building for social change'. Lupton (1995) draws our attention to a number of contradictions and dilemmas in the community model of health promotion. These include the assumption that the state is a neutral arbiter of community needs and interests. Whereas, given that the agenda of health promotion is set by the state, public health professionals often find themselves in conflict between very different agendas in mediating between the state and community. For example, the needs of communities for effective and accessible services are not necessarily transferable to government health targets to reduce risk behaviours or implement cost-rationalisation. Community based health promotion remains primarily focused on personal health promotion and communities are co-opted into professionally defined health agendas, which are primarily disease-focused. Drawing on the work of Rissel (1994), Amos (2000) points to another distinction that is often conflated in community health promotion projects, that is, the distinction between psychological empowerment (the personally empowering approach noted above) and community empowerment, which represents a shift in resources and power to the community.

HIV/AIDS prevention strategies
Since the advent of AIDS, sexual behaviour has been redefined as a health risk. However, the risk label has a particular stigmatising effect on groups identified as high risk, particularly gay men. Although there remains much dispute about the origins of AIDS and its transmission routes, it was first identified as a distinct syndrome in 1981 following the emergence of a cluster of cases amongst a visible gay community across a number of US cities and was referred to as Gay Related Immunodeficiency Syndrome (GRID) (Fieldhouse, 2001). Public hysteria ensued around the notion of a

gay plague and there were calls for mandatory testing of suspected communities and quarantine policies (Fieldhouse: 2001). Media coverage inflamed public prejudices against the gay community, which was presented as a public health threat. While the identification of risk populations is a central strategy of epidemiological surveillance, the focus on risk groups instead of risk behaviours is considered by some to be problematic because of the way in which labels reinforce stereotypes and discriminatory practices towards minority groups. Patton (1990), for example, notes that in the 1980s a hierarchy operated in the distinction between high and low risk groups in public health AIDS campaigns. While high risk groups (gay and bisexual men, IV drug users, sex-workers and immigrants) were targeted on the ethical assumption that they have an obligation to know their HIV status in order to protect the public against infection, the public (those who do not self-identify as high risk), on the other hand, was targeted on the ethical assumption of the right to know and the right to protect themselves. So, for example, sex workers are often targeted because of the assumed risk that they pose for their clients as opposed to the risk that clients pose for sex-workers in demanding unprotected sex. Gay men are unambiguously seen as high risk and, as Waldby notes, treated 'as if they themselves were the virus' (1996: 13). In heterosexual relationships, women are seen as the guardians of safe sex (Waldby, 1996; Hyde and Howlett, in press), while penetrative sex is only problematised as dangerous for gay men (Watney, 1991). However, one of the main criticisms of dispensing with risk group categorisation is that targeted interventions become diluted and mass hysteria is created by the misconception that everyone is equally at risk of HIV/AIDS (Fieldhouse, 2001). At the same time, the assumptions that underlie these classifications deny the complexity of sexual identity, sexual practices and relationships. The binary distinction between high and low risk groups reinforces cultural assumptions about normal and deviant sexual behaviour in a way that privileges heterosexuality over homosexuality and men over women, and allocates responsibility in terms of assumptions of guilt or innocence (Waldby, 1996).

While the gay movement has been active in health promotional strategies at grassroots level since the early 1980s, it has been reluctant to endorse testing as the best preventative strategy. This is not surprising given that risk categories become fixed in public perceptions as to who constitutes a risk, and taking the test reveals an individual's identity as a member of a risk group that is already stigmatised irrespective of HIV status. Insurance companies, for example, interpret having taken the HIV antibody test as an indication of a risky lifestyle. In 1999, the Irish Insurance Federation gave an undertaking to change the formulation of its question on whether an individual has undertaken a HIV antibody test to whether an individual has tested positive (DoHC, 2000b). Since 1996, improvements in treatment protocols and the availability of Highly Active Antiretroviral Therapy (HAART) have given a new impetus to the HIV test as a preventative strategy. HAART may also change the definition of AIDS and HIV from terminal diseases to chronic illness, with the expectation that people living with HIV will have a normal life span (Fieldhouse, 2001).

Following Finland, Ireland has the lowest incidence of HIV/AIDS in Europe. While the incidence of AIDS has levelled off since 1996, the incidence of HIV continues to rise. Between 1985 and the end of 1999 there were 2,195 HIV cases: IV drug users represent 41.6 per cent of the cumulative cases; homosexuals, 22.7 per cent, and heterosexuals, where the risk is unspecified, represent 18.8 per cent. Approximately 150 new HIV cases emerge every year representing an incidence rate of about .04 per cent per 1000 of the population. Recent trends suggest that while the incidence rate continues to rise for gay and bisexual men, the greatest increase is in the heterosexual population (DoHC, 2000b). A 22 per cent increase in HIV infections was reported between 2001 and 2002. For the year 2002, 63.5 per cent of HIV infections were acquired heterosexually (National Disease Surveillance Centre, 2003).

In the absence of a cure or vaccine, health policy is primarily focused on prevention through risk awareness. Risk awareness and prevention campaigns focus on risk reduction, for example, methadone and needle exchange programmes, condom campaigns and the distribution of free condoms to targeted risk groups. In Ireland, risk reduction campaigns were constrained by the fact that while condoms had been demedicalised under the 1985 Family Planning (Health) Amendment Act, distribution outlets were limited to health authorities and pharmacies. In the light of public concerns about AIDS, the sale of condoms was deregulated in 1993 and vending machines soon began to appear in social outlets. In 1993, the Eastern Health Board established a Gay Men's Health Project, but the full impact of such outreach programmes depend on a wider policy response to the discrimination and social marginalisation of the gay community. The first important step in this respect was the decriminalisation of homosexuality under the 1993 Criminal Law Sexual Offences Act. In the new AIDS strategy, we note a shift in the terminology from HIV prevention to sexual health promotion. This would suggest a movement away from defining the problem of sexual health in terms of a narrow disease prevention model towards the inclusion of a more positive view of sex and sexual identity, as well as endorsing a wider community approach to sexual health. The Gay Community in Ireland has been particularly active in promoting peer education and community mobilisation in its advocacy and political lobbying work on sexual health and identity in the context of gay rights. One effect of gay activism has been to challenge public health strategies that discriminate against those associated with the disease (that is, those categorised as high risk irrespective of HIV status) and those living with AIDS/HIV. The Gay HIV Strategies funded by the Department of Health and Children since 1997 have allowed the gay community to strike out with preventative initiatives that use sexually explicit images and gay cultural idioms to frankly discuss social taboos such as anal intercourse, anonymous and casual sex, to target outreach work at the cruising, backroom and commercial sex scenes, and to build the capacity of community mobilisation to sustain health promotional practices.

Breast cancer screening
As part of the National Cancer Strategy (1997), a national breast cancer screening programme is underway in Ireland. While the proponents of breast cancer screening argue that early detection has led to a decline in mortality rates, this view has also been contested. Professor Michael Baum who was a member of the British breast cancer screening advisory group has argued that the decline in mortality rates from breast cancer is more likely linked to the introduction of the drug Tamoxifen in the treatment of breast cancer (Baum, 1995 cited in Fitzpatrick, 2001). There are also conflicting views on health promotional policies that mainly focus on individual behaviours and lifestyles, while ignoring the environmental risks associated with the increasing risk of breast cancer, in particular exposure to radiation, environmental pollutants and contaminants such as growth hormones found in dairy and meat products (Lee Davis et al, 1998; WEN (Women's Environmental Network), June 1999).

In a book entitled *Follies and Fallacies in Medicine* (1989), Skrabanek and McCormick reviewed the criteria for screening and noted the following: an effective test should be able to distinguish between those who have and who do not have the disease; effective treatment ought to be available to cure or arrest the disease; and the benefits of early diagnosis should outweigh the harm induced by incorrect results (false positives or false negatives). They argue that mammography as a screening tool does not meet with the above criteria. Screening for cancer is based on the assumption that an early diagnosis (before symptoms occur) enhances the probability of a cure – in other words, an assumption that the stage at which the disease is diagnosed is critical. This, Skrabanek and McCormick suggest, is not universally true, because the type of tumour and whether it forms metastases (secondary growths) early also affects the outcome. They go on to note that 'the nature of the growth is a much more powerful predictor of outcome than the time of diagnosis, whether relatively early or relatively late' (1989:99). They argue that by the time a malignant tumour becomes palpable with a diameter of approximately 1 cm, it has actually been growing for about eight years on average. If it had been detected by mammography two years earlier, this would be of benefit only if metastatic spread was restricted to years six to eight. If the cancer has spread to other parts of the body before year six, then it is already too late. Furthermore, they note that fast-growing tumours are likely to appear as interval cancers between screens in any case.

Skrabanek and McCormick (1989) suggest that the positive predictive value of mammography is between 5-10 per cent, that is, for every 100 positive tests between 90-95 per cent are false positives. In addition, they argue that screening tests are repeated at increasingly close intervals, increasing a woman's chance of becoming the victim of a 'false positive' result. In reviewing some of the medical trials that have been conducted on survival from breast cancer, the authors propose that as techniques for mammography have become more sophisticated, ironically the benefits of screening have lessened (see Box 14.2).

Box 14.2 *Benefits of mammography*

	HIP (New York)	Two-counties (Sweden)	UK	Malmo
Relative risk reduction from dying from breast cancer	35%	29%	14%	5%
Absolute risk reduction of dying from breast cancer	0.02%	0.008%	0.006%	0.001%
How many women would have to be screened for one to benefit?	5,061	12,755	18,315	67,568

Source: Skrabanek and McCormick (1989: 101)

Skrabanek and McCormick contend that mammography leads to over-diagnosis and over-treatment. (This means that women are diagnosed and treated for cancer when they do not really have the disease). They support this point with reference to the UK trial, which occurred in Edinburgh and Guildford and where 51 per cent more cancers were diagnosed in the screened group compared with the control group. They also refer to over-diagnosis (40 per cent) in the Swedish (Two-counties) trial, and in the Malmo trial (30 per cent). In addition, they criticise the effectiveness of the treatment offered for breast cancer, noting the dramatic increase in rates of mastectomy in the USA compared to the UK, yet the incidence and mortality rates are not much different in the two countries. As technology gets more sophisticated, Skrabanek and McCormick (1989) anticipate that the problems with mammography will increase insofar as smaller tumours of uncertain nature and prognosis will be diagnosed and treated as cancer. The most contentious aspect of their argument is that mammography can do harm as it creates anxiety for women, subjects then to unnecessary tests and interventions, yet, they argue, makes little difference to their health outcome.

Remennick (1998) referred to evidence from the Canadian National Breast Screening Study, which documented the outcomes of screening among 90,000 women who participated in the study during 1980-87. Remennick summarises the results as follows:

> This trial showed that, among women aged 40-49 at entry, there was a higher number of deaths from breast cancer among those having an annual mammogram compared to women subject to physical examination alone (38 vs 28 deaths). Among women aged 50-59 at entry, there was a slightly lower number of deaths among those randomly assigned to an annual mammogram plus physical examination relative to physical examination alone (38 vs 39 deaths). Altogether, the picture emerging from this representative trial was highly discouraging for many screening enthusiasts (1998: 98-99).

The claim that mammography significantly reduces mortality from breast cancer was more recently challenged by a Danish study team that assessed evidence from screening programmes in Sweden, Scotland, Canada and the USA involving 500,000 women (Gotzsche and Olsen, 2000 cited in Fitzpatrick, 2001). These critical reassessments have not, however, dented public policy endorsement of national screening programmes.

Dilemmas in health promotion

As an emerging paradigm of care, health promotion faces a number of dilemmas concerning issues of responsibility, risk, competing philosophies of health, and a shift in power relations between the state and citizens, between health professionals and the state, and between patients and health professionals, in new models of governance. Here, we reflect on some of the key issues that are the subject of debate in health promotion and that raise important questions for the future of healthcare.

The risk-responsibility quagmire

A major debate in health promotion concerns the tension between responsibility and control: to what extent can individuals take responsibility for their health when the means of health are beyond their control (Sidell et al, 1997)? There are different dimensions to this debate. Firstly, if we accept the argument that individual risk behaviours such as unhealthy eating, smoking, alcohol consumption, sedentary lifestyles, unprotected sex, and so forth, are not only detrimental to individual health but also carry a significant social cost, should we hold those individuals responsible for their behaviour? Where do we draw the line in operating the principle of individual responsibility? Should those who engage in risk behaviours be denied protection and treatment? How far should we stretch our normative ideal of the healthy and, thus, responsible individual? In considering these questions, we also have to reflect on the argument that the evidence about the causal link between lifestyle behaviours associated with ill health and disease is sometimes spurious and that lifestyle factors are more often selected over social and environmental factors in the construction of risk (Nettleton, 1997; Fitzpatrick, 2001).

Secondly, while everyone is at risk of ill health, not everyone's identity is constructed in terms of risk status. However, as we discussed in Chapter 11, the promise held out by genetic screening and diagnostic testing is that risk profiling will increasingly be refined in population health programmes. This has already led to a changing definition of risk from actual risk to potential risk, where populations can be profiled according to their at-risk health status in relation to their genetic dispositions. Kenen (1997) argues that as the at-risk health status becomes institutionalised, its role will be seen as analogous to Parsons' 'sick role' (see Chapters 2 and 8). The difference between the at-risk health role and the sick role is that the former does not entail the right to be free of social obligations because the individual, of course, is not sick. To fulfil this role, however, the individual is obliged to take responsibility for his or her health by taking up diagnostic tests and, armed with the knowledge of their risk status, go about changing their lifestyles. Kenan (1997) argues that implicit in the new role is that individuals' entitlement to the rights accompanying the sick role should they fall ill will be determined by their willingness to fulfil the obligations of the at-risk health role in the first place.

Thirdly, the economic rationale of health prevention strategies entails a number of dilemmas. A political dilemma in the implementation of a radical reorientation of health policy towards preventative strategies is that they are future orientated and the costs and benefits are often intangible and difficult to calculate (Godfrey, 1997). Furthermore, in times of fiscal restraint, the health services are faced with the dilemma of committing resources to preventative strategies while public patients with chronic conditions carry the burden of cutbacks in basic health and social services. While health promotion is a cost-saving mechanism for rationalising demands on the health system by transferring responsibility, at least in part, to individuals to maintain health, it finds itself supporting conflicting philosophies of health.

Conflicting philosophies of health

Beattie (1991) notes that there is a tension between paternalistic, top-down approaches and bottom-up, participatory models of health promotion, and between an emphasis on problems and solutions as individual or collective. Within the framework of these two axes, individually focused health promotion strategies understand the problem of health to be associated with individual risk behaviours and the solution is to alter individual behaviours through health persuasion techniques. Here, both the definition of the problem and solution lie with the health expert. Alternatively, health promotion may adopt a more personally empowering approach through personal counselling for health, where there is a greater level of negotiation between professionals and participants about the complexity of health problems for the individual and how they might be overcome. Collectively focused health promotion includes legislative reform such as the recent work-place smoking ban in Ireland or the development of medical services such as screening and immunisations. Policy makers and experts in public health lead the agenda and actions associated with this kind of health promotion. More negotiated, collective forms of health promotion are community-based initiatives. As we saw above, community development is regarded as central to the vision of the WHO health promotion strategy on identifying and meeting needs and of empowering communities to participate in their own health through health policy actions.

Care or governance?
While the emphasis on health promotion opens up new therapeutic spaces for a wide range of health and allied professionals working in the community sector under a social model of health, the shift to health promotion holds a number of tensions for the medical profession. In Ireland, the medical academic Petr Skrabenek was the most vocal against the NPH agenda. In his book, *The Death of Humane Medicine and the Rise of Coercive Healthism* (1994) (see Chapter 6), he argued that the role of medicine should not be about the policing of lifestyle and personal behaviours. Elsewhere, we have discussed the crisis of modern medicine when faith in the biomedical model began to flounder in the face of modern chronic and debilitating conditions. This crisis of confidence became amplified in the context of major economic and social changes from the 1970s onwards (see Chapter 13) and was highlighted by a growing body of critical work throughout the seventies (for example, in the work of Illich and McKeown discussed in Chapter 6, and feminist critiques of medical patriarchy and paternalism discussed in Chapters 7, 11 and 13). As indicated in Chapter 12, public trust in the medical profession has also been dented by such controversies as the Shipman case in Britain[24], and the retention of organs and contaminated blood product controversies. The professional autonomy of the medical profession is also being undermined by health managerialism and the introduction of the principles of clinical governance to ensure that clinical practices are cost-effective and efficient in line with managerial performance measures (see Chapter 12).

Against this background, Fitzpatrick's (2001) analysis of the emerging paradigm shift in the British context is that health promotion has become a vehicle for authoritarian state policies in a context in which the widening scope and definition of health has greatly expanded the social role of doctors. This has altered the relationship between the state and medical profession, with the latter serving the interests of state policy over the

24. The Manchester GP, Harold Shipman, was convicted in January 2000 of the murder of fifteen of his patients.

interests of the individualised care of patients. He argues that this new relationship represents a fundamental shift in power that undermines professional autonomy and that, by expanding the role of medics as agents of social control, the autonomy of the patient is also undermined. In other words, the cooption of doctors into wider social programmes for effecting change in health behaviours and directly rationing health resources subordinates the needs of patients to the agenda of the state. Rather than transferring power to the patient, medical power is reinforced as a form of governance. Scambler (2001) also argues that medicine has been co-opted into this process and that as medicine increasingly defines itself in relation to identity and lifestyle projects, it may inadvertently be subscribing to the demise of its cultural authority and professional autonomy.

Summary

- Public health emerged in the wake of societal changes in the eighteenth and nineteenth centuries that prompted a concern with containing the spread of diseases among the masses of the population. Following various shifts in emphasis since then, public health began to focus in the 1970s on the fusion of environmental measures with personal health maintenance strategies to tackle chronic illness and health inequalities. This latest phase in the history of public health has been described as the New Public Health (NPH).

- Health promotion has been embraced in many Western countries, particularly through the endorsement of the WHO's *Health for All* principles that link economic policies and structural factors to the lifestyle patterns of individuals.

- Sociology provides many perspectives for understanding the social context of New Public Health such as:
  - Understanding consumer culture and in particular analysing the way in which the absence of finding collective ways to express our expectations is replaced with a focus on consumerism and individualism.
  - Understanding NPH in the context of risk and the manner in which more and more aspects of our lives are defined as risky and how health promotion regulates levels of risk.
  - Analysing the way in which social institutions monitor or survey people, and how people monitor themselves through a process of normalisation without the need for direct coercion.

- Various sociological critiques of health promotion have emerged in recent years, including:
  - Structural critiques proposing that rooting health problems in individual lifestyle behaviours fails to address the material conditions of people's lives.
  - Critiques of the surveillance role of health promotion in socially controlling people.

- Lifestyle critiques, whereby health promotion practices are perceived to endorse a dominant form of paternalism.

- Various health promotion strategies are in use, such as strategies that (ideally) aim to address structural inequalities (such as the community development model); strategies that focus on at risk groups and/or at risk behaviours; and population-wide screening of healthy individuals. Each of these models of health promotion is potentially problematic.

- A number of dilemmas have emerged in relation to health promotion. These include the tension between the expectation of individual responsibility and the extent to which people have control over their health choices; the level at which health promotion should operate (individual or collective) and the degree of paternalism that should mediate health promotion practice; and the extent to which health professionals should exercise authority over facilitating patient autonomy.

Topics for discussion and reflection
1. Are there situations in which an authoritarian approach to health promotion might be acceptable? If so, what situations might these be?
2. Consider health scares that have entered public debates in recent years. To what extent have you, or people you know, altered patterns of normal living in response to the perceived risks?

References

Aakster, C. W. (1993) 'Concepts in alternative medicine'. In Beattie, A., Gott, M., Jones, L. and Sidell, M. (eds): *Health and Wellbeing: a Reader*. London: The Open University in association with Macmillian Press, 84-93.

Abbott, P. and Wallace, C. (1990) *An Introduction to Sociology: Feminist Perspectives*. London: Routledge.

Abbotts, J., Williams, R., Ford, G., Hunt, K. and West, P. (1997) 'Morbidity and Irish catholic descent in Britain: An ethnic and religious minority 150 years on'. *Social Science and Medicine*, 45 (1), 3-14.

Abbotts, J., Williams, R., Ford, G. (2001) 'Morbidity and Irish catholic descent in Britain – Relating health disadvantage to socio-economic position'. *Social Science and Medicine*, 52 (7), 999-1005.

Acheson, D., Barker, D., Chambers, J., Graham, H., Marmot, M., and Whitehead, M. (1998) *Independent Inquiry into Inequalities in Health: Report*. London: Stationery Office.

Adams, L., Amos, M. and Munro, J. (eds) (2002) *Promoting Health: Politics and Practices*. London: Sage.

Adamson, J., Sholma, Y. B., Chatuverdi, N. and Donovan, J. (2003) 'Ethnicity, socio-economic position and gender – do they affect reported health-care seeking behaviour?' *Social Science and Medicine*, 57 (5), 895-904.

Aday, L. A. (2000) 'An expanded conceptual framework of equity: implications for assessing health policy'. In Gary L. Albrecht, Ray Fitzpatrick and Susan C. Scrimshaw, *The Handbook of Social Studies in Health and Medicine*. London: Sage.

Ahmad W. and Atkin, K. (eds) (1996) *'Race' and Community Care*. Buckingham: Open University Press.

Ahmad, W. (ed.) (2000) *Ethnicity, Disability and Chronic Illness*. Buckingham: Open University Press.

Ahmad, W. (1996) 'The trouble with culture'. In Kelleher, D. and Hillier, S. (eds) *Researching Cultural Differences in Health*. London: Routledge.

Ahmad, W., Baker, M. and Kernohan, E. (1991) 'General practitioners' perceptions of Asian and non-Asian patients'. *Family Practice*, 8 (1), 52-6.

Ahronheim, J. C., Morrison, R. S., Baskin, S. A., Morris, J., and Meier, D. E. (1996) 'Treatment of the dying in an acute care hospital: advanced dementia and metastic cancer'. *Archives of Internal Medicine,* 156, 2094-2100.

Ainsworth-Vaughn, N. (1998) *Claiming Power in Doctor-Patient Talk*. Oxford: Oxford University Press.

Allen, D. (2002) 'Negotiating the role of *expert carers* on an adult hospital ward'. In D. Allen and D. Hughes (eds) *Nursing and the Division of Labour in Health Care*. Basingstoke: Palgrave Macmillan. 183-205.

Allen, D. (1997) 'The nursing-medical boundary: a negotiated order?' *Sociology of Health and Illness*, 19 (4), 498-520.

Allen, D. (2001) *The Changing Shape of Nursing Practice: The Role of Nurses in the Hospital Division of Labour.* London: Routledge.

Alonzo, A. and Reynolds, N. R. (1995) 'Stigma, HIV and AIDS: an exploration and elaboration of a stigma trajectory'. *Social Science and Medicine*, 41 (3) 303-315.

Amos, M. (2002) 'Community Development'. In L. Adams, M. Amos, and J. Munro, (eds) *Promoting Health: Politics and Practices.* London: Sage.

Andersen H. (2000) 'Jurgen Habermas'. In H. Andersen and L. B. Kaspersen (eds) *Classical and Modern Social Theory.* Oxford: Blackwell Publishers, 326-343.

Anderson, J. M. (2000) 'Gender, "race", poverty, health and discourses of health reform in the context of globalization: a postcolonial feminist perspective in policy research'. *Nursing Inquiry*, 7: 220-229.

Anderson, R. and Bury, M. (eds) (1998) *Living with Chronic Illness: The Experiences of Patients and their Families.* London: Unwin Hyman.

Anker-Nilssen, P. (2003) 'Household energy use and the environment – a conficting issue'. *Applied Energy*, 76, 189-196.

Annandale, E. and Clark, J. (1996) 'What is gender? Feminist theory and the sociology of human reproduction'. *Sociology of Health and Illness*, 18 (1), 17-44.

Annandale, E. (1998) *The Sociology of Health and Medicine: A Critical Introduction.* Cambridge: Polity Press.

Annandale, E. and Hunt, K. (2000) (eds) *Gender Inequalities in Health.* Buckingham: Open University Press.

Appadurai, A (2001) 'Disjuncture and difference in the global cultural economy'. In S. Seidman and J. C. Alexander (eds) *The New Social Theory Reader.* London: Routledge.

Arber S. and Cooper H. (1999) 'Gender differences in health in later life: the new paradox?' *Social Science and Medicine*, 48 (1), 61-76.

Arber, S. (1991) 'Class, paid employment and family roles: making sense of structural disadvantage, gender and health status'. *Social Science and Medicine*, 32, (4), 425-436.

Arber, S. (1997) 'Comparing inequalities in women and men's health: Britain in the 1990s'. In Lahelma, E. and Rahkonen, E. (eds) Special Issue on Health Inequalities in Modern Societies and Beyond. *Social Science and Medicine*, 44, (6), 773-787.

Aries, P. (1973) *Centuries of Childhood.* London: Peregrine.

Aries, P. (1981) *The Hour of our Death.* London: Allen Lane.

Aries, P. (1985) *Images of Man and Death.* Cambridge: Harvard University Press.

Armstead, C., Lawlor, K., Gordon, G., Cross, J. and Gibbons, J. (1989) 'Relationship of racial stressors to blood pressure responses and anger expression in black college students'. *Health Psychology*, 8 (5) 541-56.

Armstrong, D. (1983a) 'The fabrication of nurse-patient relationships'. *Social Science and Medicine*, 17 (7): 457-60.

Armstrong, D. (1983b) *Political Anatomy of the Body: Medical Knowledge in Britain in the Twentieth Century.* Cambridge: Cambridge University Press.

Armstrong, D. (1987) 'Theoretical tensions in biopsychosocial medicine'. *Social Science and Medicine*, 25 (11): 183-91.

Armstrong, D. (1993) 'From clinical gaze to a regime of total health'. In A. Beattie, M. Gott, L. Jones and M. Sidell (eds) *Health and Wellbeing: A Reader.* London: Macmillan.

Armstrong, D. (1995b) 'The rise of surveillance medicine', *Sociology of Health and Illness*, 17 (3): 393-404.

Armstrong, D. (1995a) 'The problem of the whole person in holistic medicine'. In B. Davey, A. Gray and C. Seale (eds) *Health and Disease: A Reader* (Second edition). Buckingham: Open Univerity Press.

Armstrong, D. (2002) 'Clinical autonomy, individual and collective: the problem of changing doctors' behaviour'. *Social Science and Medicine*, 55 (10), 1771-1777.

Arnstein, S. (1969) 'A ladder of citizen participation'. *Journal of the American Institute of Planners*, 35: 216-24.

Ashton, J. and Seymour, H. (1993) 'The setting for a new public health'. In A. Beattie, M. Gott, L. Jones, and M. Sidell (eds) *Health and Wellbeing: A Reader*. London: Macmillan.

Ashton, J. and Seymour, H. (1988) *The New Public Health*. Buckingham: Open University Press.

Aspinall, P. J. (2001) 'Operationalising the collection of ethnicity data in studies of the sociology of health and illness'. *Sociology of Health and Illness*, 23 (6), 829-862.

Atkinson, P. (1995) *Medical Talk and Medical Work*. London: Sage

Atkinson, P. and Heath, C. (1981) *Medical Work: Realities and Routines*. London: Gower.

Backett, K., Davison, C. and Mullen, K. (1994) 'Lay evaluation of health and healthy lifestyles: evidence from three studies'. *British Journal of General Practice*, 44, 277-80.

Bakx, K. (1991) 'The "eclipse" of folk medicine in Western society'. *Sociology of Health and Illness,* 13 (1), 20-38.

Balanda, K. P. and Wilde, J. (2001) *Inequalities in Mortality, 1989-1998 A Report on All-Ireland Mortality Data*. Dublin: Institute of Public Health.

Banerji, D. (1999) 'A fundamental shift in the approach to international health by WHO, UNICEF, and the World Bank: instances of the practice of "intellectual facism" and totalitarianism in some Asian countries'. *International Journal of Health Services*, 29 (2), 227-259.

Banks, I (2001) 'No Man's Land: Men, Illness and the NHS'. *British Medical Journal* 323: 1058-1060

Bardasi, E., Jenkins, S. P. and Rigg, J. A. (2002) 'Retirement and the income of older people: a British perspective'. *Ageing and Society*, 22, 131-159.

Barham, P. and Hayward, R. (1996) 'The lives of "users"'. In Heller, T. et al (eds) *Mental Health Matters: A Reader*. London: Macmillan.

Barrington, R. (1987) *Health, Medicine and Politics in Ireland 1900-1970*. Dublin: Institute of Public Administration.

Barry, C. A., Stevenson, F. A., Britten, N., Barber, N., Bradley, C. P. (2001) 'Giving voice to the lifeworld, more effective medical care? A qualitative study of doctor-patient communication in general pratice'. *Social Science and Medicine*, 53 (4), 487-505.

Barry, J., Hamish, S., Kelly, A., O'Loughlin, R., Handy, D., and O'Dowd, T. (2001) *Inequalities in Health in Ireland – Hard Facts*. Dublin: Department of Community Health and General Practice, Trinity College.

Bartley, M., Blane, D. and Davey-Smith, G. (1998) 'Introduction: Beyond the black report'. In Bartley, M., Blane, D. and Davey-Smith, G. (eds) *The Sociology of Health Inequalities*. Oxford: Blackwell.

Bartley, M., Poppay, J. and Plewis, I. (1992) 'Domestic conditions, paid employment and women's experience of ill health'. *Sociology of Health and Illness*, 14 (3), 313-43.

Barton, R. (1959) *Institutional Neurosis*. Bristol: Wright.

Bassett, K., Iyer, N. and Kazanjian, A. (2000) 'Defensive medicine during hospital obstetrical care: a by-product of the technical age'. *Social Science and Medicine*, 51 (4), 523-537.

Baudrillard, J. (1981) *Simulations*. New York: Semiotext.

Baum, M. (1995) 'Screening for breast cancer, time to think – and stop'. *Lancet*, 346: 436-7.

BBC Two *Newsnight* Programme 26th March 2003.

Beattie, A. (1991) 'Knowledge and control in health promotion'. In J. Gabe, M. Calnan and M. Bury (eds) *The Sociology of Health Service*. London: Routledge.

Beattie, A. (1993) 'The changing boundaries of health' in A. Beattie, M. Gott, L. Jones, and M. Sidell, (eds) (1993) *Health and Wellbeing: A Reader*. London: Macmillan.

Beattie, A., Gott, M., Jones, L. and Sidell, M. (eds) (1993) *Health and Wellbeing: A Reader*. London: Macmillan.

Beck C. T. (1994) 'Phenomenology: Its use in nursing research'. *International Journal of Nursing Studies*, 31 (6) 449-510.

Beck, U. (1992) *Risk Society*. London: Sage.

Becker, Howard. S. (1966) *Outside: Studies in the Sociology of Deviance*. New York: Free Press.

Bedell, S. E., Deitz, D. C., Leeman, D. and Delbanco, T. L. (1991) 'Incidence and characteristics of preventable iatrogenic cardiac arrests'. *Journal of the American Medical Association*, 265, 2815-20.

Begley, C. (1988) 'Episiotomy – A change in midwives' practice'. *Irish Nursing Forum and Health Services*, 34, 12-14.

Begley, C. (1997) *Midwives in the making: A longitudinal study of the experiences of student midwives during their two year training in Ireland*. Unpublished PhD Thesis. University of Dublin, Trinity College.

Begley, C. (1999a). 'Student midwives' experiences during their training programme'. In M Treacy, and A. Hyde (eds), *Nursing research: design and practice* (pp. 225-241). Dublin: University College Dublin Press.

Begley, C. (1999b) 'A study of student midwives' experiences during their two-year education programme'. *Midwifery*, 15, 194-202.

Begley, C. (1999c) 'Student midwives' views of "learning to be a midwife" in Ireland'. *Midwifery*, 15, 264-273.

Begley, C. (2001) 'Giving midwifery care: student midwives' views of their working role'. *Midwifery*, 17, 24-34.

Begley, M., Garavan, C., Condon, M., Kelly, I., Holland, K., and Staines, A. (1999) *Asylum in Ireland: A Public Health Perspective*. Dublin: Department of Public Health Medicine, University College Dublin.

Beisecker, A. E. (1988) 'Aging and the desire for information and input in medical decisions: patient consumerism in medical encounters'. *The Gerontologist*, 28, 330-335.

Beisecker, A. E. and Beisecker, T. D. (1990) 'Patient information-seeking behaviours when communicating with doctors'. *Medical Care*, 28: 19-28.

Bendelow, G. A. (1993) 'Pain perceptions, emotion and gender'. *Sociology of Health and Illness*, 15 (3), 273-94.

Bendelow, G. A. and Williams, S. J. (1995) 'Transcending dualisms: towards a sociology of pain'. *Sociology of Health and Illness*, 17, 139-65

Benner, P. (1984) *From Novice to Expert. Excellence and Power in Clinical Nursing.* Menlo Park, CA: Addison-Wesley.

Benner, P. and Wrubel, J. (1989) *The Primacy of Caring.* London: Addison-Wesley.

Bensing, J. M., Verhaak, P. F. M., van Dulmen, A. M., and Visser, A. P. (2000) 'Communication: the royal pathway to patient-centered medicine'. *Patient Education and Counselling*, 39, 1-3.

Benzeval, M., Judge, K. and Soloman, M. (1992) *The Health Status of Londoners.* London: King's Fund Institute.

Berger, P. and Berger, B. (1976) *Sociology: A Biographical Approach.* Harmondsworth: Penguin Books Ltd.

Bernard, M. (2000) *Promoting Health in Old Age: Critical Issues in Self-Health Care.* Buckingham: Open University Press.

Bhugra, D. and Bahl, V. (eds) (1999) *Ethnicity: An Agenda for Mental Health.* London: Gaskell.

Bijker, W. E. (1995) *Of Bicycles, Bakelites and Bulbs. Towards a Theory of Sociotechnical Change.* Cambridge MA: MIT Press.

Bilton, T., Bonnett, K., Jones, P., Sheard, K., Skinner, D., Stanworth, M. and Webster, A. (1996) *Introductory Sociology* (Third edition). London: Macmillan.

Birke, L. (2003) 'Shaping biology: feminism and the idea of the biological'. In Simon Williams, Lynda Birke, and Gillian Bendelow (eds) *Debating Biology: Sociological Reflections on Health, Medicine and Society.* London: Routledge, 39-52.

Blanchard, C. G., Labrecque, M. S., Ruckdeschel, J. C. and Blanchard, E. B. (1988) 'Information and decision-making preferences of hospitalised adult cancer patients'. *Social Science and Medicine*, 27 (11), 1139-1145.

Blane, D. (2003) 'The use of quantitative medical sociology'. *Sociology of Health and Illness*, 25, 115-130.

Blaxter, M. (1990) *Health and Lifestyles.* London: Tavistock/Routledge.

Blumer, Herbert (1969) *Symbolic Interactionism: Perspective and Method.* Englewood-Cliffs, New Jersey: Prentice Hall.

BMA (1986) *Report of the Board of Science and Education on Alternative Therapy.* London: BMA.

BMA (2000) *Acupuncture: Efficacy, Safety and Practice.* London: British Medical Association.

BMA (2004) *Acupuncture: Efficacy, Safety and Practice: Board of Science.* www. bma. org. uk/qp. nsf/Content/Acupuncture%3A+efficacy%2C+and+practice +28m%29?OpenDocumentandHighlight+2,acupuncture,86. (April 20th 2004).

BMA (2002) BMA Publications. www. bma. org. uk/ap. nsf/Content/_Hub+Science+ publications. (August 27, 2002).

Bolam, B., Hodgetts, D., Chamberlain, K., Murphy, S. and Gleeson, K. (2003) '"Just do it": an analysis of accounts of control over health amongst low socio-economic status groups'. *Critical Public Health*, 13 (1), 15-31.

Bolton, S. C. (2001) 'Changing faces: nurses as emotional jugglers'. *Sociology of Health and Illness*. 23 (1) 85-100.

Bond, J., Briggs, R. and Coleman, P. (1993) 'The study of ageing'. In Bond, J., Coleman, P. and Peace, S. (eds) *Ageing in Society: An Introduction to Social Gerontology* (Second edition). London: Sage, 19-52.

Boucher, G. W. (1998) *The Irish Are Friendly But ... A Report on Racism and International Students in Ireland*. Dublin: Irish Council for International Students.

Bourdieu, P. (1977) *Outline of a Theory of Practice*. Cambridge: Cambridge University Press.

Bourdieu, P. (1990) *The Logic of Practice*. Cambridge: Polity.

Bourdieu, P. (1984) *Distinctions*. London: Routledge.

Bourke, J. (1993) *Husbandry to Housewifery: Women, Economic Change, and Housework in Ireland 1890-1914*. Oxford: Clarendon Press.

Bourke, J. (2004) 'Home alone. Dublin: The Yoke Publications'. www. theyoke. net/articles/home_alone. html (April 20th 2004).

Bowler, I. (1993) '"They're not the same as us": midwives' stereotypes of South Asian descent maternity patients'. *Sociology of Health and Illness*, 15 (2), 157-78.

Bowling, A. (2002) *Research Methods in Health: Investigating health and health services*. (Second edition). Buckingham: Open University Press.

Boychuk Duchscher, J. E. (2000) 'Bending a habit: critical social theory as a framework for humanistic nurse education'. *Nurse Education Today*, 20, 453-462.

Boyle, P., Halfacree, K. and Robinson, V. (1998) *Exploring Contemporary Migration*. Harlow: Longman

Bradby, M. (1990) 'Status passage into nursing: another view of the socialization process into nursing'. *Journal of Advanced Nursing*, 15, 1220-1225.

Bradley, C. P. (1991) 'Decision-making and prescribing – a literature review'. *Family Practice*, 8, 276-87.

Breemhaar, B. Visser, A., and Kleijnen, J. (1990) 'Perceptions and behavior among elderly hospital patients: Description and explanation of age differences in satisfaction, knowledge, emotions, and behavior'. *Social Science and Medicine*, 31 (12), 1377-1385.

Breen, R., Hannan, D., Rottman, D. and Whelan, C. (1990) *Understanding Contemporary Ireland: State, Class and Development in the Republic of Ireland*. Dublin: Gill and Macmillan.

Breggin, P. R. (1993) *Toxic Psychiatry: Drugs and Electro Convulsive Therapy: The Truth and Better Alternative*. London: Fontana.

Breggin, P. R. and Breggin, G. R. (1995) *Talking Back to Prozac: What Doctors Aren't Telling You About Today's Most Controversial Drug*. New York: St Martins.

Brennan, T. A., Leape, L. L., Laird, N. et al. (1991) 'Incidence of adverse effects and negligence in hospitalised patients: Results of the Harvard Medical Practice Study 1'. *New England Journal of Medicine*, 324: 370-6.

Britten, N. and Ukoumunne, O. (1997) 'The influence of patients' hopes of receiving a prescription on doctors' perceptions and the decision to prescribe: a questionnaire survey'. *British Medical Journal*, 315, 1506-10.

Britten, N. (1996) 'Lay views of drugs and medicines: orthodox and unorthodox accounts'. In Williams S. J. and Calnan, M. (eds) *Modern Medicine: Lay Perspectives and Experiences*. London: UCL Press Ltd.

Britten, N. (2001) 'Prescribing and the defence of clinical autonomy'. *Sociology of Health and Illness,* 23 (4), 478-496.

Brockbank, W. (1970) *History of Nursing at Manchester Royal Infirmary.* Manchester: Manchester University Press.

Broom, D. and Woodward, R.V. (1996) 'Medicalisation reconsidered: towards a collaborative approach to care'. *Sociology of Health and Illness,* 18 (3), 357-378.

Broverman, I. K., Broverman, D. M., Clarkson, F. E., Rosenkrantz, P. S. and Vogel, S. R. (1970) 'Sex-role stereotypes and clinical judgements of mental health'. *Journal of Consulting and Clinical Psychology,* 34, 1-7.

Brown, G. W., Andrews, B., Harris, T. O., Adler, Z., Bridge, L. (1986) 'Social support, self-esteem and depression'. *Psychological Medicine,* 16, 813-31.

Brown, H. and Smith, H. (2001) 'Assertion, not assimilation: A feminist perspective on the normalisation principle'. In H. Brown and H. Smith (eds), *Normalisation: A Reader.* London and New York: Routledge.

Brown, P. and Chadwick, G. (1997) 'Management and the Health Professional'. In J. Robins (ed.) *Reflections on Health: Commemorating Fifty Years of The Department of Health 1947-1997.* Dublin: Department of Health.

Bullough, V. and Vought, M. (1973) 'Women, menstruation and nineteenth-century medicine'. *Bulletin of the History of Medicine,* 47, 66-82.

Bunton, R. and Burrows, R. (1995) 'Consumption and health in the "epidemiological" clinic of late modern medicine'. In R. Bunton, S. Nettleton, and R. Burrows (eds) *The Sociology of Health Promotion: Critical Analyses of Consumption, Lifestyle and Risk.* London: Routledge.

Bunton, R. and MacDonald, G. (1992) *Health Promotion: Disciplines and Diversity.* London: Routledge.

Bunton, R., Nettleton, S., and Burrows, R. (eds) (1995) *The Sociology of Health Promotion: Critical Analyses of Consumption, Lifestyle and Risk.* London: Routledge.

Burns, J. (1992) 'Mad or just plain bad: gender and the work of forensic clinical psychologists'. In J. M. Ussher and P. Nicolson (eds) *Gender Issues in Clinical Psychology.* Routledge: London.

Burnstein, J. M., Yan, R., Weller, I. and Abramson, B. L. (2003) 'Management of congestive heart failure: a gender gap may still exist. Observations from a contemporary cohort'. *BMC Cardiovascular Disorders.* 3 (1) 1.

Bury, M. (1986) 'Post constructionism and the development of medical sociology'. *Sociology of Health and Illness,* 8 (2), 137-69.

Bury, M. (1982) 'Chronic illness as biographical disruption'. *Sociology of Health and Illness,* 4 (2), 167-82.

Bury, M. (1991) 'The sociology of chronic illness: a review of research and prospects'. *Sociology of Health and Illness,* 13 (4), 451-68.

Busfield, J. (1982) 'Gender and mental illness', *International Journal of Mental Health,* 11 (1/2): 46-66

Busfield, J. (1986) *Managing Madness: Changing Ideas and practice.* London: Unwin Hyman.

Busfield, J. (1996) 'Professionals, the state and the development of mental health policy'. In T. Heller et al (eds) *Mental Health Matters: A Reader.* London: Macmillan.

Busfield, J. (2002) 'The archaeology of psychiatric disorder: gender and disorders of thought, emotion and behaviour'. In G. Bendelow, M. Carpenter, C. Vautier and

S. Williams (eds) *Gender Health and Healing: the Public/Private Divide*. London: Routledge.

Caelli, K. (2001) 'Engaging with phenomenology: Is it more of a challenge than it needs to be?' *Qualitative Health Research*, 11 (2) 273-81.

Callon, Michel (1986): 'The sociology of an actor-network: the case of an electric vehicle'. In M. Callon, J. Law, and A. Rip (eds) *Mapping the Dynamics of Science and Technology*. London: Macmillan.

Calnan, M. (1988) 'Lay evaluation of medicine and medical practice: report of a pilot study'. *International Journal of Health Services*, 18, 311-22.

Cameron, E. and Bernardes, J. (1998) 'Gender and disadvantage in health: men's health for a change'. In Bartley, M., Blane, D. and Davey-Smith, G. (eds) *The Sociology of Health Inequalities*. Oxford: Blackwell Publishers.

Campbell, P. (1996) 'The history of the user movement in the United Kingdom'. In Heller, T. et al (eds) *Mental Health Matters: A Reader*. London: Macmillan.

Campbell, R. and Porter, S. (1997) 'Feminist theory and the sociology of childbirth; a response to Ellen Annandale and Judith Clark'. *Sociology of Health and Illness*, 19, (3), 348-358.

Campbell, R. and MacFarlane, A. (1995) *Where to be Born: The Debate and the Evidence*. (Second edition). Oxford: Crown Publications.

Carpenter, M. (2000) 'Health for some: global health and social development since Alma Ata.' *Community Development Journal*, 35 (4), 336-351.

Carr-Saunders, A. M. and Wilson, P. A. (1933) *The Professions*. Oxford: Clarendon Press.

Carter, S. (1995) 'Boundaries of danger and uncertainty: an analysis of the technological culture of risk assessment'. In J. Gabe (ed.) *Medicine, Health and Risk: Sociological Approaches*. Oxford: Blackwell.

Cartner-Morley, J. (1998) 'Doctors in disgrace: one month's headlines'. *Guardian*, 22nd October, cited in Morrall, P. (2001) *Sociology and Nursing*. London: Routledge.

Cartwright, A. and Anderson, R. (1981) *General Practice Revisited: A Second Study of Parients and their Doctors*. London: Tavistock.

Cartwright, A. and O'Brien, M. (1976) 'Social class variations in health care and in the nature of general practitioner consultations'. In M. Stacey (ed.) *The Sociology of the NHS*. Keele: University of Keele, Sociological Review Monograph 22.

Cartwright, L. (1995) *Screening the Body: Tracing Medicine's Visual Culture*. Minneapolis and London: University of Minnesota Press.

Chan, C. (2000) 'A study of health services for the Chinese minority in Manchester'. *British Journal of Nursing*, 5 (3), 140-7.

Chandola, T., Bartley, M., Sacker, A., Jenkinson, C., and Marmot, M. (2003) 'Health Selection in the Whitehall II study, UK'. *Social Science and Medicine*, 56 (10), 2059-2072.

Chaney, D. (1995) 'Creating memories: some images of ageing in mass tourism'. In M. Featherstone and A. Wernick (eds) *Images of Ageing: Cultural Representations of Later Life*. London: Routledge

Chapple, A. (1998) 'Iron deficiency anaemia in women of South Asian descent: a qualitative study'. *Ethnicity and Health*, 3 (3), 199-212.

Charles, C. and DeMaio, S. (1993) 'Lay participation in health care decision making: a conceptual framework'. *Journal of Health Politics, Policy and Law*, 18, 881-904.

Charmaz, K. (1983) 'Loss of self: a fundamental form of suffering in the chronically ill'. *Sociology of Health and Illness*, 5 (2), 168-95.

Cheek, J. and Porter, S. (1997) 'Reviewing Foucault: Possibilities and problems for nursing and healthcare'. *Nursing Inquiry*, 4, 108-19.

Chesler, P. (1972) *Women and Madness*. New York: Doubleday.

CIA World Factbook (2004) *Ireland: Total Fertility Rate*. www. indexmundi. com/g/g. aspx. (April 22nd 2004)

Ciambrone, D. (2001) 'Illness and other assaults on self: the relative impact of HIV AIDS on women's lives'. *Sociology of Health and Illness*, 23, 517-40.

Clarke, A. (2001) *The Sociology of Healthcare*. London: Prentice Hall.

Clarke, A. E., Mamo, L., Fishman, J. R., Shim, J. K., and Fosket, J. R. (2003) 'Biomedicalization: Technoscientific Transformations of Health, Illness, and U. S. Biomedicine'. *American Sociological Review*, 68 (April), 161-193.

Clarke, J. and O'Neill C. (2001) 'An analysis of how *The Irish Times* portrayed Irish nursing during the 1999 strike'. *Nursing Ethics*, 8 (4), 350-59.

Cleary, A. (1997) 'Gender differences in mental health in Ireland'. In A. Cleary and M. P. Treacy (eds), *The Sociology of Health and Illness in Ireland*. Dublin: University College Dublin Press.

Coast, J. (1996) 'The Oregon plan: Technical priority setting in the USA'. In J. Coast, J. Donovan and S. Frankel (eds), *Priority Setting: The Health Care Debate*. Chichester, Wiley.

Coburn, D. (1993a) 'Professional power in decline: Medicine in a changing Canada'. In Hafferty, F. W. and McKinlay, J. B. (eds) *The Changing Medical Profession: An International Perspective*. New York: Oxford University Press.

Coburn, D. (1993b) 'State authority, medical dominance, and trends in the regulation of the health professions: the Ontario case'. *Social Science and Medicine*, 37 (2), 129-38.

Coburn, D. (2000) 'Income inequality, social cohesion and the health status of populations: the role of neo-liberalism'. *Social Science and Medicine*, 51 (1), 135-146.

Cochrane, A. L. (1995) 'Effectiveness and efficiency'. In B. Davey, A. Gray and C. Scale (eds) *Health and Disease: A Reader* (Second edition). Buckingham: Open Univerity Press.

Cockburn, J. and Pit, S. (1997) 'Prescribing behaviour in clinical practice: patients' expectations and doctors' perceptions of patients' expectations – a questionnaire study', *British Medical Journal*, 315, 520-3.

Cockerham, William C. (2000, Fifth edition) *Sociology of Mental Disorder*. New Jersey: Prentice-Hall

Cohen, D., Farley, T. and Mason K. (2003) 'Why is Poverty Unhealthy? Social and physical mediators'. *Social Science and Medicine*, 57 (9), 1631-1641.

Collins, A. (1997) 'Is Ireland meeting its international obligations towards refugees?' *Trocaire Development Review*, 1997, 93-114.

Collins, C. and Shelly, E. (1997) 'Differences in Lifestyle and Health Characteristics in Ireland'. In A. Cleary and M. P. Treacy (eds) *The Sociology of Health and Illness in Ireland*. Dublin: University College Dublin Press.

Comte, A. (1974, orig. 1830-1842) *The Essential Comte: selected from 'Cours de philosophie positive'* by A. Stanislav and M. Clarke. London: Croom Helm Originally published Paris: Bachelier.

Connell Meehan, T. (2003) 'Careful nursing: a model for contemporary nursing practice'. *Journal of Advanced Nursing,* 44 (1), 99-107.

Conrad, P. (1999) 'A mirage of genes'. *Sociology of Health and Illness,* 21 (2): 228-41.

Conrad, P. and Gabe, J. (1999) *Sociological Perspectives on the New Genetics.* Oxford: Blackwell.

Corcoran, M. and Pellion, M. (eds) *Ireland Unbound: A Turn of the Century Chronicle.* Dublin: Institute of Public Administration.

Corrigon, O. (2003) 'Empty ethics: the problem with informed consent'. *Sociology of Health and Illness,* 25 (7), pp. 768-792

Corsaro, W. A. (1997) *The Sociology of Childhood.* Thousand Oaks, CA: Pine Forge Press.

Costello, J. (2001) 'Nursing older dying patients: findings from an ethnographic study of death and dying in elderly care wards'. *Journal of Advanced Nursing,* 35 (1), 59-68.

Council of Europe (1997) *Convention on Human Rights and Biomedicine,* European Treaties, ETS No. 164.

Courtenay, W. H. (2000) 'Constructions of masculinity and their influence on men's well-being: a theory of gender and health'. *Social Science and Medicine,* 50 (10), 1385-1401.

Coutler, A. and Fitzpatrick, R. (2000) 'The patient's perspective regarding appropriate care'. In G. L. Albrecht, R. Fitzpatrick and S. C. Scrimshaw, *The Handbook of Social Studies in Health and Medicine.* London: Sage.

Coward, R. (1993) 'The myth of alternative health'. In A. Beattie, M. Gott, L. Jones and M. Sidell, (eds) *Health and Wellbeing: A Reader.* Macmillan in association with Open University Press.

Cox, C. (2001) 'Advanced nurse practitioners and physician assistants: what is the difference? Comparing the USA and the UK'. *Hospital Medicine,* 62 (3), 169-171.

Coyle, J. (1999) 'Exploring the meaning of "dissatisfaction" with health care: the importance of personal identity threat'. *Sociology of Health and Illness,* 21 (1), 95-124.

Craib, Ian (1992) *Modern Social Theory: From Parsons to Habermas.* (Second edition). London: Harverster Wheatsheaf.

Crawford, R. (1994) 'The boundaries of the self and the unhealthy other: reflections on health, culture and AIDS'. *Social Science and Medicine,* 38 (10): 1347-65.

Crotty M. (1993) 'The influence of educational theory on the development of nurse training to education in the United Kingdom'. *Journal of Advanced Nursing,* 18, 1645-1650.

Crotty, M. (1996) *Phenomenology and Nursing Research.* Melbourne: Churchill Livingstone.

CSO (1999) *Report on Vital Statistics.* Cork: Central Statistics Office.

CSO (2003a) *Statistical Yearbook of Ireland.* Cork: Central Statistics Office.

CSO (2003b) *Report on Vital Statistics.* Dublin: The Stationery Office.

CSO (2004a) *Expecatation of Life at Various Ages, 1871-1996. Table C.* Cork: Central Statistics Office.

CSO (2004b) *2002 Census of Population: Principal Demographic Results* www. cso. ie/pressreleases/pre/cenpdr2002. html. (Downloaded April 20th 2004).

CSO (2004c) *Maternal deaths D15.* Cork: Central Statistics Office.

Culley, L. and Dyson, S. (2001) 'Introduction: sociology, ethnicity and nursing practice'. In Culley, L. and Dyson, S. (eds) *Ethnicity and Nursing Practice*. Basingstoke: Palgrave.

Culley, L. (2001) 'Nursing, culture and competence'. In Culley, L. and Dyson, S. (eds) *Ethnicity and Nursing Practice*. Basingstoke: Palgrave.

Cumming, E. and Henry, W. E. (1961) *Growing Old*. New York: Basic Books.

Cunningham-Burley, S. and Boulton, M. (2000) 'The social context of the new genetics'. In G. L. Albrecht, R. Fitzpatrick and S. C. Scrimshaw, *The Handbook of Social Studies in Health and Medicine*. London: Sage.

Cunningham-Burley, S. and Kerr, A. (1999) 'Defining the "social": towards an understanding of scientific and medical discoures on the social aspects of the new human genetics'. *Sociology of Health and Illness*, 21 (5), 647-68.

Cypress, B. K. (1984) *Patterns of Ambulatory Care in Obstetrics and Gynaecology*. Hyattsville MD: US Department of Health and Human Services.

Dahl, E. (1994) 'Social inequalities in ill-health – the significance of occupational status, education and income: results from a Norwegian survey'. *Sociology of Health and Illness*, 16, 664-67.

Dallos, R. (1996) 'Psychological approaches to mental health and distress'. In Heller, T. et al (eds) *Mental Health Matters: A Reader*. London: Macmillan.

D'Arcy, P. F. and Griffin, J. P. (1986) *Iatrogenic Diseases*. Oxford: Oxford University Press.

Davey Smith, G. (1994) 'Explanations for socioeconomic differentials in mortality'. *European Journal of Public Health*, 4 (2), 131-144.

Davey, B and Seale, S. (2001) 'An historical approach to medical knowledge'. In C. Seale, S. Pattison, and B. Davey (eds) *Medical Knowledge: Doubt and Certainty*. Buckingham: Open University Press.

Davey Smith, G., Neaton, J. D., Wentworth, D., Stamler, R. and Stamler, J. (1996) 'Socio-economic differentials in mortality risk among men screened for the multiple risk-factor intervention trial: white men'. *American Journal of Public Health*, 86, 486-496.

Davies C. (1998) 'The cloak of professionalism'. In M. Allott and M. Robb (eds) *Understanding Health and Social Care: An Introductory Reader*. Sage Publications in Association with the Open University, 190-197.

Davies, C. (1995) *Gender and the Professional Predicament in Nursing*. Buckingham: Open University Press.

Davis, Fred (1975) 'Deviance disavowel: the management of strained interaction by the visibly handicapped'. In A. R. Lindesmith, A. L. Strauss and N. K. Denzin (eds) *Readings in Social Psychology* (Second edition). Hinsdale: Dryden

Davis-Floyd, R. W. (1994) 'The technocratic body: American childbirth as cultural expression'. *Social Science and Medicine*, 38 (8), 1125-40.

Davison, C. and Davey Smith, G. (1995) 'The baby and the bath water: examining social-cultural and free-market critiques of health promotion'. In R. Bunton, S. Nettleton, and R. Burrows (eds) *The Sociology of Health Promotion: Critical Analyses of Consumption, Lifestyle and Risk*. London: Routledge.

Davison, C., Frankel, S. and Davey Smith, G. (1997) 'The limits of lifestyle: re-assessing "fatalism" in the popular culture of illness prevention'. In M. Sidell, L. Jones, J. Katz, and A. Peberdy (eds) *Debates and Dilemmas in Promoting Health: A Reader*. London: Macmillan.

Daykin, N. and Clark, B. (2000) '"They'll still get the bodily care". Discourses of care and relationships between nurses and healthcare assistants.' *Sociology of Health and Illness*, 22 (3) 349-363.

De Cock, K. M., Dorothy Mbori-Ngacha, D., and Marum, E. (2002) 'Shadow on the continent: public health and HIV/AIDS in Africa in the 21st century'. *The Lancet*, 360, 67-72.

Dean, A., Kolody, B. and Wood, P. (1990) 'Effects of social support from various sources on depression in elderly persons'. *Journal of Health and Social Behaviour*, 31: 148-61.

Delanty, G. (1999) *Social Theory in a Changing World Conceptions of Modernity*. Cambridge, UK: Polity.

Deloitte and Touche (in conjuction with the York Health Economics Consortium) (June, 2001) *Value for Money Audit of the Irish Health System*.

Department of Finance (2002) *Annual Report: Ireland's Participation in the World Bank and the International Monetary Fund 2001*. Dublin: The Stationery Office.

Department of Health (Irl) (1966) *Health Services and their Future Development*. Dublin: Stationery Office.

Department of Health (Irl) (1984) *Planning for the Future: The Psychiatric Service*. Dublin: Stationery Office.

Department of Health (Irl) (1986) *Health – The Wider Dimensions*. Dublin: Stationery Office.

Department of Health (Irl) (1989) *Report of the Commission on Health Funding*. Dublin: Stationery Office

Department of Health (Irl) (1992a) *Green Paper on Mental Health*. Dublin: Stationery Office.

Department of Health (Irl) (1992b) *Putting the Patient First: A Charter of Rights for Hospital Patients*. Dublin: Department of Health.

Department of Health (Irl) (1994) *Shaping a Healthier Future: A Strategy for Effective Healthcare in the 1990s*. Dublin: Stationery Office.

Department of Health (Irl) (1995) *Developing a Policy for Women's Health*. Dublin: The Stationery Office.

Department of Health (Irl) (1996) *National Task Force on Suicide Interim Report*. Dublin: Stationery Office.

Department of Health (Irl) (1997a) *Report of the Maternity and Infant Care Scheme Review Group*. Dublin: The Stationery Office.

Department of Health (Irl) (1997b) *Report of the Tribunal of Inquiry into the Blood Transfusion Service Board*. Dublin: Department of Health.

Department of Health (UK) (1991) *The Patients' Charter*. London: Department of Health.

Department of Health (UK) (1993) *Changing Childbirth: Part 1, The Report of the Expert Maternity Group*. London: HMSO.

Department of Health (UK) (1997) *The New National Health Service*. London: Stationery Office.

Department of Health (UK) (2000) *National Health Service Plan: A Plan for Investment, A Plan for Reform*. London: Stationery Office.

Department of Health (UK) (2001a) *The Royal Liverpool Children's Inquiry Report*. London: The Stationery Office.

Department of Health (UK) (2001b) *Government Response to the House of Lords Select Committee on Science and Technology's Report on Complementary and Alternative Medicine.* London: HMSO.

Department of Health and Social Security (DHSS) (1980) *Inequalities in Health: the Report of a Working Group (The Black Report).* London: HMSO.

Dew, K. (2000a) 'Deviant insiders: medical acapuncturists in New Zealand'. *Social Science and Medicine*, 50 (12), 1785-1795.

Dew, K. (2000b) 'Apostasy to orthodoxy: debates before a Commission of Inquiry into chiropractice'. *Sociology of Health and Illness*, 22 (3), 310-330.

Di Cecco, R., Patel, U., and Upshur, R. (2002) *BMC Family Practice.* 3 (1), 8.

Dingwall, R. (2002) 'Bioethics' in A. Plinick, *Genetics and Society: An Introduction.* Buckingham and Philadelphia: Open University Press. 161-180.

Diprose, R. (1995) 'The body biomedical ethics forget'. In P. A. Komesaroff (ed.), *Troubled Bodies: Critical Perspectives on Postmodernism, Medical Ethics, and the Body*, Durham and London: Duke University Press.

Dodd, R. (2002) 'Health in poverty'. *Global Social Policy*, 2 (3) 343-360.

DoHC (Department of Health and Children) (1995) *Making the Healthier Choice the Easier Choice.* Dublin: DoHC

DoHC (1997) *A Plan for Women's Health 1997-1999.* Dublin: Stationery Office.

DoHC (1998) *Report of the Inspector of Mental Hospitals.* Dublin: Stationery Office.

DoHC (1999a) *Children First: National Guidelines for the Protection and Welfare of Children.* Dublin: The Stationery Office.

DoHC (1999b) *White Paper on Private Health Insurance.* Dublin: Stationery Office.

DoHC (2000a) *The National Health Promotion Strategy 2000-2005.* Dublin: Government Publications.

DoHC (2000b) *AIDS Strategy 2000: Report of the National AIDS Strategy Committee.* Dublin: Stationery Office.

DoHC (2001) *Working Group on Child and Adolescent Psychiatric Services, First Report.* Dublin: Stationery Office.

DoHC (2001a) *Minister Announces Plans to Regulate Complementary Therapies* (Press Release). www. doh. ie/pressroom/pr20010620. html. (April 10th 2004)

DoHC (2001b) *Quality and Fairness: A Health System for You – Health Strategy.* Dublin: Stationery Office.

DoHC (2001c) *Primary Care: A New Direction – Health Strategy.* Dublin: Stationery Office.

DoHC (2002) *Traveller Health: A National Strategy.* Dublin: Government Publications Office

DoHC (2003a) *Research Strategy for Nursing and Midwifery in Ireland.* Dublin: Stationery Office.

DoHC (2003b) *Prospectus Report – Audit of Structures and Functions in the Health System.* Dublin: Stationery Office.

DoHC (2003c) *Report of the National Task Force on Medical Staffing* (Hanley Report). Dublin: Stationery Office.

Dong, W., Colhoun, H., Ben-Sholomo, Y. and Chaturverdi, N. (1996) 'Cardiac surgery in England – do men and women have equal access?' *Journal of Epidemiology and Community Health*, 50, 590-91.

Donnison, J. (1977) *Midwives and Medical Men: A History of Inter-professional Rivalries and Women's Rights*. London: Heinemann.

Donovan, J. L. (1995) 'Patient decision making: the missing ingredient in compliance research'. *International Journal of Technology Assessment in Health Care*, 11 (3), 443-5.

Dooley, D., Dalla-Vorgia, P., Garanis-Papadatos, T. and McCarthy, J. (2003) *The New Ethics of Reproductive Technologies*. New York and Oxford: Berghahn Books.

Douglas, J. (1995) 'Developing anti-racist health promotion strategies'. In Bunton, R., Nettleton, S. and Burrows, R. (eds) *The Sociology of Health Promotion*. London: Routledge.

Douglas, J. D. (1967) *The Social Meanings of Suicide*. Princeton: Princeton University Press.

Douglas, M. (1966) *Purity and Danger: an Analysis of the Concepts of Pollution and Taboo*. London: Routledge and Kegan Paul.

Doyal, L. (1994) 'Changing medicine: gender and the politics of health care'. In J. Gabe, D. Kelleher, and G. Williams (eds) *Challenging Medicine*. London: Routledge.

Doyal, L. (1995) *What Makes Women Sick: Gender and the Political Economy of Health*. London: Macmillan.

Doyal, L. (2001). 'Sex, gender, and health: the need for a new approach'. *British Medical Journal*, 323 (3), 1061-3

Drager, N. (1999) 'Making trade work for public health'. *British Medical Journal*, 319, 1214.

du Pré, A (2002) 'Accomplishing the impossible: talking about body and soul and mind during a medical visit'. *Health Communication*, 14 (1), 1-21.

Dubos. R. (1959) *The Mirage of Health*. New York: Harper and Row.

Dunnell, K. and Cartwright, A. (1972) *Medicine Takers, Prescribers and Hoarders*. London: Routledge and Kegan Paul.

Durkheim, Émile (1952, orig. 1897 in French) *Suicide: A Study in Sociology*. Ed. George Simpson. London: Routledge and Keegan Paul.

Durkheim, Émile (1964a, orig. 1895 in French) *The Division of Labour in Society*. New York: Free Press.

Durkheim, Émile (1964b, orig. 1893 in French) *The Rules of Sociological Method*. New York: Free press.

Dyson, S. and Smaje, C. (2001) 'The health status of minority ethnic groups'. In Culley, L. and Dyson, S. (eds) *Ethnicity and Nursing Practice*. Basingstoke: Palgrave.

Ecob, R. and Davey Smith, G. (1999) 'Income and health: what is the nature of the relationship?' *Social Science and Medicine*, 48 (5), 693-705.

Edmondson, R. (1997) 'Older people and life-course construction in Ireland'. In A. Cleary and M. Treacy *Sociology of Health and Illness in Ireland*. Dublin: University College Dublin Press. 156-172

EDU, WHO (1993) 'Lifestyles and Health'. In A. Beattie et al (eds) *Health and Wellbeing: A Reader*. London: Macmillan.

Edwards, C. and Imrie, R. (2003) 'Disability and bodies as bearers of value'. *Sociology*, 37 (2), 239-256.

Edwards, P., Roberts, I., Clarke, M., DiGiuseppi, C., Pratap, S., Wentz, R. and Kwan, I. (2003) 'Methods to influence response to postal questionnaires

Cochrane Methodology Review'. In: The Cochrane Library Issue 1, Oxford.

Ehrenreich, B. and Ehrenreich, D. (1971) *The American Health Empire: Power, Profits, and Politics*. A HealthPAC Book, New York: Vintage.

Ehrenreich, B. and English, D. (1974a) *Witches, Midwives and Nurses: A History of Women Healers*. London: Glass Mountain.

Ehrenreich B. and English, D. (1974b) *Complaints and Disorders. The Sexual Politics of Sickness*. London: Compendium.

Ehrenreich, J. (1978) 'Introduction: the cultural crisis of modern medicine'. In J. Ehrenreich (ed.) *The Cultural Crisis of Modern Medicine*. New York: Monthly Review Press.

Eisenberg, L. (2002) 'Complementary and alternative medicine: what is its role?' *Harvard Review of Psychiatry*, 10 (4), 221-30.

Elias, N (1985) *The Loneliness of the Dying*. Oxford: Blackwell.

Elias, N. (1978 [1939]) *The Civilising Process: Volume 1: The History of Manners*. Oxford: Basil Blackwell.

Elias, N. (1982 [1939]) *The Civilising Process: Volume 2: State Formation and Civilization*. Oxford: Basil Blackwell.

Elston, M. A. (1991) 'The politics of professional power: medicine in a changing health service'. In Gabe, J., Calnan, M. and Bury, M. (eds) *The Sociology of the Health Service*. London: Routledge.

Emanuel, E. J. and Emanuel, L. L. (1992) 'Four models of the physician-patient relationship'. *Journal of the American Medical Association*, 267, 2221-6.

Emerson, E. (2001) 'What is normalisation?' In H. Brown and H. Smith (eds), *Normalisation: A Reader*. London and New York: Routledge.

Emerson, J. (1970) 'Behaviour in Private Places: Sustaining Definitions of reality in Gyneocological Exams'. In H. P. Dreitzel (ed.) *Recent Sociology*, 2. New York: Collier.

Emslie C., Hunt K. and Macintyre S. (1999) 'Problematizing gender, work and health: the relationship between gender, occupational grade, working conditions and minor morbidity in full-time bank employees'. *Social Science and Medicine*, 48, (1), 33-48.

Emslie, C., Hunt, K. and Wat, G. (2001) 'Invisible women? The importance of gender in lay beliefs about heart problems'. *Sociology of Health and Illness*, 23 (2), 203-234.

Engel, G. L. (1977) 'The need for a new medical model: a challenge for biomedicine'. *Science*, 196, 4286, 129-36.

Epsom, J. E. (1969) 'The mobile health clinic: a report on the first year's work'. In D Tuckett and J. M. Kaufert (eds) (1978) *Basic Readings in Medical Sociology*. London: Tavistock.

Epstein, J. (1990) *Public Services: Working for the Consumer*. Review for the European Foundation for the Improvement of Living and Working Conditions. Luxembourg: Office for Official Publications of the European Community.

Escudero, J. C. (2003) 'The health crisis in Argentina'. *International Journal of the Health Services*, 33 (1), 129-136.

Ettore, E. (2002) 'Reproductive genetics, gender and the body: "Please Doctor, may I have a normal baby?"'. In S. Nettleton and U. Gustafsson, *The Sociology of Health and Ilness*. Cambridge: Polity.

Etzioni, A. (1998) 'Teachers, nurses, social workers'. In L. Mackay, K. Soothill and K. Melia (eds), *Classic Texts in Health Care*. Oxford: Butterworth Heinemann.

Eurobarometer (1997) *Women and Men in Europe and Equal Opportunities: Summary Report*. Brussels: European Commission.

Exworthy, M., Wilkinson, E. K., McColl, A., Moore, M., Roderick, P., Smith, H. and Gabbay, J. (2003) 'The role of performance indicators in changing the autonomy of the general practice profession in the UK'. *Social Science and Medicine*, 56, 1493-1504.

Faber-Langendoen, K. (1992) 'The process of foregoing life sustaining treatment in a university hospital: an empirical study'. *Critical Care Medicine*, 20 (5) 570-577.

Faber-Langendoen, K. (1996) 'A multi-institutional study of care given to patients in hospitals: ethical and practice implications'. *Archives Internal Medicine*, 159 (18), 2130-2136.

Fahey, T. (1995) 'Family and household in Ireland'. In P. Clancy, S. Drudy, K. Lynch and L. O' Dowd (eds) *Irish Society: Sociological Perspectives*. Dublin: Institute of Public Administration.

Fahey, T. and Russell, H. (2001) *Older People's Preferences for Employment and Retirement in Ireland*. Report No 67. Dublin: National Council of Ageing and Older People.

Fanning, B. (2002) *Racism and social change in the Republic of Ireland*. Manchester: Manchester University Press.

Farmer, P. (2003) *Pathologies of Power: Health, Human Rights, and the New War on the Poor*. California: University of California Press.

Farrant, W. (1985) 'Who's for amniocentesis? The politics of prenatal screening'. In H. Homans (ed.) *The Sexual Politics of Reproduction*. Aldershot: Gower.

Farrant, W. (1997) 'Addressing the contradictions: health promotion and community health action in the United Kingdom'. In M. Sidell, L. Jones, J. Katz and A. Peberdy (eds), *Debates and Dilemmas in Promoting Health: A Reader*. London: Macmillan and Open University Press.

Fealy, G. (2001) '"The lady nurses of the Irish hospitals": being a probationer in Dublin in the 1890s'. Paper presented at the Twentieth Annual Nursing and Research Conference, Royal College of Surgeons in Ireland, Faculty of Nursing, 22nd and 23rd February.

Featherstone, M. and A. Wernick (eds) (1995) *Images of Ageing: Cultural Representations of Later Life*. London: Routledge.

Featherstone, M. and Hepworth, M. (1991) 'The mask of ageing in the postmodern lifecourse'. In M. Featherstone and M. Hepworth (eds) *The Body: Social Process and Cultural Theory*. London: Sage Publications.

Fennell, G., Phillipson, C. and Evers, H. (1988) *The Sociology of Old Age*. Milton Keynes: Open University Press.

Fenton, S. and Karlson, S. (2002) 'Explaining mental distress: narratives of meaning'. In O'Connor, W. and Nazroo, J. (eds) (2002) *Ethnic Differences in the Context and Experience of Psychiatric Illness: a Qualitative Study*. London: The Stationery Office. http://www. doh. gov. uk/public/empiric/empiricqualstudy%20.pdf (20th April 2004).

Fernando, S. (1991) *Mental Health, Race and Culture*. Basingstoke: Macmillan.

Field, D. (1976) 'The social definition of illness'. In D. Tuckett (ed.) *An Introduction to Medical Sociology*. London: Tavistock.

Field, D. (1995) '"We didn't want him to die on his own" – nurses accounts of nursing dying patients'. In B. Davey, A. Gray and C. Seale (eds) *Health and Disease: A Reader* (Second edition). Buckingham: Open Univerity Press.

Fieldhouse, R. (ed.) (2001) *AIDS Reference Manual.* (October version). London: NAM Publications.

Finch, J. and D. Groves (eds) (1983) *A Labour of Love: Women, Work and Caring.* London: Routledge.

Finch, S. (2000) 'Whose values count?' *WDM in Action,* Summer, 12-13.

Fine-Davis, M. and Clarke, H. (2002) 'The Irish experience'. In M. Fine-Davis, H. Clarke and M. Berry (eds) *Mothers and Fathers: Dilemmas of the Work-Life Balance (Conference Proceedings).* Dublin: Trinity College, University of Dublin, 51-69.

Finnane, M. (1981) *Insanity and the Insane in Post-Famine Ireland.* London: Croom Helm.

Finucane, P., Moane, G. and Tiernan, J. (1994) *Support Services for Carers of Elderly People Living at Home.* Dublin: National Council for Ageing and Older People. Report No. 40.

Firor, J. and. Jacobsen, J. E. (2002) *The Crowded Greenhouse: Population, Climate Change, and Creating a Sustainable World.* New Haven, CN: Yale University Press.

Fitzpatrick, D. (1986) 'A share of the honeycomb: education, emigration and Irish women'. *Continuity and Change,* 1, (2), 224, cited in Preston, M. (1998) 'The good nurse: women philanthropists and the evolution of nursing in the nineteenth century'. *New Hibernia Review,* 211, 91-110.

Fitzpatrick, M. (2001) *The Tyranny of Health: Doctors and the Regulation of Lifestyle.* London: Routledge.

Fleck, L. (1979 orig. 1935) *The Genesis and Development of a Scientific Fact.* Chicago: Chicago University press.

Fleming, N., Newton, E. R. and Roberts, J. (2003) 'Changes in postpartum muscle function in women with and without episiotomies'. *Journal of Midwifery and Women's Health,* 48 (1), 53-59.

Foster, J. H. (2003) 'The Irish alcohol misuser in England: ill served by research and policy. Some suggestions for future research opportunities'. *Drugs, Education, Prevention and Policy,* 10 (1), 1-11.

Foucault, M. (1967) *Madness and Civilisation: A history of insanity in the age of reason.* Translated by Richard Howard. London: Tavistock

Foucault, M. (1972) *The Archaeology of Knowledge.* Translated from the French by A. M. Sheridan Smith. London: Tavistock.

Foucault, M. (1973) *The Birth of the Clinic: An Archaeology of Medical Perception.* Translated by A. M. Sheridan Smith. London: Tavistock.

Foucault, M. (1979) *Discipline and Punish: The Birth of the Prison,* London: Penguin.

Foucault, M. (1980) 'The politics of health in the eighteenth century'. In C. Gordon (ed) *Power/Knowledge: Selected Interviews and Other Writings 1972-1977.* New York: Pantheon.

Foucault, M. (1985) *The History of Sexuality: Volume Two – The Use of Pleasure,* Harmondsworth: Penguin.

Foucault, M. (1986) *The History of Pleasure: Volume Three – The Care of the Self.* Harmondsworth: Penguin.

Foucault, M. (1990) (orig. in this translation 1978-86) *The History of Sexuality* (3 volumes). Harmondsworth: Penguin. First published in this translation, Pantheon, New York.

Foucault, M. (1994) *Power* (Essential Works of Foucault: 1954-1984: volume III). (James D. Faubion (ed.). London: Penguin Books.

Foucault, M. (2001, orig. published in this translation 1970) *The Order of Things: An archaeology of the human sciences.* London: Routledge. First published in this translation London: Tavistock.

Foucault, Power/Knowledge: Selected Interviews and Other Writings 1972-1977 by Michel Foucault, Brighton: Harvester Press.

Fox, N. (2000) 'Caring: "Postmodern reflections"'. In S. J. Williams and J. Gabe and M. Calnan (eds) *Health Medicine and Society, Key Theories, Future Agendas.* London: Routledge.

Frank, R. (2002) 'Homeopath and patient – a dyad of harmony?' *Social Science and Medicine*, 55 (8), 1285-1296.

Frankel, S., Davison, C. and Davey Smith, G. (1991) 'Lay epidemiology and the rationality of responses to health education'. *British Journal of General Practice*, 41, 428-30.

Frankenberg, K. R. (1992) 'The other who is also the same: the relevance of epidemics in space and time for prevention of HIV infection'. *International Journal of Health Services*, 22 (1) 73-88.

Freidson, E. (1970a) *The Profession of Medicine: A Study of the Applied Sociology of Knowledge.* New York: Dodd Mead.

Freidson, E (1970b) *Professional Dominance: the Social Structure of Medical Care.* Chicago: Aldine.

Freidson, E. (1985) 'The reorganisation of the medical profession'. *Medical Care Review*, 42, 11-35.

Freidson, E. (1994) *Professionalism Reborn: Theory, Prophecy and Policy.* Cambridge: Polity Press.

Frohlich, K. L., Corin, E. and Potvin, L. (2001) 'A theoretical proposal for the context of health and disease'. *Sociology of Health and Illness*, 26 (6), 776-97.

Fulder, S. and Monro, R. (1981) *The Status of Complementary Medicine in the UK.* London: Threshold Foundation.

Gabe, J. (1995) *Medicine, Health and Risk: Sociological Approaches.* Oxford: Blackwell.

Gabe, J. (1996) 'The history of tranquilliser use'. In Heller, T. et al (eds) *Mental Health Matters: A Reader.* London: Macmillan.

Gabe, J. and Calnan, M. (2000) 'Healthcare and Consumption'. In S. J Williams and J. Gabe and M. Calnan (eds) *Health Medicine and Society, Key Theories, Future Agendas.* London: Routledge.

Gabe, J., Kelleher, D. and Williams, G. (1994) *Challenging Medicine.* London: Routledge.

Gamarnikow, E. (1978) 'Sexual divisions of labour: the case of nursing'. In Kuhn, A. and Wolpe, A. M. (eds) *Feminism and Materialism.* London: Routledge and Kegan Paul, 96-123.

Garfinkel, H. (1967) *Studies in Ethnomethodology.* Engelwood Cliffs, New Jersey: Prentice Hall.

Germov, J. (1999a) 'Imagining health problems as social issues'. In J. Germov (ed) *Second Opinion: An Introduction to Health Sociology* (Revised edition). Melbourne: Oxford University Press.

Germov, J. (1999b) 'Glossary'. In J. Germov (ed.) *Second Opinion: An Introduction to Health Sociology* (Revised edition). Melbourne: Oxford University Press.

Gerrish, K. (1999) 'Inequalities in service provision: an examination of institutional influences on provision of district nursing care to minority ethnic communities'. *Journal of Advanced Nursing*, 30, 6, 1263-71.

Giddens, A. (2001a) *Sociology*. (Fourth edition). Cambridge, UK: Polity Press.

Giddens, A. (2001b) 'Dimensions of globalisation'. In S. Seidman and J. C. Alexander (eds) *The New Social Theory Reader*. London: Routledge.

Giddens, A. (1990) *The Consequences of Modernity*. Cambridge: Polity.

Giddens, A. (1991) *Modernity and Self Identity*. Cambridge: Polity.

Giorgi, A. (2000) 'Concerning the application of phenomenology to caring research'. *Scandinavian Journal of Caring Science*, 14, 3-10.

Girot, E. A. (2000) 'Graduate nurses: critical thinkers or better decision makers?' *Journal of Advanced Nursing*, 31 (2), 288-297

Glaser, B. and Strauss, A. (1965) *Awareness of Dying*. Chicago: Aldine.

Glaser, B. and Strauss, A. (1967) *The Discovery of Grounded Theory*. Chicago: Aldine.

Glaser, B. (1992) *Basics of Grounded Theory Analysis*. Mill Valley, California: Sociology Press.

Glenmullen, J. (2000) *Prozac Backlash: Overcoming the Dangers of Prozac, Zoloft, Paxil, and Other Antidepressants with Safe, Effective Alternatives*, New York: Simon and Schuster.

Godfrey, C. (1997) 'Is prevention better than cure?' In M. Sidell, L. Jones, J. Katz, and A. Peberdy (eds) *Debates and Dilemmas in Promoting Health: A Reader*. London: Macmillan.

Goffman, E (1963) *Behaviour in Public Places: Notes on the Social Organization of Gatherings*. New York: The Free Press.

Goffman, E (1969) *The Presentation of Self in Everyday Life*, Harmondsworth: Penguin.

Goffman, E. (1961). *Asylums: Essays on the Social Situation of Patients and Other Inmates*. New York, Anchor.

Goffman, E. (1968) *Stigma: Notes on the Management of Spoiled Identity*. Harmondsworth: Penguin.

Goldthorpe, J. H (with C. Llewellen and C. Payne) (1980) *Social Mobility and Class Structure in Modern Britain*. (Second edition). Oxford: Clarendon Press.

Goldthorpe, J. H. and Hope, K. (1974) *The Social Grading of Occupations: A New Approach and Scale*. Oxford: Clarendon Press.

Gomm, R. (1996) 'Mental health and inequality'. In Heller, T. et al (eds) *Mental Health Matters: A Reader*. London: Macmillan.

Goode, W. J. (1960) 'Encroachment, charlatanism and the emerging profession: psychology, medicine and sociology'. *American Sociological Review*, 25, 902-14.

Gordon, S. (1991) 'Fear of caring: the feminist paradox'. *American Journal of Nursing*, February, 44-8.

Gorer, G. (1955) 'The pornography of death'. *Encounter*, October.

Gotzsche, P. C. and Olsen, O. (2000) 'Is screening for breast cancer with mammography justifiable?' *Lancet*, 355, 129-34.

Goulet, C., Gevry, H., Gauthier, R. J., Lepage, L., Fraser, W. and Aita, M. (2001) 'A controlled clinical trial of home care management versus hospital care management for preterm labour'. *International Journal of Nursing Studies*, 38 (3), 259-269.

Government of Ireland (1989) *Report of the Commission on Health Funding.* Dublin: Stationery Office.

Government of Ireland (1998) *Report of the Commission on Nursing: a Blueprint for the Future.* Dublin: The Stationery Office.

Grace, V. M. (1991) 'The marketing of empowerment and the construction of the health consumer: a critique of health promotion'. *International Journal of Health Services,* 21 (2), 329-43.

Graham, H. (1984) *Women Health and the Family.* London: Tavistock.

Graham, H. (2002) 'Building an inter-disciplinary science of health inequalities: the example of life-course research'. *Social Science and Medicine,* 55 (11), 2006-16.

Grant, A. (1989) 'Monitoring the foetus during labour'. In Chambers, I. et al (eds) *Effective Care in Pregnancy and Childbirth.* Oxford: Oxford University Press, 854-855.

Gray, D. E. (1994) 'Coping with autism: stresses and strategies'. *Sociology of Health and Illness,* 16, 275-300.

Gray, M. and Smith, L. (1999) 'The professional socialisation of diploma of higher education in nursing students (Project 2000): a longitudinal qualitative study'. *Journal of Advanced Nursing,* 29, (3), 639-647.

Grbich, C. (1999) *Qualitative Research in Health An Introduction.* London: Sage.

Greco, M. (1993) 'Psychosomatic subjects and the "duty to be well": personal agency within medical rationality', *Economy and Society,* 22 (3), 357-372.

Green Paper on Abortion (1999) Dublin: Government Publications.

Green, C. A. and Pope, C. R. (1999) 'Gender, psychosocial factors and the use of medical services; a longitudinal analysis'. *Social Science and Medicine,* 48 (10), 1368-1372.

Green, G. (1995) 'Attitudes towards people with HIV: are they as stigmatizing as people with HIV perceive them to be?' *Social Science and Medicine,* 41 (4), 557-68.

Greenslade, L. (1997) 'The blackbird calls in grief: colonialism, health and identity among Irish immigrants in Britain'. In Mac Laughlin, J. (ed.) *Location and Disloctaion in Contemporary Irish Society: Emigration and Irish Identities.* Cork: Cork University Press.

Groneman, C. (1995) 'Nymphomania: The historical construction of female sexuality'. In J. Terry and J. Urla (eds), *Deviant Bodies: Critical Perspectives on Differences in Science and Popular Culture.* Bloomington: Indiana University Press.

Guardian newspaper, Editorial, November, 18th 2002.

Gunaratnam, Y. (2001) 'We mustn't judge people … but: staff dilemmas in dealing with racial harrassment amongst hospice service users'. *Sociology of Health and Illness,* 23 (1), 65-84.

Habermas, J. (trans. W. Rehg) (1996) *Between Facts and Norms: Contributions to a Discourse Theory of Law and Democracy,* Cambridge: Polity Press.

Habermas, J. (1984) *The Theory of Communicative Action, Volume 1: Reason and the Rationalisation of Society.* (Translated by Thomas McCarthy). Boston: Beacon Press.

Habermas, J. (1987). *The Theory of Communicative Action, Volume 2: Lifeworld and System: A Critique of Functionalist Reason* (Translated by Thomas McCarthy). Boston: Beacon Press.

Hadley, R. and Clough, R. (1991) *Care in Chaos*. London: Cassell.

Hahn, H. (1988) 'Can disability be beautiful?' *Social Policy and Administration*, Winter, 26-32.

Hall, E. M. (1992) 'Double exposure: the combined impact of home and work environments on psychosomatic strain in Swedish women and men'. *International Journal of Health Services*, 22, 239-260.

Hall, P., Brockington, I., Levings, J. and Hughes, G. H. (1993) 'Comparisons of responses to the mentally ill in two communities'. *British Journal of Psychiatry*, 162, 99-108.

Hanrahan, G. (2003) *A qualitative exploratory study: investigating the experiences of individuals with a disability label accessing open employment through Ireland's supported employment service*. MA Thesis, University of Limerick: Unpublished.

Haralambos, M. and Holborn, M. (1990) *Sociology: Themes and Perspectives*. (Third edition). London: Unwin Hyman.

Hardey, M. (1999) 'Doctor in the house: the Internet as a source of lay health knowledge and the challenge to expertise'. *Sociology of Health and Illness*, 21 (6), 820-35.

Harding, S. and Balarajan, R. (1996) 'Patterns of mortality in second generation Irish living in England and Wales: longitudinal study'. *British Medical Journal*, 312, 1389-92.

Harding, S. and Balarajan, R. (2001) 'Mortality of third generation Irish people living in England and Wales: longitudinal study'. *British Medical Journal*, 322, 466-467.

Harding, S. (1987) 'Is there a feminist methodology?' In S. Harding (ed.) *Feminism and Methodology: Social Science Issues*. Milton Keyes: Open University Press.

Harding, S. (1991) *Whose science? Whose knowledge? Thinking from women's lives*. Buckingham: Open University Press.

Harrison, S. and Dowswell, G. (2002) 'Autonomy and bureaucratic accountability in primary care: what English general practitioners say'. *Sociology of Health and Illness*, 24 (2) 208-266.

Hart, C. (2004) *Nurses and Politics: the Impact of Power and Practice*. Basingstoke, Palgrave.

Hart, N. (1982) 'Is capitalism bad for your health?' *British Journal of Sociology*, 33, 435-43.

Hartley, H. (2002) 'The system of alignments challenging physician professional dominance: an elaborated theory of countervailing powers'. *Sociology of Health and Illness*, 24 (2), 178-207.

Harvey, L. and MacDonald, M. (1993) *Doing Sociology: A practical introduction*. Basingstoke: Macmillan.

Harvey, L., MacDonald, M. and Hill, J. (2000) *Theories and Methods*. Abingdon: Hodder and Stoughten.

Hatt, G. (1998) 'Uncertainty in medical decision-making'. In A. Petersen and C. Waddell (eds) *Health Matters: A Sociology of Illness, Prevention and Care*. Buckingham: Open University Press.

Haug, M. (1973) 'Deprofessionalization: an alternative hypothesis for the future'. *Sociological Review Monograph*, 2, 195-211.

Havighurst, R. J. (1963) 'Successful ageing'. In R. H. Williams, C. Tibbitts, and W. Donohue (eds), *Processes of Ageing*, 1. New York: Atherton.

Hayes, L. (1995) 'Unequal access to midwifery care: a continuing problem?' *Journal of Advanced Nursing*, 21, 702-7.

Health Education Unit, WHO (1993) 'Life-styles and Health'. In A. Beattie et al (eds) *Health and Wellbeing: A Reader*. London: Macmillan.

Heath, C. (1981) 'The opening sequence in doctor-patient interaction'. In P. Atkinson and C. Heath (eds) *Medical Work: Realities and Routines*. Farnborough UK: Gower.

Heath, C. (1984) 'Participation in the medical consultation: The co-ordination of verbal and non-verbal behaviour between the doctor and the patient'. *Sociology of Health and Illness*, 6 (3) 311-38.

Held, P., Pauly, M. and Boubjerg, R. (1988) 'Access to kidney transplantation'. *Archives of Internal Medicine,* 148, 2594-2600.

Heller, T., Reynolds, J., Gomm, R., Muston, R. and Pattison, S. (eds) (1996) *Mental Health Matters: A Reader*. London: Macmillan.

Hepworth, M. (1995) 'Positive ageing: what is the message?' In R. Bunton, S. Nettleton, and R. Burrows (eds) *The Sociology of Health Promotion*. London: Routledge.

Herman, R. J. (1993) 'Return to sender: reintegrative stigma-management strategies of ex-psychiatric patients'. *Journal of Contemporary Ethnography*, 22 (3) 295-330.

Higgins, P. C. (1981) *Outsiders in a Hearing World: A Sociology of Deafness*. London: Sage.

Hogg, R, Pedro Cahn, P., Katabira, E. T., Lange, J., Samuel, N. M., O'Shaughnessy, M., Vella, S., Wainberg, M. A. and Montaner, J. (2002) 'Time to act: global apathy towards HIV/AIDS is a crime against humanity'. *The Lancet,* 360 1710-1711.

Holloway, I. and Wheeler, S. (2002) *Qualitative Research in Nursing* (Second edition). Oxford: Blackwell Science.

Holton, R. and Turner, B. (1989) *Max Weber on Economy and Society*. London: Routledge.

Hopper, S. (1981) 'Diabetes as a Stigmatized Condition: the case of low-income clinic patients in the United States'. *Social Science and Medicine*, 15 (b) 11-19.

Horton, R. (2004) 'A statement by the editors of *The Lancet*'. *The Lancet,* 363 (9411), 820.

Hoskins, R. (2003) 'Income and health: implications for community nursing'. In Miers, M. (ed.) *Class, Inequalities and Nursing Practice*. Basingstoke: Palgrave.

Hraba, J., Lorenz, F., Lee, G. and Pechachova, Z., (1996) 'Gender differences in health: evidence from the Czech Republic'. *Social Science and Medicine*, 43 (7), 1143-1451.

Hughes, B. (2000) 'Medicalized bodies'. In P. Hancock et al (eds) *The Body, Culture and Society*. Buckingham: Open University Press.

Hughes, B. and Paterson, K. (1997) 'The social model of disability and the disappearing body'. *Disability and Society*, 12 (3), 325-340.

Hughes, D. (1988) 'When nurse knows best: some aspects of nurse-doctor inter-action in a casualty department'. *Sociology of Health and Illness*, 10 (1) 1-22.

Hughes, D. (2002) 'Nursing and the division of labour: sociological perspectives'. In D. Allen and D. Hughes (eds) *Nursing and the Division of Labour in Healthcare*. Basingstoke: Palgrave.

Hughes, J. A., Martin, P. J. and Sharrock, W. W. (1995) *Understanding Classical Sociology Marx, Weber, Durkheim*. London: Sage.

Hunt, A. D., Litt, I. F. and Loebner, M. (1988) 'Obtaining a sexual history from adolescent girls: a preliminary report of the influence of age and ethnicity'. *Journal of Adolescent Health Care*, 9, 52-54.

Hunt, K. and Annandale, E. (1993) 'Just the job? Is the relationship between health and domestic and paid work gender specific?' *Sociology of Health and Illness*, 15 (5), 632-634.

Hunt, K., Ford, G., Harkins L. and S. Wyke (1999) 'Are women more ready to consult than men? Gender differences in family practitioner consultation for common chronic conditions'. *Journal of Health Services Research and Policy*, 4, 96-100.

Hunter, D. (1994) 'From tribalism to corporatism: the managerial challenge to medical dominance'. In J. Gabe, D Kelleher, and G. Williams (eds) *Challenging Medicine*. London: Routledge.

Husserl, E. (1960 orig. 1929) *Cartesian meditations: An introduction to phenomenology*. Translated by Dorion Cairns. Nijhoff: The Hague.

Hyde A. and Brady, D. (2002) 'Staff nurses' perceptions of supernumerary status compared to rostered service for Diploma in Nursing students'. *Journal of Advanced Nursing*, 38 (6), 624-632.

Hyde A. and Roche-Reid, B. (2004) 'Midwifery practice and the crisis of modernity: implications for the role of the midwife'. *Social Science and Medicine*, 58 (12), 2613-2623.

Hyde A. and Treacy M. P. (1999) 'Nurse education in the republic of Ireland: negotiating a new educational space'. In *Women and Education in Ireland*, Connolly B. and Ryan A. (eds). MACE Publications, Maynooth, 89-108.

Hyde, A. (1997) 'The medicalisation of childbearing norms: encounters between unmarried pregnant women and medical personnel in an Irish context'. In A. Cleary and M. Treacy (eds) *The Sociology of Health and Illness in Ireland*. Dublin: University College Dublin Press.

Hyde, A. (1998) 'From mutual pretense awareness to open awareness: single pregnant women's public encounters in an Irish context'. *Qualitative Health Research*, 8, (5), 634-643.

Hyde, A. (2000a) 'Single pregnant women's encounters in public: changing norms or performing roles?' *Irish Journal of Applied Social Studies*, 2 (2), 84-105.

Hyde, A. (2000b) 'Age and partnership as public symbols: stigma and non-marital motherhood in an Irish context'. *The European Journal of Women's Studies*, 7, 71-89.

Hyde, A. and Howlett, E. (in press) *Understanding Teenage Heterosexuality in Ireland*. Dublin: Crisis Pregnancy Agency.

Hyde, A. and Treacy, M. P. (1999) 'Ethical issues in research'. In M. Treacy and A. Hyde (eds) *Nursing Research: Design and Practice*. Dublin: UCD Press.

Hyde, P. (2000) 'Science friction: cervical cancer and the contesting of medical beliefs'. *Sociology of Health and Illness*, 22 (2), 217-23.

Illich, I. (1976) *Limits to Medicine. Medical Nemesis: The Expropriation of Health*. Middlesex: Penguin Books.

Illich, I. (1984) *Medical Nemesis*. In P. R. Lee, C. L. Estes, and N. B. Ramnsey (eds) *The Nation's Health* (Second edition). San Francisco: Boyd and Fraser Publishing Co., 134-142

Illich, I. (1995) 'The epidemics of modem medicine'. In B. Davey, A. Gray and C. Seale (eds) *Health and Disease: A Reader* (Second edition). Buckingham: Open University Press.

Immigration Council of Ireland (2003) *Labour Migration into Ireland*. Dublin: Immigrant Council of Ireland.

Inhorn, M. C. and Whittle, K. L. (2001) 'Feminism meets the "new" epidemiologies: toward an appraisal of antifeminist biases in epidemiological research on women's health'. *Social Science and Medicine*, 53, (5), 553-567.

International Reform Monitor (2004) *European Union: Very Slight Increase in the Fertility Rate*. www. reformmonitor. org/index. php3?content=docview1739. (May 1st 2004)

IPA (2002) *Report on the Regulation of Practitioners of Complementary and Alternative Medicine in Ireland*. Dublin: Institute of Public Administration.

Irish Association for the Improvement of Maternity Services (IAIMS) (1995). *A guide to maternity units in Ireland*. IAIMS, Dublin.

Irish Cancer Society (2002) 'Complementary and alternative therapies'. www. cancer. ie/information/cat. (August 12th 2002)

Irish Refugee Council (2002) 'Fact Sheet on Health Care for Asylum Seekers. Social Policy Information', Note 2 (June). http://www. irishrefugeecouncil. ie/factsheets/healthinfo2. html (18 December 2002).

Irish, J. E. (1997) 'Deciphering the physician-older patient interaction'. *International Journal of Psychiatry in Medicine*, 27 (3), 251-267.

Isla, A. (1993) 'The debt crisis in Latin America: an example of unsustainable development'. *Canadian Women's Studies*, 13 (3), 65-8.

JACM (1992) 'Damning RCP allergy report prompts an angry backlash'. *Journal of Alternative and Complementary Medicine*, 10 (1), 9.

James N. (1989) 'Emotional labour: skill and work in the regulation of feelings'. *Sociological Review*, 37, 15-41.

Jerrome, D. (1992) *Good Company: An Anthropological Study of People in Groups*. Edinburgh: Edinburgh University Press.

Jewson, N. (1976) 'The disappearance of the sick man from medical cosmology, 1770-1870'. *Sociology*, 10, 225-44.

Jewson, N. (1997) 'Inequalities and differences in health'. In S. Taylor and D. Field (eds) *Sociology of Health and Health Care* (Second edition). Oxford: Blackwell Scientific Publications.

Johanson, R., Newburn, M, and Macfarlane, A. (2002) 'Has the medicalisation of childbirth gone too far?' *British Medical Journal*, 324, 892-895.

Johnson, M. (2004) 'Real world ethics and nursing research'. Royal College of Nursing Annual International Conference. Cambridge University, March 22nd.

Johnson, T. M., Hardt, E. J. and Kleinman, A. (1995) 'Cultural factors in the medical interview'. In Lipkin Jr. M., Putnam, S. M. and Lazare, A. (eds) *The Medical Interview*. New York: Springer.

Jones, D. (2002) 'Contemporary theorising – postmodernism'. In Ian Marsh (ed.) *Theory and Practice in Sociology*. Harlow: Pearson Education Ltd.

Jones, L. (1994) *The Social Context of Health and Health Work*. London: Macmillan.

Jones, L. and Sidell, M. (1997) *The Challenge of Promoting Health: Exploration and Action*. London: Macmillan.

Jones, L. J. (1998) 'Evaluating Market Principles in Health Care'. In M. Allot and M. Robb (eds) *Understanding Health and Social Care: An Introductory Reader*. London: Sage.

Jones, P. (2003) *Introducing Social Theory.* Cambridge, UK: Polity.

Julian-Reynier, C., F. Eisinger, P. Vennin, F. Chabal, Y. Aurran, C. Nogues, Y. J. Bignor, M. Machelard-Roumagnac, C. Maugard-Louboutin, D. Serlin, B. Blanc, P. Orsoni and H. Sobol (1996) 'Attitudes towards cancer predictive testing and transmission of information to the family'. *Journal of Medical Genetics*, 33, 731-6.

Kane, P. (1994) *Women's Health: From womb to tomb* (Second edition). London: Macmillan

Kaplan, J. M. (2000) *The Limits and Lies of Human Genetic Research: Dangers for Social Policy.* London: Routledge.

Karlson, S. and Nazroo, J. (2002) 'Agency and Structure: the impact of ethnic identity and racism on the health of ethnic minority people'. *Sociology of Health and Illness*, 24, (1), 1-20.

Kass, F., Spitzer, R., Williams, Janet B. W, and Widigen, T. (1989) 'Self-Defeating Personality Disorder and DSM-III-R: Development of the Diagnostic Criteria'. *American Journal of Psychiatry*, 146 (8), 13-27.

Katz, J. and Peberdy, A. (1997) *Promoting Health: Knowledge and Practice.* London: Macmillan.

Katz, S. (1996) *Disciplining Old Age: the Formation of Gerontological Knowledge.* Charlottesville/London: University Press of Virginia.

Kawachi, I., Kennedy, B. P., and Wilkinson, R. G. (eds) (1999) *The Society and Population Health Reader: Volume 1 Income Inequality and Health.* New York: New Press.

Kelleher, C. (1997) 'Promoting Health'. In J. Robins (ed.) *Reflections on Health: Commemorating Fifty Years of The Department of Health 1947-1997.* Dublin: Department of Health.

Kelleher, C. C., Friel, S., Nic Gabhainn, S. and Tay, J. B. (2003) 'Socio-demographic predictors of self-related health in the Republic of Ireland: findings from the National Survey on Lifestyle, Attitudes and Nutrition', SLAN. *Social Science and Medicine*, 57 (3), 477-486.

Kelly, M. and Charlton, B. (1995) 'The modern and the postmodern in health promotion'. In R. Bunton, S. Nettleton, and R. Burrows (eds) *The Sociology of Health Promotion: Critical Analyses of Consumption, Lifestyle and Risk.* London: Routledge.

Kendell, R. E. (1996) 'The nature of psychiatric disorders'. In Heller, T. et al (eds) *Mental Health Matters: A Reader.* London: Macmillan.

Kenen, R. H. (1997) 'The at-risk health status and technology: a diagnostic invitation and the "gift" of knowing'. In M. Sidell, L. Jones, J. Katz, and A. Peberdy (eds) *Debates and Dilemmas in Promoting Health: A Reader.* London: Macmillan.

Kennedy, F. (2001) *Cottage to Creche: Family Change in Ireland.* Dublin: Institute of Public Administration.

Kennedy, P. (2002) *Maternity in Ireland: A woman-centred perspective.* Dublin: Liffey Press.

Kennedy, P. and Murphy-Lawless, J. (2000) *The Maternity Care Needs of Refugee and Asylum Seeking Women.* Dublin: Women's Health Unit, Northern Area Health Board.

Kennedy, P. and Murphy-Lawless, J. (2003) 'The maternity care needs of refugee and asylum seeking women in Ireland'. *Feminist Review,* Special issue on Exile and Asylum, Issue 73, 39-53.

Kerr, A., Cunningham-Burley, S. and Amos, A. (1998) 'Eugenics and the new genetics in Britain: Examining contermporary professionals' accounts'. *Science, Technology and Human Values*, 23, 175-98.

Kevles D. J. (1992) 'Out of Eugenics: The historical politics of the human genome'. In D. J. Kevles and L. Hood (eds), *Scientific and Social Issues in the Human Genome Project*. MA: Harvard University Press

Kickbusch, I. (2000) 'The development of international health policies – accountability intact?' *Social Science and Medicine*, 51 (6), 979-989.

Kiely, G. (1995) 'Fathers in families'. In McCarthy I. C. (ed) *Irish Family Studies: Selected Papers*. Dublin: UCD.

Kinsella, R. (2001) *Waiting Lists: Analysis, Evaluation and Recommendations*. Centre for Insurance Studies, Graduate School of Business, University College Dublin.

Kitson, A. (2001) 'Does nursing education have a future?' *Nurse Education Today*, 21 (2), 86-96.

Kitt, T. (2001) 'Opening Address'. In McGivern (ed) *Employment and Retirement Among the Over 55s: Patterns, Preferences and Issues*. Proceedings of a Joint Conference of the Expert Group on Future Skills Needs and the National Council on Ageing and Older People, Report No. 56, National Council on Ageing and Older People, 10-12.

Klein, R. (1990) 'Looking after consumers in the NHS'. *British Medical Journal*, 300: 1351-2.

Klein, R. D. (1989) *The Politics of the National Health Service*. (Second edition). UK: Longman.

Kleinman, A. (1988) *The Illness Narratives: Suffering, Healing and the Human Condition*. New York: Basic Books.

Klopf, D. W. (1991) *Intercultural Encounters: Fundamentals of Intercultural Communication* (Second edition). Englewood, Colorado: Morton.

Knebl, J. A., Shores, J. H., Gamber, R. G., Gray, W. T. and Herron, K. M. (2002) 'Improving functional ability in the elderly via the Spencer technique, an osteopathic manipulative treatment: a randomised controlled trial'. *Journal of the American Osteopathic Association*, 102 (7), 387-96.

Knight M. and Field, D. (1981) 'A silent conspiracy: coping with dying cancer patients on an acute surgical ward'. *Journal of Advanced Nursing*, 6, 221-229.

Kohler Riessman, C. (1983) 'Women and medicalisation: a new perspective'. *Social Policy*, Summer, 3-18.

Koivusalo, M. and Ollila, E. (1997) *Making a Healthy World*. London: Zed.

Kosteniuk, J. G. and Dickinson, H. D. (2003) 'Tracing the social gradient in the health of Canadians: primary and secondary determinants'. *Social Science and Medicine*, 57 (2), 263-267.

Kramer, P. D. (1993) *Listening to Prozac*. New York: Viking.

Krieger, N. and Fee, E. (1994) 'Social Class: the missing link in US health data'. *International Journal of Health Services*, 24, 25-54.

Krieger, N. and Sidney, S. (1996) 'Racial discrimination and blood pressure: the CARDIA study of young black adults'. *American Journal of Public Health*, 86 (10) 1370-8.

Krupat, E., Rosenkranz, S. L., Yeager, C. M., Barnard, K., Putnam, S. M. and Inui, T. S. (2000) 'The practice orientations of physicians and patients: the effect of doctor-patient congruence on satisfaction'. *Patient Education and Counselling*, 39, 49-59.

Kuhn, T. (1970 orig. 1962) *The Structure of Scientific Revolutions*. Chicago: Chicago University Press.

Lahelma, E., Martikainen, P., Rahkonen, O. and Silventoinen, K. (1999) 'Gender differences in illhealth in Finland: patterns, magnitude and change'. *Social Science and Medicine*, 48, (1), 7-19.

Langwell, K. M. (1982) 'Differences by sex in economic returns with physician specialization'. *Journal of Health, Politics, Policy and Law*, 6, 752-761.

Laing, R. D. (1960) *The Divided Self, an Existential Study in Sanity and Madness*. London: Tavistock.

Lash, S. and Urry, J. (1994) *Economics of Signs and Space*. London: Sage.

LaVeist, T. A. (2000) 'On the study of race, racism, and health: a shift from description to explanation'. *International Journal of Health Services*, 30 (1) 217-219.

Laver, M. and Garry, J. (2000) 'Estimating policy positions from political texts'. *American Journal of Political* Science, 44 (3), 619-634.

Law (1987) 'Technology, closure and heterogeneous engineering: The case of the Portuguese expansion'. In W. E. Bijker, T. Hughes and T. Pinch, *The Social Construction of Technological Systems*. Cambridge MA: MIT Press.

Lawrence, S. C. and Bendixen, K. (1992) 'His and hers: male and female anatomy in anatomy texts for US medical students, 1890-1989'. *Social Science and Medicine*, 35 (7), 925-34.

Lawton, J. (1998) 'Contemporary hospice care: the sequestration of the unbounded body and "dirty dying"', *Sociology of Health and Illness,* 20 (2), 121-143.

Lawton, J. (2003) 'Lay experiences of health and illness: past research and future agendas', *Sociology of Health and Illness*, 25: 23-40.

Layte, R. (2001) *Poverty and Deprivation Among Older Irish People*. Dublin: National Council of Ageing and Older People.

Layte, R. and Nolan, B. (2001) 'The health strategy and socio-economic inequalities in health'. In M. Wiley, *Critique of Shaping a Healthier Future: A Strategy for Effective Healthcare in the 1990s*. Dublin: Economic and Social Research Institute.

Lazarsfeld, P. F. and Rosenberg, M. (eds) (1955) *The Language of Social Research: A Reader in the Methodology of Social Research*. Glencoe, Illinois: Free Press.

Lazarsfeld, P. F. Pasnella, A. and Rosenberg, M. (eds) (1972) *Continuities in the language of social research: A reader in the methodology of social research*. New York: Free Press.

Leape, L. (2000) 'Institute of Medicine medical error figures are not exaggerated'. *Journal of the American Medical Association*, 284 (1), 95-7.

Lee Davis, D., Axelrod, D., Baily, L., Gaynor, M. and Sasco, A. J. (1998) 'Rethinking breast cancer risk and the environment: The case for the precautionary principle'. *Environmental Health Perspectives*, 106 (9): 523-29.

Lee, J. D. and Craft, E. A. (2002) 'Protecting one's self from a stigmatized diseases ... Once one has it'. *Deviant Behaviour*, 23 (3), 267-299.

Lee, K. (2000) 'The impact of globalization on public health: inplications for the UK faculty of Public Health'. *Journal of Public Health Medicine*, 22 (3), 253-262.

Leder, D. (1990) *The Absent Body*. Chicago: Aldine.

Lelie, A. (2000) 'Decision-making in nephrology: shared decision-making?' *Patient Education and Counselling*, 39, 81-89.

Lentin, R. (2001) 'Responding to the racialisation of Irishness: disavowed multiculturalism and its discontents'. *Sociological Research Online*, 5: (4) U48-U70.

Lentin, R. and McVeigh, R. (eds) (2002) *Racism and Anti-Racism in Ireland*. Belfast: Beyond The Pale Publications.

Lerman, C., Seay, J., Balshem, A. and Audrain, J. (1995) 'Interest in genetic testing among first-degree relatives of breast cancer patients'. *American Journal of Medical Genetics*, 57, 385-392.

Lerman, C., Seay, J., Balshem, A., and Audrain, J. (1996) *American Journal of Medical Genetics*, 57: 385-92. *(note: no article title is given in the original citation)*

Lewis, O. (1961) *The Children of Sanchez*. New York: Random House.

Lewith, G. T., Watkins, A. D., Hyland, M,E., Shaw, S., Broomfield, J. A., Dolan, G. and Holgate, S. G. (2002) 'Use of ultramolecular potencies of allergen to treat asthmatic people allergic to house mite dust: double blind randomised controlled clinical trial'. *British Medical Journal*. 324, 520-523.

Light, D. W. (2000) 'The Sociological Character of Health-Care Markets'. In G. L. Albrecht, R. Fitzpatrick and S. C. Scrimshaw, *The Handbook of Social Studies in Health and Medicine*. London: Sage.

Lindsey, E. (1996) 'Health within illness: experiences of chronically ill/disabled people'. *Journal of Advanced Nursing*, 24: 465-472.

Lobmayer, P. and Wilkinson, R. (2000) 'Income inequality and mortality in 14 developed countries'. *Sociology of Health and Illness*, 22 (4), 401-14.

Lockyer, L., and Bury, M. (2002) 'The construction of a modern epidemic: the implications for women of gendering of coronary heart disease'. *Journal of Advanced Nursing*, 39 (5), 432-441.

Loftus, M. (2001) 'Chairperson's welcome and introduction'. In McGivern (ed) *Employment and Retirement Among the Over 55s: Patterns, Preferences and Issues*. Proceedings of a Joint Conference of the Expert Group on Future Skills Needs and the National Council on Ageing and Older People, Report No 56, National Council on Ageing and Older People.

Lohan, M. (2000) 'Extending feminist methodologies: researching masculinities and technologies'. In A. Byrne and R. Lentin (eds) *(Re)searching Women: Feminist Research and Practice in Ireland*. Dublin: Institute of Public Administration.

Lohan, M. and Faulkner, W. (2004) 'Masculinities and Technologies: Some introductory remarks.' *Men and Masculinities*, Special edition on Masculinities and Technologies, 6, 1, 319-329.

Lomas, J. (1998) 'Social Capital and Health – Implications for Public Health and Epidemiology'. *Social Science and Medicine*, 47 (9), 1181-8.

Lorber, J. (1997) *Gender and the Social Construction of Illness*. London: Sage.

Loudon, I. (1997) 'Midwives and the quality of maternal care'. In H. Marland and A. M. Rafferty (eds) *Midwives, Society and Childbirth: Debates and Controversies of the Modern Period*. London: Routledge.

Luddy, M. (1995) *Women and Philanthropy in Nineteenth Century Ireland*. Cambridge: Cambridge University Press.

Lundström, F. and McKeown, K. (1994) *Home Help Services for Elderly People in Ireland*. Dublin: National Council for Ageing and Older People.

Lupton, D. (1994) *Medicine as Culture*. London: Sage.

Lupton, D. (1995) *The Imperative of Health: Public Health and the Regulated Body*. London: Sage.

Lupton, D. (1997) 'Foucault and the medicalisation critique'. In A. Petersen and R. Bunton (eds) *Foucault, Health and Medicine*. London: Routledge.

Lupton, D. (1998) 'The Body, Medicine and Society'. In J. Germov (ed.) *Second Opinion: An Introduction to Health Sociology*. (Revised edition). Melbourne: Oxford University Press.

Lupton, D. (2003) *Medicine as Culture Illness, Disease And The Body In Western Societies*. (Second edition). London: Sage.

Lupton, D., Donaldson, C. and Lloyd, P. (1991) 'Caveat emptor or blissful ignorance? Patients and the consumerist ethos'. *Social Science and Medicine*, 33, 559-68.

Lynch, T. (2001) *Beyond Prozac: Healing Mental Suffering without Drugs*. Dublin: Marino Books.

Lynch, J. W., Davey-Smith, G., Hillemeier, M., Shaw, M., Raghunathan, T. and Kaplan, G. (2001) 'Income inequality, the psychosocial environment and health: comparisons of wealthy nations'. *Lancet*, 358:194-200.

Lyotard, Jean-Francois (1984) *The Postmodern Condition: A Report on Knowledge*. Manchester: Manchester University Press.

Mac Éinri (2001) *Immigration into Ireland; trends, policy responses, outlook*. Irish Centre for Migration Studies, University College Cork. http://migration. ucc. ie/irelandfirstreport. htm (12 January 2004).

MacFarlane, A. and Kelleher, C. (2002) 'Concepts of illness causation and attitudes to health care among older people in the Republic of Ireland'. *Social Science and Medicine*. 54 (9), 1389-1400.

MacFarlane, A. (1978) 'Variations in number of births and perinatal mortality rates by day of the week in England and Wales'. *British Medical Journal*, 2, 1670-1673.

MacGreil, M (1996) *Prejudice in Ireland Re-visited*. Maynooth: Survey and Research Unit, Department of Social Studies, NUI Maynooth.

Macintyre S., Ford, G. and Hunt, K (1999) 'Do women "over-report" morbidity? Men's and women's responses to structured prompting on a standard question on long standing illness'. *Social Science and Medicine*, 48 (1), 89-98

Macintyre, S. (1977) *Single and Pregnant*. London: Croom Helm.

Macintyre, S. (1991) 'Who wants babies? The social construction of instincts'. In D. Leonard and S. Allen (eds), *Sexual Divisions Revisited*. London: Macmillan in association with BSA.

Macintyre, S. (1993) 'Area, class and health: should we be focusing on places or people?' *Journal of Social Policy*, 22 (2), 213-234.

Macintyre, S. (1997) 'The Black Report and beyond: what are the issues?' *Social Science and Medicine*, 44, 395-402.

Macintyre, S., Hunt, K. and Sweeting, H. (1996) 'Gender differences in health: are things as simple as they seem?' *Social Science and Medicine*, 42 (4), 617-24.

Macionis, J. and Plummer, K. (1997) *Sociology A Global Introduction*. UK: Prentice Hall.

MacKellar, C. (1997) *Reproductive Medicine and Embryological Research: A European Handbook of Bioethical Legislation*. Edinburgh: European Bioethical Research.

MacLachlan, M. (1998) 'Promoting health: thinking through context'. In E. McAuliffe and L. Joyce (eds) *A Healthier Future: Managing Healthcare in Ireland*. Dublin: Institute of Public Administration.

Maggs, C. (1980) 'Nurse recruitment to four provincial hospitals 1881-1921'. In Davies C. (ed.) *Rewriting Nursing History*. London: Croom Helm, 18-40.

Mamo, L. (1999) 'Death and dying: confluences of emotion and awareness'. *Sociology of Health and Illness*, 21 (1) 13-36.

Manber, R., Allen, J. J. and Moris, M. M. (2002) 'Alternative treatments for depression: empirical support and relevance to women'. *Journal of Clinical Psychiatry*, 63 (7), 628-40.

Manias, E. and Street, A. (2001) 'The interplay of knowledge and decision-making between nurses and doctors in critical care'. *International Journal of Nursing Studies*, 38 (2), 129-140.

Maple, E (1992) 'The great age of quackery'. In Saks, M. (ed.) *Alternative Medicine in Britain*. Oxford: Clarendon Press.

Mark, D. (2000) 'Sex bias in cardiovascular care. Should women be treated more like men?' *Journal of the American Medical Association*, 283, 659-661.

Marmot, M. G. (1984) 'Inequalities on death – specific explanations of a general pattern?' *The Lancet*, i, 103-106.

Marmot, M. G., Davey-Smith, G., Stansfeld, S., Palel, C., North, F., Head, J., White, I., Brunner, E. and Feeney, A. (1991) 'Health Inequalities among British Civil Servants: The Whitehall II Study'. *Lancet*, 337, 1387-1393.

Marsh, I., Keating, M., Eyre, A., Campbell, R. and McKenzie, J. (2000) *Sociology: Making Sense of Society*. (Second edition). London: Prentice Hall.

Martens, P. (2002) 'Health transitions in a globalising world: towards more disease or sustained health'. *Futures*, 34, 635-648.

Martin, E. (1989) *The Woman in the Body: A Cultural Analysis of Reproduction*. Milton Keynes: Open University Press.

Martin, M. (2002) *Speech by Micheál Martin, TD, at the Launch of the Report on the Regulation of Practitioners of Complementary and Alternative Medicine in Ireland*. 14 November 2002. <http:/www. doh. ie/pressroom/pr20021114. htlm> (April 18th 2004).

Martin, P. A. (1999) 'Genes as drugs: the social shaping of gene therapy and the reconstruction of genetic disease', *Sociology of Health and Illness*, 21 (5): 517-38.

Marx, K. (1867) [1971] *Das Kapital: A Critique of Political Economy*. London: Laurence and Wishartt.

Marx, K. (1977, orig. 1877) *Capital*. Translated from the original Das Kapital 1877. London: Lawrence and Wishart.

Marx, K. and Engels, F. (1848) [1975] *The Manifesto of the Communist Party*. Moscow: Progress Publishers.

Marx, K. (1954, orig. 1852) *The Eighteenth Brumaire of Louis Bonaparte*. Moscow: Progress Publishers.

Marx, K. (1963, orig. 1845) 'Theses on Feuerbach'. In T. B. Bottommore and M. Reubel (eds) *Selected Writings in Sociology and Social Philosophy*. Harmondsworth: Penguin.

Masango, D. (2004) 'Deal Paves Way for Cheaper Aids Medication'. BuaNews (Pretoria) April 6. http://allafrica. com/stories/200404060532. htlm> (April 18th 2004)

Matthews S., Manor O. and Power C. (1999) 'Social inequalities in health: are there gender differences?' *Social Science and Medicine*, 48 (1), 49-60

May, C. and Sirur, D. (1998) 'Art, science and placebo: incorporating homeopathy in general practice'. *Sociology of Health and Illness*, 20 (2) 168-190.

May, K. (1992) 'Individualised care? Power and subjectivity in therapeutic relations'. *Sociology*. 26, 589-602.

Mazer, T. (1993) *Death and Dying in A Hospice: An Ethnographic Study*. Unpublished PhD thesis, University of Edinburgh.

McAdam-O'Connell, B. (1998) 'Risk, responsibility and choice: the medical model of birth and alternatives'. In Kennedy, P. and Murphy-Lawless, J. (eds) *Returning Birth to Women: Challenging Policies and Practices*. Dublin: Centre for Women's Studies, Trinity College Dublin and Women's Education, Research and Resource Centre, University College Dublin.

McAuliffe, E. (1998) 'Towards patient-centred care: Consumer involvement in healthcare'. In E. McAuliffe and L. Joyce *A Healthier Future? Managing Healthcare in Ireland*. Dublin: Institute of Public Administration.

McDonnell, M. (1989) 'Patients' perceptions of their care at Our Lady's Hospice, Dublin'. *Palliative Medicine* 3, 47-53.

McDonnell, O. (1997) 'Ethical and social implications of technology in medicine: new possibilities and new dilemmas'. In A. Cleary and M. P. Treacy (eds) *The Sociology of Health and Illness in Ireland*. Dublin: University College Dublin Press.

McDonnell, O. (1999) 'Shifting Debates on New Reproductive Technology: Implications for Public Discourse in Ireland'. In P. O'Mahony (ed.) *Nature, Risk and Responsibility: Discourses of Biotechnology*. London: Macmillan.

McDonnell, O. (2001) *New Reproductive Technologies and Public Discourse: From Biopolitics to Bioethics*, Unpublished Ph. D. dissertation, Department of Sociology, University College Cork.

McEvoy, R. and Richardson, N. (2004) *Men's Health in Ireland – A Report from the Men's Health Forum in Ireland*. Belfast: Men's Health Forum in Ireland (MHFI)

McInerney, F. (2000) '"Requested death": a new social movement'. *Social Science and Medicine*, 50.

McKee, M. and Clarke, A. (1995) 'Guidelines, enthusiasms, uncertainty, and the limits to purchasing'. *British Medical Journal*, 310, 101-04.

McKenna, P. and Mathews, T. (2003) 'Safety of home delivery compared with hospital delivery in the Eastern Regional Health Authority in Ireland in the years 1999-2002'. *Irish Medical Journal*, 96 (7), 198-200.

McKeown, T. (1976) *The Modern Rise of Population*. London: Edward Arnold.

McKeown, T. (1984) 'Determinants of health'. In P. R. Lee, C. L. Estes and N. B. Ramsey (eds) *The Nation's Health* (Second edition). San Francisco: Boyd and Fraser Publishing Co.

McKeown, T. (1995) 'The medical contribution'. In B. Davey, A. Gray and C. Scale (eds) *Health and Disease: A Reader* (Second edition). Buckingham: Open University Press.

McKevitt, M (1998) *Managing Core Public Services*. Oxford: Blackwell.

McKevitt, M. (1990) *Health Care Policy in Ireland: A Study in Control*. Cork: Hibernian University Press.

McKinlay, J. and Stoeckle, J. (1988) 'Corporatisation and the social transformation of doctoring'. *International Journal of Health Services*, 18, 191-205.

McKinlay, J. B. (1993) 'The promotion of health through planned sociopolitical change: challenges for research and policy'. *Social Science and Medicine*, 36 (2), 109-117.

McManus, J. (2001) Royal Academy of Medicine Lecture. Oct 23rd (Cited in Wren, 2003).

McNamara, M. (2000) *So What Do You Do Exactly? Illuminating The Role Of The Clinical Placement Co-Ordinator On Registration/Diploma Programmes In General Nursing*. Unpublished Masters Dissertation. Dublin: National University of Ireland, University College Dublin.

McNaught, A. (1987) *Health Action and Ethnic Minorities*. London: Bedford Square Press/NCHR.

McQueen, D. (1989) 'Thoughts on the ideological origins of health promotion'. *Health Promotion*, 4, (4), 339-42.

McVeigh R. and Binchy, A. (1999) 'Travellers, Refugees and Racism in Tallaght'. Dublin: West Tallaght Resource Centre.

Mead, G. H. (1967, orig. 1934) *Mind, Self and Society from the Standpoint of a Social Behaviorist*, Chicago: University of Chicago Press. Originally published Chicago. University of Chicago Press

Meadows, S. H. (1961) 'Social class migration and chronic bronchitis'. *British Journal of Preventive and Social Medicine*, 15, 171-6.

Mechanic, D. and Meyer, S. (2000) 'Concepts of trust among patients with serious illness.' *Social Science and Medicine*, 51 (5) 657-668.

Medical Council (March 1989) *A Guide to Ethical Conduct and Behaviour and to Fitness to Practise* (Second edition).

Medical Council (January 1994) *A Guide to Ethical Conduct and Behaviour and to Fitness to Practise* (Third edition).

Medical Council (November 1998) *A Guide to Ethical Conduct and Behaviour and to Fitness to Practise* (Fourth edition).

Medical News Today (2004) 'Complementary therapists to be regulated in UK says Minister'. http//www. medicalnewstoday. com. (April 14th 2002)

Meerabeau, L. (1991) 'Husband's participation in fertility treatment. They also serve who stand and wait'. *Sociology of Health and Illness*, 13 (3), 396-410.

Melia, K. (1987) *Learning and Working: the Occupational Socialization of Nurses*. London: Tavistock Publications.

Mellor, P. and Shilling, C. (1993) 'Modernity, self-identity and the sequestration of death'. *Sociology*, 27, 411-32.

Mellor, P. A. (1993) 'Death in high modernity: the contemporay presence and absence of death'. In D. Clark (ed.) *The Sociology of Death*, Oxford: Blackwell Publishers.

Merleau-Ponty, M. (1962) *The Phenomenology of Perception* (transl. by C. Smith). London: Routlege and Kegan Paul.

Miers, M. (2000) *Gender Issues and Nursing Practice*. London: Macmillan Press Ltd.

Miers, M. (2003) 'Measuring class and researching health'. In Miers, M. (ed.) *Class, Inequalities and Nursing Practice*. Basingstoke: Palgrave.

Miles, A. (1991) *Women, Health and Medicine*. Milton Keynes: Open University Press.

Mills, C. W. (1978) 'The sociological imagination'. In Peter Worsley (ed.) *Modern Sociology* (Second edition). UK: Penguin.

Mills, C. W. (1970) *The Sociological Imagination.* Harmondsworth: Penguin.

Mishler, E. (1984) *The Discourse of Medicine: Dialectics of Medical Interviews.* Norwood, N. J: Ablex.

Moller, D. (1996) *Confronting Death: Values, Institutions and Human Mortality.* Oxford: Oxford University Press.

Moller Okin, S. (1989) *Gender, Justice and the Family.* New York: Basic Books.

Moore, R. and Porter, S. (1998) 'Poverty in health care'. In Birchenall, M. and Birchenall, P. (1998) *Sociology as Applied to Nursing and Health Care.* London: Balliere Tindall in association with the RCN.

Morrall, P. (2001) *Sociology and Nursing.* London: Routledge.

Mort, F. (2000) *Dangerous Sexualities: Medico-Moral Politics in England since 1830.* (Second edition). London: Routledge and Kegan Paul.

Moscucci, O. (1990) *The Science of Woman: Gynaecology and Gender in England, 1800-1929.* Cambridge: Cambridge University Press.

Moynihan, C. (1998). 'Theories in Health Care and Research: Theories of Masculinity'. *British Medical Journal,* 317, 1072-1075.

Mulkay, M. (1997) *The Embryo Research Debate: Science and the Politics of Reproduction.* Cambridge: Cambridge University Press.

Murch, S. H., Anthony, A., Casson, D. M., Malik, M., Berelowitz, M., Dhillon, A. P., Thomson, M. A., Valentine, A., Davies, S. E. and Walker-Smith, J. A. (2004) 'Retraction of an interpretation.' *The Lancet,* 363, 750.

Murdoch-Eaton, D. and Crombie, H. (2002) 'Complementary and alternative medicine in the undergraduate curriculum'. *Medical Teacher,* 24 (1), 100-2.

Murphy, A. (2001) 'Participation of the over 55s in the labour force in Ireland'. In McGivern, Y. (ed.) *Employment and Retirement Among the Over 55s: Patterns, Preferences and Issues.* Proceedings of a Joint Conference of the Expert Group on Future Skills Needs and the National Council on Ageing and Older People, Report No 56, National Council on Ageing and Older People, 14-21.

Murphy-Lawless, J. (1988) 'The obstetric view of feminine identity: a nineteenth century case history of the use of forceps on unmarried women in Ireland'. In, A. D. Todd and S. Fisher, *Gender and Discourse: The Power of Talk.* Norwood, N. J.: Aldex Publishing Corporation.

Murphy-Lawless, J. (2003) *Establishing the Rationales for Gender-Specific Strategies to Improve Women's Health: The Evidence from Research.* Dublin: Department of Social Policy and Social Work, University College Dublin.

Murphy-Lawless, J. (1998) *Reading Birth and Death: A History of Obstetric Practice.* Cork: Cork University Press.

Murray, C. (1989) 'Underclass'. *Sunday Times Magazine,* 26th November, 56.

Mussa, M. (2003) 'Meeting the challenges of globalisation'. *Journal of African Economies,* 12, 14-34.

Naidoo, J. and Wills, J. (2000) *Health Promotion: Foundations for Practice* (Second edition). London: Baillière Tindall.

Nathanson, C. (1980) 'Social roles and health status among women: the significance of employment'. *Social Science and Medicine,* 14a, 463-71.

National Council on Ageing and Older People (1999) *What Works in Health Promotion for Older People?* Report No. 58. Dublin: National Council for Ageing and Older People.

National Council on Ageing and Older People (2004) *Demography: Ageing in Ireland: Fact File No. 1.* Dublin: National Council on Ageing and Older People.

www. ncaop. ie/publications/research/factfiles/ff/demography. pdf (April 22nd 2004)

National Disease Surveillance Centre (2003) *HIV and AIDS statistics: 2002 Annual Summary.* National Disease Surveillance Centre, Dublin.

National Economic and Social Forum (April 2002) *Equity of Access to Hospital Care.* Dublin: NESF.

Navarro, V. (1976) *Medicine Under Capitalism.* London: Croom Helm.

Navarro, V. (1980) 'Work, ideology and science'. *International Journal of Health Services,* 10 (4), 523-50.

Navarro, V. (1986) *Crisis, Health and Medicine: A Social Critique.* London: Tavistock.

Nazroo, J. Y. (1998) 'Genetic, cultural or socio-economic vulnerability? Explaining ethnic inequalities in health'. *Sociology of Health and Illness,* 20 (5), 710-30.

Nazroo, J. Y. (1997) *The Health of Britain's Ethnic Minorities.* London: Policy Studies Institute.

NCCRI (National Consultative Committee on Racism and Interculturalism) (1999) *Submission to the Working Group on the Integration of Refugees,* February 1999. http://www. nccri. com (10 February 2003).

NCCRI (National Consultative Committee on Racism and Interculturalism) (2001a) *Refugees and Asylum Seekers.* http://www. nccri. com/refugees. html (10 February 2003).

NCCRI (National Consultative Committee on Racism and Interculturalism) (2001b) *Raising Awareness of Diversity and Racism,* http://www. nccri. com (10 February 2003)

NCCRI (National Consultative Committee on Racism and Interculturalism) (2002) *Migration Policy in Ireland: Reform ad Harmonisation,* Advocacy Paper One (December) http://www. nccri. com/migration. html (10 February 2003)

Nelkin, D. and Brown, M. J. (1984) *Workers at Risk: Voices from the Workplace.* Chicago: University of Chicago Press.

Nelkin, D. and Lindee, M. S. (1995) 'The media-ted gene: stories of gender and race'. In J. Terry and J. Urla (eds) *Deviant Bodies.* Bloomington and Indianapolis: Indiana University Press.

Nelson S. (1997) 'Pastoral care and moral government: early nineteenth century nursing and solutions to the Irish question'. *Journal of Advanced Nursing,* 26, 6-14.

Nettleton, S. (1995) *The Sociology of Health and Illness.* Cambridge: Polity.

Nettleton, S. (1997) 'Surveillance, health promotion and the formation of a risk identity'. In M. Sidell, L. Jones, J. Katz, and A. Peberdy (eds) *Debates and Dilemmas in Promoting Health: A Reader,* London: Macmillan.

Nettleton, S. and R. Bunton (1995) 'Sociological critiques of health promotion'. In R. Bunton, S. Nettleton, and R. Burrows (eds) *The Sociology of Health Promotion: Critical Analyses of Consumption, Lifestyle and Risk.* London: Routledge.

Newton, K. M., Buist, D. S., Keenan, N. L., Anderson, L. A. and LaCroix, A. Z. (2002) 'Use of alternative therapies for menopause symptoms: results of a population-based survey'. *Obstet Gynecol,* 100 (1), 18-25.

Nietzsche, F. (1967, orig. 1901) *The Will to Power.* Translated by W. Kaufmann. New York: Random House.

Nightingale, F. (1860) *Notes on Nursing: What it is and What it is Not.* London: Harrison.

Nolan, B. and Whelan, C. T. (1997) 'Unemployment and health'. In A. Cleary and M. P. Treacy (eds) *The Sociology of Health and Illness in Ireland*. Dublin: University College Dublin Press.

Nolan, B. and Wiley M. (2000) *Private Practice in Irish Public Hospitals* (General Research Series Paper, 175 ESRI). Dublin: Oak Tree Press.

O'Farrell, C. (1989) *Foucault: Historian or Philosopher?* London: Macmillan.

Ó Ceallaigh, A. (2000) 'Summary of events from November 1996 to the present March 2000'. http:// iol/. ie/~rayd/Ann/summary. hml (April 18th 2004)

O'Connor, A., Hyde, A., and Treacy, M. (2003) 'Nurse teachers' constructions of reflection and reflective practice'. *Reflective Practice*, 4 (2), 107-119.

O'Connor, M (1995) *Birth Tides: Turning Towards Home Birth*. London: Pandora.

O'Connor, M. (2001) 'Equal rights in the birth chamber: the need for a midwife-based system of maternity care in Europe'. *MIDIRS midwifery digest*, 11 (1), 129-132.

O'Connor, M. (2004) 'Truth or fiction? A review of a new medical 'study' on home birth in Dublin'. www. ireland. iol. ie/~hba/homebirth_truth_fiction. htm. (April 10th 2004)

O'Connor, P. (1998) *Emerging Voices: Women in Contemporary Irish Society*. Dublin: Institute of Public Administration.

O'Donovan, O. (1997) 'Contesting concepts of care: the case of the home help service in Ireland'. In Treacy, M. P. and Clery, A. (eds) *The Sociology of Health and Illness in Ireland*, 141-155.

O'Driscoll, K. and Meagher, D. (1980) *Active Management of Labour*. London: W. B. Saunders.

O'Farrell, N. (2002) 'Genital Ulcers, stigma, HIV and STI control in sub-Saharan Africa'. *Sexually Transmitted Infections*, 78 (2):143-146.

O'Ferrall, F. (2000) *Citizenship and Public Service: Voluntary and Statutory Relationships in Irish Healthcare*. Dublin: Dundalgan Press.

O'Hara, T. (1998) 'Current structure of the Irish health care system – Setting the context'. In A. Leahy and M. M. Wiley (eds) *The Irish Health System in the 21st Century*. Dublin: Oak Tree Press.

O'Hare, A., Whelan, C. T. and Commins, P. (1991) 'The development of an Irish census-based social class scale'. *The Economic and Social Review*, 22, (2) 135-156.

O'Shea, E. and Kelleher, C. C. (2001) 'Health Inequalities in Ireland'. In Cantillon, S., Corrigan C., Kirby P. and O'Flynn. J. (eds) *Rich and Poor: perspectives on tackling inequality in Ireland*. Dublin: Oak Tree Press in association with Combat Poverty.

O'Sullivan, T. and Butler, M. (2002) *Current Issues in Irish Health Management: A Comparative Review*, Dublin: Institute of Public Administration.

Oakley, A. (1974) *Housewife*. London: Allen Lane.

Oakley, A. (1980) *Women Confined: Towards a Sociology of Childbirth*. Oxford: Martin Robinson.

Oakley, A. (1993) *Essays on Women, Health and Medicine*. Edinburgh: Edinburgh University Press.

Oakley, A. (1995) 'Doctor knows best'. In B. Davey, A. Gray and C. Seale (eds) *Health and Disease: A Reader* (Second edition). Buckingham: Open University Press, 332-337.

Oakley, A. (1998) 'The importance of being a nurse'. In L. Mackay, K. Soothill, and K. Melia (eds) *Classic Texts in Health Care*. Oxford: Butterworth Heinemann.

OECD (1997) *OECD Economic Surveys: Ireland 1997*. Paris: OECD.

Oliver, M. (1990) *The Politics of Disablement*. Basingstoke: Macmillan.

Oliver, M. (1992) 'Changing the social relations of research production?' *Disability, Handicap and Society*, 7 (2): 101-15.

Oliver, M. (1996) *Understanding Disability: from Theory to Practice*. Basingstoke: Macmillan.

ONS (Office of National Statistics) (2002) *Social Trends No. 32*. London: The Stationery Office.

Oppenheimer, M. (1973) 'The proletarianisation of the professional'. *Sociological Review Monograph*, 20, 213-37.

Othman, N. and Kessler, C. S. (2000) 'Capturing globalization: prospects and projects'. *Third World Quarterly*, 21 (6) 1013-1026.

Oudshoorn, N. (1994) *Beyond the Natural Body: An Archeology of Sexhormones*. London: Routledge.

Owusu, F. (2003) 'Pragmatism and the gradual shift from dependency to neoliberalism: the World Bank, African leaders and development policy in Africa.' *World Development*, 31 (10) 1655-1672.

Parish, R. (1995) 'Health promotion: rhetoric and reality'. In R. Bunton, S. Nettleton and R. Burrows (eds) *The Sociology of Health Promotion: Critical Analyses of Consumption, Lifestyle and Risk*. London: Routledge.

Parsons, Talcott (1951a) 'Illness and the role of the physician: A sociological perspective'. *American Journal of Orthophyschiatry*, 2, 452-60.

Parsons, T. (1951b) *The Social System*. New York: Free Press, Glencoe.

Parsons, T. (1975) 'The sick role and the role of the physician reconsidered'. *Milbank Memorial Fund Quarterly*, Summer, 257-78.

Paterson, K. and Hughes, B. (2000) 'Disabled bodies'. In P. Hancock, E. Jagger, K. Paterson, R. Russel, E. Tulle-Winton and M. Tyler. *The Body, Culture and Society*. Buckingham: Open University Press.

Patton, C. (1990) *Inventing AIDS*. London: Routledge.

Pavee Point (2003) www. paveepoint. ie/ (20 February 2003).

Pearson, M. (1986) 'The politics of ethnic minority health studies'. In Rathwell, T. and Phillips, D. (eds) *Health, Race and Ethnicity*. London: Croom Helm.

Peillon, M. (1982) *Contemporary Irish Society: An Introduction*. Dublin: Gill and Macmillan.

Pendleton, A. (2003) 'This tomato is Italian. It costs you 10p, but to a farmer called Charles it is costing everything'. *The Independent on Sunday*, 14/9/2002, 12-13.

Petersen, A. (2001) 'Biofantasies: genetics and medicine in the print news media'. *Social Science and Medicine*, 52 (8), 1255-1268.

Petersen, A. and Bunton, R. (2002) *The New Genetics and the Public's Health*. London and New York: Routledge.

Petersen, A. and Waddell, C. (1999) *Health Matters: A Sociology of Illness, Prevention and Care*. Buckingham: Open University Press.

Petticrew, M., McKee, M. and Jones, J. (1993) 'Coronary artery surgery: are women discriminated against?' *British Medical Journal*, 306, 1164-1166.

Pharoah, C. (1995) *Primary Health Care for Elderly People from Black and Minority Ethnic Communities. Studies in Ageing*. London: Age Concern/Institute of Gerontology, King's College, HMSO.

Pierret, J. (2003) 'The illness experience: state of knowledge and perspectives for research'. *Sociology of Health and Illness*, 25, 4-22.

Pilgrim, D. and Rogers, A. (1993) *Sociology of Mental Health and Illness*. Buckingham: Open University Press.

Pilnick, A. (2003) *Genetics and Society an Introduction*. Buckingham: Open University Press.

Pollack, A. (1999) 'An invitation to racism? Irish daily newspaper coverage of the refugee issue'. In D. Kiberd (ed) *Media in Ireland: The Search for Ethical Journalism*. Dublin: Open Air.

Pollard, T. M. and Brin Hyatt, S. (1999) *Sex, Gender and Health*. Cambridge: Cambridge University Press.

Pollock, E. and Daly, D. (1998) 'Mapping maternity care in Northern Ireland'. In Kennedy, P. and Murphy-Lawless, J. (eds) *Returning Birth to Women: Challenging Policies and Practices*. Dublin: Centre for Women's Studies, Trinity College Dublin and Women's Education, Research and Resource Centre, University College Dublin, 17-20.

Popay, J., Bartley, M. and Owen, C. (1993) 'Gender inequalities in health: social position, affective disorders and minor physical morbidity'. *Social Science and Medicine*, 36 (1), 21-32.

Popay, J., Bennett, S., Thomas, C., Williams, G., Gatrell, A. and Bostock, L. (2003) *Sociology of Health and Illness*, 25 (1), 1-24.

Popper, K. (1980, orig. 1959) *The Logic of Scientific Inquiry*. London: Hutchinson. Originally published London: Routledge and Keegan Paul.

Porter, S. (1991) 'A participant observation study of power relations between nurses and doctors in a general hospital'. *Journal of Advanced Nursing*, 16, 728-735.

Porter, S. (1993) 'Critical realist ethnography: the case of racism and professionalism in a medical setting'. *Sociology* 27 (4), 591-609.

Porter, S. (1995) 'Northern nursing: the limits of idealism'. *Irish Journal of Sociology*, 5, 22-42.

Porter, S. (1997) 'The patient and power: sociological perspectives on the consequences of holistic care'. *Health and Social Care in the Community*, 5 (1), 17-20.

Porter, S. (1998a) *Social Theory and Nursing Practice*. Basingstoke: Macmillan.

Porter, S. (1998b) 'Women in a woman's job: the gendered experience of nursing '. In, W. Cockerham, W. Glaser and L. Heusor, *Readings in Medical Sociology*. New Jersey: Prentice Hall.

Porter, S. (1999) 'Working with doctors'. In Geoff Wilkinson and Margaret Miers (eds) *Power and Nursing Practice*. London: Macmillan.

Potter, J. (1996) *Representing Reality: Discourse Rhetoric and Social Construction*. London: Sage.

Potter, J. and Wetherell, M. (1987) *Discourse and Social Psychology: Beyond Attitudes and Behaviour*. London: Sage.

Prättälä, R., Karisto, A. and Berg, M. A. (1994) 'Consistency and variation in unhealthy behaviour among Finnish men, 1982-1990'. *Social Science and Medicine*, 39, (1) 53-64.

Preston, M. (1998) 'The good nurse: women philanthropists and the evolution of nursing in the nineteenth century'. *New Hibernia Review*, 211, 91-110.

Preston-Whyte, M. E., Fraser, R. C. and Beckett, J. L. (1983) 'Effect of a principal's gender on consultation patterns'. *Journal of the Royal College of General Practitioners, 33,* 654-658.

Priestly, M. (2003) *Disability: A Life Course Approach.* Cambridge: Polity.

Prior, L. (2003) 'Belief, knowledge and expertise: the emergence of the lay expert in medical sociology'. *Sociology of Health and Illness.* 25, 41-57.

Prior, L. (1989) *The Social Organisation of Death.* London: Macmillan.

Prior, L. (1991) 'Community versus hospital care: the crisis in psychiatric provision'. *Social Science and Medicine,* 324 (4), 483-9.

Prior, L. (1993) *The Social Organisation of Mental Illness.* London: Sage.

Prior, L. (1997) 'Following in Foucault's footsteps: text and context in qualitative research'. In D. Silverman (ed.) *Qualitative Research: Theory, Method and Practice.* London: Sage.

Prowse, M. and Allen, D. (2002) '"Routine" and "emergency" in the PAUC: the shifting contexts of nurse-doctor interaction.' In D. Allen and D. Hughes (eds) *Nursing and the Division of Labour in Healthcare.* Basingstoke: Palgrave.

Purvis Cooper, C. and Yukimura, D. (2002) 'Science writers' reactions to a medical "breakthrough" story'. *Social Science and Medicine.* 52 (12), 1887-96.

Putnam, R. D. (1995) 'Bowling Alone: America's Declining Social Capital'. *Journal of Democracy,* 61, 65-78.

Putnam, R. D. (2000) *Bowling Alone: The Collapse and Revival of American Community.* New York: Simon and Schuster,

Quaid, K. and Morris, M. (1993) 'Reluctance to undergo predictive testing: The case of Huntington Disease'. *American Journal of Medical Genetics,* 45: 59-71.

Quin, S. (1999) 'Improving health care: health policy in Ireland' in S. Quinn, P. Kennedy, A. O'Donnell, G. Kiely (eds), *Contemporary Irish Social Policy.* Dublin: University College Dublin Press.

Radley, A. (1994) *Making Sense of Illness. The Social Psychology of Health and Disease.* Sage: London.

Raftery J., Jones, D. R. and Rosato, M. (1990) 'The mortality of first and second generation Irish immigrants in the UK'. *Social Science and Medicine,* 3, 577-84.

Reay, D. (1997) 'Feminist theory, habitus, and social class: Disrupting notions of classlessness'. *Women's Studies International Forum,* 20: 225-33.

Refugee Resettlement Research Project. *Report of a Survey of the Vietnamese and Bosnian Communities in Ireland,* (1998) http://www. nccri. com/refugees. html (13 February 2003).

Remennick, L. (1998) 'The preventive potential'. *Current Sociology,* 46 (1), 71-83.

Report of the Assisted Reproduction Sub-Commitee of the executive Council of the Institute of Obstetricians and Gynaecologists. (May 1999).

Rhodes, R. M. (1992) *Women and the Family in Post-Famine Ireland: Status and Opportunity in a Patriarchal Society.* New York: Garland Publishing.

Rier, D. A. (2000) 'The missing voice of the critically ill: a medical sociologist's first person account'. *Sociology of Health and Illness,* 22 (7), 68-93.

Riska, E. (2002) 'From Type A Man to the hardy man: masculinity and health'. *Sociology of Health and Illness,* 24 (3), 347-358.

Rissel, C. (1994) 'Empowerment: the holy grail of health promotion?'. *Health Promotion International,* 9 (1), 39-44.

Robert, S. A. and House, J. S. (2000) 'Socioeconomic inequalities in health: integrating individual-, community-, and societal-level theory and research'. In G.

L. Albrecht, R. Fitzpatrick and S. C. Scrimshaw. *The Handbook of Social Studies in Health and Medicine.* London: Sage.

Roberts, H. (1985) *The Patient Patients: Women and Their Doctors.* London: Pandora.

Robins, J. (1986) *Fools and Mad: A History of the Insane in Ireland,* Dublin: Institute of Public Administration.

Robins, J. (1995) *The Miasma: Epidemic and Panic in Nineteenth Century Ireland.* Dublin: Institute of Public Administration.

Robins, J. (2000) *Nursing and Midwifery in Ireland in the Twentieth Century.* Dublin: An Bord Altranais.

Robson, C. (2002) *Real World Research: A Resource For Social Scientists And Practitioner-Researchers.* Oxford: Blackwell.

Rodmell, S. and Watt, A. (1992) *The Politics of Health Education.* London: Routledge.

Rogers, A. and Pilgrim, D. (1991) 'Pulling Down Churches: Accounting for the British Mental Health Users Movement'. *Sociology of Health and Illness,* 13 (2): 129-148.

Roos, G., Prättälä, R. and Koski, K. (2001) 'Men, masculinity and food: interviews with Finnish carpenters and engineers'. *Appetite* 37 (1) 47-56.

Roter, D. (2000) 'The enduring and evolving nature of the patient-physician relationship'. *Patient Education and Counselling.* 39, 5-15.

Rubery J. et al (1995) *Changing Patterns of Work and Working Time in the European Union and the Impact on Gender Divisions.* Brussels: EC DG:V.

Ryan, S. (1997) 'Interventions in childbirth: the midwives' role'. In A. Byrne and M. Leonard (eds) *Women and Irish Society: A Sociological Reader.* Belfast: Beyond the Pale Publications. 255-267.

Sabo, D. and Gordon, D. F. (1995) 'Rethinking men's health'. In Sabo, D. and Gordon, D. F. (eds) *Men's Health and Illness Gender, Power and the Body.* London: Sage.

Sacker, A., Bartley, M., Firth, D. and Fitzpatrick, R. (2001) 'Dimensions of Social Inequality in the health of women in England: occupational, material and behavioural pathways'. *Social Science and Medicine,* 52 (5), 763-781.

Saks, M. (1994) 'The alternatives to medicine'. In Gabe, J., Kelleher, D. and Williams, G. (eds) *Challenging Medicine.* Routledge: London, 84-103.

Salmon, P. (2000) 'Patients who present physical symptoms in the absence of physical pathology: a challenge to existing models of doctor-patient interaction'. *Patient Education and Counselling,* 39 105-13.

Saltonstall, R. (1993) 'Healthy bodies, social bodies: men's and women's concepts and practices of health in everyday life'. *Social Science and Medicine,* 36 (1) 7-14.

Salvage, J. (1990) 'The theory and practice of "New Nursing"'. *Nursing Times,* 86 (4), 42-45.

Saris, A. J. (1997) 'The asylum in Ireland: A brief institutional history and some local effects'. In A. Cleary and M. P. Treacy (eds) *The Sociology of Health and Illness in Ireland.* Dublin: University College Dublin Press.

Scambler, G., Scambler, A. and Craig, D. (1981) 'Kinship and friendship networks and women's demand for primary care'. *Journal of the Royal College of General Practitioners,* 26, 746-50.

Scambler, G. (1989) *Epilepsy.* London: Routledge.

Scambler, G. (2002) *Health and Social Change: A Critical Theory*. Buckingham: Open University Press.

Schafer, T., Riehle, A., Wichmann, H. E. and Ring, J. (2002) 'Alternative medicine in allergies – prevalence, patterns of use, and costs'. *Allergy*, 57 (8), 694-700.

Scheff, T. J. (1966) *Being Mentally Ill: A Sociological Theory*. Chicago: Aldine.

Schiebinger, L. (1987) 'Skeletons in the closet: the first illustrations of the female skeleton in eighteenth century anatomy'. In C. Gallagher and T. Laqueur (eds) *The Making of the Modern Body: Sexuality and Society in the Nineteenth Century*. Berkeley: University of California Press.

Schutz, A. (1962) *The Problem of Social Reality*. The Hague; Nijhoff.

Schutz, Alfred (1966) *Collected Papers, Volume 3*. Nijhoff, The Hague: Martinus.

Schwartz, R. K., Soumerai, S. B. and Avorn, J. (1989) 'Physician motivations for non-scientific drug prescribing'. *Social Science and Medicine*, 28 (6), 577-82.

Scott, Wilbur J. (1990) 'Post traumatic stress disorder in DSM-II: A case in the politics of diagnosis and disease'. *Social Problems*, 37 (3), 294-310.

Scriven, A. and Orme, J. (1996) *Health Promotion: Professional Perspectives*. London: Macmillan.

Seale C. (1995a) 'Dying alone'. *Sociology of Health and Illness*, 17 (3), 374-392.

Seale, C. (2000) 'Changing patterns of death and dying'. *Social Science and Medicine*, 51 (6), 917-930.

Seale, C. (1995b) 'Heroic death'. *Sociology*, 29 (4), 597-613.

Seale, C. (2001) 'Doctor-patient interaction'. In C. Sease, S. Pattison and B. Davey (eds), *Medical Knowledge: Doubt and Certainty*. Buckingham: Open University Press.

Seedhouse, D. (1986) *Health: The Foundations for Achievement*. Chichester: John Wiley and Sons.

Seyfang, G. (2003) Environmental mega-conferences – from Stockholm to Johannesburg and beyond. *Global Environmental Change*, 13, 223-228.

Seymour, J. E. (2000) 'Negotiating natural death in intensive care'. *Social Science and Medicine*, 51 (8) 1241-1250.

Seymour, W. (1989) *Bodily Alterations: An Introduction to a Sociology of the Body for Health Workers*. Allen and Unwin: Sydney.

Shand, H. (2001) 'Gene Giants: Understanding the "Life Industry"'. In B. Tokar *Redesigning Life? – The Worldwide Challenge to Genetic Engineering*. London and New York: Zed Books.

Sharma, U. (1992a) *Complementary Medicine Today: Practitioners and Patients*. London: Routledge.

Sharma, U. (1992b) 'Professionalism in complementary medicine today: an overview'. Paper presented at International Sociological Association Conference on Professions in Transition, University of Leicester/De Montfort University, Leicester, 21-23rd April.

Sharp, K. (1994) 'Sociology and the nursing curriculum: A note of caution'. *Journal of Advanced Nursing*, 20, 391-395.

Shaw, M., Dorling, D., Gordon, D. and Smith, D. (1999) *The Widening Gap: Health Inequalities and Policy in Britain*. Bristol: The Policy Press.

Shaw, M., Dorling, D. and Mitchell, R. (2002) *Health, Place and Society*. London: Prentice Hall.

Sheldon, S. (1997) *Beyond Control: Medical Power and Abortion Law*. London: Pluto Press.

Shilling, C. (1993) *The Body and Social Theory*. London: Sage

Shilton, H. (1999) 'Men's health and culture'. In T. Harrison and K. Dignan (eds) *Men's Health: An Introduction for Nurses and Health Professionals.* UK: Churchill Livingstone.

Shostak, S. (2003) 'Locating gene-environment interaction: at the intersections of genetics and public health'. *Social Science and Medicine,* 56 (11), 2327-2342.

Sidell, M., Jones, L., Katz, J. and Peberdy, A. (eds) (1997) *Debates and Dilemmas in Promoting Health: A Reader.* London: Macmillan.

Siegrist, J. and Marmot, M. (2004) 'Health Inequalities and the psychosocial environment', *Social Science and Medicine,* 58 (8), 1463-1473.

Simmel, G. (1964, orig. 1950) 'The sociology of Georg Simmel/ translated from the German!' Edited and with an introduction by Kurt H. Wolff, Free Press of Glencoe: Collier-Macmillan. Originally published under this translation Free Press of Glencoe.

Simpson, G. (1952) 'Editor's introduction The aetiology of suicide'. In Durkheim, Émile (1952, orig. 1897 in French) *Suicide.* Edited by George Simpson. London: Routledge and Keegan Paul.

Skeggs, B. (1997) *Formations of Class and Gender: Becoming Respectable.* London: Sage.

Skrabanek, P. and McCormic, J. (1989) *Follies and Fallacies in Medicine.* Glasgow: The Tarragon Press.

Skrabanek, P. (1994) *The Death of Humane Medicine and the Rise of Coercive Healthism.* Suffolk: The Social Affairs Unit.

Sleep, J. et al (1984) 'West Berkshire perineal management trial'. *British Medical Journal,* 289, 587-590.

Slevin O. (1995) 'Knowledge and theory'. In *Theory and Practice of Nursing,* Baseford L. and Slevin O. (eds). Edinburgh: Campion Press.

Smaje, C. (1995) *Health, 'Race' and Ethnicity: Making Sense of the Evidence.* London: King's Fund.

Smaje, C. (2000) 'A place for race? Medical sociology and the critique of racial ideology'. In Williams, S. J., Gabe, J. and Calnan, M. (eds) (2000) *Health Medicine and Society Key Theories, Future Agendas.* London and New York: Routledge, 67-86.

Smartt, U. (2000) 'Euthanasia and the law', (British Broadcasting Corporation) http://news. bbc. co. uk/1/hi/health/background_briefings/euthanasia/1044740. stm (28/11/2000)

Snelgrove, S. and Hughes, D. (2002) 'Perceptions of teamwork in acute medical wards'. In D. Allen and D. Hughes (eds) *Nursing and the Division of Labour in Healthcare.* Basingstoke: Palgrave.

Speed, E. (2002) 'Irish Mental Health Social Movements: A Consideration of Movement Habitus'. *Irish Journal of Sociology,* 11: 62-80.

Stakelum, A. and Boland, J. (2001) *Men's Health in Focus: A Qualitative Study on Men's Beliefs and Attitudes in the North Eastern Health Board.* Meath: NEHB.

Stein, L. (1967) 'The doctor-nurse game'. *Archives of General Psychiatry* 16, 699-703. [Reprinted in L. Mackay, K. Soothill, K. Melia (eds) *Classic Texts in Healthcare.* Oxford: Butterworth Heinemann].

Stein, L., Watts, D. and Howell, T. (1990) 'The doctor-nurse game revisited'. *Nursing Outlook,* 36, 264-8.

Steingart, R. M., Packer, M., Hamm, P., Coglianese, M. E., Gersh, B., Geltman, E. M., Sollano, J., Katz, S., Moye, L., Basta, L. L. et al (1991) 'Sex differences in the management of coronary artery disease. Survival and ventricular enlargement investigators'. *The New England Journal of Medicine*, 325, 226-230.

Stevenson, F. A., Barry, C., Britten, N., Barber, N. and Bradley, C. P. (2000) 'Doctor-patient communication about drugs: the evidence for shared decision making'. *Social Science and Medicine*, 50 (6), 829-840.

Stimson, G. V. (1974) 'Obeying doctors' orders: a view from the other side'. *Social Science and Medicine*, 8, 97-104.

Stockdale, A. (1999) 'Waiting for the cure: mapping the social relations of human gene therapy research'. *Sociology of Health and Illness*, 21 (5): 579-96.

Strauss, A. L. (1987) *Qualitative Analysis for Social Scientists*. New York: Cambridge University Press.

Strauss, B. and Corbin, J. (1998) *Basics of Qualitative Research: Techniques and Procedures for Developing Grounded Theory* (Second edition). Thousand Oaks, CA: Sage.

Strong, P. (1979) *The Ceremonial Order of the Clinic*. London: RKP

Sullivan, O. (2000) 'The domestic division of labour: twenty years of change?' *Sociology*, 34, (3) 437-456.

Surlis, S. and Hyde, A. (2001) 'HIV-positive patients' experiences of stigma during hospitalisation'. *Journal of the Association of Nurses in AIDS Care*, 12 (6), 45-54.

Susman, J. (1994) 'Disability, stigma and deviance'. *Social Science and Medicine*, 38 (1) 15-22.

Svensson, R. (1996) 'The interplay between doctors and nurses – a negotiated order perspective'. *Sociology of Health and Illness*, 18 (3), 379-398.

Szasz, T. (1961) *The Myth of Mental Illness: Foundations of a Theory of Personal Conduct*. London: Secker.

Szreter, S. (1995) 'The importance of social intervention in Britain's mortality decline c. 1850- 1914: a reinterpretation of the role of public health'. In B. Davey, A. Gray and C. Scale (eds) *Health and Disease: A Reader* (Second edition). Buckingham: Open University Press.

Task Force on the Travelling Community (1995) *Report of the Task force on the Travelling Community, Department of Equality and Law Reform*. Dublin: Government Publications.

Tauli-Corpuz, V. (2001) 'Biotechnology and indigenous peoples'. In B. Tokar (ed.) *Redesigning Life? The World Challenge to Genetic Engineering*. London, New York: Zed Books.

Taylor, B. (2001) 'HIV, Stigma, and Health: integration of theoretical concepts and the lived experiences of individuals'. *Journal of Advanced Nursing*, 35 (5), 792-798.

Taylor, B., Miller, E., Lingam, R., Andrews, N., Simmons, A. and Stowe, J. (2002) 'Measles, mumps, and rubella vaccination and bowel problems or developmental regression in children with autism: population study'. *British Medical Journal*. 324, 393-6.

Taylor, S. and Field, D. (1993) *Sociology of Health and Health Care*. Oxford: Blackwell Science.

Taylor, S. (1997) 'Approaches to health and health care'. In S. Taylor and D. Field (eds) *Sociology of Health and Health Care* (Second edition). London: Blackwell Science.

Terry, J. and Urla, J. (eds) (1995) *Deviant Bodies*. Bloomington and Indianapolis: Indiana University Press.

Tew, M. (1998) *Safer Childbirth? A Critical History of Maternity Care* (Second edition). New York: Free Association Books.

Thane, P. (1982) *Foundations of the Welfare State*. London: Longman.

Thomas, C. (1993) 'Deconstructing concepts of care'. *Sociology*, 27:649-70.

Thorogood, N. (1992) 'What is the relevance of Sociology for Health Promotion?' In R. Bunton and G. MacDonald (eds). *Health Promotion: Disciplines and Diversity*. London: Routledge.

Throsby, K. and Gill, R. (2004) '"It's different for men": Masculinity and IVF'. In Lohan, M. and Faulkner, W. (eds) 'Masculinities and Technologies' Special Edition of *Men and Masculinities*, 6 (4), 330-348

Timmermans, S. (1994) 'Dying of awareness: the theory of awareness contexts revisited'. *Sociology of Health and Illness*, 16 (1), 22-39.

Tobin, J., Wassertheil-Smolter, S. and Wexler, J. et al (1987) 'Sex bias in considering coronory bypass surgery'. *Annals of Internal Medicine*, 107, 19-25.

Tormey, W. P. (Winter 1992-1993) 'Two-speed public and private medical practice in the Republic of Ireland'. *Administration*, 40 (4), 371-81.

Treacy, M. P. (1989) 'Gender prescription in nurse training: its effects on health care provision'. *Recent Advances in Nursing*, 25, 70-90.

Treacy, M. and Hyde, A. (1999) 'Contextualising Irish nursing reseach'. In M. Treacy and A. Hyde (eds) *Nursing Research: Design and Practice*. Dublin: University College Dublin Press.

Treacy, M. (1987) 'Some aspects of the hidden curriculum'. In P. Allan and M. Jolley (eds) *The Curriculum in Nursing Education*. London: Chapman and Hall.

Trohler, U. (1999) 'Women under the knife – another history of surgery'. *Gynakologisch-Geburtshilfliche Rundschau*, 39 (4), 199-206.

Tucker. V. (1997) 'From biomedicine to holistic health: towards a new health model'. In Cleary. A. and Treacy, M. P. (eds) *The Sociology of Health and Illness in Ireland*. Dublin: University College Dublin Press.

Tuckett, D., Boulton, M. Olson, C. and Williams, A. (1985) *Meetings Between Experts*. London: Tavistock.

Turner, B. S. (1987) *Medical Power and Social Knowledge*. London: Sage.

Turner, R. J. (1981) 'Social support as a contingency in psychological well-being', *Journal of Health and Social Behaviour*, 22, 357-67.

Twinn S. and Davies S. (1996) 'The supervision of Project 2000 students in the clinical setting: issues and implications for practitioners'. *Journal of Clinical Nursing*, 5, 177-183.

Tussig, M., Michello, J. and Subedi, S. (1999) *A Sociology of Mental Illness*. New Jersey: Prentice Hall.

UK Office for National Statistics http://www. statistics. gov. uk/methods_quality/ns_ sec/default. asp (25 January 2004)

Umberson, J. D., Chen, M. D., House, J. S., Hopkins and K. Slater, E. (1996) 'The effect of social relationships on psychological well-being. Are men and women really so different?' *American Sociological Review*, 61, 837-857.

Ungerson, C. (1987) *Policy is Personal: Sex, gender and informal care*. London: Tavistock.

United Kingdom Central Council (1986) *Project 2000: A New Preparation for Practice*. London: United Kingdom Central Council for Nursing, Midwifery and Health Visiting.

United Nations (2003) *Human Development Report 2003*. United Nations: New York.

UPIAS (1976) *Fundamental Principles of Disability*, London: Union of Physically Impaired against Segregation/Disability Alliance /Disability Alliance.

Urata, Y., Yoshida, S., Irie, Y., Tanigawa, T., Amayasu, H., Nakabayashi, M. and Akahori, K. (2002) 'Treatment of asthma patients with herbal medicine TJ-96: a randomised controlled trial'. *Respiratory Medicine*, 96 (6), 469-74.

Ussher, J. (1991) *Women's Madness: Misogyny or Mental Illness?* Hertfordshire: Harvester Wheatsheaf.

van Ryn, M. and Burke, J. (2000) 'The effect of patient race and socio-economic status on physicians' perceptions of patients'. *Social Science and Medicine*, 50 (6), 813-828.

Verbrugge, L. M. (1985) 'Gender and health: an update on hypotheses and evidence'. *Journal of Health and Social Behaviour*, 26, 156-82.

Verbrugge, L. M. and Wingard, D. L. (1987) 'Sex differentials in health and mortality'. *Women and Health*, 12, 103-145.

Verhoef, M. J., Casebeer, A. L. and Hilsden, R. J. (2002) 'Assessing efficacy of complementary medicine: adding qualitative research methods to the "Gold Standard"'. *Journal of Alternative and Complementary Medicine*, 8 (3), 275-81.

Victor, C. R. (1994) *Old Age in Modern Society: A Textook of Social Gerontology* (Second edition). London: Chapman and Hall.

Waddington, I. (1984) *The Medical Profession in the Industrial Revolution*. London: Gill and Macmillan

Wadsworth, M. E. (1986) 'Serious illness in childhood and its association with later life achievement'. In R. G. Wilkinson (ed.) *Class and Health: Research and Longitudinal Data*. London: Tavistock.

Wagner, M. (1994) *Pursuing the Birth Machine: The Search for Appropriate Birth Technology*. Sevenoaks, Kent: ACE Graphics.

Wainwright, D. (1996) 'The political transformation of the health inequalities debate'. *Critical Social Policy*, 49, 16 (4), 6-82.

Wajcman, J. (May, 2002) 'Addrssing technological change: the challenge to social theory'. *Current Sociology*, 50 (3), 347-63.

Wakefield, A. J., Murch, S. H., Anthony, A., Linnell, J., Casson, D. M., Malik, M., Berelowitz, M., Dhillon, A. P., Thomson, A. P., Harvey, P., Valentine, A., Davies, S. E. and Walker-Smith, J. A. (1998) 'Ileal-lymphoid-nodular hyperplasia, non-specific colitis, and pervasive developmental disorder in children'. *The Lancet*, 351, 637-41.

Wakefield, A. J., Harvey, P. and Linnell, J. (2004) 'MMR – responding to retraction'. *The Lancet*, 363 (9417), 1327.

Walby, S. and Greenwell, J. (1994) *Medicine and Nursing: Professions in a Changing Health Service*. London: Sage.

Walby, S. (1990) *Theorising Patriarchy*. Oxford: Basil Blackwell.

Waldby, C. (1996) *AIDS and the Body Politic: Biomedicine and Sexual Difference*. London and New York: Routledge.

Waldron, I. (1995) 'Contributions of changing gender differences in behavior and social roles to changing gender differences in mortality'. In Sabo, D. and Gordon, D. F. (eds) *Men's Health and Illness Gender, Power and the Body*. London: Sage.

Walker, A. (1999) 'Political participation and representation of older people in Europe'. In A. Walker and G. Naegele (eds) *The Politics of Old Age in Europe*. Buckingham: Open University Press.

Wallman, S. (1986) 'Ethnicity and the boundary process in context'. In Rex. J. and Mason, D. (eds) *Theories of Race and Ethnic Relations*. Cambridge: University Press.

Walsh, D. (1997) 'Mental health care in Ireland 1954-1997 and the Future'. In J. Robins (ed.) *Reflections on Health: Commemorating Fifty Years of The Department of Health 1947-1997*. Dublin: Institute of Public Administration.

Walter, T., Littlewood, J. and Pickering, M. (1995) 'Death in the news: the public invigilation of private emotion'. *Sociology*, 29, (4), 579-596.

Wang, X. and Feng, Z. (2003) 'Energy consumption with sustainable development in a developing country: a case in Jiangsu, China'. *Energy Policy*, 31, 1679-1684

Watney, S. (1991) 'AIDS: the second decade: "risk", research and modernity'. In P. Aggleton, G. Hart and P. Davies (eds) *AIDS: Responses, Interventions and Care*. London: Falmer.

Watson, D. and Williams, J. (2001) 'Perceptions of the Quality of Health Care in the Public and Private Sectors in Ireland' *(Report to The Centre for Insurance Studies, Graduate Business School, University College Dublin)*. Dublin: ESRI.

Watson, J. (1979) *The Philosophy and Science of Caring*. Boston: Little Brown.

Watson, J. (1985) *Nursing: Human Science and Human Care: A Theory of Nursing*. New York: Appleton-Century-Crofts.

Watson, J. (2000) *Male Bodies: Health, Culture and Identity*. Buckingham: Open University Press.

Watt, P. (1997) 'Reporting on refugees'. *Focus on Ireland and the Wider World*. 57/8, 29-30.

Webb, M. (2000) 'Ethics in Psychiatry'. In K. Kearon and F. O'Ferrall (eds) *Medical Ethics and the Future of Healthcare*. Dublin: Columba Press.

Weber, M. (1948) *From Max Weber: Essays in Sociology*. Edited and translated by H. H. Gerth and C. Wright Mills. London: Routledge and Keegan Paul.

Weber, M. (1978) *Economy and Society: An Outline of Interpretive Sociology* edited from the original (1929) by G. Roth and C. Wittich and translated by E. Fischoff. Berkeley: University of California Press.

Webster, A. (2002) 'Innovative health technologies and the social: redefining health, medicine and the body'. *Current Sociology*, 50 (3), 443-57.

Weitzman, L. et al (1972) 'Sex role socialisation in picture books for pre-school children'. *American Journal of Sociology*, 77 (6), 1125-1150.

Wendell, S. (1996) *The Rejected Body: Feminist Philosophical Reflections on Disablity*. New York, London: Routledge.

Whelan, C. T., Hannan, D. F. and Creighton, S. (1991) *Unemployment, Poverty and Psychological Distress*, General Research Series, No. 150, Dublin: Economic and Social Research Institute.

White, D. (2000) 'Consumer and community participation: a reassessment of process, impact, and value'. In Gary L. Albrecht, R. Fitzpatrick and S. C. Scrimshaw, *The Handbook of Social Studies in Health and Medicine*. London: Sage.

White, K. (2002) *An Introduction to the Sociology of Health and Illness*. London: Sage.

Whitehead, M. (1988) *The Health Divide*, and Townsend, P. and Davidson, N (1982) (eds) *The Black Report*, published together as *Inequalities in Health* (1988). London: Penguin Books.

WHO (1946) *Constitution of the World Health Organisation*. New York: World Health Organisation.

WHO (1978) *Alma Ata Declaration*. Geneva: World Health Organisation.

WHO (1984) *Health Promotion: A Discussion Document on the Concepts and Principles*. Copenhagen: World Health Organisation.

WHO (1985) *Targets for Health for All by the Year 2000*. Geneva, World Health Organisation.

WHO (1986) *The Ottowa Charter for Health Promotion*. Copenhagen: WHO.

WHO (2002) *The World Health Report: Reducing Risks: Promoting Healthy Life*. Geneva: World Health Organisation.

WHO (2003) *Global school health initiative*. http://www. who. int/school_youth_health/gshi/en> (April 18th 2004)

WHOQOL-HIV Group (2003) 'Prelininary development of the World Health Organisation's Quality of Life instrument'. (WHOQOL-HIV): analysis of the pilot version. *Social Science and Medicine*, 57 (7), 1257-1275.

Wicks, D. (1998) *Nurses and Doctors at Work: Rethinking Professional Boundaries*. Buckingham: Open University Press.

Wild, S. and McKeigue, P. (1997) 'Cross sectional analysis of mortality by country of birth in England and Wales, 1970-92'. *British Medical Journal*, 314, 705-710.

Wiley, M. M. (2001) *Critique of Shaping a Healthier Future: A strategy for Effective Healthcare in the 1990s*. Dublin: Economic and Social Research Institute.

Wilkinson, R. G. (1996) *Unhealthy Societies: The afflictions of inequality*. London: Routledge.

Wilkinson, R. G., Kawachi, I. and Kennedy, B. (1998) 'Mortality, the social environment, crime and violence'. In Bartley, M., Blane, D. and Davey-Smith, G. (eds) *The Sociology of Health Inequalities*. Oxford: Blackwell Publishers, 19-38.

Williams, G. (1984) 'The Genesis of Chronic Illness: Narrative re-construction'. *Sociology of Health and Illness*, 6 (2), 175-200.

Williams, R., and Ecob, R. (1999) 'Regional mortality and the Irish in Britain: findings from the ONS Longitudinal Study'. *Sociology of Health and Illness*, 21 (3), 344-67.

Williams, G. H. (2003) 'The determinants of health: structure, context and agency'. *Sociology of Health and Illness*, 25 (Silver Anniversary Issue), 131-154.

Williams, R. (1990) *A Protest Legacy: Attitudes to Death and Illness Among Older Aberdonians*. Oxford: Clarendon Press.

Williams, R. (1993) 'Health and length of residence among South Asians in Glasgow: a study controlling for age'. *Journal of Public Health Medicine*, 15, (1), 52-60.

Williams, S. (1996) 'The vicissitudes of embodiment across the chronic illness trajectory'. *Body and Society*, 2, 23-4.

Williams, S. J. (2000) 'Chronic illness as biographical disruption or biographical disruption as chronic illness? Reflections on a core concept'. *Sociology of Health and Illness*, 22 (1), 40-67.

Williams, S. J. (2003) *Medicine and the Body*. London: Sage.

Williams, S. J. and Bendelow, G. (1998) *The Lived Body: Sociological Themes, Embodied Issues*. London: Routledge.

Wilson A. (1989) 'A new role for staff nurses: the effects of supernumerary students'. *The Professional Nurse*, 5 (2), 105

Wilson, A. (1998) 'Getting Help'. In O'Dowd, T. and Jewell, D. (eds) *Men's Health*. Oxford: Oxford University.

Witz A. (1994) 'The challenge of nursing'. In Gabe, J., Kelleher, D. and Williams, G. (eds) *Challenging Medicine*, London

Witz, A. (1992) *Professions and Patriarchy*. London: Routledge.

Wolf, N. (1991) *The Beauty Myth: How Images of Beauty are Used against Women*. London: Vintage/Random House.

Wolpe, P. R. (1985) 'The maintenance of professional authority: acupuncture and the American physician'. *Social Problems*, 32, 409-424.

Women's Environmental Network (June, 1999) *Putting Breast Cancer on the Map Report*. London: WEN. www. wen. org. uk (20 November 2003)

Wood, B. (2000) *Patient Power?: The Politics of Patients' Associations in Britain and America*. Buckingham: Open University Press.

World Statistics (2004) *Crude Marriage Rates for Selected Countries*. www. infoplease. com/ipa/a0004385. htlm (April 18th 2004).

Wray, S. (2003) 'Women growing older: agency, ethnicity and culture'. *Sociology*, 37 (3), 511-527.

Wren, M-A. (2003) *Unhealthy State: Anatomy of a Sick Society*. Dublin: New Island.

Wyke, S., Hunt, K. and Ford, G. (1998) 'Gender differences in consulting a general practitioner for common symptoms of minor illness'. *Social. Science and Medicine*, 46 (7), 901-906.

Yip I. and Duran, N. (2001) 'The role of complementary medicine in the treatment of prostate cancer'. *Current Urology Report*s, 2 (3), 231-6.

Youngs, R. (2003) 'European approaches to democracy assistance: learning the right lessons?' *Third World Quarterly*, 24 (1), 127-139.

Zola, I. K. (1984) 'Healthism and disabling medicalisation'. In P. R. Lee, C. L. Estes, and N. B. Ramsey (eds) *The Nation's Health* (Second edition). San Francisco: Boyd and Fraser Publishing Co.

Zola, I. K. (1972) 'Medicine as an institution of social control'. *Sociological Review*, 20, 487-504.

Index